Poptropica® English

TEACHER'S EDITION 5

Ice Island

Laura Miller • John Wiltshier
Series advisor: David Nunan

Contents

Scope and sequence

Welcome

Vocabulary: **Time:** two days ago, yesterday, today, now, tomorrow

Structures:
I played tennis on Monday morning.
We cleaned our rooms on Saturday morning.
He/She danced at the party on Friday evening.
They went to the movies on Saturday afternoon.

1 Friends

Vocabulary: **Physical appearance:** dark hair, light hair, spiky hair, bald, handsome, beautiful, good-looking, cute
Adjectives to describe personality: bossy, creative, sporty, lazy, smart, patient, talkative, helpful, friendly, hard-working

Structures:
What does he/she look like? He's/She's good-looking.
He/She has straight, dark hair and brown eyes.
What do they look like? They're tall and good-looking.
They have short, light hair and blue eyes.
He/She doesn't have light hair.
They don't have light hair.
What's he/she like? He's sporty and he's smart.
She's bossy but hard-working.
I like him because he's patient. I like her because she's friendly.

Values: Help your friends in class.

Cross-curricular:
Art: Warm and cool colors

2 My life

Vocabulary: **Daily activities:** brush my teeth, make my bed, wash my face, clean my room, do my homework, meet my friends, study before a test, take notes in class, take out the trash, be on time
Adverbs of frequency: always, usually, often, sometimes, never

Structures:
You must brush your teeth. *(Order)*
You should brush your teeth. *(Advice)*
I always brush my teeth. / He usually brushes his teeth. / She often brushes her teeth. / They sometimes brush their teeth. / We never brush our teeth.

Values: Giving is great.

Cross-curricular:
Social science: Being healthy

3 Free time

Vocabulary: **Activities and hobbies:** hitting, kicking, throwing, catching, diving, going shopping, telling jokes, reading poetry, jumping on the trampoline
More activities and hobbies: playing video games, in-line skating, playing chess, playing the drums, acting, singing karaoke, running races, singing in a choir

Structures:
What am I good at? I'm good at hitting.
What's he/she good at? He's/She's good at hitting.
What are they good at? They're good at hitting.
He/She isn't good at catching. / They aren't good at catching.
What does he/she like/love doing? He/She likes/loves going shopping.
What were you doing yesterday at 7:00? I was drawing pictures.
What was he/she doing yesterday at 7:00? He/She was drawing pictures.
What were they doing yesterday at 7:00? They were drawing pictures.
Were you drawing pictures? Yes, I was. / No, I wasn't.
Was he/she drawing pictures? Yes, he/she was. / No, he/she wasn't.
Were they drawing pictures? Yes, they were. / No, they weren't.

Values: It's good to try new things. You should have a hobby.

Cross-curricular:
Music: Musical instruments

4 Around the world

Vocabulary:	**Countries:** China, Korea, Japan, Australia, the United States, Mexico, Colombia, Brazil, Argentina, the United Kingdom, Spain, Italy, Egypt, India **Places:** pyramid, statue, cave, volcano, city, town, farm, factory, castle	**Values:** Teamwork is important. **Cross-curricular:** **Geography:** Seasons
Structures:	There's a rain forest in Brazil. / There isn't a rain forest in Korea. There are some penguins in Argentina. / There aren't any penguins in Italy. Is there a pyramid in the city? Yes, there is. / No, there isn't. Are there any beaches in Australia? Yes, there are some beautiful beaches in Australia. Are there any volcanoes in the United Kingdom? No, there aren't.	

5 Shopping

Vocabulary:	**Clothing and accessories:** jacket, swimsuit, watch, bracelet, wallet, handbag, umbrella, gloves, sunglasses, hoodie, belt **Adjectives to describe clothing and accessories:** cheap, expensive, tight, baggy, old-fashioned, modern	**Values:** Dress correctly for each occasion. **Cross-curricular:** **Science:** Properties of materials
Structures:	How much is this/that jacket? It's ninety dollars and fifty cents. How much are these/those sunglasses? They're thirty dollars. Whose watch is this? It's Maddy's/mine/yours/his/hers. Whose pens are these? They're Dan's/mine/yours/his/hers.	

6 Party time

Vocabulary:	**Irregular past tense verbs:** make/made, have/had, come/came, give/gave, get/got, sing/sang, bring/brought, meet/met, eat/ate, see/saw **Ordinal numbers:** first, second, third, fourth, fifth, sixth, seventh, eighth, ninth, tenth, eleventh, twelfth, thirteenth, fourteenth, fifteenth, sixteenth, seventeenth, eighteenth, nineteenth, twentieth, thirtieth	**Values:** Be a creative problem solver. **Cross-curricular:** **History:** The first Thanksgiving
Structures:	I made a cake. / I didn't make a cake. Where did you go? I went to Ghana. When did you go to Ghana? I went on August 1st. What did you see? I saw giant butterflies. Who did you meet? I met my relatives.	

7 School

Vocabulary:	**Adjectives:** interesting, boring, exciting, scary, funny, difficult, easy, romantic, relaxing **School subjects:** computer science, math, geography, science, history, art, music, P.E.	**Values:** Learn about your older family members' youths. **Cross-curricular:** **Social science:** Life experiences
Structures:	Was it interesting? Yes, it was. / No, it wasn't. Was there an alien in it? Yes, there was. / No, there wasn't. Were there any exciting stories? Yes, there were. / No, there weren't. Did you have computer science on Tuesday? Yes, I did. / No, I didn't. Was P.E. relaxing? Yes, it was. / No, it wasn't. It was difficult.	

8 Entertainment

Vocabulary:	**Nationalities:** Chinese, Korean, Japanese, Australian, American, Mexican, Colombian, Brazilian, Argentinian, British, Spanish, Italian, Egyptian, Indian **Occupations:** cowboy, king, queen, scientist, spy, soldier, sailor, waiter, actor, musician	**Values:** Be a good role model for others. **Cross-curricular:** **Technology:** Video games
Structures:	Is he/she from the United States? Yes, he/she is. / No, he/she isn't. Where's he/she from? He's/She's from Argentina. He's/She's Argentinian. Where are they from? They're from Australia. They're Australian. He's a cowboy. He likes playing the guitar. He's a cowboy who likes playing the guitar. It's an American movie. It's very famous. It's an American movie that's very famous.	

Introduction

Dear Teachers,

Welcome!

It is my pleasure to introduce you to *Poptropica English*. This is the most exciting and important series for teaching English to young learners on the market today. It is designed to educate learners for the twenty-first century. This involves more than teaching learners to communicate in English. It also involves helping learners to socialize and work cooperatively, to have a sense of responsibility to others, to develop their ability to reflect on their learning processes, and to begin learning and using English independently.

The series is based on some key educational principles. The most important of these is that of catering to the whole learner. This means that you are not just responsible for developing the ability of learners to communicate through English, you are also responsible for their emotional, social, and moral development. This is a very challenging task, but *Poptropica English* will provide you with resources to help you meet that challenge.

Through these materials, learners engage with English by using it in a wide range of interesting and fun situations that relate to their everyday lives. Yes, they have to learn vocabulary and master the pronunciation and grammar of the language, but they do so through engaging tasks that keep them motivated and show them the relevance of English to their lives beyond the language classroom.

The journey from infancy to adulthood is an amazing adventure, of which language learning is a part. I hope that you enjoy taking your students on the adventure with *Poptropica English*.

David Nunan
Series Advisor
Poptropica English

Ice Island is a six-level course for children learning English at primary level. It offers best practice methodology in the classroom, while also offering teachers and students an innovative digital environment in the shape of the unique **Poptropica English World**.

Poptropica English is designed to provide teachers and students with a truly blended English language learning environment. It takes into account the current movement towards using an increased amount of technology in the classroom, and also at home, as more and more families use computers and want safe, effective, educational material for their children.

Poptropica English motivates children by introducing them to **Poptropica English World**, an online area which extends and enhances their learning. Students are introduced to a group of **Poptropicans** in an **Island Adventure Game** that echoes their books. Children follow the characters through their book, while listening to stories, singing songs, communicating, and playing games along the way. Most importantly, students will enjoy themselves, and make their own discoveries in English.

Methodology

Poptropica English assumes no previous knowledge of English and takes a "5Ps" approach to communication in order to provide support and encourage production from an early stage. The PPP (Presentation, Practice, and Production) method is a tried and tested approach which is favored by many teachers in the primary classroom. The lesson sequence is clear and easy to follow and works in a structured way. The **Poptropica English** "5Ps" approach adds also Personalization and Pronunciation.

Presentation is the first stage. The teacher demonstrates the key language, while providing a model (on audio or **Poptropica English World**) for students to hear the correct pronunciation.

Practice is provided in the form of controlled and more open activities, using the presented language.

Production activities encourage students to use the language either to speak or write something. These activities encourage students to become more autonomous, and to manipulate the language in order to communicate.

Personalization activities are also included in the lesson structure to engage students further with the unit language, and to help them with language recall.

Pronunciation is a key area in language teaching, and it is addressed in all units. Students practice it through fun and engaging songs and chants that help them acquire the stress, rhythm, and intonation of English.

Cross-Curricular Teaching

Children are naturally curious about the world around them. They want to know how nature works (natural science), how man's inventions function (technology), they are drawn to the exciting stories behind man's achievements and artistic creations (history/art), as well as the fascinating landscapes and customs of far-away places (geography/social science). Therefore, it seems natural and appropriate for their foreign language classroom to provide opportunities for them to explore this world, and to integrate the resulting knowledge and understanding with language learning.

Here are some other reasons for integrating content with language learning, and some tips for making the most of the cross-curricular pages in **Poptropica English**:

- Young students already bring an incredible amount of previous knowledge of the world to the language-learning classroom.

Tip 1: Start the lesson by inviting students to focus on the images on the page and ask a few warm-up questions, e.g., *What can you see on the page? What is the lesson about? What do you know about the topic? What else would you like to know?* Use the children's first language if necessary.

- What the students hear or read about a topic can later provide realistic reasons for speaking and writing about it.

Tip 2: As the students do the activities in the lesson, highlight any new vocabulary relating to the topic, and gather it in a simple diagram on the board. At the end of the lesson, invite the students to copy the diagram into their notebooks for later reference.

- Cross-curricular lessons can lead to very motivating individual or small group projects.

Tip 3: Invite students to read the instructions and help them visualize what the end product will be (a written list of physical exercises, possibly illustrated with drawings or photos, or a poster with pictures, captions, and a short text describing an animal from their country). Help students think about what to write, how to draft and edit and, finally, how to make it look nice (layout, design). Depending on the time available, allow students to do the project in class, or write a draft in class and complete the project at home.

- Mini projects can lead to research opportunities.

Tip 4: Help the students brainstorm sources of information for their mini project (the school library, the Internet, an "expert" from school, a relative or family friend). Teach them to gather – and check the relevance and reliability of – information.

Tip 5: You might like to give students feedback. You could give students two stars and one wish e.g., *Beautiful pictures!, Excellent coloring! Add one more picture label*. This could be given in L1.

Classroom Management Tips

Poptropica English presents different classroom dynamics. It goes from individual work to pairwork, group work, and whole-class activities. When working in pairs, groups, or in a whole-class setting, students foster cooperative learning, where they learn with and from each other. The following suggestions focus on different ways of grouping or pairing students. All the activities presented here are suited to any group size, age, or interest.

Ideas on how to divide students into pairs and groups

Grouping by Order: Organize students in a specific order and then divide them up. Ask students to get in line in alphabetical order (according to their first or last name, or the number of letters in their name), order of birthdays (grouped either by month or by their day of birth), months of the year, days of the week, or height.

Animal Sounds: This is a loud but fun way to divide students up. Have names of animals on slips of paper. Distribute them and ask students not to show their slip to each other. When they are ready, ask them to start making the sound of that animal that they have on the slip of paper. They have to find the other members of their animal family.

Pick and Mix: Students can be divided into groups or pairs by having them pick objects from a bag. Then you will ask them to find their team mates. Some examples of objects you can use are:

Colored chips: (e.g., ask students to team with same colors together; different colors together; two same color chips and two different ones, etc.).

Colored pencils: (e.g., students who get the same colors are in the same group/pair, light and dark of the same color makes a pair, four different colors makes a group, etc.)

Numbered popsicle sticks: Prepare popsicle sticks by writing a number at the end of each stick and placing them number down in a small can or container. Each student picks one and finds their group/pair (e.g., same numbers, sequential numbers, odd numbers, etc.).

Word jumble: Write vocabulary words from a topic on sheets of paper and put them in a bag or box. Ask students to pick one and find the rest of their group or pair. Students should look for others who have similar words or things (e.g., animals – all dogs together, all birds together, all cats together), others who group together (e.g., jungle animals, farm animals, sea animals) or others whose word starts with the same letter (e.g., roses, rainbow, rain, rock).

Strategic Grouping: Depending on the activity, you may want to group students using one of these combinations: stronger and weaker students together, stronger students together, weaker students together, talkers and listeners together. Whatever you choose, do not let students know what your strategy is.

Signaling that the activity has finished

When assigning speaking activities and playing games in large classes, it can often be hard to grab students' attention. With this in mind, here are some suggestions to help you deal with this situation.

Can You Hear Me? Start talking to them in a very low voice and say, *If you can hear me raise your hand.* Students who hear you raise their hand, which will call the other ones' attention and they will do the same.

Clapping: Clap your hands in different patterns and speed. Students have to join you in clapping. Say, *Clap once if you can hear me.* Some students join you. Then say, *Clap twice if you can hear me.* And finally, *Clap three times if you can hear me.* At this point, students will notice that the activity has finished.

Eyes on Me: Count to three saying, *One, two, three… eyes on me!* Students stop the activity and say, *One, two, three… eyes on you!* This way, if the other students have not heard you, they will hear the students and then notice that the activity is finished.

Give Me Five: Raise your hand and say, *Give me five.* Students put their hands up and say, *five.* Then they start to count from one to five. If that does not call everyone's attention, say, *Give me five again.* Students repeat the count.

Raising Hands: Raise your hands. Wait until students notice your hands up and gradually stop talking.

Ring a Bell: Set a timer for the amount of time you would like the activity to last, or ring a bell. When students hear the sound, they stop the activity.

Silent Request: Create a signal for silence. Then practice the signal with your students until they know that every time you make that signal it is time to stop the activity.

Singing: Play or sing a **Poptropica English** song or chant. Have students join you.

Stop Light: Make a stop light with removable color circles. When in green, students can talk in pairs or in groups. When in yellow, they must be ready to end the conversation. When in red, it is time to stop talking. If they are too loud, you can quickly go from green to red. If they are quieter again, go back to green.

What is Assessment for Learning?

Poptropica English includes elements of **Assessment for Learning** methodology, which help to enhance learning by supporting students in understanding what they know and what they need to do next, empowering them to move themselves forward, and making them active in their own learning, as well as helping teachers understand where their students are. **Assessment for Learning** is looking for ways to understand how students are doing, and using this information to help them improve, and to also help teachers make decisions about how to help students improve.

Assessment: isn't this testing?

It can be, but when we talk about **Assessment for Learning**, we're really talking about assessing students formatively, watching and listening to our students to see how far they understand, and using this to help decide what we need to do next. This can be during any activity in class, the kind of assessment you already do every day!

Why is Assessment for Learning important in Poptropica English?

Poptropica English provides fun and engaging material to help your students have an exciting and motivating early experience with English. A handful of **Assessment for Learning** techniques and activities have been integrated into each lesson, to build on this positive experience. These activities give students an awareness of what and how they are learning, and give you, the teacher, lots of opportunities to assess how each student is doing. Introducing the **learning adventure** in your classes to talk about students' learning, makes each step along their English language adventure visible and interactive, engaging and motivating students while also developing self-assessment skills.

What is the learning adventure?

The **learning adventure**, based on each of the **Poptropica English Islands**, is a path which represents how confident the student feels about a particular learning objective. Using this poster in class enables students to develop self-assessment skills, by reflecting on how well they can remember vocabulary, for example, from the lesson or unit. It can also help gather evidence for the teacher on who is confident about the lesson, and who needs more practice.

Where is the learning adventure used?

The **learning adventure** is used in *Vocabulary*, *Cross-curricular*, *I can do it!*, and *Wider World* lessons.

How do I introduce the learning adventure to my students?

It's a good idea to model with students how to use the **learning adventure** poster. The **learning adventure** poster can be put in the classroom, and the image is used in a sequence of activities, using both the Student Book and accompanying teacher's notes, and in **Poptropica English World** for class presentation.

There are four steps on the **learning adventure**:

1. ***Let's go!*** – This means that students have started a new learning objective and are at the beginning of their learning; maybe they know one or two words.
2. ***I'm on my way!*** – This means that students are moving along their journey with increasing understanding or knowledge; maybe they know five or six words.
3. ***I'm almost there!*** – This means that students are feeling increasingly confident about what they have learned, and have a good (though not necessarily 100%) knowledge or understanding.
4. ***I've arrived!*** – This means that students are very confident about what they have learned, and have a good (though not necessarily 100%) knowledge or understanding.

How do I use the poster with my class?

It's really useful if you can have the poster on the wall for every class. The poster is used in two different ways.

For Vocabulary, Cross-curricular, and Wider World lessons.

The poster works in the same sequence each time and the lesson plans show you exactly when and how. Every lesson begins with ***student-friendly objectives*** – these will appear in the teacher's notes for each lesson. You can write these on the board, or if you are using **Poptropica English World**, the objectives appear on screen at the start of each lesson sequence. The first activity in these classes is ***What do you know?*** – this is a Student Book activity asking students which words they know on this topic before the main class presentation. This will find out what students already know about a topic, engage them, and give students confidence that they know something already. Now, using the poster, ask the students, *Where are you on your learning adventure?* Ask students to think about how many words they know, and to say which stage on the poster they think they are at, e.g., if they know two or three words, they might say, *Let's go!* as they are at the beginning of their learning. You should respond positively, as they are already moving along their learning adventure! At the end of the lesson, ask the students again, *Where are you on your learning adventure?* Students think how many words they know now, and choose a stage on the poster, e.g., if they know eight words they might say, *I know teddy bear, car, kite, doll, boat, bike, ball, train*. It's a good idea to remind students of where they were at the beginning of the lesson, and where they are now, to really emphasize the progress they are making.

I can do it!

The poster is used to help students develop the skills needed to identify what they know and what they don't know, to help them focus and move themselves forward. With practice, this should make learning more efficient, produce confident students not afraid to ask for help from teachers and classmates, and underline that everyone can make progress. As with every lesson, we begin with ***Student-friendly objectives***. We ask students, *What can you remember?* This activity asks students to recall what topics/language they learned in the previous unit. Ask students, *Where are you on your learning adventure?* For each topic/language area, ask students to say where they are on their learning adventure. The students then complete a set of activities to help them review and consolidate the unit topic/language.

What other Assessment for Learning activities are there, and why should I use them?

What do you know? – Asks students if they know any words associated with the unit topic before the main class presentation.

Students will feel confident that they already know some words from the topic so they aren't at the beginning of their learning.

Pop Quiz – Gives you a quick end-of-lesson activity to help you check where who has "got it" and who needs more help.

Provides opportunities to see where students are in their learning, and helps you provide useful feedback and adjust your teaching in line with individual needs.

Extension questions – Asks students a question to help extend their thinking and learning.

Requires more than only remembering what they have learned, and illustrates that they have understood it.

I can do it! – Self-assessment lessons develop students' skills to assess where they are in their learning, and what they need to do next to achieve their learning goals, motivating them to continue learning.

Developing the skills to identify what you know and what you don't forms a huge part of learning. With practice, this should facilitate learning and produce confident students, not afraid to ask for help from teachers and their classmates.

When can I use the learning adventure?

You can use the **learning adventure** in any lesson with any learning objectives. For students new to this concept, it's good to begin with vocabulary, as it's easy to identify what you know and have learned.

What if my students do not use the learning adventure accurately?

It doesn't matter too much about accuracy. They aren't giving themselves grades, they are simply increasing their awareness about their own learning. What matters is helping your students to increase their awareness by modelling how to use the poster, using examples to show how many words you might know for each stage on the poster. Also, by encouraging students to think of their progress more positively if they underestimate on the **learning adventure**. Or, if students indicate too confidently where they are, ask students to think a little more carefully about how many words they can remember, for example. For strong students, keep them motivated by asking them to find out more about the topic or new words on the topic. Also, using the poster regularly in class will help students integrate this into their learning more easily.

What if my students are very shy?

If students don't want to say where they are, you can make cards that students can hold up in class. Each student can make a card for each stage, e.g., *Let's go*.

Components

For the student

- Four *Wider World* units;
- Four *Review* units;
- *Goodbye* unit to consolidate and wrap up;
- Wordlist;
- Verb list.

Poptropica English World is an online area where students can find a variety of resources which enhance their learning:

- the **Poptropica English Island Adventure Game**, which provides a safe, engaging, and highly-motivating environment where students meet the characters from the Student Book plus a host of other exciting characters, and follow them on an adventure. Students will engage in safe, "closed-chat" dialogs with the characters they meet, and will practice target language from the units. They will also follow instructions to help them solve puzzles, and learn supplementary language along the way. The **Poptropica English Island Adventure Game** is a great tool to make learning happen in an interactive way, and it further consolidates and extends the language learning process. Most of all, students will enjoy learning through play and will absorb English without realizing it!
- **homework** assigned by their teachers and automatically graded;
- **extra online games** to consolidate the language introduced in the classroom;
- **songs and chants** for the course;
- **videos** for the course, which contain four animated stories with **Poptropica English** characters.

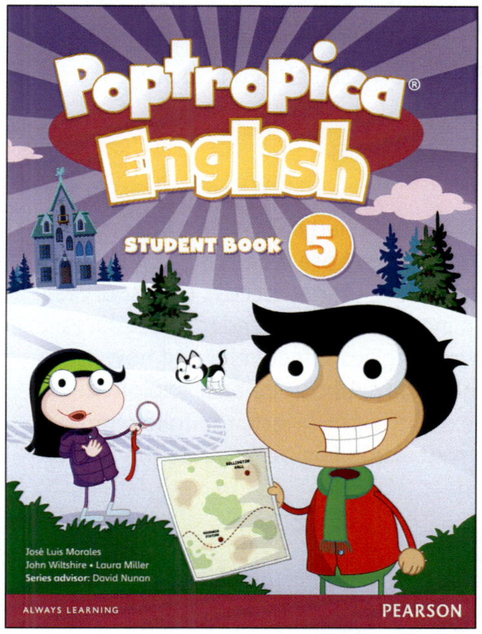

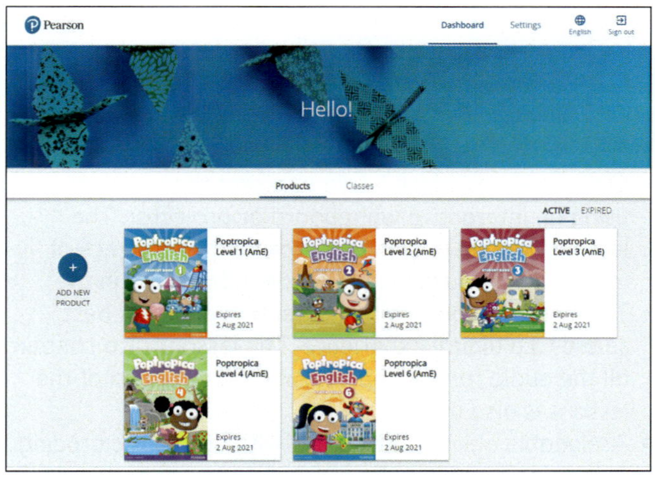

For the parent

Parents also have access to **Poptropica English World**, through their child's account and can track their children's achievements.

The **Workbook** provides reinforcement and consolidation of the language presented in the Student Book. It contains controlled and freer practice, plus personalization, further listening, and reading texts.

The accompanying **CD** contains all the audio for the listening activities in the Workbook.

For the teacher

The **Teacher's Edition** provides step-by-step lesson plans covering all the Student Book material.

Each lesson plan is clearly structured into stages:

- Warm-up activities;
- Step-by-step lesson plans;
- Pop Quiz.

The lesson notes are designed to be flexible support for all teachers, including those who may lack time for planning or who have limited access to resources. The Introduction includes recommended procedures for using games and stories effectively, and how **Poptropica English World** can be best exploited. For maximum flexibility and variety, the following **photocopiable materials** can be found in the Teacher's Edition:

- Story Cards;
- Activity Sheets;
- Tests.

Poptropica English World is one online location where teachers, students, and parents can find all the materials and tools which can be used inside and/or outside the classroom with **Poptropica English**. Teachers can use it for lesson preparation, for delivering lessons, to assign and track homework, to monitor students' performance, and to manage their classes. The resources available to teachers include:

- Online lessons which let you present the material using an interactive whiteboard or projector. The lessons contain activities mirroring the sequence of material introduced in the Student Book and in the Teacher's Edition but in an interactive format best suited to a digital experience. The lessons also contain all the audio for the course. An offline version of the lessons is also available.
- Assignable online **homework** with automatic grading;
- A tool for **tracking the performance** of both individual students and the whole class;
- Extra resources like **tests, worksheets, videos, posters,** and **Picture Cards**;
- Access to the **Poptropica English Island Adventure Game**, in which students can meet characters from the book in a safe, engaging, and motivating environment. The game consolidates and extends the material covered in the Student Book.
- **Poptropica English World** can also be used by parents and students at home. It will allow students to access extra activities and will give parents the opportunity to monitor their child's progress.

You will find more information on **Poptropica English World** on pages 13–15.

The **Class Audio CDs** contain all the songs (including karaoke versions), chants, stories, and listening activities which appear in the Student Book. They also contain audio for tests which are available in the Teacher's Edition. All the audio is also available online as part of **Poptropica English World**.

The **Picture Cards** present main target vocabulary in each unit. The teaching notes in the Teacher's Edition clearly explain how the Picture Cards can be used to present, practice, and consolidate language through games and activities. The Picture Cards are also available online as part of **Poptropica English World**.

The **posters** accompanying the course are of two types. **Learning adventure** posters help students and teachers gain awareness of what and how the students are learning. **Vocabulary** posters serve as another tool for teaching and consolidating vocabulary. All posters are also available online as part of **Poptropica English World**.

The **videos** are available in **Poptropica English World**. They give students a new context in which to recycle the language of the Student Book.

The **Tests** (Placement Test, Unit Tests, Review Tests, and End of Level Test) can be found at the back of the Teacher's Edition. The audio for these tests is on the Audio CD. These tests and the audio are also available online, as part of **Poptropica English World**.

Poptropica English World

Poptropica English has been designed as a course in which all the components are aligned to provide best practice methodology and an innovative digital environment, both inside and out of the classroom. The print components and the **Poptropica English World** environment allow teachers to choose varying degrees of blended learning approach in their lessons, depending on their situation.

What is Poptropica English World?

Poptropica English World is one online location where teachers, students, and parents can find materials and tools which can be used inside and/or outside the classroom with **Poptropica English**.

Poptropica English World consists of two main areas:

Teacher area

This is an area that teachers can use for lesson preparation, for delivering lessons, to assign and track homework, to monitor students' performance, and to manage their classes. It contains online lessons, which enable lessons to be delivered with an interactive whiteboard or projector. An offline version of the lessons is also available. It also contains **assignable online homework**. It has a tool for **tracking the performance** of both individual students and the whole class. It also has **extra resources** to use in the class, such as tests, videos, posters, and Picture Cards, and allows teachers download access to the **Poptropica English Island Adventure Game**.

How can I use the print and digital components of Poptropica English?

Poptropica English can be used in all classrooms, whatever the level of technology. The lesson flow is the same irrespective of which medium you use, but you can use the components in different ways, depending on whether you have access to the Internet and/or to an interactive whiteboard.

Scenario 1

I have no Internet and no interactive whiteboard in my classroom. How can I benefit from Poptropica English World?

As long as you can get Internet access somewhere (in the staffroom, at home), you can set online homework for students to do at home. Students' homework will be graded, and their achievements will be visible to you. You will be able to see how well the whole class and individual students are doing, and which structures or vocabulary still need further practice.

You can access extra resources such as tests to print and use with your class.

You can encourage your students to get more practice and/or use English outside of class, by asking them to explore other areas of **Poptropica English World**. They can do homework, play the **Poptropica English Island Adventure Game** or mini games at home in their free time, thus gaining extra exposure to the language covered in class. In the **Poptropica English Island Adventure Game**, they will meet characters from their coursebooks, and will be able to join them in their adventures. Students can also play extra games available for each unit of the book.

Finally, you can encourage students to return to the songs, chants, and videos covered in class, which are all available in **Poptropica English World**, to consolidate their learning.

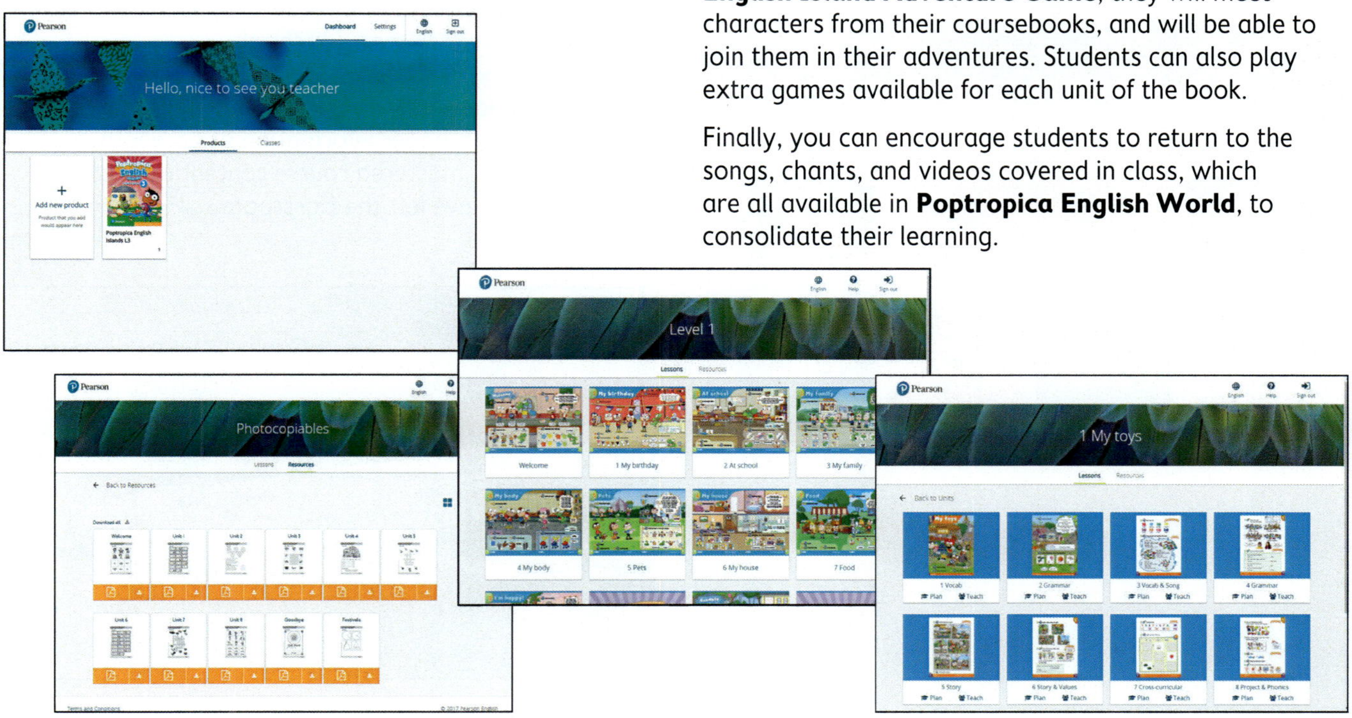

Scenario 2

I have an interactive whiteboard or projector but no Internet in the classroom. How can I benefit from Poptropica English World?

- You can do everything that teachers in scenario 1 can do.
- You can use the offline version of the lessons in the class via the interactive whiteboard. The lessons reflect the sequence of activities in the Teacher's Edition but using digital media. The activities themselves will sometimes have a slightly different format than in the book, in order to make them interactive and make the best of the digital medium. The parts of the lesson when children need to do individual practice can still be done in the Student Book or Workbook.

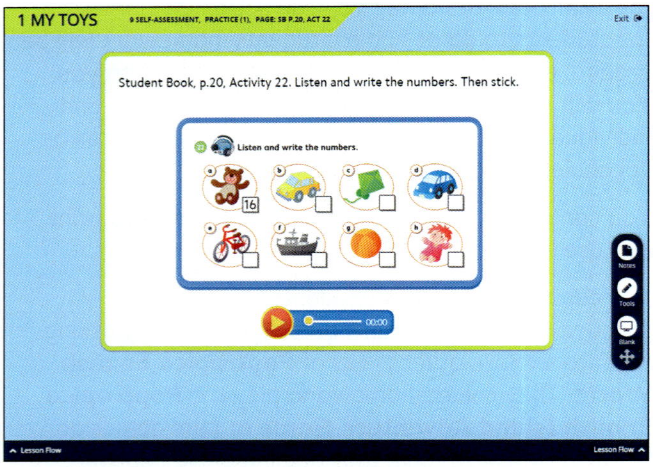

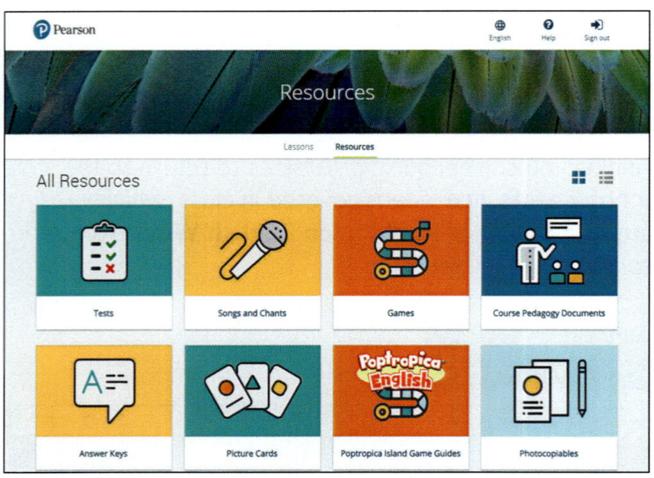

Scenario 3

I have a classroom with an interactive whiteboard and Internet. How can I benefit from Poptropica English World?

- You can do everything that teachers in scenario 2 can do.
- All the media that you need to deliver your lessons will be available in one location, and you can use them at any moment. In addition, you can preview and assign homework, access the additional resources, and student area content directly from the lesson.
- You can share in-class content with students.
- You can receive content updates.

Where can I find more information on how to use Poptropica English World?

There are help notes and help videos available in **Poptropica English World** to guide you through common questions.

What are the benefits of using both the print components and Poptropica English World?

- Your students will spend more time on their English exploring the student area outside of class, and reinforcing their in-class learning via a mixture of printed and interactive homework activities;
- Your students will get extra language practice via a different medium, which is attractive to them;
- Your students will be more engaged with their learning process as a result of a variety of media and fun activities, and will have some choice over how and what they learn;
- The use of **Poptropica English World** strengthens the link between home and school;
- As a result, your students will be more confident about their language skills;
- You will have broader information as to whether students have mastered course content and retained it after they have left the classroom.

Student area

This is an area where students can access resources applicable to them. They can do homework set by their teachers, which will be automatically graded, and reported to a performance area, where they can track their achievements. They can also play extra games, listen to songs, or watch videos linked to the units they are working on.

In addition, students can play the **Poptropica English Island Adventure Game** relevant to their level, in which they meet characters from the Student Book and follow them on an adventure. Students will engage in safe "closed-chat" with the characters they meet, and will practice and consolidate the language of the units. They will also follow instructions to help them solve puzzles, and learn supplementary language along the way. Within the game, they need to find cards like ones hidden in the opening pages of each Student Book unit. Clicking on them in the game will unlock additional games, which will give them extra rewards.

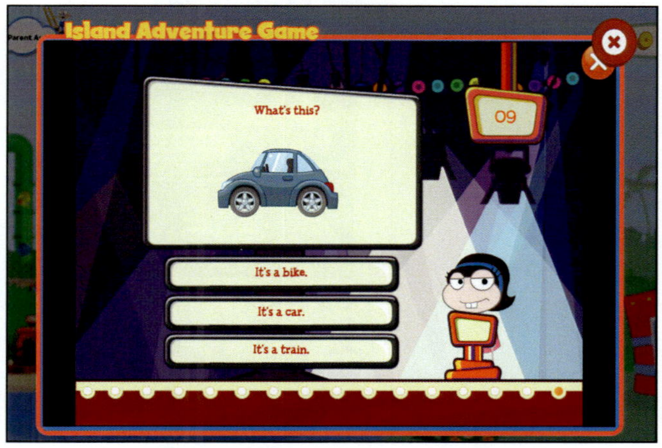

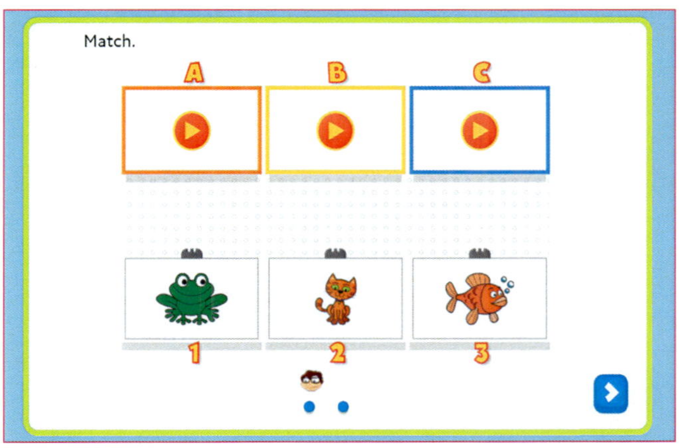

Unit Walkthrough

Lesson 1

Presentation and practice of vocabulary with audio support

Previous knowledge of the topic is activated through an **Assessment for Learning** activity.

Lesson 2

Presentation and practice of grammar with audio support

The new grammar content is summarized in a *Look!* box on the Student Book page, and in the grammar presentation on the lessons in **Poptropica English World**.

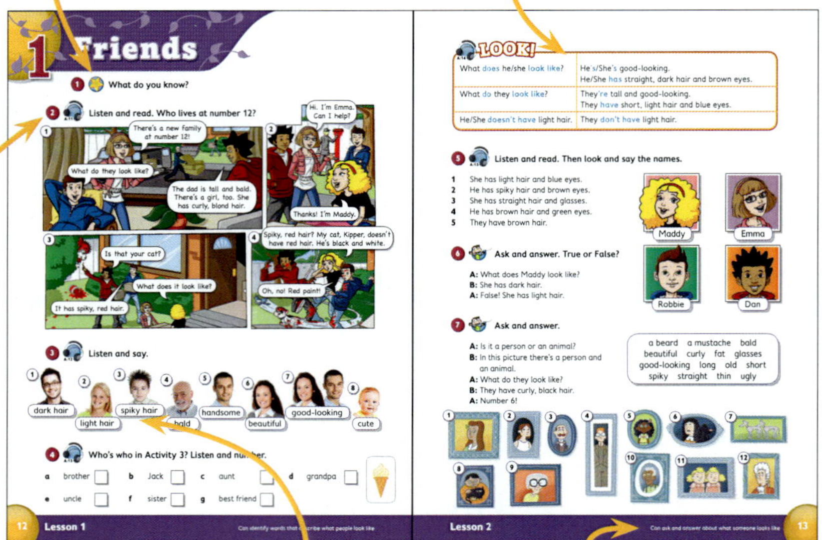

Students listen to the key unit vocabulary in the context of a dialog between the characters.

Target vocabulary from the opening story is illustrated and labeled.

Clear and concise learning objectives help clarify the aim of the lesson for the teacher and parent.

Further practice of the target language is provided in the Workbook for **all** lessons.

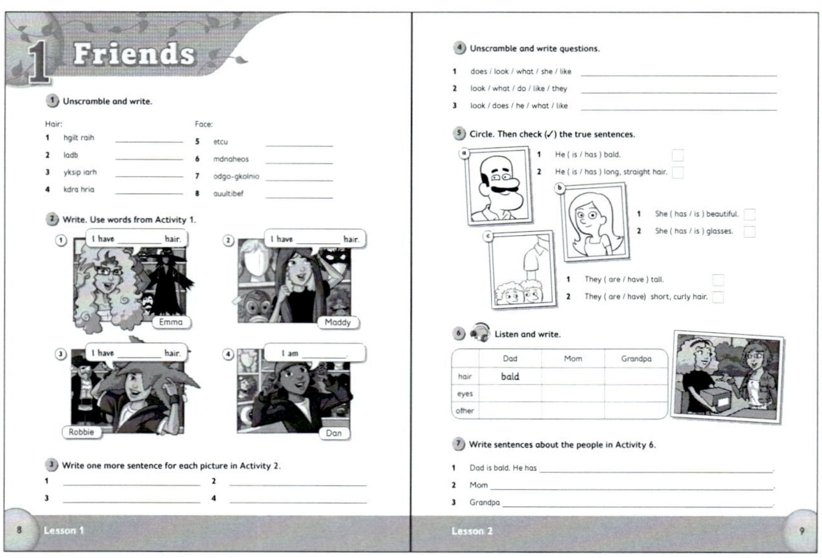

Lesson 3

Presentation and practice of vocabulary with audio support

Students learn a new set of vocabulary which is linked to the unit topic. This may be additional words or a separate vocabulary set. The language of the unit is then practiced in a song. Karaoke versions of the songs are included in the class audio and on **Poptropica English World**.

Extra individual practice of both vocabulary sets is provided via the **Poptropica English World** homework activity.

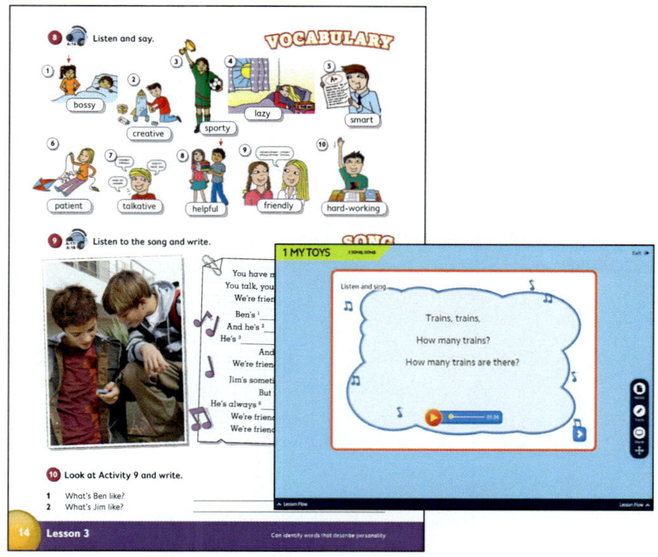

Lesson 4

Presentation and practice of grammar with audio support

The new structure is presented with a listening activity, and further consolidated with a skills activity. The new grammar content is summarized in a *Look!* box on the Student Book page, and in the grammar presentation on the lessons in **Poptropica English World**.

A skills activity helps to consolidate the grammar and vocabulary of the unit.

Extra individual practice of both grammar points is provided via the **Poptropica English World** homework activity.

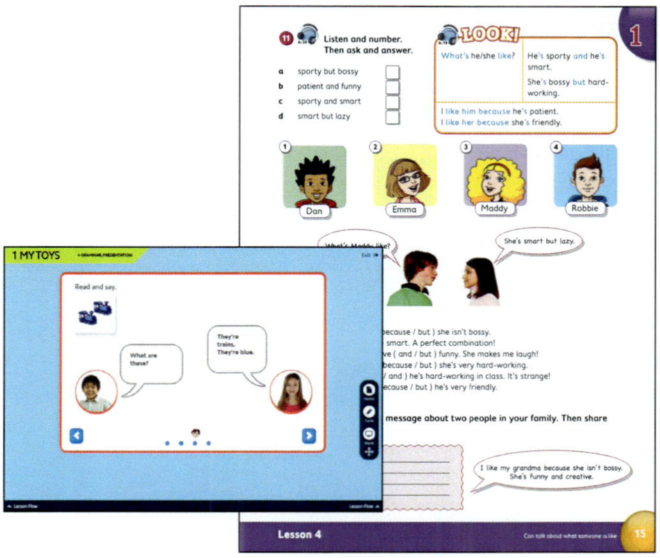

Lesson 5

Story

The story is provided with speech bubbles and audio support. It consolidates vocabulary and structures from previous lessons, and introduces new functional language.

Lesson 6

Story comprehension and value

Students review the story before doing a comprehension activity to check understanding. The values topic for the unit is usually linked to the story, and is summarized in the **Values** box on the Student Book page.

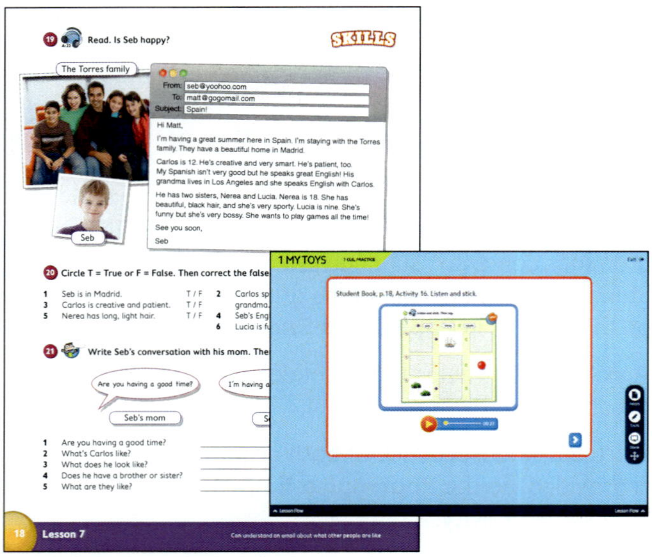

Lesson 7

Skills

Target language is practiced and extended through skills in English.

Lesson 8

Cross-curricular content

Target language is practiced and extended through a cross-curricular topic in English. The material may be related to art, music, geography, science, history, or technology.

A project encourages further exploration of the topic and provides the opportunity for personalization of the unit language.

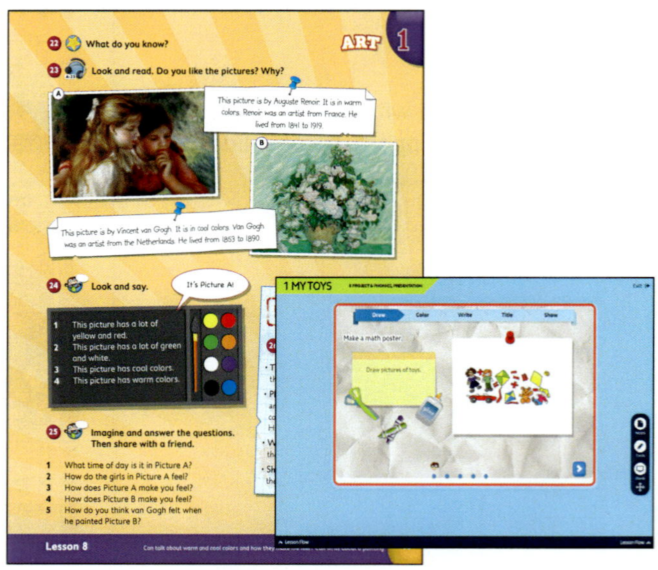

Lesson 9

Self-assessment and review

Students complete a self-assessment in every unit. This involves students completing three activities – one vocabulary, one grammar, and one communicative. After completing each activity, students are invited to self-assess. They check the boxes in the I CAN feature according to how confident they feel about each statement.

The **Poptropica English World** homework activity provides additional consolidation and practice of the unit language.

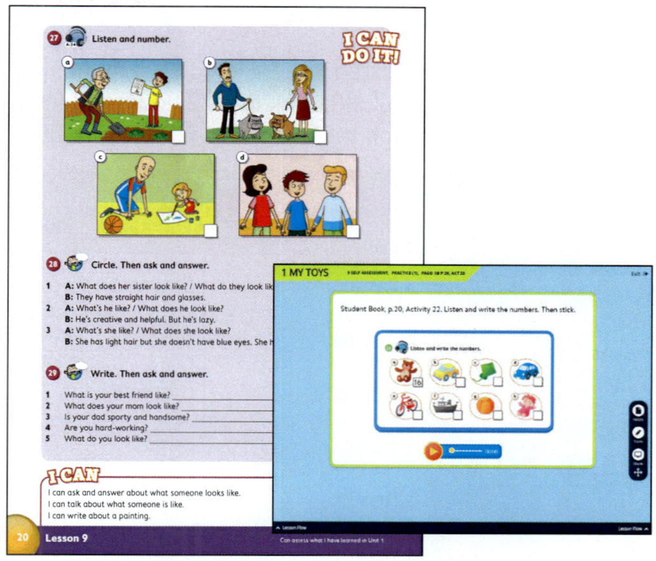

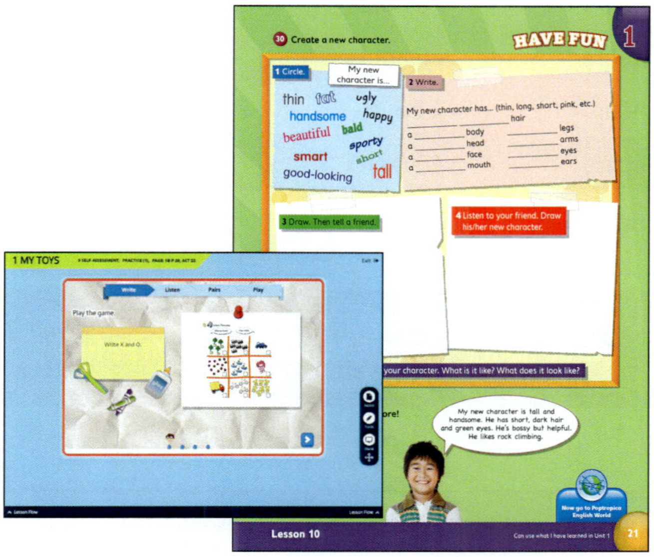

Lesson 10

Review and consolidation

Students consolidate and practice the unit language through a fun language game.

A final self-assessment is provided in **Poptropica English World** via a three-step activity. This activity involves students assessing the words they know or don't know, reviewing the words they don't know, and a final check activity to gauge the accuracy of their self-assessment.

Review

After Units 2, 4, 6, and 8, students complete a Review lesson. This provides practice and consolidation of the language from the previous two units.

Wider World

Culture lesson

After Units 1, 3, 5, and 7, students complete a Wider World lesson. Students read a text that explores an element of international culture linked to one of the unit topics. Each Wider World lesson includes a writing task, which encourages personalization and extension of the topic.

Course Planning

The following are suggested hour schedules, depending on the number of hours allocated to a course. We assume five basic scenarios of 52, 62, 80, 104, or 122 hours per level of a course. If more hours are available, the course can be extended further through the use of the variety activities found in **Poptropica English World** and other components.

	52 hours per level	62 hours per level	80 hours per level	104 hours per level	122 lessons per level
Welcome	3 hours	3 hours	4 hours	6 hours	6 hours
Unit 1	5 hours	6 hours	8 hours	10 hours	12 hours
Unit 2	5 hours	6 hours	8 hours	10 hours	12 hours
Review	1 hour	1 hour	1 hour	2 hours	2 hours
Unit 3	5 hours	6 hours	8 hours	10 hours	12 hours
Unit 4	5 hours	6 hours	8 hours	10 hours	12 hours
Review	1 hour	1 hour	1 hour	2 hours	2 hours
Unit 5	5 hours	6 hours	8 hours	10 hours	12 hours

Depending on the number of lessons you have to cover each unit, we suggest that you divide your time in the following way:

	5 lessons per unit/52 hours per level	6 lessons per unit/62 hours per level	8 lessons per unit/80 hours per level	10 lessons per unit/104 hours per level	12 lessons per unit/122 hours per level
Lesson 1 – Presentation	1	1	1	1	1
Lesson 2 – Presentation		2	2	2	2 3
Lesson 3 – Presentation/Song	2	3	3	3	4 5
Lesson 4 – Presentation/Skills			4	4	6
Lesson 5 – Consolidation (Story)	3	4	5	5	7
Lesson 6 – Comprehension/ Values				6	8
Lesson 7 – Skills	4	5	6	7	9
Lesson 8 – Cross-curricular			7	8	10
Lesson 9 – Self-Assessment	5	6	8	9	11
Lesson 10 – Review				10	12

	52 hours per level	62 hours per level	80 hours per level	104 hours per level	122 lessons per level
Unit 6	5 hours	6 hours	8 hours	10 hours	12 hours
Review	1 hour	1 hour	1 hour	2 hours	2 hours
Unit 7	5 hours	6 hours	8 hours	10 hours	12 hours
Unit 8	5 hours	6 hours	8 hours	10 hours	12 hours
Review	1 hour	1 hour	1 hour	2 hours	2 hours
Goodbye	3 hours	3 hours	3 hours	5 hours	5 hours
Festivals	1 hour	2 hours	2 hours	2 hours	3 hours
Wider World	1 hour	2 hours	3 hours	3 hours	4 hours

Here is a suggestion of what components can be covered in various lessons of a unit, depending on the time available. The practice activities in the core material can be covered faster or in more detail depending on the students' capabilities, class size, and the length of the lesson.

The core material for each lesson is the same:

- **Poptropica English World** presentation and practice
- Student Book presentation and practice
- Workbook page practice

	Extension material
Lesson 1	Picture Cards on **Poptropica English World** Extra activities from games and extension banks Presentation of the **Poptropica English Island Adventure Game** in the class to set the scene for the unit
Lesson 2	Picture Cards on **Poptropica English World** Extra activities from games and extension banks
Lesson 3	Picture Cards on **Poptropica English World** Extra activities from games and extension banks Extra work on the song with karaoke versions
Lesson 4	Extra activities from games and extension banks
Lesson 5	Extra activities from games and extension banks Extra time devoted to role-playing the story
Lesson 6	Extra activities from games and extension banks
Lesson 7	Picture Cards on **Poptropica English World** Extra activities from games and extension banks
Lesson 8	Extra time devoted to doing and presenting the project in the class
Lesson 9	**Learning adventure** poster Games and songs used in the unit
Lesson 10	Test Video available via **Poptropica English World**

How to Use Stories

Stories are an essential part of language learning because they allow students to absorb information in a fun and stimulating way. Learning outside the normal boundaries of a teacher-based classroom environment creates the opportunity for students to develop their creative and communicative skills. Using stories in the classroom greatly enhances students' ability to listen, and to actively respond to target language and structures in a fun and relaxed atmosphere. Stories increase motivation, and encourage less confident students to contribute with their ideas and opinions because they are not confined to the limits of a certain structure. They provide larger chunks of language in a context, and provide an opportunity for students to produce language.

There's a story in Lesson 5 of each unit, featuring the characters. These stories serve to review and reinforce the target language and structures of the unit. The artwork is visually stimulating, and the audio effects ensure students listen avidly from start to finish. Below is a four-step method for using stories in the classroom that starts with anticipation and ends with (assisted) performance.

Stage 1 – Anticipating the story

Before listening to the audio, ask students questions or carry out a simple discussion to get them thinking about the story. This can enable students to begin forming an idea of the theme of the story and how it might develop. It also provides an opportunity to introduce any new vocabulary or to review previously learned language, allowing teachers to assess how thoroughly students have absorbed the target language of the unit. Teachers should not provide any answers at this stage but rather allow students to think for themselves.

Stage 2 – Hearing and seeing the story

At this stage, students listen to the story and work through it to find answers to your questions. If access to technology is limited or if it fails during the lesson, teachers can simply read from the book.

Stage 3 – Checking the story

Some suggested questions to be asked after listening to the story are provided in the teaching notes. This gives teachers the possibility to further assess the depth of students' comprehension of the story and of the language used. It also sparks students' creativity and imagination by encouraging them to visualize how the story develops.

Stage 4 – Role-playing the story

After listening to the story several times, students are ready to role-play it in groups, providing them with the opportunity to say larger chunks of language. Props can be brought to class and used to make the experience even more stimulating. Teachers may play the audio, or read the audio script from the Teacher's Edition, while students role-play, or students may recite the story from memory. Try to ensure that, as far as possible, every student gets an opportunity to be involved in the role-play.

Below are some suggestions for extra work with the stories:

- While students listen to the story, they perform a specific action for target vocabulary (e.g., students clap when they hear the word purple, or stamp their feet when they hear the word blue).
- Students draw a new picture for any frame of the story.
- Students create a new ending for the story.
- Students draw or describe their favorite character.
- Students discuss real-life situations with connotations to the story.
- Students comment on how they would feel or how they would behave if they were in a similar situation to one of the story characters.
- You might like to give students feedback. You could give students two stars and one wish, e.g., *Fantastic actions!, Great teamwork!, Speak a little louder next time.* This could be given in L1.

Game Bank

Picture Card games

Guess the card: Cut out a small square in the center of a sheet of paper. Hold the sheet in front of a Picture Card, allowing students to see only a small part of the picture through the hole. Students guess the item.

Memory game: Stick Picture Cards on the board. After students memorize the cards, remove them and students list the items. To make the game more challenging, ask students to say the cards in the order they appeared on the board, or only remove one.

Picture Card mime: Invite a student to the front. Show him/her a card or a written word while hiding it from the rest of the class. He/She mimes the word silently. The student who correctly guesses the word is the next one to come forward. Alternatively, split the class into two teams, and ask a member of each team to mime the same word for their teams.

Sort the cards: Divide the class into small groups. Mix Picture Cards from different units, and divide them into piles according to the number of groups. Students arrange them back into categories. The first group to finish wins.

Tic-Tac-Toe: Divide the class into two teams. One is "O" and the other is "X". Draw a large grid on the board with nine spaces. Stick one Picture Card in each space. Students select a card, and say the word on the Picture Card. If it is correct, remove the Picture Card and write an "O" or an "X" accordingly.

Hot seat: A student sits with his/her back to the class. The teacher shows the class a Picture Card, e.g., lion. Students make sentences about the animal, e.g., *They live in Africa. They can run fast. They eat meat.* The student in the hot seat has to guess the animal as quickly as possible. Set a limit for the number of sentences students can make.

TPR games

Aye, aye, Captain! You are the Captain. Give orders to the class. This is a useful activity to review actions, parts of the body, colors, numbers, and classroom objects. For example, you say, *Jump three times. Touch your head. Turn around. Then s*tudents say, *Aye, aye, Captain!* and carry out the action. Model a few times and then invite students to be the captain.

Basketball: Ask a question to a student. If he/she answers correctly, he/she has a shot at the basket. If the student gets the ball in the basket (or box), he/she wins two points. If he/she only hits the basket, he/she wins one point. The student with the most points is the winner.

Pass the ball: Students stand in a large circle. Make a paper ball (or use a soft ball), then call out a category, e.g., *family*, and throw the ball to a student. He/She must say a word in the category you mentioned. He/She then throws the ball to another student, who says another word in the same category. If a student drops the ball, he/she must sit down. Continue until one student remains. This game can also be used to have students ask and answer questions or practice vocabulary that follows a sequence, e.g., days of the week, months of the year, etc.

Teacher says: Give the students instructions but tell them to follow the instructions only if they are preceded by "Teacher says." If you say, *Pick up a pencil*, students should do nothing, but if you say, *Teacher says pick up a pencil*, students must pick up a pencil. They are out of the game if they do an action when they should not.

Team games

Category writing: Divide the class into groups. Each group chooses their "captain". Write the name of a vocabulary category on the board, e.g., sports, food, or animals. Each group helps their captain to write as many words as they can which belongs to that category in two minutes.

Drawing race: Divide the class into two teams and invite a student from each team to the front of the class. Whisper a word to the two students. Each student draws the item on the board. The first team to identify the picture correctly wins a point.

Parachute: Play a guessing game in teams. Draw a large parachute on the board with some strings leading to a stick figure hanging from the parachute. Think of a word students have learned, and draw a dash inside the parachute for each letter in the word. Students from one team try to guess the word. For each incorrect guess, erase one of the parachute's strings. Award points to the team when they guess the word correctly. If all the parachute's strings are erased before students guess the word, the other team can try.

Reading race: Write sets of sentences on strips of paper describing Picture Cards, e.g., *It's big. It's black and white. It has four legs*. Divide the class into teams and ask each team to stand in a line. Place a set of sentences face down at the front of each line. Stick the Picture Cards on the board. When you say, *Go!* one student from each team picks up a sentence, sticks it below the appropriate Picture Card on the board, and goes back to his/her team. The first team to stick all its sentences under the correct cards wins.

Phonics and spelling games

Spelling bee: Divide the class into two teams. The first player on Team A is given a word to spell. If correct, the team gets a point. This can also be done as a class competition, by having students line up to be given words one by one. When they make a mistake, they sit down. The last student standing is the winner.

Little books labeling: Do an activity to practice spelling words with the target sounds/graphemes. Give each student a sheet of paper and have them fold and tear it in half lengthways, and join the ends of the two strips with tape. Now fold the paper like a fan and stick some tape along the spine to make an eight-page book. Students write their name on the cover and then draw four simple illustrations on alternate pages. Next they switch books with a partner and label the illustrations in each other's books. Then check the books together.

Letter mess: Write a selection of letters on the board. Explain to the class that they have to make as many words as possible from the given letters. Model one or two examples on the board for them. Then give students a time limit to do the activity in pairs or small groups.

Speedy sounds: Make letter cards to review the key sounds from a unit. Show the cards in random order and have students chorus the letter sounds. Gradually increase the speed. Then show a card and elicit a word containing that sound. Repeat with the other cards.

Rhyming tennis: Play a game to practice spelling words with target sounds that rhyme, (e.g., *ou, ow, all, aw, ew*, or *y* graphemes). Put the class in two teams with a different set of letter cards. The first team must make a word using their first letter card, e.g., *y* and write it on the board, e.g., *try*. The second team must make a word that rhymes with *try* and write it on the board, e.g., *my*. The first team must hit back with another rhyming word, e.g., *fly*. The teams go back and forth until one team can't make a word. The game is over when all the cards are gone.

Spin the pencil: Play a game to practice spelling words with target sounds/graphemes. Put the students in pairs. Have them draw a large circle on a sheet of paper with graphemes around the edge of the circle (like a clock face). They take it in turns spinning a pencil in the circle and spelling a word from the letter sound that the pencil is pointing to.

Spell check: Do an activity to practice spelling words with target sounds and to focus on punctuation. Write five sentences on the board, each with two errors, e.g. the sentence does not begin with a capital letter, the final punctuation is missing or wrong, sample words are misspelled. In pairs, students correct the mistakes.

Miscellaneous games

Bingo: Play bingo with any topic. Ask students to draw the bingo grids. Then they write or draw in the boxes the vocabulary items you wish to review. The winner is the first student to check off all the items on his/her grid.

Drawing game: Students draw pictures of target vocabulary on the board. They must do this slowly, line by line. The class tries to guess what he/she is drawing before he/she finishes the picture. The first student to guess draws the next item.

I spy: Choose something you can see and say, *I spy with my little eye something beginning with (g)*. Students guess the object. The student who guesses correctly has a turn at choosing an item.

Pass the secret: Have students sit in a circle. Start the secret by whispering a simple sentence to the student next to you, e.g., *I have a yellow hat*. The students whisper the secret around the circle. The last student says the secret out loud. Compare how close it is to your original secret sentence. If necessary, write the original secret sentence on the board.

Picture dictation: Divide the class into pairs. Student A describes a picture for Student B to draw. Then they switch roles. This game can be played with any lexical set.

Stop the bus: Write a letter on the board and shout, *Start the bus!* Students write as many words beginning with this letter as they can think of. When you shout, *Stop the bus!*, everyone stops writing. Students get one point for each word.

Song or Chant extension: Have students work in pairs or small groups. Prompt them to write a new verse for the song, using the lyrics on the Student Book pages. You can change just some words or all the lyrics depending on their level.

Extension Bank

Welcome

My weekend schedule: Give students a sheet of paper and ask them to write down their weekend schedule. Students then ask and answer questions about each other's schedules. Invite some pairs to come to the front and talk about their partner's schedule.

My special friend: Give each student a sheet of paper. They draw a picture of a friend from outside the class, as well as some smaller pictures of things that person likes, or can do. They label the items and title the picture. Then have students come to the front to introduce their friend. Display the pictures in the classroom.

Unit 1

Find your match: Have each student think of two adjectives of character that describe themselves. Then ask all students to stand up and mingle around the classroom. They have to find their match by sharing their description, e.g., *I am shy and clever.* If the other student uses one of their adjectives too, they can stay together. When everyone has a match, the pairs take turns describing their partner, e.g., *He is sporty and patient. I am friendly and creative.*

Guess who? Cut out or photocopy pictures of famous people or movie/cartoon characters that the students will know. Have them work in small teams to describe the different appearance and personality traits of the people/characters, e.g., *Look at this picture. She has dark hair and glasses. She is old. She looks friendly.* After practicing, students can choose their favorite two, and make a poster describing them.

Unit 2

***Always, Sometimes, Never* game:** Write the headings *Always, Usually, Sometimes, Often, Never* on the board. Divide the class in half and have them stand in two circles. Get in the middle of one circle and say, *Always! I always brush my teeth.* then quickly point to a student and say, *Never!*, and then help them to say a *never* sentence as quickly as possible. They then point to someone else and say, e.g., *Sometimes!* That person has to quickly say a sentence with *sometimes*. Repeat until everyone has a turn.

My school life: Give a sheet of paper to each student and give them time to draw and label a poster about their life: hobbies, favorite subjects at school, friends, etc. Have students present their posters to the class, and encourage others to ask questions. Display the posters in the classroom.

Review Units 1 & 2

Comic strip: Give each student a large piece of poster paper and ask them to divide it in four squares. Tell students they are going to create a comic strip story about a person. They need to talk about who they are, and their daily routines, in the story. In the first box, ask students to either draw a picture of their character or cut one from a magazine. In the second box, they should draw a picture showing the kind of person they are (e.g., sporty, helpful, friendly, etc.). In the third box, they should draw a picture of some things they always, usually, often, or sometimes. And in the fourth box, they draw something they never do. Students should write a sentence underneath each box. Display the pictures in the classroom.

Unit 3

Animal world: Divide students into groups of four. Give each group an animal picture, or have them draw one, and then ask them to make a presentation on what they know about the animal. Ask them to talk about what they like and don't like, and what actions the animal can and can't do. Have groups present to the class orally.

Whisper game: Divide the students into small teams and have them stand in line. The last student in the line whispers two sentences about someone in class to the student in front of them, using target language, e.g., *The teacher had a busy day yesterday. She was running races and going shopping.* When the messages reach the first student in each line, the students all say the sentences aloud. The last student in the line verifies if it is correct. Correct answers get a point. The last student in the line then goes to the front of the line, and the game is repeated until everyone has a turn at being the 'whisperer'.

Unit 4

My country / My city poster: Give each student a sheet of paper and ask them to design a poster about their country or city, drawing and labeling things and places that can be found in their country or city. Students come to the front and present their poster to the class. Display the posters in the classroom.

Crossword puzzle: Give each student a sheet of paper and ask them to design a crossword puzzle with at least six countries in it. Tell them to leave the squares blank, and have them draw pictures or flags as clues for each answer. Circulate and help as needed. When students are done, they have to pass their crossword puzzles to another student to do.

Review Units 3 & 4

Show and tell: Have students prepare a poster about themselves for show and tell in the classroom. They should include pictures of themselves and information about their favorite hobbies and activities. Have students present their poster to the whole class, individually or in small teams. Encourage other students to ask questions.

Unit 5

The fashion show game: Give each student a sheet of paper and have them draw and color a picture of a boy or girl with interesting and fashionable clothes. Then have them walk like a model down the runway with their picture in front of them, as other students suggest sentences using target language. Then display the pictures in the classroom.

Ad design: Pair students and give each pair a sheet of paper. Ask them to design an advert for a shop of their choice. Tell them to use a question in their ad (e.g., *Are you looking for the perfect pet?*) When they are done, pairs can present their ad by reading it dramatically, as if they were presenting it on the radio. Have students vote for the best ad. Display the ads in the classroom.

Unit 6

Irregular verb memory chant: Have students sit in a circle on chairs. Start a chant rhythm by tapping your lap, then say, *On Monday, I made a cake*, and elicit a repeat as a practice try. Start again, then have the next student repeat, and then add their own statement about something they did in the past. Continue around the circle. If a student forgets one part, they have to sit out.

A problem month: Pair students. Photocopy Activity Sheet 12 (see Poptropica English World) and give each student a copy, which they have to cut into strips. Tell the pairs to match up an irregular past tense verb they have learned in this unit to a number, think of a problem, and say a sentence using both the number and the verb: *On the fifteenth, I met a mean dog.* Then they have to think of a creative solution, and use a later number. *On the eighteenth, I saw him again and gave him a cookie. Now the dog is my friend.* Invite confident students to share their problems and solutions.

Review Units 5 & 6

My vacation: Place Picture Cards 78–104 around the classroom. Tell students they are going to talk about an imaginary vacation. Brainstorm some places that you might go on vacation, and the kinds of things you might do. Ask students to create a poster of their vacation. Then ask them to write a short story, talking about what they did, and what kind of clothes they wore.

Unit 7

Family tree: Ask students to research their family history as homework. In class, give each student a sheet of paper. Tell the students to draw their family tree and label it. Have students talk about their families and their family history in pairs. Then have some students present their family tree to the class. Display the family trees in the classroom.

What school is like for me: Pair students. Photocopy Activity Sheet 14 (see Poptropica English World) and give each pair a copy, which they have to cut into pieces. Students take turns handing their partner a card. The other student has to then say what they think about the subject, using the target language, e.g., *Last year, math was easy for me. Now it is difficult.*

Unit 8

TV show guessing game: Divide the class in half and start each team with five points. Invite a student to think of a TV show others may know of. The other students ask questions, e.g., *Is it funny? Is it about soldiers? Is it at night?*, etc. The student answers, yes or no. If a student thinks they know the TV show, they may guess, but if they are wrong their team loses a point.

Family picture: Have students draw, label, and color a picture of a family they know living overseas. Students then present their picture to the class. Encourage other students to ask questions. Later, display the pictures in the classroom.

Review Units 7 & 8

Word Association game: Pair students. Tell them they will play a word matching game using words from these categories: *countries and nationalities, school, jobs, describing how we feel about something.* Place a Picture Card on the board to illustrate each category. Ask one student to join you at the front to model the game. Tell them you will say a word and they have to say another word that matches it. For example, *Korea – Korean; interesting – boring; queen – king.* Continue until you deliberately make a mistake and students catch you out. Now have students play in pairs. Keep a tally of how many times each pair wins a round.

Goodbye

Spelling quiz: In a reading activity, have students circle words from the texts that are new to them. Brainstorm the list together, and write the words on the board. Give students a minute or two to study the list then erase it. Hold a two-team spelling bee game or a mini spelling quiz on paper.

Word game: Say a word connected to the topic, *School*, e.g., *math*. A volunteer says any word they associate with *math*, e.g., *numbers*, or *difficult*. Another student continues, saying any one word they associate with the previous one. Continue around the class. If students hesitate or say an inappropriate word, they are out!

Unit Overview

Unit Objective

- I can talk about time, and activities now and in the past

Language

Target Vocabulary	Time: two days ago, yesterday, today, now, tomorrow
Target Structures	I played tennis on Monday morning. We cleaned our rooms on Saturday morning. He/She danced at the party on Friday evening. They went to the movies on Saturday afternoon.

Skills

Reading	• Can understand a story • Can identify when people did activities in the past
Writing	• Can complete simple sentences about the characters in a story • Can write about what people are doing now • Can write about when I did activities in the past • Can complete simple sentences about regular activities *(Workbook)*
Listening	• Can understand a story • Can identify characters in a story • Can recognize at what time people do regular activities
Speaking	• Can talk about when I did activities in the past

Lesson 1 SB pages 6–7 or Poptropica English World

Learning Objective
Can understand a story

Additional Language
diamonds, incredible, of course, follow it!

Warm-up

- Pre-teach the word *skidoo* and find out what students know about traveling over snow and ice. Ask students, *What other ways are there to travel over snow and ice?* Ask students to open their books and find a skidoo in the story. Ask, *Does it look new or old?*

Open books and ask students to look at the pictures. Ask, *What are we learning today?* Write the lesson objective on the board: *We're reading a story.*

1 A:02 Talk about the pictures. Then listen and read.

- Ask the class questions about each picture. Students answer or guess. Ask, e.g., *What can you see in Picture 1? What time of day is it? Who's on TV in Picture 2? What does the man want? What are they traveling on in Picture 3?*
- Play the audio and have students listen and follow. Ask questions to check comprehension, e.g., *Who wants the diamonds? (Hector Frost) Where are the diamonds? (in the town) Who lives above the supplies store? (Polly and her mom) What is Mike's dog's name? (Gizmo) What wakes Polly up? (the skidoo) What does Gizmo find outside? (a red ribbon)*, etc.

Point to the lesson objective on the board. Ask students, *What happened in the story?* Give students a minute to tell their partner.

- Ask students, *Where are you on your learning adventure?* Ask them which words they find easiest or most difficult to remember. Tell students, *Good job!* to reinforce the progress they are making.

Pop Quiz: Say the name of each character, and ask students to say a sentence about that character, e.g., *Smith (Smith drives the skidoo.)*.

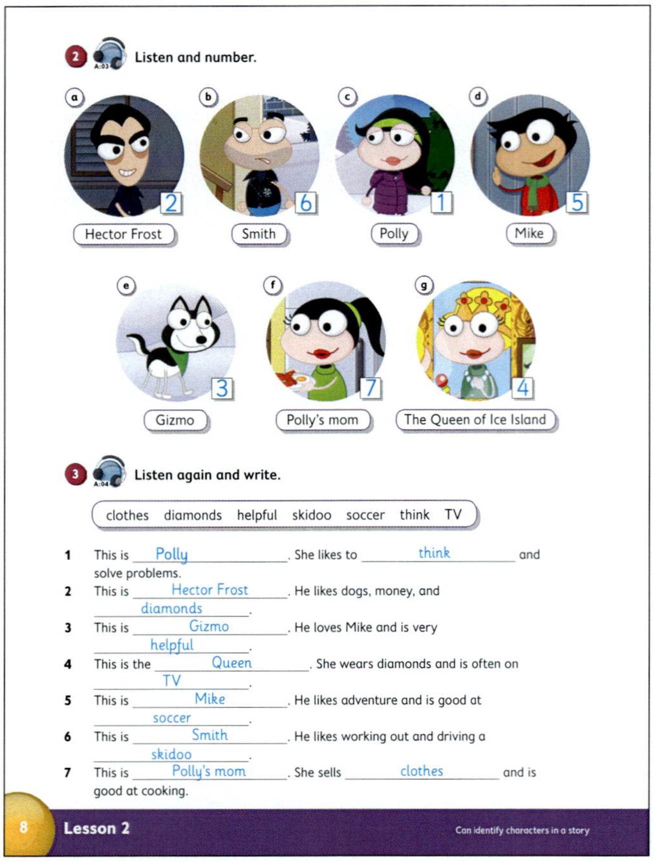

2 Listen and number.

a	b	c	d	e	f	g
Hector Frost 2	Smith 6	Polly 1	Mike 5	Gizmo 3	Polly's mom 7	The Queen of Ice Island 4

3 Listen again and write.

clothes diamonds helpful skidoo soccer think TV

1 This is Polly. She likes to think and solve problems.
2 This is Hector Frost. He likes dogs, money, and diamonds.
3 This is Gizmo. He loves Mike and is very helpful.
4 This is the Queen. She wears diamonds and is often on TV.
5 This is Mike. He likes adventure and is good at soccer.
6 This is Smith. He likes working out and driving a skidoo.
7 This is Polly's mom. She sells clothes and is good at cooking.

8 Lesson 2 Can identify characters in a story

Lesson 2 SB page 8 or Poptropica English World

Learning Objective
Can identify characters in a story

Additional Language
clothes, diamonds, helpful, skidoo, soccer, think, TV

Warm-up

- Review introductions. Invite a student to come forward and then say to the class, *This is (name). He/She likes...* . Have the student introduce you to the class.
- Invite students to pair up to practice introductions. Then go around the class and have students introduce their partner to you.

Open books and ask students to look at the book. Ask, *What are we learning today?* Write the lesson objective on the board: *We're learning to talk about the characters in the story.*

2 A:03 Listen and number.

- Have students look at the pictures. Review the names of the characters.
- Tell students they will listen to some numbered introductions for the characters, and they have to write the numbers in the correct boxes. Play the audio and have students match the character to the introduction they hear. You may want to pause the audio between each numbered item, to give students time to write the answers.

1 This is Polly. She likes to think and solve problems.
2 This is Hector Frost. He likes dogs, money, and diamonds.
3 This is Gizmo. He loves Mike and is very helpful.
4 This is the Queen. She wears diamonds and is often on TV.
5 This is Mike. He likes adventure and is good at soccer.
6 This is Smith. He likes working out and driving a skidoo.
7 This is Polly's mom. She sells clothes and is good at cooking.

3 A:04 Listen again and write.

- Draw students' attention to the words in the word box. Have students say the words chorally.
- Give students time to read the incomplete introductions. Then play the audio again and have students complete the introductions.
- To check answers, have students switch their books, and read the sentences chorally.

Pop Quiz: Pair students and ask them to prepare introductions for each other, including their names and what they like, e.g., *This is Sally. She likes singing and snowboarding.* Ask them to introduce each other to the class.

Homework WB page 4

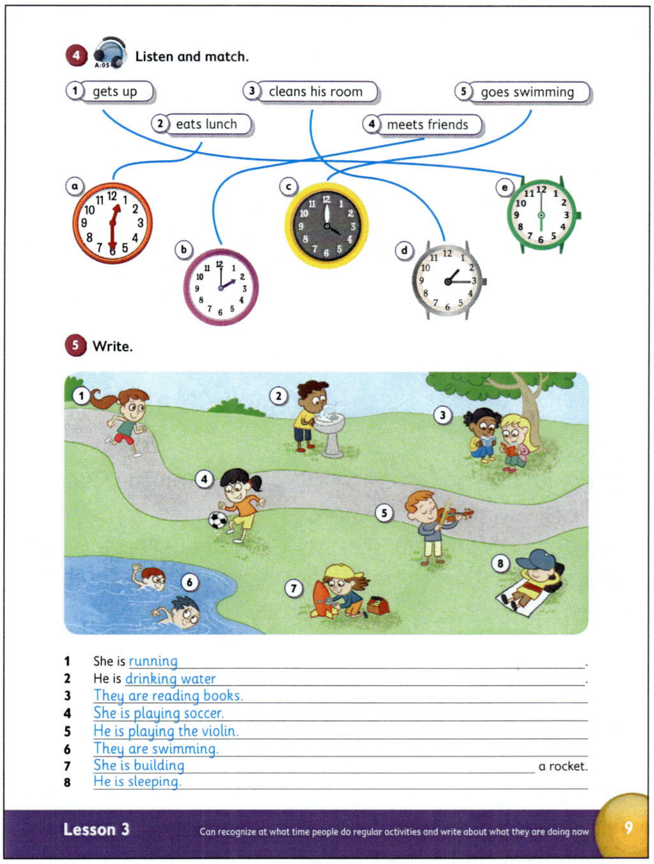

4 Listen and match.

1 gets up
2 eats lunch
3 cleans his room
4 meets friends
5 goes swimming

a b c d e

5 Write.

1 She is running.
2 He is drinking water.
3 They are reading books.
4 She is playing soccer.
5 He is playing the violin.
6 They are swimming.
7 She is building a rocket.
8 He is sleeping.

Lesson 3 Can recognize at what time people do regular activities and write about what they are doing now 9

Lesson 3 SB page 9 or Poptropica English World

Learning Objective
Can recognize at what time people do regular activities and write about what they are doing now

Additional Language
gets up, eats lunch, cleans his room, meets friends, goes swimming

Warm-up

- Review expressions of time with Picture Cards 1–4. Have students listen and repeat as you show the picture side, then the word side of the Picture Cards. Write jumbled versions on the board, and have students guess the answer. Then invite them to spell the words chorally.

Open books and ask students to look at the book. Ask, *What are we learning today?* Write the lesson objective on the board: *We're learning to talk about when people do regular activities and write about what they are doing now.*

4 Listen and match.

A:05

- Read the numbered texts chorally. Then draw students' attention to the clocks. Ask, *What time is it?*, and have students answer chorally.
- Play the audio. Tell students to listen only.

1 She gets up at six o'clock.
2 He eats lunch at twelve thirty.
3 He cleans his room at a quarter after one.
4 She meets friends at two o'clock.
5 She goes swimming at four o'clock.

- Play the audio again, and have students match the activity to the time of day.
- Have students check their answers in pairs. Play the audio again, and stop after each item to ask students questions about each item, e.g., *What time does she get up? (She gets up at six o'clock.).*

5 Write.

- Give students time to study the picture. Ask students questions about the picture, *Look at 1. What is she doing?* Elicit, *She's running.*
- Give students time to complete the activity.
- To check answers, have students pair up and switch books. Invite volunteers to stand and ask a question about an item, e.g., *Look at 2. What is he doing?*, and choose a student to answer.

Pop Quiz: Have students take turns miming an action for the class. The other students have to guess what he/she is doing, e.g., *He's playing the piano./She's sleeping.*

Materials
Picture Cards 1–4

Homework WB page 5

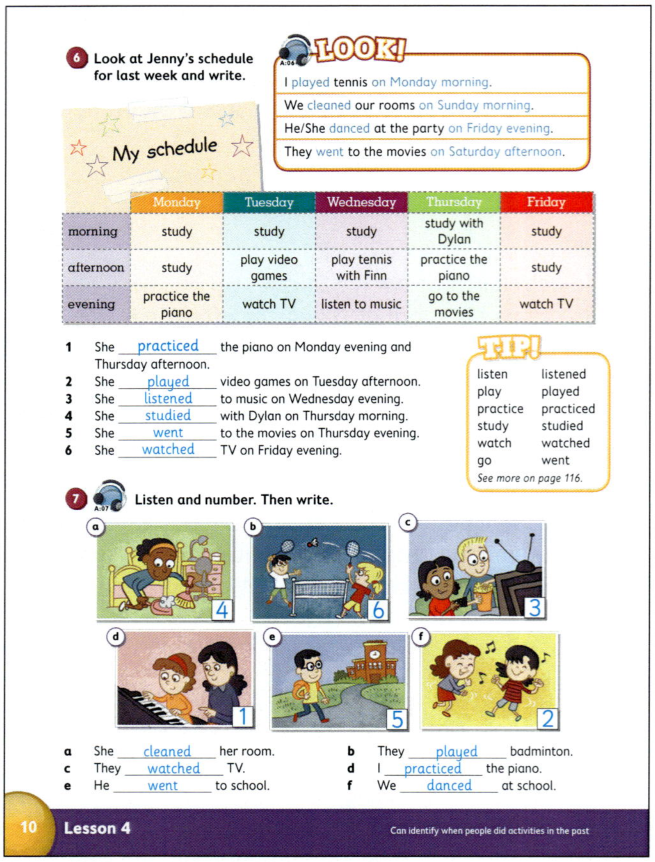

6 Look at Jenny's schedule for last week and write.

LOOK!

A:06

I played tennis on Monday morning.
We cleaned our rooms on Sunday morning.
He/She danced at the party on Friday evening.
They went to the movies on Saturday afternoon.

My schedule

	Monday	Tuesday	Wednesday	Thursday	Friday
morning	study	study	study	study with Dylan	study
afternoon	study	play video games	play tennis with Finn	practice the piano	study
evening	practice the piano	watch TV	listen to music	go to the movies	watch TV

1 She practiced the piano on Monday evening and Thursday afternoon.
2 She played video games on Tuesday afternoon.
3 She listened to music on Wednesday evening.
4 She studied with Dylan on Thursday morning.
5 She went to the movies on Thursday evening.
6 She watched TV on Friday evening.

TIP!

listen	listened
play	played
practice	practiced
study	studied
watch	watched
go	went

See more on page 116.

7 A:07 Listen and number. Then write.

a 4 b 6 c 3 d 1 e 5 f 2

a She cleaned her room.
b They played badminton.
c They watched TV.
d I practiced the piano.
e He went to school.
f We danced at school.

10 Lesson 4 Can identify when people did activities in the past

Lesson 4 SB page 10 or Poptropica English World

Learning Objective
Can identify when people did activities in the past

Warm-up

- Put students into pairs to talk about their school schedules. Tell them they can look at the schedule on page 10 of their Student Book as a guide. Give students time to ask and answer questions.
- Invite students to come to the front to talk about themselves, and each other.

Open books and ask students to look at the book and the Look! box. Ask, *What are we learning today?* Write the lesson objective on the board: *We're learning to talk about when people did activities in the past.*

6 Look at Jenny's schedule for last week and write.

- Draw students' attention to the Look! box and play the audio (track A:06).
- Point to the schedule and ask students, *What is this?* Elicit, *It's Jenny's schedule.*
- Give students time to study the schedule. Ask, *What did Jenny do on Friday afternoon?* (*She studied.*) Invite one or two volunteers to ask similar questions.
- Give students time to write the missing words.
- To check answers, have students say the sentences chorally. Students check their own work.

Tip!

Draw students' attention to the Tip! box on the page. Read the verbs together chorally, and mime an action for students to copy as you say each one. Direct students' attention to additional verbs on pages 116–119, and say some of them chorally.

7 A:07 Listen and number. Then write.

- Ask students to look at the pictures. Point and ask, *What did he/she do? What did they do?*, and elicit answers.
- Play the audio, giving students time to write the numbers in the correct boxes.

1 I practiced the piano.
2 We danced at school.
3 They watched TV.
4 She cleaned her room.
5 He went to school.
6 They played badminton.

- After students have numbered the boxes, draw their attention to the incomplete sentences. Give students time to complete the activity. To check answers, have students say the sentences chorally. Students check their own work.
- Give each student the Welcome Worksheet (see page 34) and give them time to do the activity. To check answers, have students pass their worksheet to a partner. Invite volunteers to say the answers.

Pop Quiz: Write a schedule on the board similar to the one from Student Book, page 10. Complete the schedule with different activities, e.g., *play soccer, practice the violin, do homework, study with Annie, walk my dog*. Tell students it is Evan's schedule. Ask students to make statements about Evan, e.g., *Evan walked his dog on Friday morning. He played soccer on Saturday.*, etc.

Materials
Welcome Worksheet

Homework WB page 6

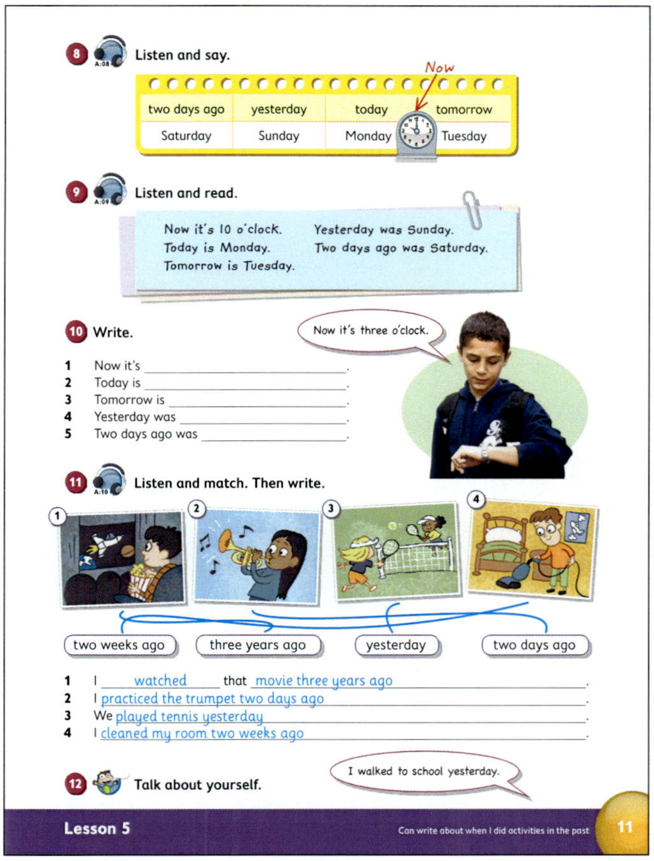
8 Listen and say.

two days ago	yesterday	today	tomorrow
Saturday	Sunday	Monday	Tuesday

Now

9 Listen and read.

Now it's 10 o'clock.
Today is Monday.
Tomorrow is Tuesday.
Yesterday was Sunday.
Two days ago was Saturday.

10 Write.

Now it's three o'clock.

1 Now it's ___.
2 Today is ___.
3 Tomorrow is ___.
4 Yesterday was ___.
5 Two days ago was ___.

11 Listen and match. Then write.

two weeks ago | three years ago | yesterday | two days ago

1 I watched that movie three years ago.
2 I practiced the trumpet two days ago.
3 We played tennis yesterday.
4 I cleaned my room two weeks ago.

12 Talk about yourself.

I walked to school yesterday.

Lesson 5 Can write about when I did activities in the past 11

Lesson 5 SB page 11 or Poptropica English World

Learning Objective
Can write about when I did activities in the past

Target Language
Two days ago was Saturday.

Warm-up

- Write *today*, *tomorrow*, *yesterday*, and *two days ago* on the board. Have students read chorally then have them say what day it is today, what day it was yesterday, what day it will be tomorrow, and what day it was two days ago.

Open books and ask students to look at the book. Ask, *What are we learning today?* Write the lesson objective on the board: *We're learning to write about what we did in the past.*

8 Listen and say.

A:08

- Direct students' attention to the memo.
- Play the audio, and have students listen and repeat.

9 Listen and read.

A:09

- Direct students' attention to the memo.
- Play the audio, and have students listen and read along.

10 Write.

- Direct students' attention back to the memo in Activity 9.
- Give students time to complete the sentences. Check answers as a class.

11 Listen and match. Then write.

A:10

- Direct students' attention to the pictures and the expressions of time in the boxes below.
- Play the audio, and have students follow and match the pictures to the text.

1 I watched that movie three years ago.
2 I practiced the trumpet two days ago.
3 We played tennis yesterday.
4 I cleaned my room two weeks ago.

- Now ask students to write the sentences as they heard them. Play the audio again if students are having difficulty remembering.
- To check answers, put students in pairs and have them switch books. Read the sentences chorally.

12 Talk about yourself.

- Direct students' attention to the speech bubble. Invite a volunteer to read it, then read chorally.
- Put students into small groups, and allow them time to complete the activity. Randomly ask students to say something to the class about themselves.

Pop Quiz: Write *yesterday, three days ago, one week ago,* and *ten years ago,* on the board. Ask students to pretend they are someone famous, and to say statements about themselves using the phrases on the board. Other students guess who they are, e.g., *Ten years ago I was in a Harry Potter movie. One week ago I met Rupert Grinch and Daniel Radcliffe for lunch. Three days ago I went to the U.S.A. Yesterday I cleaned my room. (Emma Watson)*

Are you ready for Unit 1?

- Ask students how they feel about their learning in this unit. Ask students to tell you what they found easy and what they found the most difficult to learn in the unit.
- Ask students, *Where do you think you are on your learning adventure?* Ask students if they are ready to move on to the next unit. Tell students that it is fine if they do not remember everything as they will continue to practice throughout the level.
- Encourage students to ask if they have any questions about what they learned in the Welcome unit. Tell students, *Good job!* to reinforce the progress they are making.

Homework WB page 7

Welcome Worksheet

Name ______________________ Class ____________

Write about the children's busy week.

1 SUNDAY	2 MONDAY	3 TUESDAY

4 WEDNESDAY	5 THURSDAY	6 FRIDAY	7 SATURDAY

1 She practiced the piano on Sunday.

2 They ______________________________.

3 ______________________________.

4 ______________________________.

5 ______________________________.

6 ______________________________.

7 ______________________________.

1 Friends

Unit Overview

Unit Objective

- I can talk about physical appearance and personality

Language

Target Vocabulary	Physical appearance: dark hair, light hair, spiky hair, bald, handsome, beautiful, good-looking, cute Adjectives to describe personality: bossy, creative, sporty, lazy, smart, patient, talkative, helpful, friendly, hard-working
Target Structures	What does he/she look like? He's/She's good-looking. He/She has straight, dark hair, and brown eyes. What do they look like? They're tall and good-looking. They have short, light hair, and blue eyes. He/She doesn't have light hair. / They don't have light hair. What's he/she like? He's sporty and he's smart. She's bossy, but hard-working. I like him because he's patient. I like her because she's friendly.
Features	**Cross-curricular:** Art: Warm and cool colors **Values:** Help your friends in class.

Skills

Reading	• Can identify words that describe what people look like • Can understand a simple story • Can understand details of a story • Can understand an email about what other people are like
Writing	• Can write short sentences about what people are like • Can write about a painting • Can write short sentences that describe what people look like *(Workbook)* • Can write short sentences about what makes good and bad friends *(Workbook)* • Can write an online profile about myself *(Workbook)*
Listening	• Can identify words that describe what people look like • Can identify words that describe personality
Speaking	• Can ask and answer about what someone looks like • Can talk about what someone is like • Can discuss a story • Can talk about helping my friends in class • Can talk about warm and cool colors and how they make me feel

Lesson 1 SB page 12 or Poptropica English World

Learning Objective
Can identify words that describe what people look like

Target Language
dark hair, light hair, spiky hair, bald, handsome, beautiful, good-looking, cute

1 What do you know?

- Open books and ask students to look at the pictures. Ask, *What are we learning today?* Write the lesson objective on the board: *We're learning about what people look like.*
- Close books. Ask students what English words they know for describing people. Introduce students to the learning adventure poster. Use this poster with students to help them indicate how confident they feel about the lesson objective and show the teacher who may need more help. See pages 8–9 of the Introduction for how to use this with your classes.
- Refer to the learning adventure poster and say, *Great! You are already moving along your learning adventure!*

2 A:11 Listen and read. Who lives at number 12?

- Play the audio and have students listen. Ask students to identify the characters.

3 A:12 Listen and say.

- Focus on the people's faces. Play the audio and have students repeat.
- Put Picture Cards 5–12 on the board. In pairs, one student points to a person in the class and says, *What does (name) look like?* His/her partner has to say a word to describe that person. Students use as many different adjectives as possible.

4 A:13 Who's who in Activity 3? Listen and number.

- Play the audio again. Have students number the boxes.

> **a** This is my brother, Joe. / He has short dark hair and glasses. Cool!
> **b** This is my friend Jack. He has spiky hair. Do you like it? / Yes, I do.
> **c** My aunt Sara is great. She's very beautiful.
> **d** This is my grandpa. He's bald.
> **e** The handsome man is my uncle.
> **f** And this is my baby sister Rose. She's cute. / So cute!

> **g** I know this one. She has light hair and is very beautiful! / Yes! She's my best friend and I think she's very beautiful!

- Check answers as a class.

Ask students, *How many words do you know for describing what people look like now?* Give students a minute to tell their partner the new words they know.

- Ask students to say where they are on their adventure now. Ask students which words they find easiest or most difficult to remember. Tell students, *Good job!* to reinforce the progress they are making.

Pop Quiz: Show students a selection of pictures of people from magazines and ask them to describe the people using words from the lesson.

- Direct students' attention to the ice cream card on page 12. Tell students to go online to the Poptropica English Island Adventure Game and find the item. Once students click on it, they are taken to a supplementary language task.

Materials
Poster, Picture Cards 5–12, pictures of people (cut from magazines)

Homework WB page 8

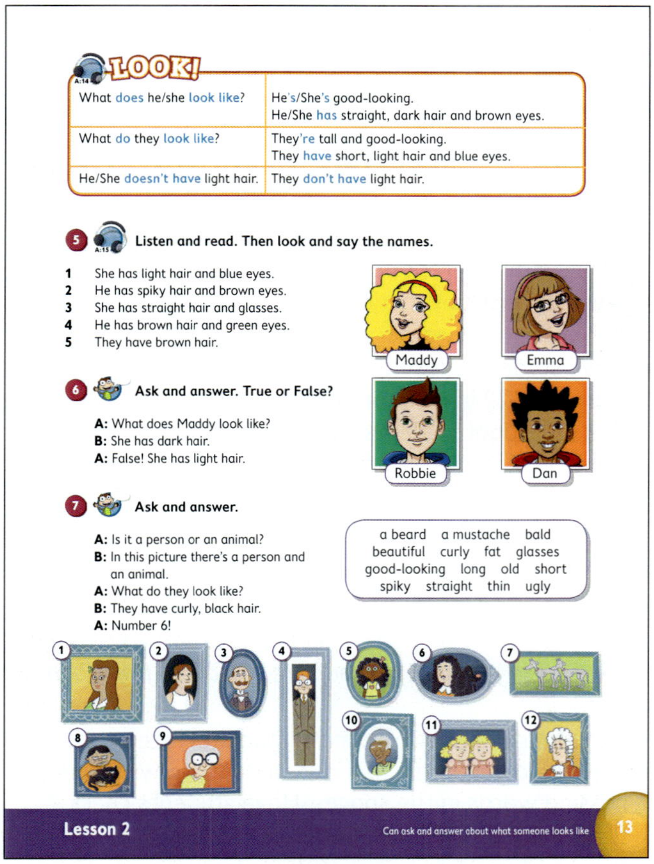

LOOK! A:14

What does he/she look like?	He's/She's good-looking. He/She has straight, dark hair and brown eyes.
What do they look like?	They're tall and good-looking. They have short, light hair and blue eyes.
He/She doesn't have light hair.	They don't have light hair.

5 A:15 Listen and read. Then look and say the names.

1 She has light hair and blue eyes.
2 He has spiky hair and brown eyes.
3 She has straight hair and glasses.
4 He has brown hair and green eyes.
5 They have brown hair.

6 Ask and answer. True or False?

A: What does Maddy look like?
B: She has dark hair.
A: False! She has light hair.

7 Ask and answer.

A: Is it a person or an animal?
B: In this picture there's a person and an animal.
A: What do they look like?
B: They have curly, black hair.
A: Number 6!

a beard a mustache bald beautiful curly fat glasses good-looking long old short spiky straight thin ugly

Lesson 2 Can ask and answer about what someone looks like 13

Lesson 2 SB page 13 or Poptropica English World

Learning Objective
Can ask and answer about what someone looks like

Warm-up

- Ask the class, *What does (name of your school principal) look like?* Elicit responses from students (ensuring they are polite). Continue this game, using well-known people.

Open books and ask students to look at the activities and the Look! box. Ask, *What are we learning today?* Write the lesson objective on the board: *We're learning to ask and answer questions about what people look like.*

5 A:15 Listen and read. Then look and say the names.

- Draw students' attention to the Look! box and play the audio (track A:14). Students repeat chorally.
- Review the names of the characters.
- Play the audio and have students match the description to the character by saying the name/names after each statement.
- To review comprehension, say a name, e.g., *Maddy!* and elicit a description, e.g., *She has light hair and blue eyes.*

6 Ask and answer. True or False?

- Ask students to practice the exchange in Activity 6 in pairs. Tell them to repeat with the remaining pictures, and to continue with well-known people if there is time.

7 Ask and answer.

- Point to the word box. Read the words chorally. Pre-teach *straight hair* and review *long, short, curly, fat, thin, ugly, old, young, glasses, mustache,* by saying, for example, *(Name) has long straight hair.*
- Help students to find a different partner and practice the exchange in Activity 7. Tell them to repeat the exchange with the remaining pictures and to continue with well-known people if there is time.

Pop Quiz: Show the same selection of pictures of people from Lesson 1, but now with names written at the top of each picture. Ask students to play a guessing game in pairs. The first student describes one of the people. The second student guesses who it is.

Materials
Pictures of people from Lesson 1 (cut from magazines)

Homework WB page 9

8 Listen and say. **VOCABULARY**

1 bossy 2 creative 3 sporty 4 lazy 5 smart

6 patient 7 talkative 8 helpful 9 friendly 10 hard-working

9 Listen to the song and write. **SONG**

You have me, and I have you.
You talk, you listen, and I do, too.
We're friends. We're friends.
Ben's 1 lazy at home,
And he's 2 shy at school.
He's 3 sporty and 4 clever,
And very cool.
We're friends. We're friends.
Jim's sometimes 5 bossy,
But that's OK.
He's always 6 helpful in every way.
We're friends. We're friends.
We're friends. We're friends.

10 Look at Activity 9 and write.

1 What's Ben like? Ben is lazy and shy. He's sporty and clever, too.
2 What's Jim like? Jim is bossy but helpful.

14 Lesson 3 Can identify words that describe personality

Lesson 3 SB page 14 or Poptropica English World

Learning Objective
Can identify words that describe personality

Target Language
bossy, creative, sporty, lazy, smart, patient, talkative, helpful, friendly, hard-working

Open books and ask students to look at the pictures. Ask, *What are we learning today?* Write the lesson objective on the board: *We're learning words that describe personality.*

- Close books. Ask students what English personality adjectives they know, e.g., *nice, polite.* Write these on the board.
- Refer to the learning adventure poster and say, *Great! You are moving along your learning adventure!*

Warm-up

- Review appearance words. Describe three or four students to the class (being sensitive with your descriptions) without saying their names. Students guess who they are.

8 A:16 Listen and say.

- Play the audio and ask students to listen and look. Play the audio again and have students repeat the new vocabulary.
- Ask, *Who is lazy? (The girl in Picture 4 is lazy.)* Ask two students to stand up. One student asks a question and the other responds. Repeat the exchange a few more times with different pairs of students.
- Ask the class to practice this matching game in pairs for all the new words.
- Have students close their books. Hold up Picture Cards 13–22 in turn for students to say the words. Ask individual students to come to the front and write the words on the board.

9 A:17 A:18 Listen to the song and write.

- Introduce the song by saying, *This is a song about friends/friendship. Everyone has friends. What kind of friend are you? Are you a helpful friend? Are you a good friend? Are you a lazy friend? Are you a bad friend? Think about it!*
- Play the song audio and have students listen.
- Play the audio again and ask students to write the missing words in the spaces. Have students check their answers with partners.
- Play the karaoke version of the song and encourage students to sing along if they feel confident enough.

10 Look at Activity 9 and write.

- Ask students questions about the picture. Say, *This is Ben and Jim. The song is about Ben and Jim. What are they like? Look at the words to the song.*
- Remind students the difference between *and* and *but* (They both add information, but *but* is used when the added information contrasts with the first piece of information.)
- Tell students to answer the questions in Activity 10. Have students check answers in pairs.

Ask students, *How many personality adjectives do you know now?* Give students a minute to tell their partner the new words they know.

- Ask students to say where they are on their adventure now. Ask students which words they find easiest or most difficult to remember. Tell students, *Good job!* to reinforce the progress they are making.

Pop Quiz: Ask students to describe someone they know to the class. Why do they like this person?

Materials
Poster, Picture Cards 13–22

Homework WB page 10

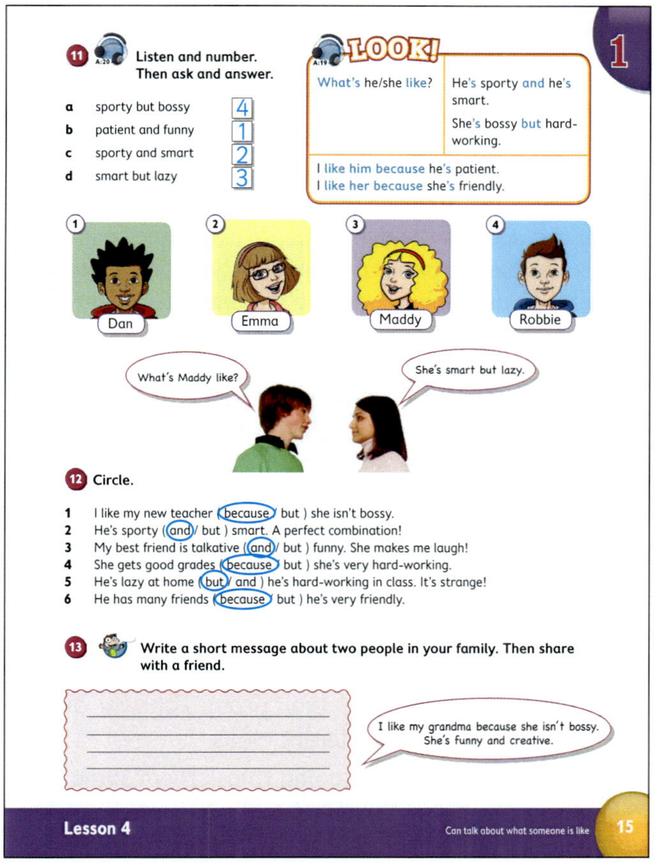
11 Listen and number. Then ask and answer.

a	sporty but bossy	4
b	patient and funny	1
c	sporty and smart	2
d	smart but lazy	3

LOOK!

What's he/she like?	He's sporty and he's smart. She's bossy but hard-working.

I like him because he's patient.
I like her because she's friendly.

12 Circle.

1 I like my new teacher (because / but) she isn't bossy.
2 He's sporty (and / but) smart. A perfect combination!
3 My best friend is talkative (and / but) funny. She makes me laugh!
4 She gets good grades (because / but) she's very hard-working.
5 He's lazy at home (but / and) he's hard-working in class. It's strange!
6 He has many friends (because / but) he's very friendly.

13 Write a short message about two people in your family. Then share with a friend.

Lesson 4 Can talk about what someone is like 15

Lesson 4 SB page 15 or Poptropica English World

Learning Objective
Can talk about what someone is like

Warm-up

- Ask students to sit in a circle on chairs and have one student stand in the center. Explain that when you show a Picture Card, the student has to say the word, then point to a person and say a sentence, *(Name) is (smart).* He/She may also point to him/herself. The person who is named should go into the circle next. Repeat the process, so everyone has a turn.

Open books and ask students to look at the activities and the Look! box. Ask, *What are we learning today?* Write the lesson objective on the board: *We're learning to talk about what people are like.*

11 Listen and number. Then ask and answer.

- Draw students' attention to the Look! box and play the audio (track A:19). Students repeat chorally.
- Play the audio, and have students say the sentences along with the audio. Ask them to write the numbers in the boxes.

> **1** Dan has spiky hair and brown eyes. He's patient and funny.
> **2** Emma has gray eyes and wears glasses. She's sporty and smart.
> **3** Maddy has blond hair and blue eyes. She's smart but lazy.
> **4** Robbie has green eyes. He's sporty but sometimes bossy.

- Remind students that the use of the word *because* leads into a reason for something.
- Pair students and have them ask each other about the characters. Ask, *What's Maddy like?* Help students answer, *Maddy is smart, but lazy.* Partners play until they have practiced all the target items.

12 Circle.

- Ask students to read the sentences and circle the correct word, *and, but* or *because*.
- Have students switch books with a partner for marking, and invite students to read the answers.

13 Write a short message about two people in your family. Then share with a friend.

- Show a picture of someone you know well and say, *I like (name) because he isn't lazy. He is helpful and friendly.* Ask students to read the example at the bottom right corner of page 15 chorally. When students have completed the activity, they can share the information with a friend.
- To extend the lesson, pair students and give each student Activity Sheet 1 (see page 152), which they cut out. Let them play *Concentration* using the strips; if they get a match, they keep the pair of strips, but must make a statement using the word. Alternatively, have pairs categorize the adjectives (physical appearance and personality), select one from each category, then make a statement using both words in a sentence.

Pop Quiz: Write the start of a number of sentences on the board and get students to complete them, either by writing on the board or in a spoken sentence. For example, *I like my soccer coach..., My friend is hard-working..., Eric is sporty...,* etc.

Materials
Picture Cards 5–22, Activity Sheet 1, scissors, a picture of someone you know well

Homework WB page 11

Lesson 5 SB page 16 or Poptropica English World

Learning Objectives
Can understand a simple story
Can discuss a story

Additional Language
thieves, plan

Functional Language
Poor (Gizmo)! Follow him quick!

Warm-up

- Review the characters in the story, *Hector Frost, Smith, Polly, Mike, Gizmo, the Queen, Polly's mother.* Ask, *Who is this?* Invite students to describe them, by prompting, *What does Polly look like? What is she like?*

Open books and ask students to look at the story. Ask, *What are we learning today?* Write the lesson objective on the board: *We're reading and discussing a story.*

14 A:21 Talk about the pictures. Then listen and read.

- Direct students' attention to the pictures and ask questions about the characters and the scenes: *Who can you see in Picture 1?* (*Mike, Polly and Gizmo*) *What are they doing?* (*looking for the skidoo*)
- Play the audio and have students listen and follow.
- Check students' understanding of the story by asking questions and pointing to the pictures, e.g., *Who is the man in Picture 6?* (*It's Smith.*) *What does he look like?* (*He is bald.*) *What is he holding?* (*shopping bags*)
- Play the audio again. Divide students into two groups and assign each group a role (Polly, Mike). Groups read aloud with the audio and mime their character's actions.

15 Why do Polly and Mike think the skidoo has something to do with the missing diamonds? Discuss your answers.

- Have students discuss the question in groups and then invite one person to write their group's answer on the board. Discuss all the different ideas.

Tell students you are going to ask them some questions about the story, and you want them to work in pairs to think of an answer. Tell students that there isn't one correct answer to each question, but you would like them to give a reason or reasons for their answer.

- Write the following questions on the board: *Do Mike and Polly know who the thieves are? Do you (the students) know who the thieves are? What do they look like? Is it safe to follow someone who might be a thief? Would you follow the skidoo? Why? Why not?* Students might like to write their answers/ideas in their notebooks. Write their answers to the last question on the board in two categories. See how many students in the class would/wouldn't follow the skidoo.

Pop Quiz: Say a line of text/statement from the story, e.g., *I love strawberry ice cream.*, and ask students to put their hands up if they know who said it. Repeat with statements/text said by each character to aid recall of the story.

Homework WB page 12

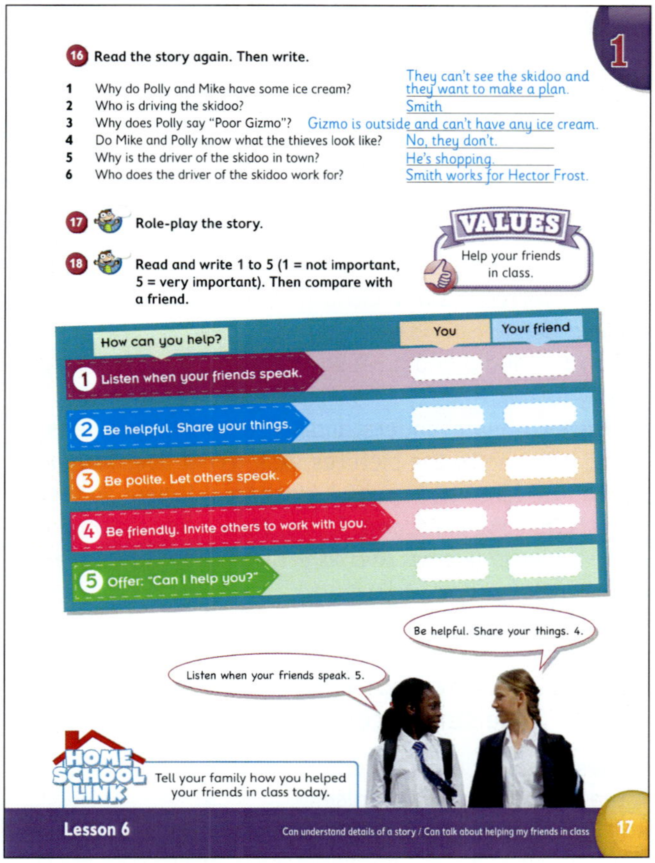
1

16 Read the story again. Then write.

1 Why do Polly and Mike have some ice cream? They can't see the skidoo and they want to make a plan.
2 Who is driving the skidoo? Smith
3 Why does Polly say "Poor Gizmo"? Gizmo is outside and can't have any ice cream.
4 Do Mike and Polly know what the thieves look like? No, they don't.
5 Why is the driver of the skidoo in town? He's shopping.
6 Who does the driver of the skidoo work for? Smith works for Hector Frost.

17 Role-play the story.

18 Read and write 1 to 5 (1 = not important, 5 = very important). Then compare with a friend.

VALUES
Help your friends in class.

How can you help?	You	Your friend
1 Listen when your friends speak.		
2 Be helpful. Share your things.		
3 Be polite. Let others speak.		
4 Be friendly. Invite others to work with you.		
5 Offer: "Can I help you?"		

HOME SCHOOL LINK Tell your family how you helped your friends in class today.

Lesson 6 Can understand details of a story / Can talk about helping my friends in class 17

Lesson 6 SB page 17 or Poptropica English World

Learning Objectives
Can understand details of a story
Can talk about helping my friends in class

Value
Help your friends in class.

Warm-up

- Have students sit in a circle and spread Picture Cards 5–22 on the floor inside the circle. Model the activity by taking Picture Card 13 and saying, e.g., *They are friends. The girl is tall and the boy is short. The girl is sometimes bossy. She is always talking. Sometimes she is not a good friend. Listen when your friends speak.*
- Give students time to look at the cards and think about what they want to say. Then go around the circle, giving everyone a chance to speak about one of the Cards.

Open books and ask students to look at the activities on the page. Ask, *What are we learning today?* Write the lesson objectives on the board: *We're reviewing the story, and we're learning about how to help our friends in class.*

16 Read the story again. Then write.

- Give students time to read the story on Student Book page 16 again. Then invite students to read the six questions in the activity.
- Give students time to write their answers then ask the questions one by one. Invite students to share their answers, and have students answer.

17 Role-play the story.

- You might like to elicit from students *What makes a good role-play?* Write their ideas on the board and/ or add these to a wall display for future role-play activities e.g., *speak clearly, use actions.* Choose one of their ideas (e.g., use actions), and tell students to try to use a lot of actions when they do their role-play.
- See the "How to use stories" section on page 23 for more ideas on how to build your students' confidence with role-plays.
- Divide students into groups of five. Give each group a set of cut-out Story Cards (see page 46), and have students place them in order.
- Play the audio again (track A:21) and have students follow. Put the class into groups to role-play the story.
- Give groups time to practice the role-play, then ask them to show the class.

You might like to give students feedback on their role-play.

18 Read and write 1 to 5 (1 = not important, 5 = very important). Then compare with a friend.

- Read the value, *Help your friends in class*, and have students repeat. Discuss some ways they can do this.
- Draw students' attention to the chart for Activity 18. Read the heading and the five sentences that follow. Have students repeat.
- Explain that they and a friend will discuss and rate these ideas. One means it is not important. Five means it is important. Give pairs time to discuss and fill in the chart.
- Discuss the results as a class. Come to an agreement about the ratings and invite a student to come to the front to write the results.

- **Home-School link:** Read the instruction with the class: *Tell your family how you helped your friends in class today.* Ask students to do this at home.

Pop Quiz: Play charades. In pairs, students role-play different ways of helping a friend in class. The class guesses what they are doing.

Materials
Picture Cards 5–22, Unit 1 cut-out Story Cards

Homework WB page 13

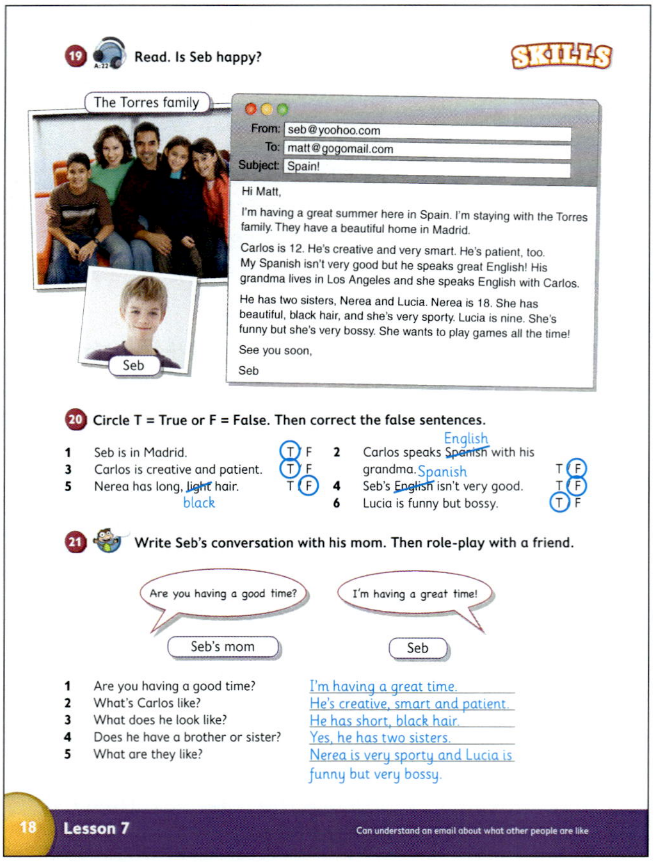

19 A:22 Read. Is Seb happy?

SKILLS

The Torres family

From: seb@yoohoo.com
To: matt@gogomail.com
Subject: Spain!

Hi Matt,

I'm having a great summer here in Spain. I'm staying with the Torres family. They have a beautiful home in Madrid.

Carlos is 12. He's creative and very smart. He's patient, too. My Spanish isn't very good but he speaks great English! His grandma lives in Los Angeles and she speaks English with Carlos.

He has two sisters, Nerea and Lucia. Nerea is 18. She has beautiful, black hair, and she's very sporty. Lucia is nine. She's funny but she's very bossy. She wants to play games all the time!

See you soon,

Seb

Seb

20 Circle T = True or F = False. Then correct the false sentences.

1 Seb is in Madrid. (T) / F
2 Carlos speaks ~~Spanish~~ English with his grandma. Spanish T / (F)
3 Carlos is creative and patient. (T) / F
4 Seb's ~~English~~ Spanish isn't very good. T / (F)
5 Nerea has long, ~~light~~ black hair. T / (F)
6 Lucia is funny but bossy. (T) / F

21 Write Seb's conversation with his mom. Then role-play with a friend.

1 Are you having a good time? I'm having a great time.
2 What's Carlos like? He's creative, smart and patient.
3 What does he look like? He has short, black hair.
4 Does he have a brother or sister? Yes, he has two sisters.
5 What are they like? Nerea is very sporty and Lucia is funny but very bossy.

18 Lesson 7 Can understand an email about what other people are like

Lesson 7 SB page 18 or Poptropica English World

Learning Objective
Can understand an email about what other people are like

Additional Language
Spain, Spanish, Los Angeles

Warm-up

- Review the adjectives of personality. Describe one child for the class to guess. Ask students to volunteer and continue.

Open books and ask students to look at the activities. Ask, *What are we learning today?* Write the lesson objective on the board: *We're learning to find information in a letter.*

19 A:22 Read. Is Seb happy?

- Direct students' attention to the pictures. Ask, *Who are they?* (*They are the Torres Family.*) *What is his name?* (*His name is Seb.*)
- Explain the concept of foreign exchange visits. Give students time to quickly scan the email for names and places. Set a time limit. Have them circle the names in the text, while volunteers write them on the board: *Spain, Torres, Madrid, Carlos, Los Angeles, Nerea, Lucia, Seb.*
- Play the audio and have students listen to the story as they follow.
- Check students' understanding by asking questions and pointing to the pictures. Ask, *What does Nerea look like?* (*She has beautiful, black hair.*) *Where do they live?* (*They live in Madrid, Spain.*) *How many sisters does Carlos have?* (*He has two sisters.*) *What is Carlos like?* (*He's creative and very smart.*)
- Play the audio again and have students speak along.

20 Circle T = True or F = False. Then correct the false sentences.

- Give students time to read the statements and circle the T for true or F for false.
- Check answers as a class.

After the listening activity, pretend you are Seb. Students ask you questions about your stay in Spain, or general questions about your likes/dislikes. Students then volunteer to come to the front and take turns being Seb or a member of the Torres family. This type of activity is designed to not only activate empathy and critical thinking skills, but to increase engagement with the listening and subject matter.

21 Write Seb's conversation with his mom. Then role-play with a friend.

- Direct students' attention to the questions that Seb's mom is asking him. Tell your students they are pretending to be Seb, and then ask some students the various questions.
- Give students time to write Seb's answers. Then pair students and have them practice the conversation, taking on both roles.
- Invite some pairs to come to the front and role-play the conversation in front of the class.

Pop Quiz: Say some statements from the text, and ask students to stand up if they think it's true, and put up their hands if they think it's false, e.g., *Lucia wants to play games all the time.* (true)

Homework WB page 14

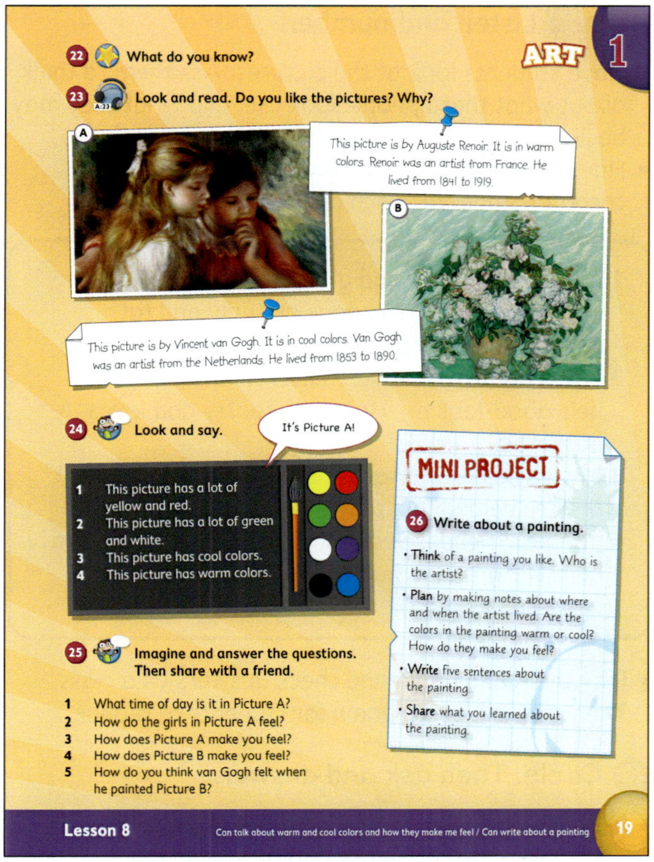
ART 1

22 What do you know?

23 Look and read. Do you like the pictures? Why?

A

This picture is by Auguste Renoir. It is in warm colors. Renoir was an artist from France. He lived from 1841 to 1919.

B

This picture is by Vincent van Gogh. It is in cool colors. Van Gogh was an artist from the Netherlands. He lived from 1853 to 1890.

24 Look and say.

It's Picture A!

1 This picture has a lot of yellow and red.
2 This picture has a lot of green and white.
3 This picture has cool colors.
4 This picture has warm colors.

25 Imagine and answer the questions. Then share with a friend.

1 What time of day is it in Picture A?
2 How do the girls in Picture A feel?
3 How does Picture A make you feel?
4 How does Picture B make you feel?
5 How do you think van Gogh felt when he painted Picture B?

MINI PROJECT

26 Write about a painting.

- **Think** of a painting you like. Who is the artist?
- **Plan** by making notes about where and when the artist lived. Are the colors in the painting warm or cool? How do they make you feel?
- **Write** five sentences about the painting.
- **Share** what you learned about the painting.

Lesson 8 Can talk about warm and cool colors and how they make me feel / Can write about a painting 19

Lesson 8 SB page 19 or Poptropica English World

Learning Objectives
Can talk about warm and cool colors and how they make me feel
Can write about a painting

Additional Language
colors, France, the Netherlands

22 What do you know?

- Open books and ask students to look at the activities. Ask, *What are we learning today?* Write the lesson objective on the board: *We're learning about warm and cool colors in art and we're writing about a painting.*
- Refer to the learning adventure poster and say, *Great! You are moving along your learning adventure!*

Warm-up

- Show some pictures of paintings by Renoir and Vincent van Gogh. Ask the students if they like the pictures. Ask, *How do they make you feel?*

23 Look and read. Do you like the pictures? Why?

- Give students time to look at the two paintings.
- Play the audio and have students listen.
- Give students time to reflect before they answer.

24 Look and say.

- Explain that some colors are warm (e.g., yellow, orange) and some are cool (e.g., blue, white).
- Pair students and give them time to match the statements to Pictures A and B.

25 Imagine and answer the questions. Then share with a friend.

- Ask, *What time of the day is it now, morning or evening?*
- Students look at the two pictures again and answer the questions.
- To extend the lesson, hand out Activity Sheet 2 (see page 153) and have the students color the six International Maritime Signal Flags. Tell the students what the meanings are for the flags and give them time to remember. Then put the class in groups and say the meanings, one by one. The groups must decide and raise a flag. Ask more confident students to describe the flags, e.g., *It's red and yellow. Red and yellow are warm colors.*

26 Write about a painting.

- Ask students what steps they will take to make sure they include all the necessary information. Remind students of the steps to success: Think, Plan, Write and Share.
  Think If they need some help, show them the examples you brought in for the warm-up.
  Plan Ask students to make some notes about when and where the artist lived.
  Write Give students time to write. Remind them to check their work afterwards.
  Share Nominate students to read their sentences.

You may also wish to give students feedback on their projects.

Ask students, *What do you know about describing art and artists now?* Give students a minute to tell their partner the new ideas and words they can remember. Ask students, *Where are you on your learning adventure?* Tell students, *Good job!* to reinforce the progress they are making.

Pop Quiz: As students are leaving the class, show them different colors (cards or objects) and ask them if they are warm or cool.

Materials
Poster, Activity Sheet 2, scissors, pictures by Renoir and Vincent van Gogh from the Internet, objects with interesting colors

Homework WB page 15

27 Listen and number.

I CAN DO IT!

a 4 b 1 c 2 d 3

28 Circle. Then ask and answer.

1 A: What does her sister look like? / What do they look like?
B: They have straight hair and glasses.
2 A: What's he like? / What does he look like?
B: He's creative and helpful. But he's lazy.
3 A: What's she like? / What does she look like?
B: She has light hair but she doesn't have blue eyes. She has dark eyes!

29 Write. Then ask and answer.

1 What is your best friend like? ______
2 What does your mom look like? ______
3 Is your dad sporty and handsome? ______
4 Are you hard-working? ______
5 What do you look like? ______

I CAN
I can ask and answer about what someone looks like.
I can talk about what someone is like.
I can write about a painting.

20 Lesson 9 Can assess what I have learned in Unit 1

Lesson 9 SB page 20 or Poptropica English World

Learning Objective
Can assess what I have learned in Unit 1

Warm up

- Divide the class into two teams. Place Picture Cards 5–22 word-side up on the board. The teams have to think of a sentence about a fictional person that includes a word from each set of cards, e.g., *(Name) has long dark hair and is always helpful*. Invite a student from each team to come to the front and say their sentence to the class. Continue until all students have taken a turn. Give two points for each correct sentence.

Open books and ask students to look at the activities. Write this lesson objective on the board: *We're thinking about our learning adventure.*

- Ask students what they have been learning in the unit. Put their ideas on the board, e.g., *personality adjectives*.
- For each idea, ask students to tell their partner where they think they are on their learning adventure. Reassure students who are less confident that they will have opportunities for more practice.

27 Listen and number.

A:24

- Have students look at the pictures. Ask them to think about what these people look like, and what they may be like.
- Have students listen to the audio and write the correct number for each picture.

1 She has light hair and glasses. He has spiky hair and a mustache. The dogs are ugly and fat. They're not very friendly.
2 She is creative and very cute! He's bald, but he's good-looking. He's very sporty and loves basketball.
3 My friends are talkative. I like them because they're helpful and they aren't bossy.
4 My best friend is very smart. He has curly brown hair. His grandpa has curly gray hair! He's old and hard-working.

- Play the audio again and check answers as a class. Then play the audio again for students to repeat.

28 Circle. Then ask and answer.

- Have students read and then circle the correct questions. Have them ask and answer in pairs.

29 Write. Then ask and answer.

- Ask confident students to read the questions aloud. Then have students write their own answers, before asking and answering in pairs.

Ask students how they feel about their learning in this unit. Ask students to tell you what they found easy and what they found the most difficult to learn in the unit.

- Read the three *I can* statements with students, and invite students to check the boxes according to how confident they feel about the language point.
- Ask students, *Where are you on your learning adventure?* Students indicate where they think they are on the learning adventure poster. Tell students, *Good job!* to reinforce the progress they are making.

Pop Quiz: In groups of four, students tell the others the answers to the following questions: *Which is your favorite activity in the unit? Why? Which activity don't you like? Why? What is your favorite new word? Which word is the most difficult for you?*

Materials
Poster, Picture Cards 5–22

Homework WB page 16

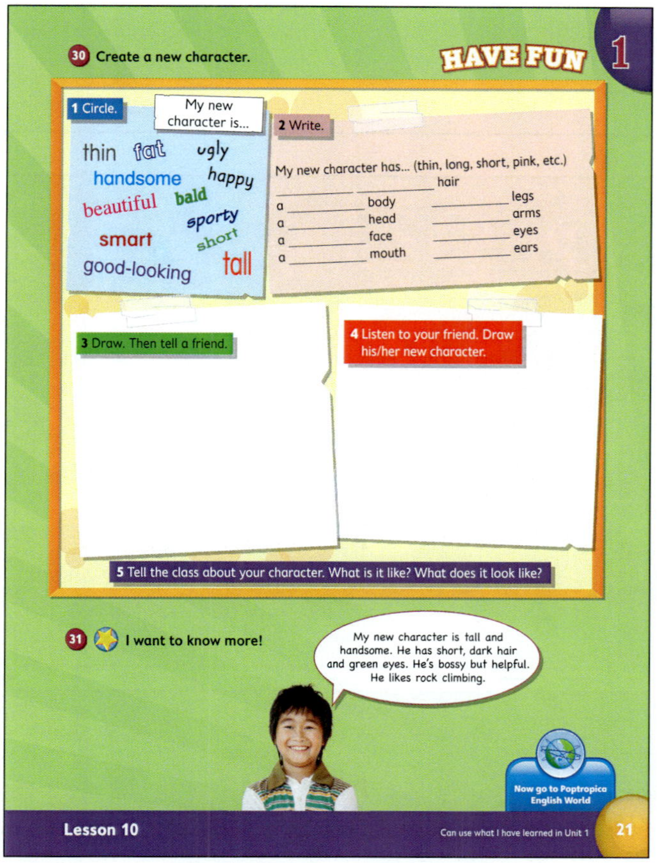

Lesson 10 SB page 21 or Poptropica English World

Learning Objective
Can use what I have learned in Unit 1

Warm-up

- Show some popular comic books to the class. Have students take turns pointing to a character in the book and describing them using target language.
- Invite students to name some other characters seen on television or movies, and then ask students to describe them.

Open books and ask students to look at the pictures. Ask, *What are we learning today?* Write the lesson objectives on the board: *We're going to create a character to review Unit 1 language.*

30 Create a new character.

- Tell students they are going to design and draw their own new character. Explain that they have to first choose the description by circling the words in Part 1. Then have students read the words aloud. Give students time to think about their design and circle the words they want to use.
- Then tell students they have to specify the look of body parts by filling the blanks in Part 2.
- Draw students' attention to the blank space for Part 3. Allow time to draw and color their new character in the space.
- When students have finished Part 3, put them into pairs. Explain that they will take turns describing their character to their partner, and the partner will draw it in the space for Part 4. Explain that they have to talk only, and not show their drawings to their partner. You can also invite pairs of students to come to the front so the class can compare how similar the drawings of the characters are.
- When this is completed, invite students to come to the front to show and talk about their new character using the adjectives of character (*helpful, bossy, smart*, etc.).

Tell students you are going to give them answers and they have to guess the questions. Allow students to work in pairs, and allow them sufficient time to work out the questions before nominating pairs to give their responses.

- Say answers to students, e.g., *They have short, light hair, and blue eyes. She isn't lazy.* and students provide the correct questions, e.g., *What do they look like? Is she lazy?* This will provide students with further reinforcement of the question form. With a confident class, you can then repeat this, with a student giving the answer.

31 I want to know more!

- Ask students to choose anything they enjoyed from the unit and to go and find out more. You might like to set this activity as homework with a quick feedback session at the beginning of the next class.
- You can also suggest that students write one or two questions about what they want to know, then switch question(s) with a partner. Students then find answer(s) to their partner's question(s) as a homework activity, with feedback the next lesson.

Are you ready for Unit 2?

- Ask students if they are ready to move on to the next unit. Tell students that it is fine if they do not remember everything as they will continue to practice throughout the level.
- Encourage students to ask if they have any questions about what they learned in Unit 1.

You may wish to give Unit 1 Test (see page 188) at this time.

Materials
Popular comic books

Homework WB page 17

Unit 1 Story Cards

Wider World 1

SB pages 22–23 or Poptropica English World

Learning Objectives
Can understand texts about families around the world
Can talk about big and small families

Additional Language
help, argue, washing machine, music practice

Warm-up

- Review adjectives of physical appearance and personality by using Picture Cards 5–22. Have students listen and repeat. Then place the Cards around the room for reference. Invite a student to come to the front and describe a person in the class. Students have to guess the student.

1 What do you know?

- Open books and ask students to look at the pictures. Ask, *What are we learning today?* Write the lesson objective on the board: *We're learning about families around the world.*
- Close books. Ask students what English words they know for describing people, e.g., *good-looking, tall.*
- Refer to the learning adventure poster and say, *Great! You are moving along your learning adventure!*

2 A:25 Listen and read. Are the families big or small?

- Point to the pictures in the Student Book and say, *What do they look like?* Ask students to point at the people in the pictures and talk about them, using the target vocabulary.
- Ask volunteers to say who they live with, e.g., *I live with my mom, my dad, and my brother.* Pre-teach *husband*, e.g., *(Name) lives with his mother and her husband.*
- Pre-teach *argue, dirty, help, practice, washing machine,* by miming or drawing.
- Give students time to look at the pairs of pictures. Point at each picture in turn and ask the class, *Is the family big or small?* Elicit responses.
- Play the audio. Students listen and follow.

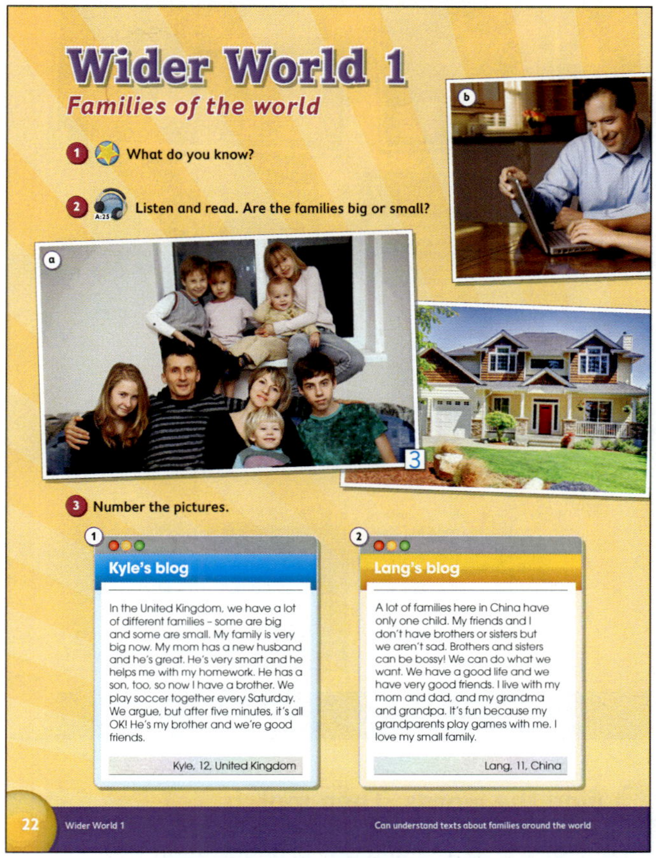
Wider World 1
Families of the world

1 What do you know?

2 A:25 Listen and read. Are the families big or small?

a b 3

3 Number the pictures.

1 **Kyle's blog**

In the United Kingdom, we have a lot of different families – some are big and some are small. My family is very big now. My mom has a new husband and he's great. He's very smart and he helps me with my homework. He has a son, too, so now I have a brother. We play soccer together every Saturday. We argue, but after five minutes, it's all OK! He's my brother and we're good friends.

Kyle, 12, United Kingdom

2 **Lang's blog**

A lot of families here in China have only one child. My friends and I don't have brothers or sisters but we aren't sad. Brothers and sisters can be bossy! We can do what we want. We have a good life and we have very good friends. I live with my mom and dad, and my grandma and grandpa. It's fun because my grandparents play games with me. I love my small family.

Lang, 11, China

22 Wider World 1 Can understand texts about families around the world

3 Number the pictures.

- Ask the class, *Do you have a blog? What do you write about?* Elicit responses.
- If you have a world map, ask a volunteer to point out the United States, China, and the United Kingdom. Find out what students know about these countries.
- Have students read the blogs aloud. Then allow them time to read the three blogs to themselves before they match the number of the blogs to the pairs of pictures.
- After checking answers, ask students if they are surprised by any of the information. Ask students if they think any of these families are similar to their own.

Say to students, *Blue-eyed people are smarter than brown-eyed people.* and *Good-looking people are always sporty*. Divide the class into two or into groups and tell students that they have to think of reasons to support whether these statements are true/false. Remind them there is no right or wrong answer, but they need to give their reasons for what they think.

Materials
Poster, Picture Cards 5–22, map of the world, sheet of paper for each student

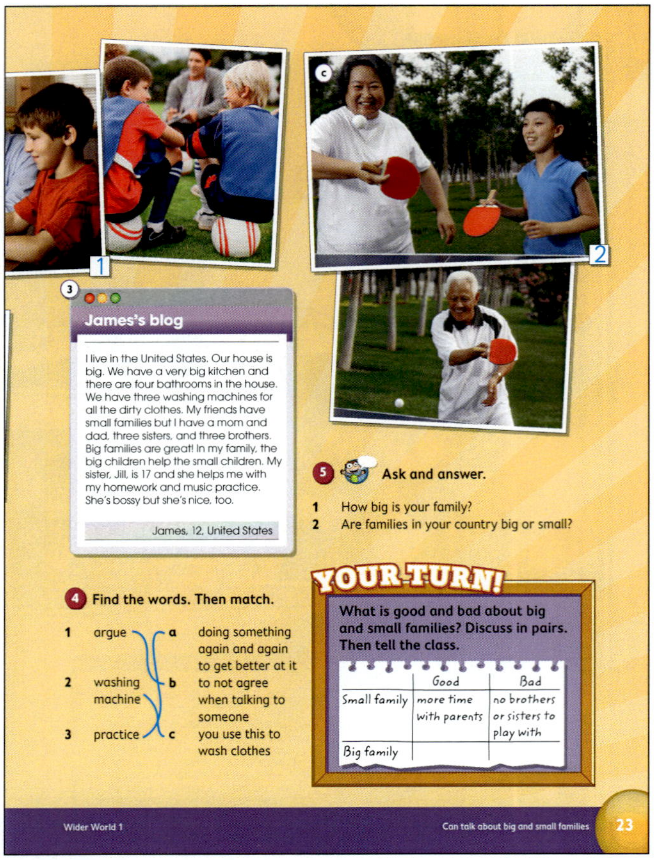

3

James's blog

I live in the United States. Our house is big. We have a very big kitchen and there are four bathrooms in the house. We have three washing machines for all the dirty clothes. My friends have small families but I have a mom and dad, three sisters, and three brothers. Big families are great! In my family, the big children help the small children. My sister, Jill, is 17 and she helps me with my homework and music practice. She's bossy but she's nice, too.

James, 12, United States

4 Find the words. Then match.

1 argue — a doing something again and again to get better at it
2 washing machine — b to not agree when talking to someone
3 practice — c you use this to wash clothes

5 Ask and answer.

1 How big is your family?
2 Are families in your country big or small?

YOUR TURN!

What is good and bad about big and small families? Discuss in pairs. Then tell the class.

	Good	Bad
Small family	more time with parents	no brothers or sisters to play with
Big family		

Wider World 1 Can talk about big and small families 23

4 Find the words. Then match.

- Look at words 1–3 and drill pronunciation with the class.
- Ask students to find the words in the blogs and then match them to their meanings. Remind students to look at the words directly before and after, and the whole sentence to help them.
- Check answers as a class.

5 Ask and answer.

- To start the discussion, ask students how many brothers and sisters they think is normal in their country. Ask, *Is it usual to live with grandparents and aunts/uncles?*
- Then put students in groups of three and give them time to do the activity.
- Invite students to the front to talk about their families, and families in their country. Encourage other students to ask questions.

YOUR TURN! Tell students that they are going to work in pairs, and talk about big and small families, and what is good or bad about them. Make sure you give students time to think through their answers before they work with their partner. To give students a reason to listen, each student will also think of one/two more questions to ask their partner.

- Ask students to share their ideas/results with another partner, if there is time.
- Ask the class if they think it is best to have a big or a small family. Take a class vote.
- If you have time, tell students to close their books and give them a sheet of paper. Then tell them they will have two minutes to scan the three blogs and write down all the different adjectives they can find. Then start the speed game. After two minutes, students put their pencils down. Have students call out their adjectives. Find out which student was able to write down the most adjectives.

Pop Quiz: Pair students and tell them that you will say a name (*Kyle, Lang,* or *James*) and in two minutes (timed) they have to write as many sentences about that person as they can, e.g., *James: He lives in the USA. His house has a big kitchen. His sister Jill is seventeen.* See which pair wrote the most sentences. Have them share their sentences with the class. Then ask whether any other students had sentences the winning pair didn't write.

2 My life

Unit Overview

Unit Objective

- I can talk about daily activities and routines

Language

Target Vocabulary	Daily activities: brush my teeth, make my bed, wash my face, clean my room, do my homework, meet my friends, study before a test, take notes in class, take out the trash, be on time Adverbs of frequency: always, usually, often, sometimes, never
Target Structures	You must brush your teeth. *(Order)* You should brush your teeth. *(Advice)* I always brush my teeth. He usually brushes his teeth. She often brushes her teeth. They sometimes brush their teeth. We never brush our teeth.
Features	**Cross-curricular:** Social science: Being healthy **Values:** Giving is great.

Skills

Reading	• Can identify daily activities and routines • Can understand a simple story • Can understand details of a story • Can assess whether someone is a morning person • Can understand a text about being healthy
Writing	• Can use *always, usually, often, sometimes, never* • Can write about how often I do things • Can create a healthy menu • Can write simple sentences about what people should and must do *(Workbook)* • Can write simple sentences about routines *(Workbook)*
Listening	• Can identify daily activities and routines • Can understand a simple story
Speaking	• Can give orders and advice using *you must* and *you should* • Can talk about how often I do things • Can discuss a story • Can talk about giving

Lesson 1 SB page 24 or Poptropica English World

Learning Objective
Can identify daily activities and routines

Target Language
brush my teeth, make my bed, wash my face, clean my room, do my homework, meet my friends, study before a test, take notes in class, take out the trash, be on time

1 What do you know?

- Open books and ask students to look at the pictures. Ask, *What are we learning today?* Write the lesson objective on the board: *We're learning about daily activities and routines.*
- Close books. Ask students what English words they know for things they do every day, e.g., *go to school, do my homework*. Write on board.
- Refer to the learning adventure poster and say, *Great! You are already moving along your learning adventure!*

2 A:26 Listen and read. Who is hard-working? Who is lazy?

- Ask students to look at the scenes in their books and listen as you play the audio.
- Play the audio again and have students read along.
- Point to the last picture. Say, *Maddy needs Kipper now. Where is Kipper?* Elicit, *Kipper is in the tree. He ran away.* Ask, *Why does Maddy need Kipper?* Elicit, *The homework asks, "How long is your pet's tail"?*
- Ask the class, *Who is hard-working?* (*Emma and Dan*) *Who is lazy?* (*Maddy and Robert*) *Who is naughty?* (*Kipper*). Then ask, *Are you hard-working? Are you lazy?*

3 A:27 Listen and say.

- Play the audio and have students repeat.
- Put Picture Cards 23–32 on the board. Write the headings *Hard-working at home* and *Hard-working at school* on the board. Ask students to write activities under each heading as appropriate.
- Say, *I am hard-working at home. I make my bed and clean my room. I take out the trash.* Point to the heading and the pictures as you say it. Then invite students to come to the front and talk about themselves.

4 A:28 Work with a friend. Listen and play the memory game.

- Ask students to find a partner. Play the audio and have students listen.

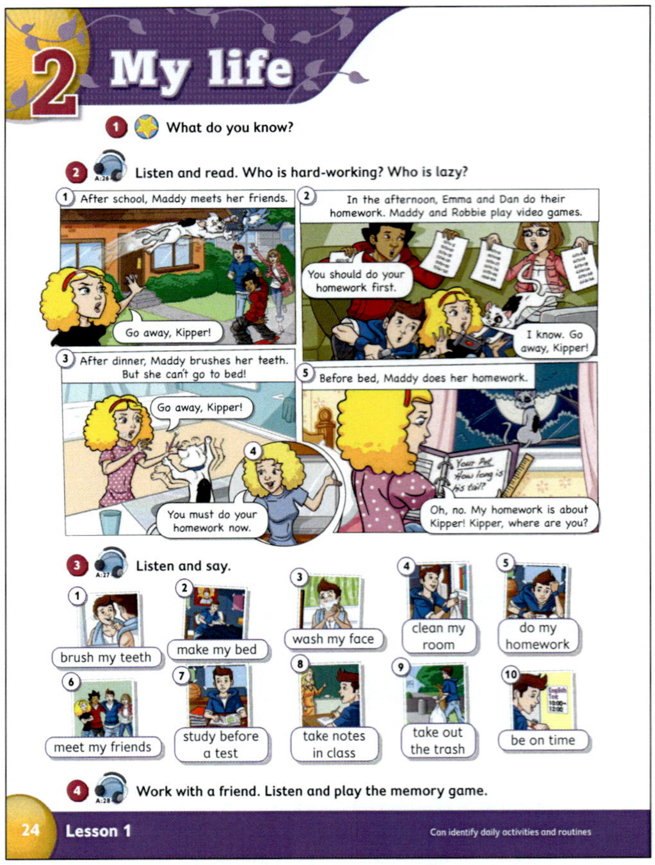

Boy 1: After school, I should brush my teeth.
Girl 1: After school, I should brush my teeth and make my bed.
Boy 2: After school, I should brush my teeth, make my bed, and wash my face.

- Play the audio again. Have students play the memory game, and continue it by pointing to the pictures and adding to the list of things to do.

Ask students, *How many words for daily activities do you know now?* Give students a minute to tell their partner the new words they know.

- Ask students to say where they are on their adventure now. Ask students which words they find easiest or most difficult to remember. Tell students, *Good job!* to reinforce the progress they are making.

Pop Quiz: Ask students what they do before/after certain daily activities. Ask, *What do you do before you brush your teeth? What do you do after you make your bed?*

Materials
Poster, Picture Cards 23–32

Homework WB page 18

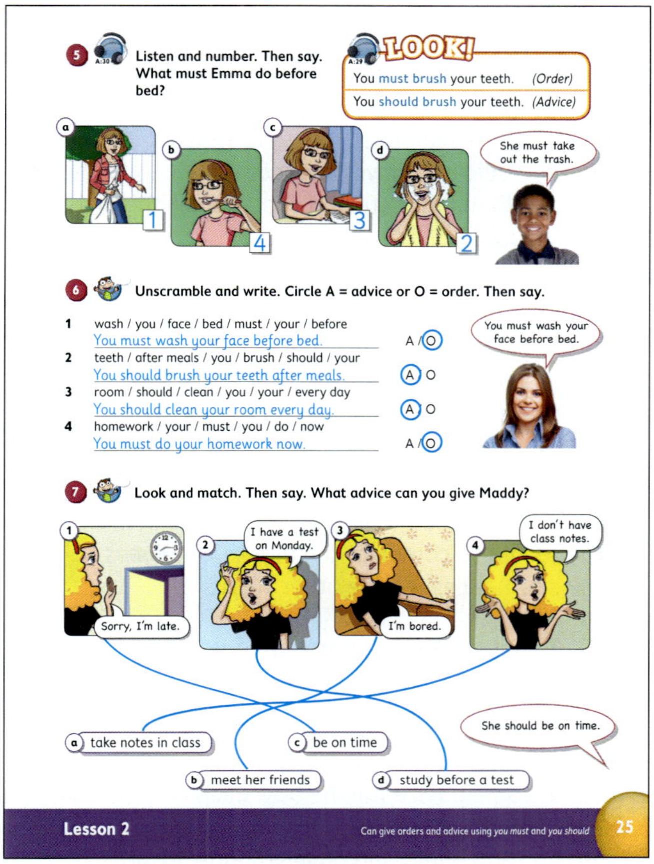

5 Listen and number. Then say. What must Emma do before bed?

LOOK!

You must brush your teeth. (Order)

You should brush your teeth. (Advice)

6 Unscramble and write. Circle A = advice or O = order. Then say.

1 wash / you / face / bed / must / your / before
You must wash your face before bed. A / (O)

2 teeth / after meals / you / brush / should / your
You should brush your teeth after meals. (A) / O

3 room / should / clean / you / your / every day
You should clean your room every day. (A) / O

4 homework / your / must / you / do / now
You must do your homework now. A / (O)

7 Look and match. Then say. What advice can you give Maddy?

Lesson 2 Can give orders and advice using *you must* and *you should* 25

Lesson 2 SB page 25 or Poptropica English World

Learning Objective
Can give orders and advice using *you must* and *you should*

Warm-up

- Review the daily activity terms using Picture Cards 23–32. Show the pictures to the class and have them say the words.

Open books and ask students to look at the activities and the Look! box. Ask, *What are we learning today?* Write the lesson objective on the board: *We're learning to give orders and advice.*

5 A:30 Listen and number. Then say. What must Emma do before bed?

- Draw students' attention to the Look! box and play the audio (track A:29). Students repeat chorally.
- Play the audio. Allow students time to match the picture to the statement by writing the number in the correct box. Then ask the class, *What must Emma do before bed?* (*She must brush her teeth.*)

> **1** She must take out the trash.
> **2** She should wash her face.
> **3** She must do her homework.
> **4** She should brush her teeth.

- Put students in pairs to practice asking and answering questions related to the pictures.

6 Unscramble and write. Circle A = advice or O = order. Then say.

- Draw students' attention to the mother on page 25. Ask, *What is mom saying?* And let the class read the speech bubble aloud. Then, write a scrambled sentence on the board: *your / must / You / homework school / do / after* and invite students to unscramble the sentence and say it (*You must do your homework after school.*).
- Ask students to unscramble each sentence and decide if each one is giving advice or an order.
- Check answers as a class.

7 Look and match. Then say. What advice can you give Maddy?

- Say, *Look at Maddy. Maddy is not happy. What advice do you have for Maddy?* Allow students time to match the advice to the picture.
- Have students work in pairs to role-play the exchanges. Remind students to use *You* instead of *She.*
- To extend the lesson, have students go in pairs and hand each pair Activity Sheet 3 (see page 154). Students cut the parts into pieces, then place the pictures in one row and words in another row. Students make logical sentences by pairing up a picture card and a word card and then saying the sentence. Encourage early finishers to continue the activity by adding additional terms.

Pop Quiz: Make statements similar to those in Activity 7. Students can give you advice/orders in response to the statements. Say, *The kitchen smells bad.* (*You should take out the trash.*) *I forgot what the teacher said in class.* (*You must take notes in class.*)

Materials
Picture Cards 23–32, Activity Sheet 3, scissors

Homework WB page 19

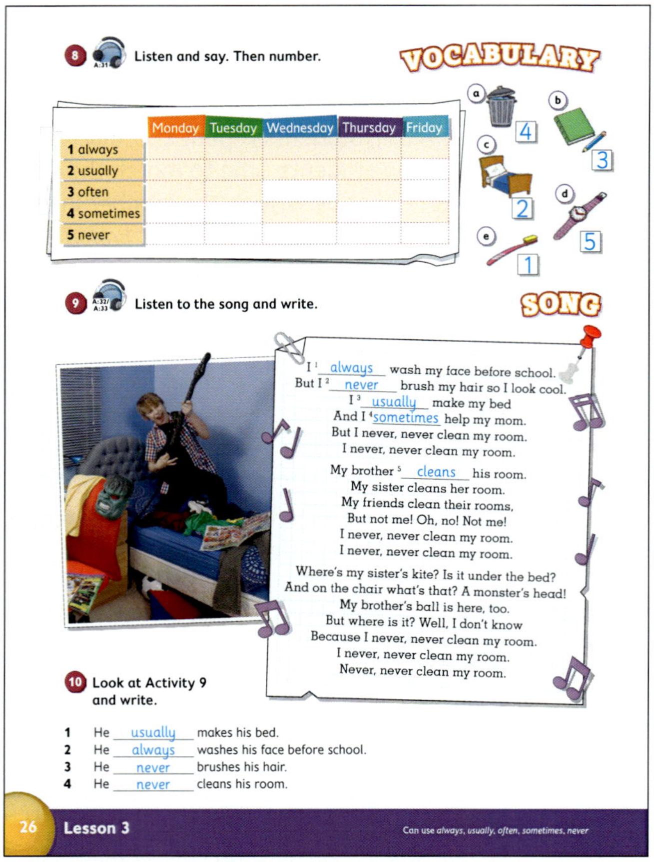

8 Listen and say. Then number. VOCABULARY

	Monday	Tuesday	Wednesday	Thursday	Friday
1 always					
2 usually					
3 often					
4 sometimes					
5 never					

a 4 b 3 c 2 d 5 e 1

9 Listen to the song and write. SONG

I [1] always wash my face before school.
But I [2] never brush my hair so I look cool.
I [3] usually make my bed
And I [4] sometimes help my mom.
But I never, never clean my room.
I never, never clean my room.

My brother [5] cleans his room.
My sister cleans her room.
My friends clean their rooms,
But not me! Oh, no! Not me!
I never, never clean my room.
I never, never clean my room.

Where's my sister's kite? Is it under the bed?
And on the chair what's that? A monster's head!
My brother's ball is here, too.
But where is it? Well, I don't know
Because I never, never clean my room.
I never, never clean my room.
Never, never clean my room.

10 Look at Activity 9 and write.

1 He usually makes his bed.
2 He always washes his face before school.
3 He never brushes his hair.
4 He never cleans his room.

26 Lesson 3 Can use *always, usually, often, sometimes, never*

Lesson 3 SB page 26 or Poptropica English World

Learning Objective
Can use *always, usually, often, sometimes, never*

Target Language
always, usually, often, sometimes, never

Warm-up

- Review modals of advice and obligation. Put Picture Cards 23–32 on the board and invite students to come to the front to choose a card and say a *must/should* statement, e.g., *I must study before a test. I should study before a test.*

Open books and ask students to look at the pictures. Ask, *What are we learning today?* Write the lesson objective on the board: *We're learning adverbs of frequency.*

- Close books. Ask students what English adverbs of frequency they know, e.g., *always, never.* Write on board.
- Refer to the learning adventure poster and say, *Great! You are moving along your learning adventure!*

8 Listen and say. Then number.

- Introduce the adverbs of frequency, *always, usually, often, sometimes,* and *never* with Picture Cards 33–37. Hold them up and ask students to repeat.
- Play the audio and have students repeat. Play the audio again and ask students to number the pictures.

> **1** always He always brushes his teeth.
> **2** usually He usually makes his bed.
> **3** often He often does his homework.
> **4** sometimes He sometimes takes out the trash.
> **5** never He is never on time.

- To check understanding, say, *Maddy plays tennis on Monday and Tuesday. She* [pause] *plays tennis.* and wait for students to complete the blank (*sometimes*). Elicit similar sentences for the other words.

9 Listen to the song and write.

- Ask students questions about the picture. Ask, *What is the boy doing?* Elicit, *He's playing the guitar.* Ask students to look at the bedroom and see if they can think of some advice for the boy. Elicit responses. *(He should clean his room.)*
- Play the song audio and have students listen.
- Play the audio again and ask students to write the missing words. Have students check their answers with partners.
- Play the karaoke version of the song and have students sing along if they feel confident enough.

10 Look at Activity 9 and write.

- Stick Picture Cards 33–37 on the board, word-side up. Say, *I always clean my room. The boy...* and wait for the word *never* from students. Point to the card *always* and elicit a response. *(He always washes his face before school.)*
- Give students time to do Activity 10. Check answers by reading them chorally.

Ask students, *How many adverbs of frequency do you know now?* Give students a minute to tell their partner the new words they know.

- Ask students to say where they are on their adventure now. Ask students which words they find easiest or most difficult to remember. Tell students, *Good job!* to reinforce the progress they are making.

Pop Quiz: Mime different daily activities and students have to guess what you're doing. The student who guesses first does the next mime.

Materials
Poster, Picture Cards 23–37

Homework WB page 20

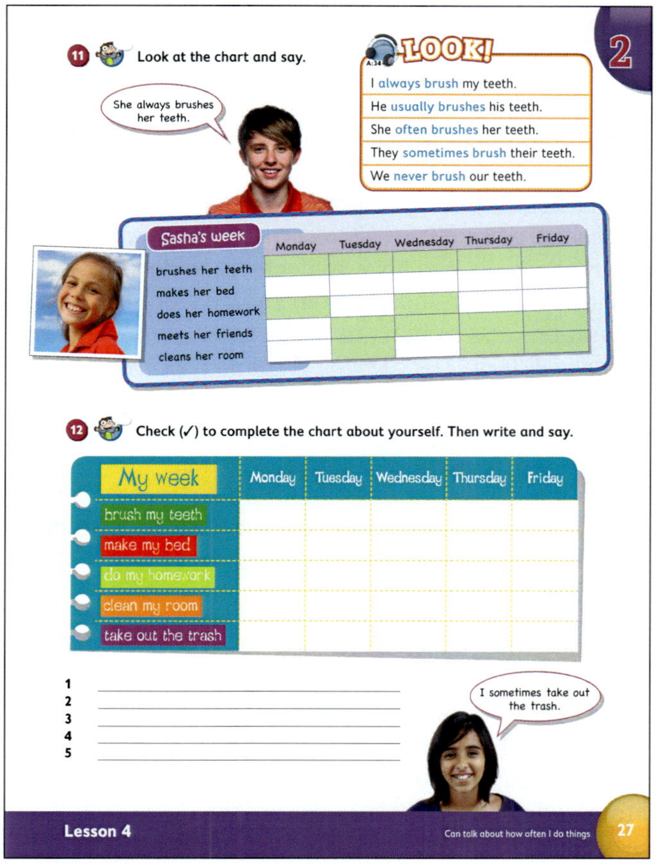

Lesson 4 SB page 27 or Poptropica English World

Learning Objective
Can talk about how often I do things

Target Language
always, usually, often, sometimes, never

Warm-up

- Assign students a word: *always, usually, often, sometimes, never.* Ask students to sit in a circle on chairs and have one student stand in the center. Explain that you are going to talk about yourself, and that when you say one of these words, any students assigned that word have to change seats. Meanwhile, the student in the middle will try and grab a chair to sit on. The aim of the game is to get a seat. To extend the activity, you can ask students to talk about themselves and then say an adverb of frequency. (Remember to take one student's place in the circle.)

Open books and ask students to look at the activities and the Look! box. Ask, *What are we learning today?* Write the lesson objective on the board: *We're using adverbs of frequency to talk about daily things.*

11 Look at the chart and say.

- Draw students' attention to the Look! box and play the audio (track A:34). Students repeat chorally.
- Draw students' attention to the picture of the girl and the chart. Say, *This is Sasha. What does she do?* Point at the boy and his speech bubble, and elicit, *She always brushes her teeth.* Point at the row of green boxes across the week.
- Allow students time to think of sentences for the remaining four activities.
- Pair students and have them ask each other about Sasha's routine.
- To check answers, elicit sentences from volunteers. *(She never makes her bed. She sometimes does her homework. She usually meets her friends. She often cleans her room.)*

12 Check (✓) to complete the chart about yourself. Then write and say.

- Ask students to look at the chart for Activity 12. Say, *Your turn!* Give students time to complete the chart.
- When students have finished, tell them to write about each activity on the lines provided.
- Pair students and have them learn about each other by asking and answering questions. Invite each student to stand up and say one or two things about their friend.

Pop Quiz: Write a new schedule on the board, similar to the one in Activity 12. Change the activities to: *takes out the trash, washes his face, studies before a test, meets his friends, brushes his teeth.* Point to each activity, and the class can respond together or as individuals with: *He always brushes his teeth.*, etc.

Lesson 5 SB page 28 or Poptropica English World

Learning Objectives
Can understand a simple story
Can discuss a story

Additional Language
training camp, hide, igloo, work out, stay awake, ribbons

Functional Language
He's one strong guy! Hey, come on.

Warm-up

- Say, *Let's talk about Smith.* Write an adverb of frequency on the board and then choose a Picture Card from Picture Cards 23–32. Show the class, and have someone say, e.g., *Smith sometimes does his homework.* The student who makes a sentence can pick the next student to have a turn by writing an adverb and choosing a card.

Open books and ask students to look at the story. Ask, *What are we learning today?* Write the lesson objective on the board: *We're reading and discussing a story.*

13 Talk about the pictures. Then listen and read.

- Direct students' attention to the pictures, and ask questions about the characters and the scenes: *Who can you see in Picture 3?* (*Mike, Polly, Gizmo, and Smith*) *What are they doing?* (*watching Smith working out*) *Where are they?* (*in an igloo/at the training camp*).
- Play the audio and have students listen and follow.
- Check students' understanding of the story by asking questions and pointing to the pictures, e.g., *Who is the man in Picture 1?* (*It's Smith.*) *What do the children build?* (*an igloo*) *What do the children make in the igloo?* (*a fire*)
- Play the audio again. Encourage students to read along and mime their character's actions.

14 Why are Polly and Mike excited to find red ribbons in Smith's shopping bag? Discuss your answers.

- Have students discuss the question in groups and then invite one person to write their group's answer on the board. Discuss all the different ideas.

Write the following statement on the board, *Mike and Polly should not make a fire.* Divide students into groups and ask them to discuss the statement. They might like to write their answers/ideas in their notebooks.

- Ask groups who agree with the statement to say why they agree, and write their reasons on the board. Ask groups who disagree with the statement to say why they disagree, and write their reasons on the board. See how many students in the class would/wouldn't have made a fire.

Pop Quiz: Divide the class into two teams. Say one word from the text (e.g., *strong*) and students put up their hands to say which character said the word, and to read the whole sentence out loud (*Mike: He's one strong guy!*). The first person with their hand up who gets everything correct wins a point.

Materials
Picture Cards 23–37

Homework WB page 22

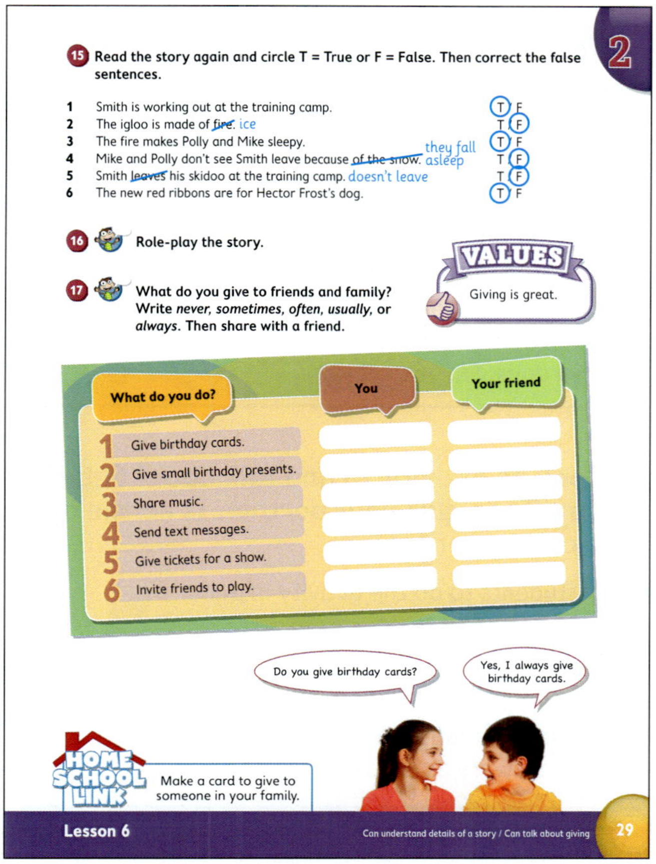
2

15 Read the story again and circle T = True or F = False. Then correct the false sentences.

1 Smith is working out at the training camp. T / F
2 The igloo is made of ~~fire~~. ice T / F
3 The fire makes Polly and Mike sleepy. T / F
4 Mike and Polly don't see Smith leave because ~~of the snow~~. they fall asleep T / F
5 Smith ~~leaves~~ his skidoo at the training camp. doesn't leave T / F
6 The new red ribbons are for Hector Frost's dog. T / F

16 Role-play the story.

17 What do you give to friends and family? Write *never, sometimes, often, usually,* or *always*. Then share with a friend.

VALUES
Giving is great.

What do you do?	You	Your friend
1 Give birthday cards.		
2 Give small birthday presents.		
3 Share music.		
4 Send text messages.		
5 Give tickets for a show.		
6 Invite friends to play.		

HOME SCHOOL LINK Make a card to give to someone in your family.

Lesson 6 Can understand details of a story / Can talk about giving 29

Lesson 6 SB page 29 or Poptropica English World

Learning Objectives
Can understand details of a story
Can talk about giving

Value
Giving is great.

Warm-up

- Ask students to think about what Polly, Mike, and Smith are like. Ask what a friend should give each one as a present. *(Mike likes playing soccer. Polly should give him a soccer shirt.)*

Open books and ask students to look at the activities on the page. Ask, *What are we learning today?* Write the lesson objectives on the board: *We're reviewing the story, and we're learning about giving.*

15 Read the story again and circle T = True or F = False. Then correct the false sentences.

- Give students time to look at the story and play the audio again.
- Allow students time to do the activity.
- Check answers by having students switch books with another student. Read the statement and elicit answers from the class. Ask students to correct the false statements then check again with their partners.

16 Role-play the story.

- See the "How to use stories" section on page 23 for more ideas on how to build your students' confidence with role-plays.
- Divide students into groups of three. Give each group a set of cut-out Story Cards (see page 60), and have students place them in order.
- Play the audio again (track A:35), and have students follow. Put the class into groups to role-play the story.
- Give groups time to practice the role-play then ask them to show the class.

You might like to give students feedback on their role-play.

17 What do you give to friends and family? Write *never, sometimes, often, usually,* or *always.* Then share with a friend.

- Read the value, *Giving is great.* Say, *I always give my friend a gift on her birthday.* Invite students to say what they do.
- Draw students' attention to the chart. Ask, *What do you do?* Then say the six items chorally. Tell students to fill out the chart under the *You* column.
- Tell students to find a partner and ask how often they give the items to friends and family, and record the answers in their chart.
- Invite volunteers to stand and talk about their partners. Then invite some pairs to come to the front and talk about each other, based on the information in the chart.

- **Home-School link:** Read the instruction with the class: *Make a card to give to someone in your family.* Ask students to do this at home.

- To extend the lesson, divide class into pairs. Give each pair Activity Sheet 4 (see page 155) and have them cut out the pieces. One person says a sentence, for example, *Gizmo never sends texts messages.* The partner must line up the correct cards. Take turns and have fun!

Pop Quiz: Suggest various situations and ask students what they would/could give in that situation. For example, *Your friend left his school lunch at home.* (*Give him some of your lunch.*) *Your grandma cannot see well enough to read anymore.* (*Read to her aloud.*) *It is your mom's birthday. (Buy her some flowers. Make her a card. Give her breakfast in bed.)*

Materials
Unit 2 cut-out Story Cards, Activity Sheet 4, scissors

Homework WB page 23

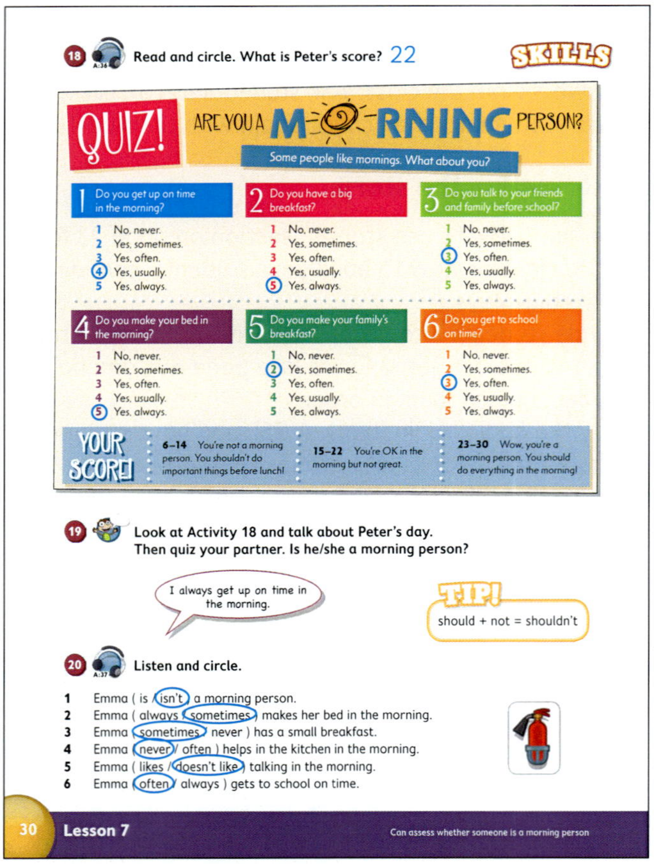

18 Read and circle. What is Peter's score? 22 SKILLS

QUIZ! ARE YOU A MORNING PERSON?

Some people like mornings. What about you?

1 Do you get up on time in the morning?
1 No, never.
2 Yes, sometimes.
3 Yes, often.
(4) Yes, usually.
5 Yes, always.

2 Do you have a big breakfast?
1 No, never.
2 Yes, sometimes.
3 Yes, often.
4 Yes, usually.
(5) Yes, always.

3 Do you talk to your friends and family before school?
1 No, never.
2 Yes, sometimes.
(3) Yes, often.
4 Yes, usually.
5 Yes, always.

4 Do you make your bed in the morning?
1 No, never.
2 Yes, sometimes.
3 Yes, often.
4 Yes, usually.
(5) Yes, always.

5 Do you make your family's breakfast?
1 No, never.
(2) Yes, sometimes.
3 Yes, often.
4 Yes, usually.
5 Yes, always.

6 Do you get to school on time?
1 No, never.
2 Yes, sometimes.
(3) Yes, often.
4 Yes, usually.
5 Yes, always.

YOUR SCORE!
6–14 You're not a morning person. You shouldn't do important things before lunch!
15–22 You're OK in the morning but not great.
23–30 Wow, you're a morning person. You should do everything in the morning!

19 Look at Activity 18 and talk about Peter's day. Then quiz your partner. Is he/she a morning person?

I always get up on time in the morning.

TIP! should + not = shouldn't

20 Listen and circle.

1 Emma (is / (isn't)) a morning person.
2 Emma (always / (sometimes)) makes her bed in the morning.
3 Emma ((sometimes) / never) has a small breakfast.
4 Emma ((never) / often) helps in the kitchen in the morning.
5 Emma (likes / (doesn't like)) talking in the morning.
6 Emma ((often) / always) gets to school on time.

30 Lesson 7 Can assess whether someone is a morning person

Lesson 7 SB page 30 or Poptropica English World

Learning Objective
Can assess whether someone is a morning person

Additional Language
morning person, shouldn't

Warm-up

- Have students say sentences about their routine.

Open books and ask students to look at the activities on the page. Ask, *What are we learning today?* Write the lesson objective on the board: *We're learning to find if someone is a morning person.*

18 Read and circle. What is Peter's score?

A:36

- Play the audio. Allow students time to complete the quiz for Peter and calculate his score.

1 So, Peter, do you get up on time in the morning? / I sleep late on Saturdays and Sundays! But I'm usually early during the week. So, I guess my answer is yes, I usually get up on time. **2** Do you have a big breakfast? / I eat toast, eggs, cereal, yogurt, and fruit for breakfast every day! Wow! **3** Do you talk to your friends and family before school? / I talk to my parents, and I sometimes call a friend to make plans for after school. So, yes, I often talk before school. I'm only quiet before exams! **4** Do you make your bed in the morning? / Of course! You must make your bed every day! **5** Do you make your family's breakfast? / Not usually. I guess I sometimes do. When it's someone's birthday or a special day! **6** Do you get to school on time? / Four out of five days. So, yes, often.

19 Look at Activity 18 and talk about Peter's day. Then quiz your partner. Is he/she a morning person?

- Ask students to do the activity in pairs.

20 Listen and circle.

A:37

- Play the audio and have students listen.
- Play the audio again for students to circle the words.
- Check answers as a class.

Woman: Hi, Emma. Do you get up on time in the morning?
Emma: No, never. I love my bed! I'm not a morning person at all.
Woman: Do you make your bed in the morning?
Emma: Yes, sometimes. But I don't always have time to make my bed.
Woman: Do you have a big breakfast?
Emma: No, never. I drink juice, and I sometimes eat an apple, but I don't like big breakfasts.
Woman: Do you make your family's breakfast?
Emma: No, never. I sometimes help in the kitchen in the evening, but never in the morning.
Woman: Do you talk to your friends and family before school?
Emma: Yes, sometimes but not usually. I don't like talking in the morning.
Woman: Do you get to school on time?
Emma: I often get to school on time, but not always!

Pop Quiz: Pretend to be Peter/Emma and provide answers. Students have to work out the questions.

- Direct students' attention to the fire extinguisher card on page 30. Tell students to go online to the Poptropica English Island Adventure Game and find the item. Once students click on it, they are taken to a supplementary language task.

Homework WB page 24

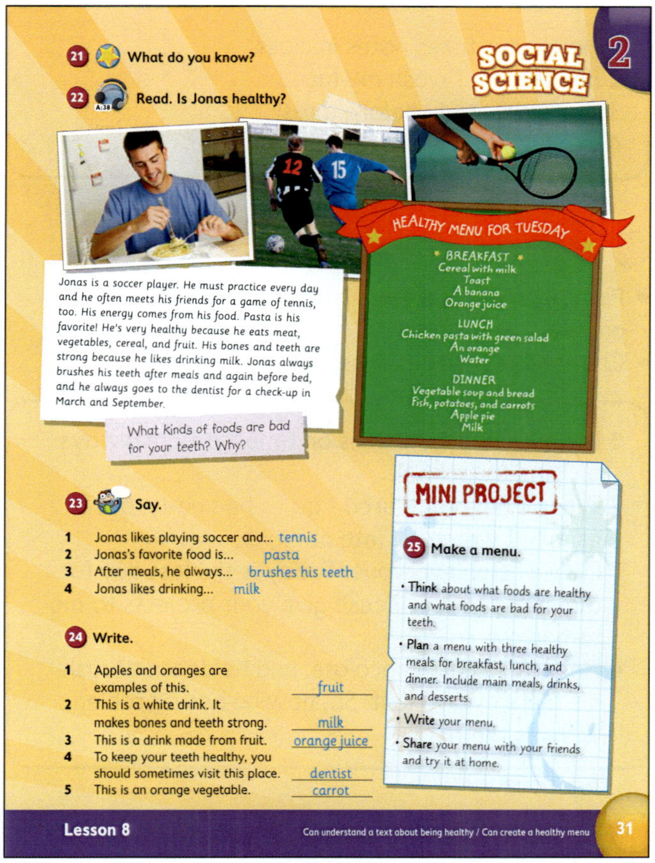

SOCIAL SCIENCE 2

21 What do you know?

22 A:38 Read. Is Jonas healthy?

Jonas is a soccer player. He must practice every day and he often meets his friends for a game of tennis, too. His energy comes from his food. Pasta is his favorite! He's very healthy because he eats meat, vegetables, cereal, and fruit. His bones and teeth are strong because he likes drinking milk. Jonas always brushes his teeth after meals and again before bed, and he always goes to the dentist for a check-up in March and September.

What kinds of foods are bad for your teeth? Why?

HEALTHY MENU FOR TUESDAY

BREAKFAST
Cereal with milk
Toast
A banana
Orange juice

LUNCH
Chicken pasta with green salad
An orange
Water

DINNER
Vegetable soup and bread
Fish, potatoes, and carrots
Apple pie
Milk

23 Say.

1 Jonas likes playing soccer and... tennis
2 Jonas's favorite food is... pasta
3 After meals, he always... brushes his teeth
4 Jonas likes drinking... milk

24 Write.

1 Apples and oranges are examples of this. fruit
2 This is a white drink. It makes bones and teeth strong. milk
3 This is a drink made from fruit. orange juice
4 To keep your teeth healthy, you should sometimes visit this place. dentist
5 This is an orange vegetable. carrot

MINI PROJECT

25 Make a menu.

- **Think** about what foods are healthy and what foods are bad for your teeth.
- **Plan** a menu with three healthy meals for breakfast, lunch, and dinner. Include main meals, drinks, and desserts.
- **Write** your menu.
- **Share** your menu with your friends and try it at home.

Lesson 8 Can understand a text about being healthy / Can create a healthy menu 31

Lesson 8 SB page 31 or Poptropica English World

Learning Objectives
Can understand a text about being healthy
Can create a healthy menu

Additional Language
soccer player, energy, pasta, bones, dentist, check-up

Warm-up

- Write *Healthy food* and *Unhealthy food* on the board. Invite students to come to the front to write a food under one of the headings.

21 What do you know?

- Open books and ask students to look at the activities. Ask, *What are we learning today?* Write the lesson objectives on the board: *We're learning about healthy food.*
- Refer to the learning adventure poster and say, *Great! You are moving along your learning adventure!*

22 A:38 Read. Is Jonas healthy?

- Ask about the pictures. Say, *What is Jonas doing?* (*He's eating pasta. He's playing soccer. He's playing tennis.*)
- Play the audio and have students read along.
- Have students read the text. Then draw attention to the menu. Ask, *What does Jonas eat for breakfast?* and elicit responses. Repeat for the whole menu.

23 Say.

- Say, *Jonas likes playing soccer and tennis.* Elicit a similar statement from a student.
- Put students into small groups and have them continue to say statements about Jonas, using the sentence starters in Activity 23.

Explain to students that there is no correct answer in this activity. They just need to provide a good argument. Write *eggs vs cereal / milk vs juice / banana vs chocolate croissant* on the board, then tell students that one is right and one is wrong in each pair. Students have to argue how that is true.

24 Write.

- Give students time to read the five statements and write their answers.
- Check answers by having students switch books, and eliciting answers from different pairs.

25 Make a menu.

- Ask students what steps they will take to make sure they include all the necessary information. Remind students of the steps to success: Think, Plan, Write and Share.
  Think Refer students back to the ideas in the warm-up.
  Plan Ask students to think carefully about what foods to include.
  Write Give students time to write out their menus. Remind them to check they have included the information they need.
  Share Ask students to share their menu with a partner. Does their partner think it's healthy?
- Encourage students to try their menus at home and feedback to the class.

You may also wish to give students feedback on their projects.

Ask students, *What do you know about healthy eating now?* Give students a minute to tell their partner the new ideas and words they can remember. Ask students, *Where are you on your learning adventure?* Tell students, *Good job!* to reinforce the progress they are making.

Pop Quiz: As students are leaving the class, call out different foods and have students say whether they are healthy or unhealthy.

Materials
Poster, sheet of paper for each student

Homework WB page 25

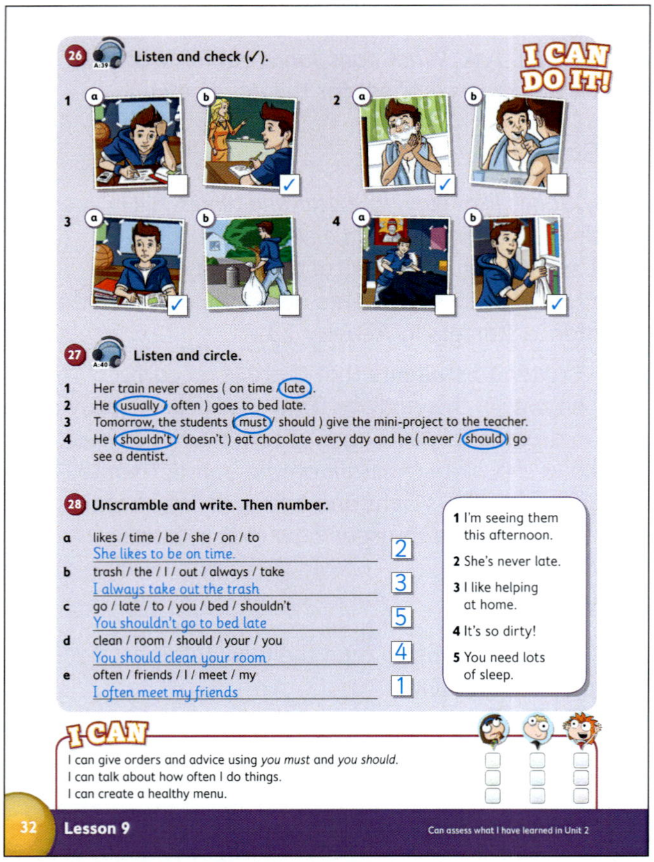

26 Listen and check (✓).

I CAN DO IT!

1 a b 2 a b 3 a b 4 a b

27 Listen and circle.

1 Her train never comes (on time / late).
2 He (usually / often) goes to bed late.
3 Tomorrow, the students (must / should) give the mini-project to the teacher.
4 He (shouldn't / doesn't) eat chocolate every day and he (never / should) go see a dentist.

28 Unscramble and write. Then number.

a likes / time / be / she / on / to
She likes to be on time. 2
b trash / the / I / out / always / take
I always take out the trash 3
c go / late / to / you / bed / shouldn't
You shouldn't go to bed late 5
d clean / room / should / your / you
You should clean your room 4
e often / friends / I / meet / my
I often meet my friends 1

1 I'm seeing them this afternoon.
2 She's never late.
3 I like helping at home.
4 It's so dirty!
5 You need lots of sleep.

I CAN
I can give orders and advice using *you must* and *you should*.
I can talk about how often I do things.
I can create a healthy menu.

32 Lesson 9 Can assess what I have learned in Unit 2

Lesson 9 SB page 32 or Poptropica English World

Learning Objective
Can assess what I have learned in Unit 2

Warm-up

- Do a quick review with Picture Cards 23–32. Invite some students to come to the front and give them a Card. They mime the activity and other students guess.

Open books and ask students to look at the activities. Write this lesson objective on the board: *We're thinking about our learning adventure.*

- Ask students what they have been learning in the unit. Put their ideas on the board, e.g., *daily activities*.
- For each idea, ask students to tell their partner where they think they are on their learning adventure. Reassure students who are less confident that they will have opportunities for more practice.

26 Listen and check (✓).

- Have students listen to the audio and check the best option.
- Have students switch books with a partner. Play the audio again for students to check answers. Ask the class to agree on the correct response.

1 He always takes notes in class.
2 Before bed, I wash my face.
3 You must study before a test.
4 He should clean his room more often.

27 Listen and circle.

- Play the track and have students circle the correct answer.
- Check answers as a class.

1 My train always comes on time, so I am always on time for school.
2 When I am really tired I go to bed early, but usually I watch TV late at night.
3 Please listen everyone. Today is the last day for the mini-project. Please give your projects to me tomorrow.
4 He always eats chocolate, and he doesn't brush his teeth every night. So, now he has a problem with his teeth.

28 Unscramble and write. Then number.

- Have students look at the words on each line. Ask them to put the words in the correct order, then number them.
- Get students to check answers in pairs by asking and answering, e.g., *Are your friends coming this afternoon? (Yes, I often meet my friends.) Is she often late? (No, she's never late. She likes to be on time.)*

Ask students how they feel about their learning in this unit. Ask students to tell you what they found easy and what they found the most difficult to learn in the unit.

- Read the three *I can* statements with students, and invite students to check the boxes according to how confident they feel about the language point.
- Ask students, *Where are you on your learning adventure?* Students indicate where they think they are on the learning adventure poster. Tell students, *Good job!* to reinforce the progress they are making.

Pop Quiz: In groups of four, students tell the others the answers to the following questions: *Which is your favorite activity in the unit? Why? Which activity don't you like? Why? What is your favorite new word? Which word is the most difficult for you?*

Materials
Poster, Picture Cards 23–32

Homework WB page 26

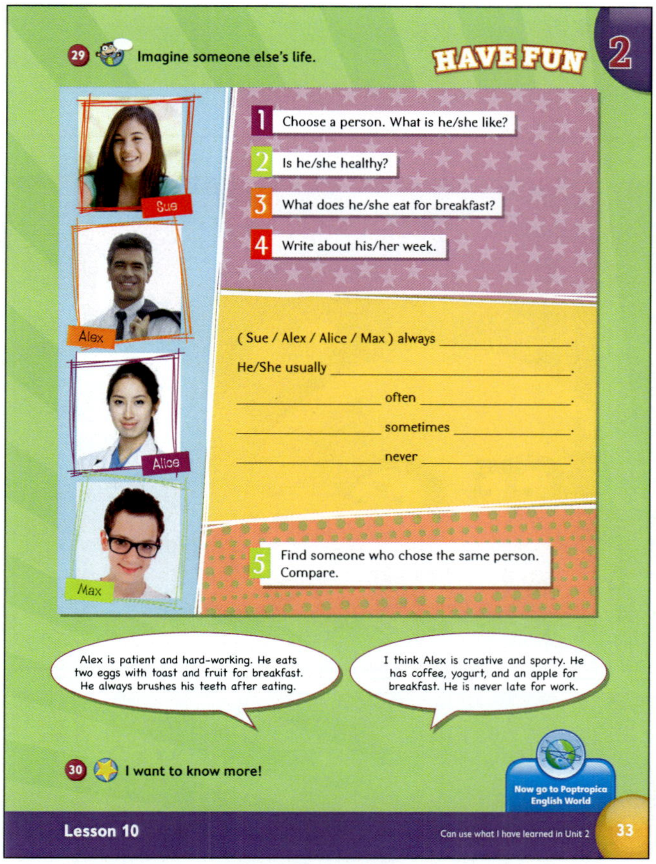

Lesson 10 SB page 33 or Poptropica English World

Learning Objective
Can use what I have learned in Unit 2

Warm-up

- Display Picture Cards 23–37 to review daily activities and adverbs of frequency. Then, write some scrambled words on the board and have students say the answers.

Open books and ask students to look at the pictures. Ask, *What are we learning today?* Write the lesson objective on the board: *We're going to review Unit 2 language, and imagine someone's life.*

Show students a range of breakfast pictures including a continental breakfast with pastries/hot chocolate/muesli/yogurt; an "American" breakfast with bacon, eggs, hashbrowns, tomatoes; a Japanese breakfast with salmon, miso soup, veggies; a single cup of black coffee; and a "healthy" breakfast with fruit salad, glass of orange juice, Greek yogurt, toast with poached egg, and asparagus. Ask students, *Which is the one that doesn't belong?* or *Which is the healthiest?*

Ask students to work in pairs to make sentences/questions with target language, based on their school schedules. Use the adverbs of frequency *always*, *often*, *usually*, *sometimes*, *never*, e.g., *I'm never late for class. / I always help my classmates.* Give pairs a few minutes, and ask them to share their sentences with the class.

- This activity helps build students' confidence as they are using the language they have learned in a different context.

29 Imagine someone else's life.

- Ask students to choose one of the pictures and imagine that person's life, e.g., *Does he/she wake up early/eat a big breakfast/always brush his/her teeth?* Students can decide whether the person is healthy or not healthy, and what they eat for breakfast. Remind them that their breakfast choice in question 3 should reflect their answer in question 2.
- Once students have written about their person's week, ask them to find someone who chose the same picture, and compare their answers.

30 I want to know more!

- Ask students to choose anything they enjoyed from the unit and to go and find out more. You might like to set this activity as homework with a quick feedback session at the beginning of the next class.
- You can also suggest that students write one or two questions about what they want to know, then switch question(s) with a partner. Students then find answer(s) to their partner's question(s) as a homework activity, with feedback the next lesson.

Are you ready for Unit 3?

- Ask students if they are ready to move onto the next unit. Tell students that it is fine if they do not remember everything as they will continue to practice throughout the level.
- Encourage students to ask if they have any questions about what they learned in Unit 2.

You may wish to give Unit 2 Test (see page 190) at this time.

Materials
Picture Cards 23–37, range of breakfast pictures (cut from magazines)

Homework WB page 37

Unit 2 Story Cards

Review Units 1 and 2

SB pages 34–35 or Poptropica English World

Learning Objectives
Can talk about physical appearance and personality
Can talk about daily activities and routines

Review Units 1 and 2

1 Read, look, and number.

1 My brother is seven. He has curly, brown hair and gray eyes. He's very funny but he's lazy.

2 My mom has long, light hair and blue eyes. She's sporty. She plays tennis every day. She's talkative and sometimes bossy.

3 My teacher isn't very tall. She has long, straight hair. She's a good teacher because she's smart and always very patient.

4 My friend is in my class at school. He's short and has light hair and glasses.

Amy

a Fergus 4 b Mrs. Taylor 2 c Ben 1 d Mrs. Picton 3

2 Ask and answer.

A: What does Amy's teacher look like? B: She has long, straight hair.
A: What's Amy's teacher like? B: She's smart and patient.

3 Ask and answer.

1 What must you do in the morning?
2 What should you do after school?
3 What must you do before bed?
4 What should you do every day?

I must make my bed in the morning.

34 Review Units 1 and 2 Can talk about physical appearance and personality

Warm-up

- Review adjectives of physical appearance and personality, using Picture Cards 5–22. Have students listen and repeat. Then place the cards around the room for reference. Invite students to come forward and describe a person in the class. Students have to guess the student.

Open books and ask students to look at the pages. Ask, *What are we learning today?* Write the lesson objective on the board: *We're reviewing language from Units 1 and 2.*

Direct students to pages 12–15 if they should like to refresh their memories on the vocabulary and grammar structures needed for Activities 1 and 2. To challenge students further, ask them to write a description for Amy's father.

- Activities 3–5 are based on vocabulary and grammar structures from pages 24–27. To challenge students further, ask them to write five sentences about Amy's father, using *always*, *never*, *often*, *sometimes* and *usually*.

1 Read, look and number.

- Draw students' attention to the pictures of the people. Pointing to each picture in turn, have the class repeat the names after you. Then ask the class, *What does he/she look like?* Elicit responses.
- Give students time to do the activity, matching Amy's speech bubbles to the correct person, by writing numbers in the boxes.
- To check answers, have students read the texts and say the answers chorally.

2 Ask and answer.

- Invite confident students to read the exchange chorally.
- Give students time to do the activity. Challenge a strong class by asking students to cover the speech bubbles in Activity 1 while they complete the activity. Students needing support can refer to the text for reference.

3 Ask and answer.

- Read the text in the speech bubble chorally. Then, have students read the questions chorally. Invite a confident pair of students to model the first exchange.
- Allow students time to do the activity in pairs.
- Ask the class the questions in this activity and have them answer together. Ask additional questions if time allows, e.g., *What must you do every Monday/ weekend?*

Materials
Picture Cards 5–22, 33–37

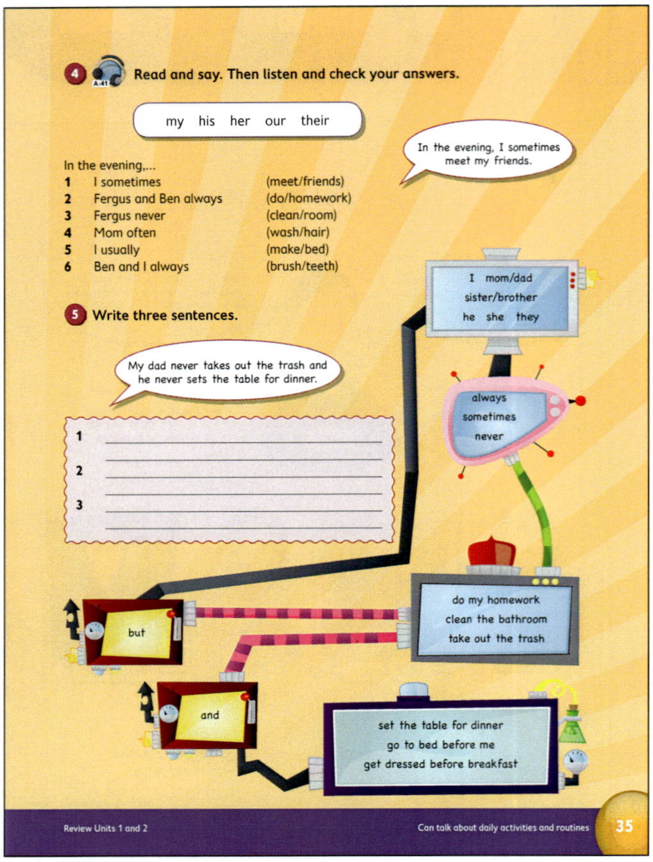

4 A:41 Read and say. Then listen and check your answers.

my his her our their

In the evening, I sometimes meet my friends.

In the evening,...
1 I sometimes (meet/friends)
2 Fergus and Ben always (do/homework)
3 Fergus never (clean/room)
4 Mom often (wash/hair)
5 I usually (make/bed)
6 Ben and I always (brush/teeth)

5 Write three sentences.

My dad never takes out the trash and he never sets the table for dinner.

1 ______
2 ______
3 ______

I mom/dad sister/brother he she they

always sometimes never

do my homework clean the bathroom take out the trash

but

and

set the table for dinner go to bed before me get dressed before breakfast

Review Units 1 and 2 Can talk about daily activities and routines 35

4 Read and say. Then listen and check your answers.

- Draw students' attention to the possessive pronouns in the word box. Ask volunteers to use one in a sentence.
- Next, have students read the text in the speech bubble chorally. Finally give students time to read all the words in parenthesis.
- Pair students and have them make sentences. Invite confident students to say a sentence to the class.
- Play the audio. Students listen and follow.

1 In the evening, I sometimes meet my friends.
2 In the evening, Fergus and Ben always do their homework.
3 In the evening, Fergus never cleans his room.
4 In the evening, Mom often washes her hair.
5 In the evening, I usually make my bed.
6 In the evening, Ben and I always brush our teeth.

- Invite students to read the statements, this time without the audio as a guide. Check answers by eliciting the correct statement from individual students.

5 Write three sentences.

- Ask students to look at the "sentence machine". Explain that they need to choose words and phrases from each section of the machine to make three sentences.
- Read the text in the speech bubble chorally. Draw students' attention to the word *never*. Review the adverbs of frequency, using Picture Cards 33–37. You can quickly elicit the spellings of these words if time allows.
- Draw students' attention to the words *but* and *and*, checking for comprehension. Ask some students to use these words in a sentence, along with daily activities target language.
- Allow students time to do the activity, writing three statements about family members.
- Pair students and have them say their sentences to each other. Invite some students to talk about their partner's family members, or read their own sentences.
- To end the lesson, ask students which game they've enjoyed most from Units 1 and 2. Play it again.

- Watch the video story *Meet Finn and Jenny* on Poptropica English World. Ask students what happened in the story. Watch again, stopping at key points, and ask them about the language, the images, or the story. Ask the students to role-play the story. Assign the roles of two of the characters to confident speakers and let other students play the other parts. Encourage them to say as much of the dialog as they can and prompt them where necessary.

Pop Quiz: You take the part of Fergus, Mrs. Taylor, Ben or Mrs. Picton, without telling the students who you are. Students have to ask you questions (e.g., *Do you wear glasses? Do you clean your room?*), and guess who you are from your answers. Students can also take turns at playing the different characters and being asked questions.

You may wish to give Review Test 1 (see page 204) at this time.

3 Free Time

Unit Overview

Unit Objective

- I can talk about free-time activities and hobbies

Language

Target Vocabulary	Activities and hobbies: hitting, kicking, throwing, catching, diving, going shopping, telling jokes, reading poetry, jumping on the trampoline, playing video games, in-line skating, playing chess, playing the drums, acting, singing karaoke, running races, singing in a choir
Target Structures	What am I good at? I'm good at hitting. What's he/she good at? He's/She's good at hitting. What are they good at? They're good at hitting. He/She isn't good at catching. They aren't good at catching. What does he/she like/love doing? He/She likes/loves going shopping. What were you doing yesterday at 7:00? I was drawing pictures. What was he/she doing yesterday at 7:00? He/She was drawing pictures. What were they doing yesterday at 7:00? They were drawing pictures. Were you drawing pictures? Yes, I was. / No, I wasn't. Was he/she drawing pictures? Yes, he/she was. / No, he/she wasn't. Were they drawing pictures? Yes, they were. / No, they weren't.
Features	**Cross-curricular:** Music: Musical instruments **Values:** It's good to try new things. You should have a hobby.

Skills

Reading	• Can identify free-time activities and hobbies • Can understand a simple story • Can understand details of a story • Can recognize what people are good at and what they like doing • Can understand an interview with a musician
Writing	• Can complete simple sentences about what people are good/not very good at • Can write interview questions for a musical person • Can write simple sentences giving advice *(Workbook)*
Listening	• Can identify free-time activities and hobbies • Can understand a simple story
Speaking	• Can talk about what people are good at and not good at doing • Can talk about what people were doing yesterday at different times • Can discuss a story • Can talk about trying new things

Lesson 1 SB page 36 or Poptropica English World

Learning Objective
Can talk about free-time activities

Target Language
hitting, kicking, throwing, catching, diving, going shopping, telling jokes, reading poetry, jumping on the trampoline

1 What do you know?

- Open books and ask students to look at the pictures. Ask, *What are we learning today?* Write the lesson objective on the board: *We're learning about free-time activities.*
- Close books. Ask students what English words they know for activities and hobbies, e.g., *playing soccer, reading*. Write on board.
- Refer to the learning adventure poster and say, *Great! You are already moving along your learning adventure!*

2 Listen and read. Is Robbie good at throwing?

A:42

- Play the audio and ask students to look and listen.
- Divide the class into two groups (Emma and Robbie). Play the audio again, pausing for groups to repeat.

3 Listen and say.

A:43

- Focus attention on the action pictures. Play the audio and have students repeat.
- Put Picture Cards 38–46 on the board for students to refer to. Number them from 1 to 9. Pair students and have them play a game. One student in each pair says a number. His/her partner has to mime the activity and then say it.

4 Listen and number using the words in Activity 3.

A:44

- Ask students to look at the pictures in Activity 3 again. Play the audio and have students listen.

a She loves reading poetry. She has lots of poetry books.
b He's good at diving. He loves the ocean, and is good at swimming, too.
c He's good at tennis. He's fast and is good at hitting the ball.
d They like going shopping. They usually go shopping on Saturday afternoon.
e He's really good at throwing because he practices throwing every week.

f He's good at catching. He often plays baseball after school.
g She's good at kicking a ball. She likes playing outside every day.
h He's really good at telling jokes. He always makes his friends laugh!
i She loves jumping on the trampoline. She practices jumping on the trampoline after school every day.

- Play the audio again. Have students number the boxes according to what they hear.
- To check answers, ask students to switch books, then elicit answers from the class.

Ask students, *How many words for activities and hobbies do you know now?* Give students a minute to tell their partner the new words they know.

- Ask students to say where they are on their adventure now. Ask students which words they find easiest or most difficult to remember. Tell students, *Good job!* to reinforce the progress they are making.

Pop Quiz: Show students a selection of pictures of people doing different activities and hobbies and ask individual students what they are doing.

Materials
Poster, Picture Cards 38–46, pictures of people doing different activities and hobbies (cut from magazines)

Homework WB page 28

Lesson 2 SB page 37 or Poptropica English World

Learning Objective
Can talk about what people are good at and not good at doing

Open books and ask students to look at the activities and the Look! box. Ask, *What are we learning today?* Write the lesson objective on the board: *We're learning to talk about what people are good and not good at doing.*

Warm-up

- Ask the class to stand in a circle. Say, e.g., *I love dancing/throwing.* Tell students to give you the "thumbs up" sign if they think you are good at dancing/throwing, and "thumbs down" if they think you are bad at it. Say, *I'm not good at dancing/ throwing.* Then, they mime dancing/throwing badly.
- Repeat with various activities so students are introduced to the idea of being "good at" something.

5 A:46 Listen and number.

- Draw students' attention to the Look! box and play the audio (track A:45). Students repeat chorally.
- Have students look at the scene. Tell them they will listen to some statements and they have to write the number in the correct box.

1 She's good at diving.
2 He's good at throwing.
3 She isn't good at dancing.
4 They aren't good at climbing.
5 He isn't good at hitting.
6 They're good at riding.
7 He isn't good at jumping on the trampoline.
8 They aren't good at running.

- To check answers, ask students to switch books then elicit answers from the class. Point to character *h*, ask and elicit, *Is he good at hitting? (No, he isn't good at hitting.)*

6 Look at Activity 5. Ask and answer.

- Divide the class into pairs and ask them to look at Activity 5 to ask and answer questions.
- To extend the lesson, pair students and give them each Activity Sheet 5 (see page 156) for them to cut into pieces. One person talks about what they like and can/can't do, and the partner matches the activity picture to the ✗ (am not good at) or the check mark ✓ (am good at). Students take turns being the speaker. Fast finishers can also use the papers to ask questions, talk about others, etc.

Pop Quiz: Use the same activity pictures from the Pop Quiz in Lesson 1. Ask 10 students to help. Get eight students to hold one picture each in front of the class. The last picture is held by two students. The students stand in a row. Tell them to put their thumb up if they decide they can do the activity, or down if they can't. Students don't have to be honest! The two students holding the same picture have to choose the same thumb direction. The other students in the class take turns asking and answering questions about the students holding the pictures, e.g., *Can she catch?* (Thumb down – *No, she can't.*) *Is he good at hitting?* (Thumb up – *Yes, he is.*) *What are they good at?* (Thumbs up – *They're good at shopping.*)

Materials
Activity Sheet 5, scissors, pictures of people from Lesson 1 (cut from magazines)

Homework WB page 29

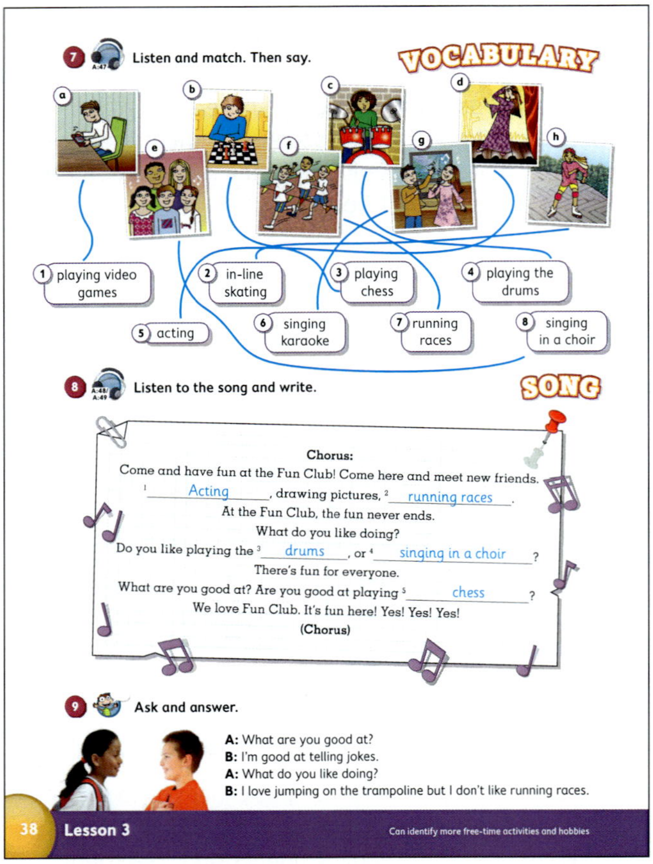

7 Listen and match. Then say. VOCABULARY

1 playing video games
2 in-line skating
3 playing chess
4 playing the drums
5 acting
6 singing karaoke
7 running races
8 singing in a choir

8 Listen to the song and write. SONG

Chorus:
Come and have fun at the Fun Club! Come here and meet new friends.
1 Acting, drawing pictures, 2 running races.
At the Fun Club, the fun never ends.
What do you like doing?
Do you like playing the 3 drums, or 4 singing in a choir?
There's fun for everyone.
What are you good at? Are you good at playing 5 chess?
We love Fun Club. It's fun here! Yes! Yes! Yes!
(Chorus)

9 Ask and answer.

A: What are you good at?
B: I'm good at telling jokes.
A: What do you like doing?
B: I love jumping on the trampoline but I don't like running races.

38 Lesson 3 Can identify more free-time activities and hobbies

Lesson 3 SB page 38 or Poptropica English World

Learning Objective
Can identify more free-time activities and hobbies

Target Language
playing video games, in-line skating, playing chess, playing the drums, acting, singing karaoke, running races, singing in a choir

Warm-up

- Review the activities from Lesson 1 using Picture Cards 38–46. Stick them on the board and divide students into two teams. Ask a student from each team to come to the front and explain what they like/don't like to do and what they are good/not good at. Repeat until all students have had a go. Keep notes.
- Then ask the teams true/false questions about their classmates, such as, *Joe is good at diving. Nina likes reading poetry.* Give points for correct answers.

Open books and ask students to look at the pictures. Ask, *What are we learning today?* Write the lesson objective on the board: *We're learning more activity and hobby words.*

- Close books. Ask students what English words they know for hobbies/activities, e.g., *watching TV, reading books.* Write on board.
- Refer to the learning adventure poster and say, *Great! You are moving along your learning adventure!*

7 A:47 Listen and match. Then say.

- Introduce the new vocabulary with Picture Cards 47–54. Hold them up, then turn them to the word-side and ask the students to repeat.
- Play the audio and ask students to look and listen. Play the audio again and ask students to match the vocabulary items to the pictures as they listen.
- Play the audio a final time and have students repeat.

8 A:48 A:49 Listen to the song and write.

- Do a TPR activity to review some activities and hobbies. Have some students come to the front to mime an action and teach the mime to the class, e.g., *acting, jumping on the trampoline, running races, playing the drums, singing in a choir, playing chess.*
- Play the song audio and have students listen.
- Play the audio again and ask students to write the correct word in the spaces. Have students check their answers with partners.
- Play the karaoke version of the song and ask students to sing the song and mime if they feel confident enough.

9 Ask and answer.

- Put students in small groups and have them ask and answer questions about what they like, and what they are good at.

Ask students, *How many words for activities/hobbies do you know now?* Give students a minute to tell their partner the new words.

- Ask students to say where they are on their adventure now. Ask students which words they find easiest or most difficult to remember. Tell students, *Good job!* to reinforce the progress they are making.

Pop Quiz: Ask students questions, e.g., *Do you like (playing video games)?* for each of the eight new activities. Students raise their hands if they do. Ask two students to count the hands and keep a tally on the board under each activity. This tally can be turned into a graph of which activities the class likes best.

Materials
Poster, Picture Cards 38–54

Homework WB page 30

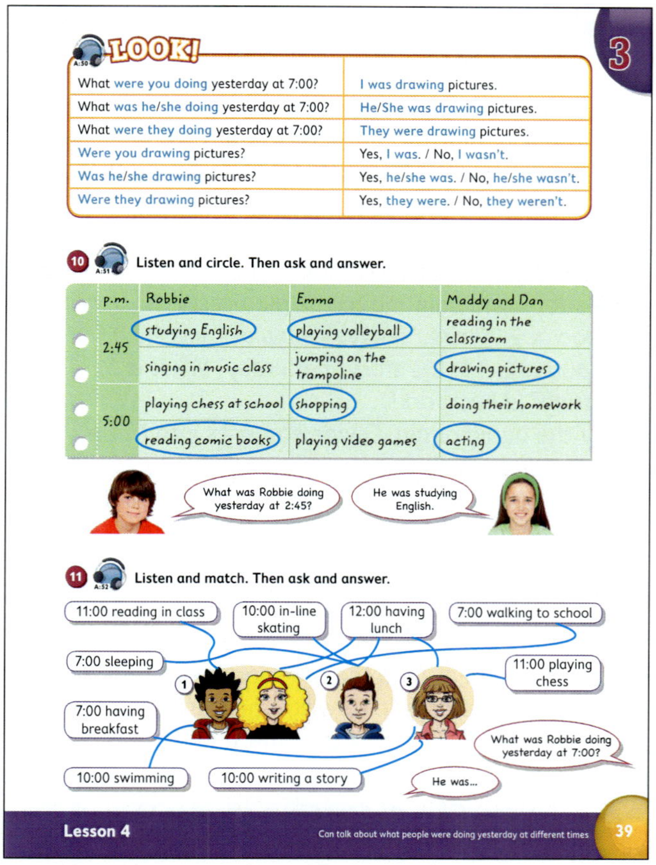

LOOK!

What were you doing yesterday at 7:00?	I was drawing pictures.
What was he/she doing yesterday at 7:00?	He/She was drawing pictures.
What were they doing yesterday at 7:00?	They were drawing pictures.
Were you drawing pictures?	Yes, I was. / No, I wasn't.
Was he/she drawing pictures?	Yes, he/she was. / No, he/she wasn't.
Were they drawing pictures?	Yes, they were. / No, they weren't.

10 Listen and circle. Then ask and answer.

p.m.	Robbie	Emma	Maddy and Dan
2:45	studying English	playing volleyball	reading in the classroom
	singing in music class	jumping on the trampoline	drawing pictures
5:00	playing chess at school	shopping	doing their homework
	reading comic books	playing video games	acting

11 Listen and match. Then ask and answer.

Lesson 4 Can talk about what people were doing yesterday at different times 39

Lesson 4 SB page 39 or Poptropica English World

Learning Objective
Can talk about what people were doing yesterday at different times

Warm-up

- Pass students Picture Cards 38–54. Say, *I am good at (activity).* The student with that card stands up. Repeat for all the activities.

Open books and ask students to look at the activities and the Look! box. Ask, *What are we learning today?* Write the lesson objective on the board: *We're talking about what people were doing yesterday.*

10 A:51 Listen and circle. Then ask and answer.

- Draw students' attention to the Look! box and play the audio (track A:50). Students repeat chorally.
- Have students listen to the audio and circle the correct activity.

What were they doing yesterday in the afternoon?
At two forty-five, Robbie was studying English.
Emma was playing volleyball.
And Maddy and Dan were drawing pictures in art class.
At five o'clock, Robbie was reading comic books.
Emma was shopping with her mom.
And Maddy and Dan were acting in a play.

- Have students check answers in pairs. Play the audio. Students say the answers along with the audio.

11 A:52 Listen and match. Then ask and answer.

- Have students listen to the audio and match the activity to the person.

Woman: What were they doing yesterday morning?
Boy 1: At seven o'clock, Robbie was sleeping.
Emma was having breakfast.
And Maddy and Dan were walking to school.
Girl 1: At ten o'clock, Emma was writing a story.
Robbie was in-line skating.
And Maddy and Dan were swimming.
Boy 1: At eleven o'clock, Maddy and Dan were reading in class.
Robbie was making a project.
And Emma was playing chess.
Girl 1: At twelve o'clock, Maddy and Dan were having lunch.
Robbie and Emma were having lunch, too.

Pop Quiz: Ask individual students, *What were you doing yesterday at 6:00/10:00/8:00? (I was...)* Then get students to ask their partners and to tell the class *(He/She was...).* Finally, invite students to ask you what you were doing at certain times yesterday.

Materials
Picture Cards 38–54

Homework WB page 31

Lesson 5 SB page 40 or Poptropica English World

Learning Objectives
Can understand a simple story
Can discuss a story

Additional Language
tracks, wolf

Functional Language
Eat your breakfast, guys. Why don't we go and have a look? Oh, come on! Yes, it sure is!

Open books and ask students to look at the story. Ask, *What are we learning today?* Write the lesson objective on the board: *We're reading and discussing a story.*

Warm-up

- Close books. Review the previous episode of the story. Prepare questions such as, *Where does Smith work out? What did Polly and Mike hide inside? What did they make in the igloo?* before class.
- Divide the class into teams and ask the questions. Teams take turns to answer questions within 20 seconds. A wrong answer means the question passes to the next team for a bonus point.

12 A:53 Talk about the pictures. Then listen and read.

- Direct students' attention to the pictures and ask questions about the characters and the scenes, e.g., *Who can you see in Picture 1?* (*Mike, Polly and Polly's mom*) *What are they doing?* (*eating breakfast*)
- Play the audio and have students listen and follow.
- Check students' understanding of the story by asking questions and pointing to the pictures: *Who heard the skidoo at 2:00 a.m.?* (*Polly*) *Who plays soccer?* (*Mike*) *What day is it in the story?* (*Saturday*) *What is Mike wearing? (a backpack)*
- Play the audio again. Divide students into three groups and assign each group a role (Polly, Mike, Polly's mom). Groups read along with the audio, and mime their character's actions.

13 Are the tracks that Polly and Mike see really wolf tracks? Discuss your answers.

- Have students discuss the question in groups, and then invite one person to write their group's answer on the board. Discuss all the different ideas.

Pretend to be Mike and invite students to ask you questions. Give students two minutes to work with a partner and think of questions to ask, e.g., *Who made you breakfast? What are you following? Which way was it going? Do you want to go have a look in the mountains? What do you usually do on Saturdays?* Then have students take turns being Mike and answering the questions. This type of activity activates empathy and critical thinking skills, and increases engagement with the story characters and plot.

Pop Quiz: Close books. Say a line of text/statement from the story, e.g., *Well, you're good at finding thieves, too!*. Students put their hands up if they know who said it *(Polly)*. Repeat with statements/text said by each character, to aid recall of the story.

Homework WB page 32

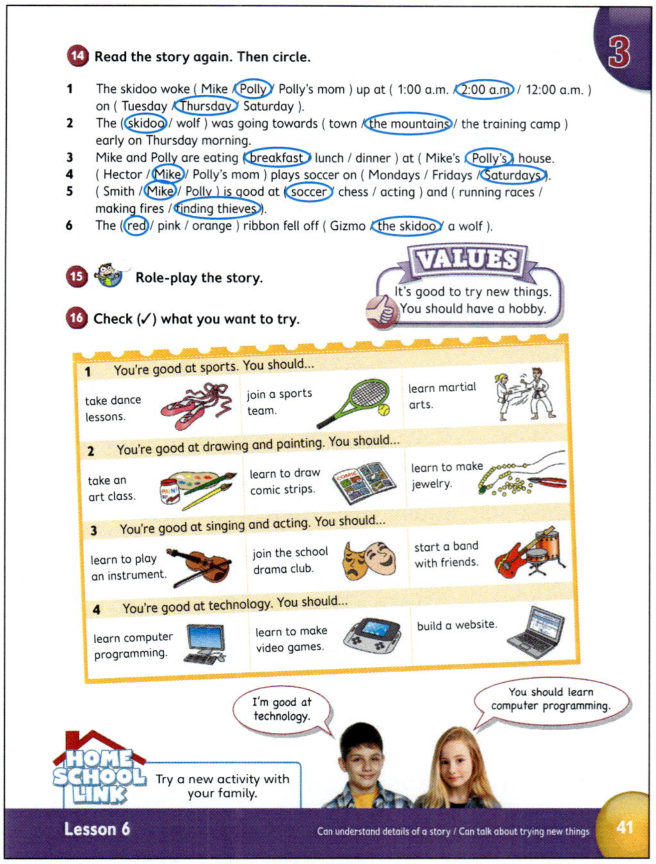
3

14 Read the story again. Then circle.

1 The skidoo woke (Mike / Polly / Polly's mom) up at (1:00 a.m. / 2:00 a.m. / 12:00 a.m.) on (Tuesday / Thursday / Saturday).
2 The (skidoo / wolf) was going towards (town / the mountains / the training camp) early on Thursday morning.
3 Mike and Polly are eating (breakfast / lunch / dinner) at (Mike's / Polly's) house.
4 (Hector / Mike / Polly's mom) plays soccer on (Mondays / Fridays / Saturdays).
5 (Smith / Mike / Polly) is good at (soccer / chess / acting) and (running races / making fires / finding thieves).
6 The (red / pink / orange) ribbon fell off (Gizmo / the skidoo / a wolf).

15 Role-play the story.

VALUES
It's good to try new things. You should have a hobby.

16 Check (✓) what you want to try.

1 You're good at sports. You should...
take dance lessons. | join a sports team. | learn martial arts.

2 You're good at drawing and painting. You should...
take an art class. | learn to draw comic strips. | learn to make jewelry.

3 You're good at singing and acting. You should...
learn to play an instrument. | join the school drama club. | start a band with friends.

4 You're good at technology. You should...
learn computer programming. | learn to make video games. | build a website.

I'm good at technology.
You should learn computer programming.

HOME SCHOOL LINK Try a new activity with your family.

Lesson 6 Can understand details of a story / Can talk about trying new things 41

Lesson 6 SB page 41 or Poptropica English World

Learning Objectives
Can understand details of a story
Can talk about trying new things

Additional Language
learn martial arts, make jewelry, build a website

Value
It's good to try new things. You should have a hobby.

Warm-up

- Invite students to talk about what they like to do and what they're good at. Repeat for all students.
- Divide the class into two. Try a class quiz by asking students to stand up and ask the class a question about someone (they have to know the answer).

Open books and ask students to look at the activities on the page. Ask, *What are we learning today?* Write the lesson objectives on the board: *We're reviewing the story, and we're learning how it's good to try new things.*

14 Read the story again. Then circle.

- Give students time to read the story again and complete the activity.
- Pair students to have them discuss answers and check their work.

15 Role-play the story.

- See the "How to use stories" section on page 23 for more ideas on how to build your students' confidence with role-plays.
- Divide students into groups of three. Give each group a set of cut-out Story Cards (see page 74), and have students place them in order.
- Play the audio again (track A:53), and have students follow along. Put the class into groups to role-play the story.
- Give groups time to practice the role-play, then ask them to show the class.

You might like to give students feedback on their role-play.

16 Check (✓) what you want to try.

- Read the value, *It's good to try new things. You should have a hobby.* Tell students about a new hobby you have. Ask, *Do you have a new hobby?* and elicit responses.
- Draw students' attention to Activity 16 and read item 1 together chorally. Check for comprehension. Allow students time to do the activity on the page.
- Draw students' attention to the children in the bottom right-hand corner of the page. Model the speech bubble language with a volunteer. Put students in pairs to discuss their choices together, using the target language.

- **Home-School link:** Read the instruction with the class: *Try a new activity with your family.* Ask students to do this at home.

Pop Quiz: Make statements to the class and ask them to give you advice on new things to try. For example say, *I like music. (You should learn a musical instrument / learn to play the piano / start a band.) I'm good at jumping. (You should play basketball / try jumping on the trampoline / learn how to skip.)*

Materials
Unit 3 cut-out Story Cards

Homework WB page 33

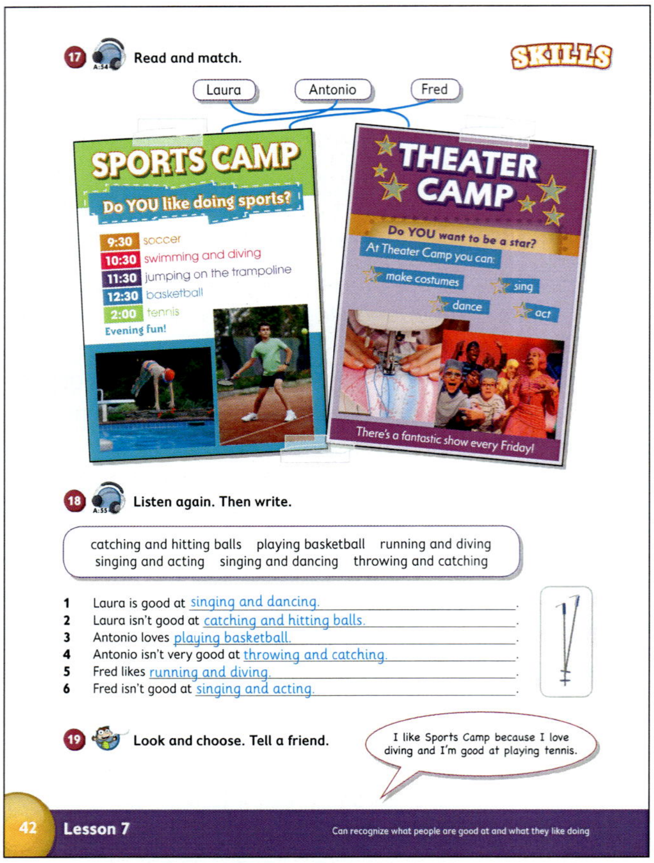
17 Read and match.

SKILLS

Laura Antonio Fred

SPORTS CAMP
Do YOU like doing sports?
9:30 soccer
10:30 swimming and diving
11:30 jumping on the trampoline
12:30 basketball
2:00 tennis
Evening fun!

THEATER CAMP
Do YOU want to be a star?
At Theater Camp you can:
make costumes
sing
dance
act
There's a fantastic show every Friday!

18 Listen again. Then write.

catching and hitting balls playing basketball running and diving
singing and acting singing and dancing throwing and catching

1 Laura is good at singing and dancing.
2 Laura isn't good at catching and hitting balls.
3 Antonio loves playing basketball.
4 Antonio isn't very good at throwing and catching.
5 Fred likes running and diving.
6 Fred isn't good at singing and acting.

19 Look and choose. Tell a friend.

I like Sports Camp because I love diving and I'm good at playing tennis.

42 Lesson 7 Can recognize what people are good at and what they like doing

Lesson 7 SB page 42 or Poptropica English World

Learning Objective
Can recognize what people are good at and what they like doing

Additional Language
theater camp, star, make costumes

Warm-up

- Pair students and have them ask and answer questions about their own schedules, using the target language from page 39. Then ask each student to stand up and talk about their partner's schedule.

Open books and ask students to look at the activities on the page. Ask, *What are we learning today?* Write the lesson objective on the board: *We're learning to find information about what people are good at and what they like doing.*

17 Read and match.

- Direct students' attention to the posters and ask, *Have you ever been to a sports camp or a theater camp?* Say, *Let's see where Laura, Antonio, and Fred went, and what they are good at.*
- Play the audio and have students listen and follow.

> Hi, I'm Laura! I don't like playing ball sports because I'm not good at catching and hitting balls. I can't swim, but I love dancing! I love singing and dancing to music in my bedroom.
> I'm Antonio. I love playing soccer. It's my favorite activity. I'm good at kicking balls. I love playing basketball, too, but I'm not very good at throwing and catching.
> Hello, I'm Fred. I like running, swimming, and diving. I'm in a swim club at school. I can't sing or act, and I don't like making things.

- Check students' understanding by asking questions and pointing to the names of the children.
- Play the audio again. Give students time to match the person to the camp they went to.

18 Listen again. Then write.

- Play the audio and have students complete the sentences with words from the box.
- Have students check their answers in pairs.

19 Look and choose. Tell a friend.

- Say, *I like Sports Camp because I love diving and I'm good at playing tennis.* Have students repeat chorally.
- Pair students and have them talk about themselves, using this target language. Invite students to stand up and say which camp they like best.

Write on the board, *You should only play a sport you are good at. You can't act if you can't sing.*

- Divide the class into small groups and get them to discuss the statements. Ask the groups to share whether they agree/disagree with the statements, and their reasons. Remind students there is no right or wrong answer.
- To extend the lesson, divide students into pairs and distribute one copy of Activity Sheet 6 (see page 157) to each pair. Ask students to ask four classmates what they are good at, not good at, and what activities they would like at a 'dream' camp. Tell them they must use full sentences. Invite pairs to come forward to tell what they've discovered.

Pop Quiz: Say some statements from the listening, and ask students to stand up if they think it's true, and put up their hands if they think it's false, e.g., *Laura is good at hitting balls.* (false)

- Direct students' attention to the ski sticks card on page 42. Tell students to go online to the Poptropica English Island Adventure Game and find the item. Once students click on it, they are taken to a supplementary language task.

Materials
Activity Sheet 6

Homework WB page 34

MUSIC 3

20 What do you know?

21 Read. Then write T = True or F = False.

This is Harry Gregson-Williams. He writes music for movies and video games.

What movies is your music in?
The *Shrek* movies, the *Narnia* movies, and a lot of others.

You write music for video games, too. Do you like playing video games?
Video games are OK but they aren't my favorite thing. I write my music on computers so I don't like playing on computers when I'm at home.

What instruments can you play?
I'm good at playing the piano and I can play the drums. I'm good at singing, too.

What's your favorite music?
Oh... I can't answer that question. I love listening to violins and trumpets but I love a lot of music!

1 He's good at playing the piano. T
2 He ~~can't~~ sing. can F
3 He likes violin music. T
4 He writes the ~~stories~~ for movies. music F
5 He ~~loves~~ playing video games. doesn't like F

22 Correct the false sentences in Activity 21. Say.

23 Listen to the music and number.

MINI PROJECT

24 Write interview questions.

- **Think** Do you know any musical people like Harry Gregson-Williams?
- **Plan** Choose one musical person and the things you want to know about him/her.
- **Write** Create five questions for a "Discover a great musician" interview. Are good interview questions short or long, polite or rude? Check your questions.
- **Share** Present your interview to the class with a friend.

Lesson 8 Can understand an interview with a musician / Can write interview questions for a musical person 43

Lesson 8 SB page 43 or Poptropica English World

Learning Objectives
Can understand an interview with a musician
Can write interview questions for a musical person

Additional Language
Shrek, Narnia, instruments, interview questions, polite, rude, violins, drums, piano, trumpet

20 What do you know?

- Open books and ask students to look at the activities. Ask, *What are we learning today?* Write the lesson objectives on the board: *We're learning about a musician, and we're writing interview questions for a musical person.*
- Close books. Ask students, *What types of music do you like? What is your favorite piece of music from a movie?*
- Refer to the learning adventure poster and say, *Great! You are moving along your learning journey!*

Warm-up

- Review musical instruments (violin, piano, drum, trumpet).

21 Read. Then write T = True or F = False.

- Say, *Making music for movies is very important. Let's learn about Harry Gregson-Williams.*
- Play the audio and have students read along.
- Play the audio again. Ask students to write T or F.

22 Correct the false sentences in Activity 21. Say.

- Have students correct the false sentences. Check answers as a class.

23 Listen to the music and number.

- Play the audio. Allow students time to number the boxes.

1 [Music: a trumpet fanfare]
2 [Music: something jazzy on the piano]
3 [Music: classical orchestral violin music]
4 [Music: drum kit doing a dramatic sequence in rock band]

- Have students check their answers with partners.

24 Write interview questions.

- Ask students what steps they will take to make sure they include all the necessary information. Remind students of the steps to success; Think, Plan, Write and Share.
  Think Ask students to think of a musical person (a composer or a musician).
  Plan Ask students to think about what they would want to know about the person they have chosen.
  Write Give students time to write five questions for their interview. Remind them to check their questions aren't too long, and are polite.
  Share Nominate students to role-play their interviews in class.

You may also wish to give students feedback on their projects.

Ask students, *What do you know about music and musical people now?* Give students a minute to tell their partner the new ideas and words they can remember. Ask students, *Where are you on your learning adventure?* Tell students, *Good job!* to reinforce the progress they are making.

Pop Quiz: As students are leaving the class, play a few seconds of the start of the pieces of music you brought. Ask students which instruments they hear in each piece.

Materials
Poster, recordings of four different types of music

Homework WB page 35

25 Listen and number. (First = 1, Second = 2.)

I CAN DO IT!

What were they doing yesterday?

	1 Emma	2 Dan	3 Maddy	4 Mom and Dad
a	1	2	2	1
b	2	1	1	2

26 Unscramble and write questions. Then write the answers.

1 Emma / playing / was / chess
Was Emma playing chess?
Yes, she was.

2 the / drums / was / playing / Emma
Was Emma playing the drums?
No, she wasn't.

3 were / shopping / Mom / and / Dad
Were Mom and Dad shopping?
Yes, they were.

4 comic / Mom / were / and / reading / Dad / books
Were Mom and Dad reading comic books?
No, they weren't.

27 Think of an activity each person or pair did yesterday. Write it down. Then ask and answer.

You	Your mom/dad	Your friend	Your brother/sister

Was Tom in-line skating yesterday?

No, he wasn't. Guess again!

I CAN

I can talk about what people are good at and not good at doing.

I can talk about what people were doing yesterday at different times.

I can write interview questions for a musical person.

44 Lesson 9 Can assess what I have learned in Unit 3

Lesson 9 SB page 44 or Poptropica English World

Learning Objective
Can assess what I have learned in Unit 3

Warm-up

- Write the word *YESTERDAY* on the board. Say, *I was running yesterday after school. What were you doing?* Point to the first person in each row and have students reply, one by one.

Open books and ask students to look at the activities. Write this lesson objective on the board: *We're thinking about our learning adventure.*

- Ask students what they have been learning in the unit. Put their ideas on the board, e.g., *activities/hobbies*.
- For each idea, ask students to tell their partner where they think they are on their learning adventure. Reassure students who are less confident that they will have opportunities for more practice.

25 Listen and number. (First = 1, Second = 2.)

A:58

- Have students listen to the audio and write 1 or 2.
- Play the audio again for students to check their answers.

Yesterday was Saturday.
Emma was acting in the morning and playing video games in the afternoon.
Dan is good at soccer. Yesterday he was practicing kicking and throwing with friends. In the evening, he was reading his favorite comic book.
Maddy was dancing in the morning. Then, she was jumping on the trampoline with friends in the afternoon.
Mom and dad had a relaxed day yesterday. In the morning, they were reading. Then, in the evening they were watching TV.

- Play the audio again and have students speak along.

26 Unscramble and write questions. Then write the answers.

- Have students unscramble and write the questions then the answers.
- Pair students and have them practice the questions and answers. Invite some pairs to model the language to the class.

27 Think of an activity each person or pair did yesterday. Write it down. Then ask and answer.

- Ask students to look at the names and then write down an activity for each person.
- In pairs, have students ask and answer questions to find out their activities. Draw their attention to the model dialog.

Ask students how they feel about their learning in this unit. Ask students to tell you what they found easy and what they found the most difficult to learn in the unit.

- Read the three *I can* statements with students and invite students to check the boxes according to how confident they feel about the language point.
- Ask students, *Where are you on your learning adventure?* Students indicate where they think they are on the learning adventure poster. Tell students, *Good job!* to reinforce the progress they are making.

Pop Quiz: In groups of four, students tell the others the answers to the following questions: *Which is your favorite activity in the unit? Why? Which activity don't you like? Why? What is your favorite new word? Which word is the most difficult for you?*

Materials
Poster

Homework WB page 36

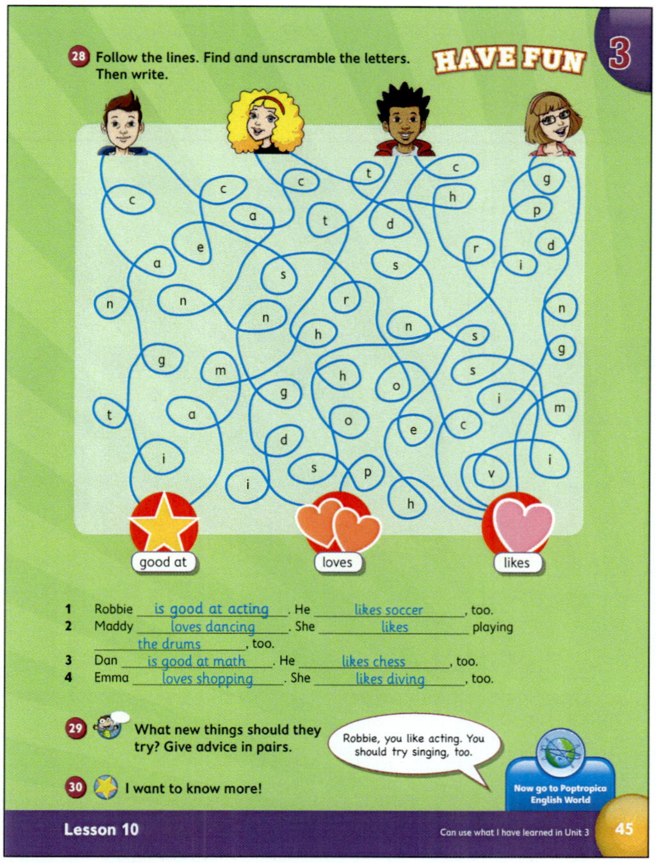

Lesson 10 SB page 45 or Poptropica English World

Learning Objective
Can use what I have learned in Unit 3

Warm-up

- Place Picture Cards 38–54 in a big bag. Go around the room and give each student a chance to pick a Picture Card out of the bag. Everyone asks chorally, *What are you good at?* And the student responds, *I am good at (activity on the card).* Repeat until everyone has a turn.

Open books and ask students to look at the pictures. Ask, *What are we learning today?* Write the lesson objective on the board: *We're going to review Unit 3 language with a game.*

28 Follow the lines. Find and unscramble the letters. Then write.

- Direct students' attention to the game-board and ask questions about the picture/activity. Ask, *What's this? What should we do?* Prompt students to answer, *It's a game. Follow the line. Unscramble the letters.*
- Allow students time to do the activity and fill in the blanks in the sentences.
- Pair students and have them discuss the answers. Check answers by inviting students to read chorally.

Say answers such as, *He is good at acting. He likes chess.* and ask students to provide the correct questions, e.g., *What is Robbie good at? What does Dan like?* This will provide students with further reinforcement of the question form.

29 What new things should they try? Give advice in pairs.

- Draw students' attention to the example sentence and have a student read it out.
- In pairs, have students decide what new hobbies the others should try, giving a reason. Nominate pairs to give their ideas.

30 I want to know more!

- Ask students to choose anything they enjoyed from the unit and to go and find out more. You could set this activity as homework with a quick feedback session at the beginning of the next class.
- You can also suggest that students write one or two questions about what they want to know, then switch question(s) with a partner. Students then find answer(s) to their partner's question(s) as a homework activity, with feedback the next lesson.

Are you ready for Unit 4?

- Ask students if they are ready to move onto the next unit. Tell students that it is fine if they do not remember everything as they will continue to practice throughout the level.
- Encourage students to ask if they have any questions about what they learned in Unit 3.

You may wish to give Unit 3 Test (see page 192) at this time.

Materials
Picture Cards 38–54, big bag

Homework WB page 37

Unit 3 Story Cards

Wider World 2

SB pages 46–47 or Poptropica English World

Learning Objectives
Can understand texts about funny sports
Can talk about funny or unusual sports

Target Language
I want to do cheese rolling. (Why?) Because I'm good at running and I love eating cheese!

Additional Language
mud racing, cheese rolling, reindeer racing, elephant polo

Wider World 2
Funny sports

1 What do you know?

2 A:59 Listen and read. What are the people doing?

3 Look and say.

It's elephant polo!

1 This is a ball sport. 4
2 This is a sport with food. 2
3 This is a winter sport. 3
4 People ride in this sport. 4
5 People run in this sport. 1

1 **Mud racing**
Hi. I live in Scottsdale, Arizona. Every year there's a mud race. It's for children only. They can run, climb, swim, and dive in mud. It's really funny. That's my brother in the picture. He loves mud!
Bianca, 11, United States

2 **Cheese rolling**
Every May, people roll a big cheese wheel down Cooper's Hill. Then everyone runs to catch the cheese. The winner can eat it! My dad likes doing the race but he never wins. He isn't very good at running!
Freddy, 11, United Kingdom

46 Wider World 2 Can understand texts about funny sports

Warm-up

- Ask different volunteers to find and point at the United States, the United Kingdom, India, and Norway on your world map.

1 What do you know?

- Open books and ask students to look at the pictures. Ask, *What are we learning today?* Write the lesson objective on the board: *We're learning about sports in different cultures.*
- Close books. Ask students what English words they know for sports, e.g., *tennis, swimming.*
- Refer to the learning adventure poster and say, *Great! You are moving along your learning adventure!*

2 A:59 Listen and read. What are the people doing?

- Give students time to look at the pictures.
- Ask the class questions about each picture in turn. Students speculate, e.g., *What are the people doing in Picture 3? (Three people are wearing skiis. I see three animals. It's cold.)*
- Elicit or say, *reindeer.* Ask students to say what they know about reindeer. (They may talk about Santa, Christmas, etc.)
- Play the audio and have students listen and follow.
- Play the audio again and pause after each item for students to answer the question.
- Play the audio again. Ask students to close their eyes while they listen, and to imagine the scene. Then have a class discussion about these four activities. Invite students to say what they feel about these strange activities.

3 Look and say.

- Ask students to read the statements chorally before they silently read the texts. In pairs, students identify the correct sports.
- To extend this activity, put students into pairs to talk to each other about the pictures. Invite some students to share their comments about a picture with the class.

Tell students you are going to give them an answer relating to the blogs and they have to guess the correct question e.g., *United Kingdom.* (*Where do they do cheese rolling?*) If necessary, allow students some time to work in pairs to think what the question could be, before asking for ideas.

Materials
Poster, world map

3

Reindeer racing

People love doing this sport in winter here in Tromso. The people don't ride the reindeer. They go on skis. The races are in the streets of the town and everyone shouts for their favorite reindeer. I love watching reindeer racing.

Ingrid, 11, Norway

4

Elephant polo

People usually play polo on horses but, here in Jaipur, people sometimes play polo on elephants. They hit the ball with very long sticks. I don't play because I'm not good at hitting the ball. But I like watching.

Rajeev, 12, India

4 Read again and choose. Tell a friend.

A: I want to do cheese rolling.
B: Why?
A: Because I'm good at running and I love eating cheese!

YOUR TURN!

- Does your country have any unusual or funny sports? Discuss in pairs.
- Tell the class.

5 Write.

In our country, people love…

Wider World 2 Can talk about funny or unusual sports 47

4 Read again and choose. Tell a friend.

- Invite two confident students to model the exchange. Then have students read it chorally.
- Pair students and give them time to do the activity. Invite some pairs to report back to the class about their partner.
- Have each student stand and tell the class which activity they want to do, and why. Have students vote for their favorite funny sport out of the four sports covered in this unit.

YOUR TURN! Tell students that they are going to work with their partner to ask and answer questions about sports from their country. Tell students that their questions and answers will help them prepare Activity 5. Make sure you give students time to think through their answers before they work with their partner. Have students present their ideas to the class. To give students a reason to listen, each student/pair will also think of one/two more questions to ask their partner.

5 Write

- Ask students to use their ideas from YOUR TURN! to write about something people love doing in their country, e.g., a funny sport from their country.
- Remind students to check their work for spelling and punctuation when they've finished.

Pop Quiz: Play a definitions team game – the teacher writes a sport on the board behind a student, and his/her team members need to describe it, *It's from India. You play it with…*, so that the student can guess the game

4 Around the world

Unit Overview

Unit Objective

- I can talk about countries and places of interest

Language

Target Vocabulary	Countries: China, Korea, Japan, Australia, the United States, Mexico, Colombia, Brazil, Argentina, the United Kingdom, Spain, Italy, Egypt, India Places: pyramid, statue, cave, volcano, city, town, farm, factory, castle
Target Structures	There's a rain forest in Brazil. / There isn't a rain forest in Korea. There are some penguins in Argentina. / There aren't any penguins in Italy. Is there a pyramid in the city? Yes, there is. / No, there isn't. Are there any beaches in Australia? Yes, there are some beautiful beaches in Australia. Are there any volcanoes in the United Kingdom? No, there aren't.
Features	**Cross-curricular:** Geography: Seasons **Values:** Teamwork is important.

Skills

Reading	• Can understand a simple story • Can understand details of a story • Can understand a blog post about seasons
Writing	• Can write simple sentences about things that can only be done in a team • Can write a blog post about seasons in my country • Can write simple sentences about places and countries *(Workbook)* • Can write questions and answers using *Is there…? / Are there…? (Workbook)* • Can complete simple sentences about what I can give to a team *(Workbook)*
Listening	• Can identify countries, continents, and places of interest • Can understand a simple story
Speaking	• Can talk about countries and places using *There is/isn't* and *There are/aren't* • Can ask and answer about places using *Is there a…* and *Are there any…?* • Can discuss a story • Can talk about the importance of teamwork • Can talk about places to visit in Egypt and my country

Lesson 1 SB page 48 or Poptropica English World

Learning Objective
Can identify countries and continents

Target Language
China, Korea, Japan, Australia, the United States, Mexico, Colombia, Brazil, Argentina, the United Kingdom, Spain, Italy, Egypt, India

1 What do you know?

- Open books and ask students to look at the pictures. Ask, *What are we learning today?* Write the lesson objective on the board: *We're learning different country and continent names.*
- Close books. Ask students what English words they know for countries, e.g., *China, Brazil.* Write on board.
- Refer to the learning adventure poster and say, *Great! You are already moving along your learning adventure!*

2 Listen and read. Does Dan like crocodiles?

- Ask students to look at the scene in their books and listen as you play the audio.
- Divide the class into two groups (Maddy and Dan). Play the audio again, pausing for groups to repeat their lines.
- Ask comprehension questions: *What is the competition about? (a round-the-world trip) What does the winner do? (go to the United Kingdom, Egypt, China, Australia, Brazil) Where are some beautiful beaches? (Australia and Brazil) What else is in Australia? (crocodiles, sharks, spiders)*

3 Listen and say.

- Focus on the flag pictures. Play the audio and have students repeat the audio after each word they hear.
- Put Picture Cards 55–68 on the board and number them. Pair students and have them play a game. One student in each pair says a number. His/her partner has to say the country's name.

4 Which continent is your country in?

- Write the names of the continents on the board, and have students listen and repeat after you. Ask, *Which continent is not here? (Antarctica) Why isn't Antarctica here? (Because there are no people in Antarctica... except scientists.)*
- Ask, *Which continent is your country in?,* and elicit answers. Draw students' attention to Activity 3, flag 1. Ask, *Which continent is China in?,* and elicit the answer. Repeat for all the countries listed.

4 Around the world

1 What do you know?

2 Listen and read. Does Dan like crocodiles?

ROUND-THE-WORLD Holiday

COMPETITION

Dan: Look! There's a competition for a round-the-world trip. The winner goes to the United Kingdom, Egypt, and China, then Australia and Brazil.
Maddy: Wow, there are a lot of interesting places you can see in the United Kingdom. In Egypt there are the Pyramids, and in China there's the Great Wall.
Dan: Sounds great! And in Brazil and Australia there are some beautiful beaches.
Maddy: But, mmm, Dan... there are crocodiles, sharks, and big spiders in Australia, too.
Dan: What?!
Maddy: Don't worry. There are a lot of children in this competition. There's little chance of winning!

3 Listen and say.

1 China 2 Korea 3 Japan 4 Australia 5 the United States
6 Mexico 7 Colombia 8 Brazil 9 Argentina 10 the United Kingdom
11 Spain 12 Italy 13 Egypt 14 India

4 Which continent is your country in?
Africa Asia Australia Europe North America South America

48 Lesson 1 Can identify countries and continents

- To extend the lesson, use Activity Sheet 7 (see Poptropica English World), and have students cut the flags and words out. First, students play *Concentration* by using the two sets of flags. They must say the word each time they turn over a flag. Matching flags are kept as points. For the second version, students use one set of flags and one set of country names.

Ask students, *How many countries and continents do you know now?* Give students a minute to tell their partner the new words they know.

- Ask students to say where they are on their adventure now. Ask students which words they find easiest or most difficult to remember. Tell students, *Good job!* to reinforce the progress they are making.

Pop Quiz: Use flags from the lesson printed out as large cards. Say, *Which country is this?* Students put their hands up to answer. Vary the game by saying, *This is Japan.* when holding up the wrong flag, e.g., the Australian flag. Students have to correct you: *No, it isn't. It's Australia.*

Materials
Poster, Picture Cards 55–68, Activity Sheet 7, scissors, large pictures of flags

Homework WB page 38

5 Listen and ✓ (= There are) or ✗ (= There aren't). Then say.

LOOK!

There's a rain forest in Brazil.
There isn't a rain forest in Korea.
There are some penguins in Argentina.
There aren't any penguins in Italy.

WILD VACATIONS

See these beautiful animals in the wild!

	penguins	monkeys	snakes
Argentina	✓	✓	✓
Italy	✗	✗	✓
China	✗	✓	✓

There are some penguins in Argentina.

6 Play the game.

A: There aren't any penguins. There aren't any monkeys. There are some snakes.
B: It's Italy!

7 Look and say.

boat dog monkey people rocks shark in the ocean in the tree on the beach

There's a dog on the beach. There aren't any people in the tree.

Lesson 2 Can talk about countries and places using There is/isn't and There are/aren't 49

Lesson 2 SB page 49 or Poptropica English World

Learning Objective
Can talk about countries and places using *There is/isn't* and *There are/aren't*

Warm-up

- Review countries by using Picture Cards 55–68. Divide the class into two lines. Show one of the Picture Cards. The first two students in the line raise their hand to say the name of the country. The first person to answer gets a point for their team. Repeat with other Cards.

Open books and ask students to look at the activities and the Look! box. Ask, *What are we learning today?* Write the lesson objective on the board: *We're learning to say what there is/are and isn't/aren't in countries and places.*

5 Listen and write ✓ (= There are) or ✗ (= There aren't). Then say.

B:05

- Draw students' attention to the Look! box and play the audio (track B:04). Students repeat chorally.
- Tell students they will listen to some statements. They have to listen and write a ✓ or a ✗.

> There are some penguins in Argentina.
> There aren't any penguins in Italy.
> There are some snakes in Italy.
> There aren't any penguins in China.
> There are some snakes in Argentina.
> There are some monkeys in China.
> There aren't any monkeys in Italy.
> There are some snakes in China.
> There are some monkeys in Argentina.

- Have students switch books to check answers. Elicit answers from the class by asking students to say a correct *There are/There aren't* statement. Then ask students to practice saying these statements in pairs.

6 Play the game.

- Divide the class into pairs and give them time to do the activity, using the exchange in Activity 6 as a model.

7 Look and say.

- Ask a confident student to read the example statement.
- Divide the class into pairs and allow time to do the activity.
- If your class needs support, do the activity as a whole class.

Pop Quiz: Where are the wild animals? Divide the class into groups of four. Give each group some Picture Cards 55–68 until they are all given out. Ask students to brainstorm a list of animals that are in the countries they have. Give students time to do the activity then invite students to stand up and each give a sentence using *There are…* . Repeat with *There aren't…* if there's time.

Materials
Picture Cards 55–68

Homework WB page 39

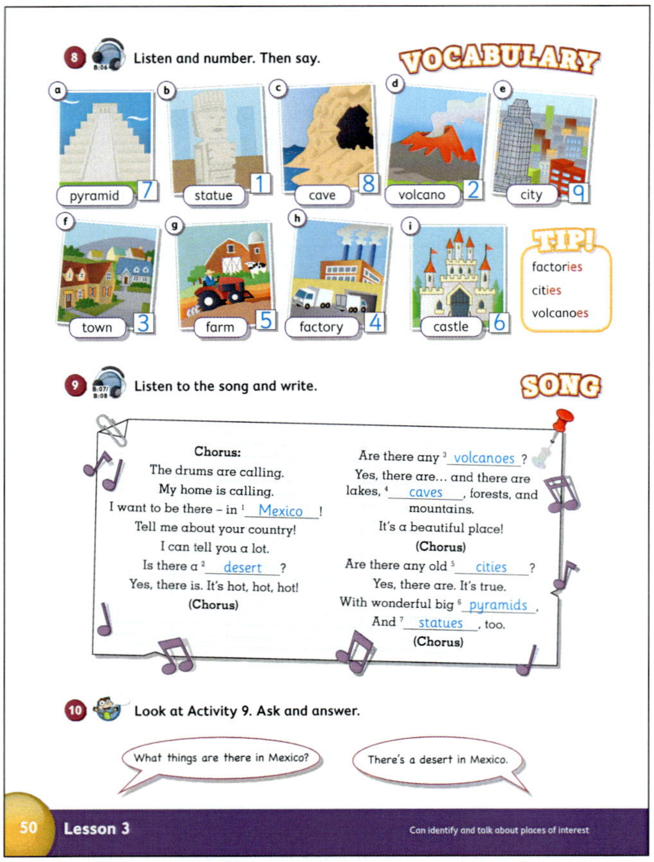
8 Listen and number. Then say.

VOCABULARY

a pyramid 7 | b statue 1 | c cave 8 | d volcano 2 | e city 9
f town 3 | g farm 5 | h factory 4 | i castle 6

TIP!
factories
cities
volcanoes

9 Listen to the song and write.

SONG

Chorus:
The drums are calling.
My home is calling.
I want to be there – in [1] Mexico !
Tell me about your country!
I can tell you a lot.
Is there a [2] desert ?
Yes, there is. It's hot, hot, hot!
(Chorus)

Are there any [3] volcanoes ?
Yes, there are… and there are lakes, [4] caves , forests, and mountains.
It's a beautiful place!
(Chorus)
Are there any old [5] cities ?
Yes, there are. It's true.
With wonderful big [6] pyramids ,
And [7] statues , too.
(Chorus)

10 Look at Activity 9. Ask and answer.

What things are there in Mexico?
There's a desert in Mexico.

50 Lesson 3 Can identify and talk about places of interest

Lesson 3 SB page 50 or Poptropica English World

Learning Objective
Can identify and talk about places of interest

Target Language
pyramid, statue, cave, volcano, city, town, farm, factory, castle

Warm-up

- Review countries and animals by saying, *There are snakes in Argentina.*, and eliciting similar statements. Repeat for, *There aren't…* statements.

Open books and ask students to look at the pictures. Ask, *What are we learning today?* Write the lesson objective on the board: *We're learning words for places of interest.*

- Close books. Ask students what English words they know for places, e.g., *house, school.* Write on board.
- Refer to the learning adventure poster and say, *Great! You are moving along your learning adventure!*

8 Listen and number. Then say.

- Introduce the new vocabulary with Picture Cards 69–77. Hold them up one by one, then turn them to the word-side and ask the students to repeat. Also, mention the word *desert* and draw a picture on the board. Ask, *Is it hot in the desert?*, and elicit, *Yes, it is.* Then ask students to look in their books and match the words to the pictures.
- Play the audio and have students number the pictures as they listen.

1 statue	**4** factory	**7** pyramid
2 volcano	**5** farm	**8** cave
3 town	**6** castle	**9** city

- Play the audio again and have students repeat.

Tip!
Draw students' attention to the Tip! box regarding the spelling of plurals.

9 Listen to the song and write.

- Say, *I can tell you a lot about my country. It is hot/ cold*, etc. Say, *Tell me about your country.*, and elicit responses.
- Draw students' attention to Activity 9. Play the song audio and have students listen.
- Play the audio again and ask students to write the correct word in the spaces. Have students check their answers with partners.
- Play the karaoke version and ask students sing along if they feel confident enough.

10 Look at Activity 9. Ask and answer.

- Draw students' attention to the example dialog at the bottom of page 50. Model the language with a confident student. Pair students, and have them ask and answer about Mexico.

Ask students, *How many words for places do you know now?* Give students a minute to tell their partner the new words they know.

- Ask students to say where they are on their adventure now. Ask students which words they find easiest or most difficult to remember. Tell students, *Good job!* to reinforce the progress they are making.

Pop Quiz: Show students Picture Cards 69–77 and ask students to say sentences about what there is/isn't or are/aren't in different countries/places, e.g., *There are volcanoes in Japan. There are factories in India.*

Materials
Poster, Picture Cards 69–77

Homework WB page 40

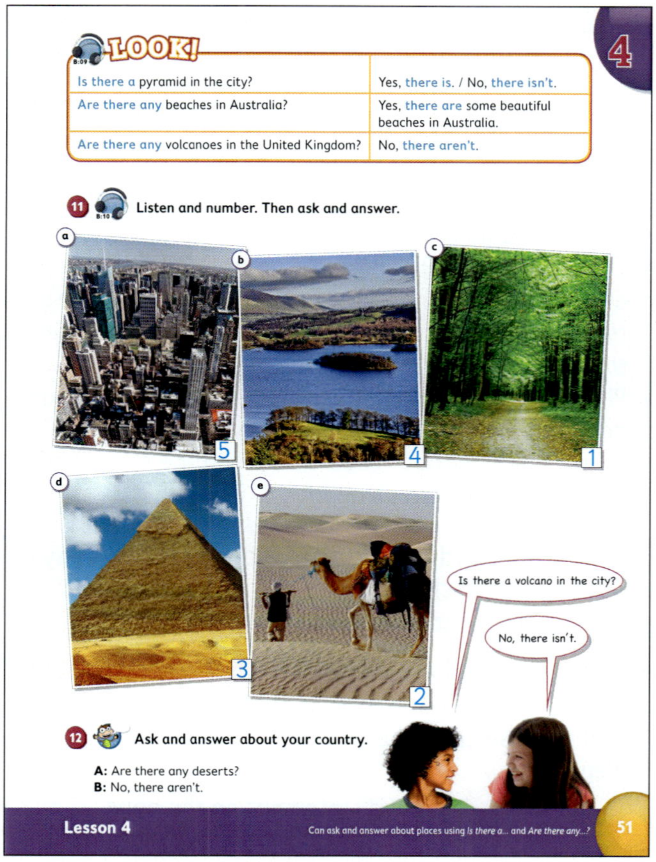
LOOK!

Is there a pyramid in the city?	Yes, there is. / No, there isn't.
Are there any beaches in Australia?	Yes, there are some beautiful beaches in Australia.
Are there any volcanoes in the United Kingdom?	No, there aren't.

11 Listen and number. Then ask and answer.

12 Ask and answer about your country.

A: Are there any deserts?
B: No, there aren't.

Lesson 4 Can ask and answer about places using *Is there a...* and *Are there any...?* 51

Lesson 4 SB page 51 or Poptropica English World

Learning Objective
Can ask and answer about places using *Is there a…* and *Are there any…?*

Warm-up

- Pass Picture Cards 55–77 to all students and have them show their pictures. Invite a student with a country Card to ask, *What things are there in (India)?* Students with appropriate cards have to answer, e.g., *There are factories in India.*

Open books and ask students to look at the activities and the Look! box. Ask, *What are we learning today?* Write the lesson objective on the board: *We're learning to ask and answer questions about what there is/are and isn't/aren't* in different places.

11 B:10 Listen and number. Then ask and answer.

- Have students read the Look! box and play the audio (track B:09). Students repeat chorally.
- Draw students' attention to the pictures in Activity 11. Point to Picture *a* and ask, *What is it?,* and elicit responses. Ask, *Is there a pyramid in the city?,* and elicit, *No, there isn't.*
- Have students listen to the audio and write the correct numbers in the boxes.

1 Are there any factories in the forest? No, there aren't.
2 Are there any camels in the desert? Yes, there are some camels in the desert.
3 Are there any pyramids in Egypt? Yes, there are some pyramids in Egypt. They're beautiful.
4 Is there an island in the lake? Yes, there is.
5 Is there a volcano in the city? No, there isn't.

- Have students switch books for checking. Play the audio again, and have students say answers along with the audio.
- Pair students and have them ask each other additional questions about the pictures, using the target language.

12 Ask and answer about your country.

- Put students in pairs to ask and answer questions about their countries. Invite confident students from different pairs to exchange information in front of the class.
- Divide class into small groups and give each group Activity Sheets 7 and 8 (see Poptropica English World) and have them cut out the pieces. One student must take an item from each Activity Sheet and give it to another person in the group to say a question about, using target structures. Students take turns doing this. To make the game more challenging, students can pick three times for their team mate to talk about.

Pop Quiz: Have four students come to the front and choose a country from Lesson 1. Give them two appropriate cards from Picture Cards 69–77 making sure that the pictures represent something in the country. Ask each student to tell the class what country he/she is, e.g., *I am Mexico.* The other students take turns to work in pairs, asking and answering about what is/isn't in each country, according to the pictures held, e.g., ask, *Are there any statues in Mexico?* If student labeled Mexico is holding a statue picture, then the answer is, *Yes, there are statues in Mexico.* If that student isn't holding a statue picture, then the answer is, *No, there aren't.*

Materials
Picture Cards 55–77, Activity Sheets 7–8, scissors

Homework WB page 41

Lesson 5 SB page 52 or Poptropica English World

Learning Objectives
Can understand a simple story
Can discuss a story

Additional Language
boss, suspect, the mainland

Functional Language
Get those kids away from here!

Warm-up

- Draw an outline of Australia on the board. Ask students to guess is the country. When they have guessed correctly, write *AUSTRALIA*. Invite volunteers to come to the front to write a word/sentence they associate with Australia (e.g., *hot, desert, kangaroo*). Then draw an irregular island shape and label it *Ice Island*. Ask students to do the same again (e.g., *snow, cold, ice, wolves, dangerous*).
- Depending on the words students have written, ask e.g., *Is Australia cold?* (*No, it's not.*) *Are there any deserts on Ice Island?* (*No, there aren't.*), etc.

Open books and ask students to look at the story. Ask, *What are we learning today?* Write the lesson objective on the board: *We're reading and discussing a story.*

13 Talk about the pictures. Then listen and read.

- Direct students' attention to the pictures and ask questions about the characters and the scenes: *Who can you see in Picture 5? (Hector Frost, Smith) How do they feel? (angry)*
- Play the audio and have students listen and follow.
- Check students' understanding of the story by asking questions and pointing to the pictures, e.g., *Where do the tracks go in Picture 3? (Bollington Hall) Where does the road go? (the Research Station)*
- Play the audio again. Divide students into four groups and assign each group a role (Polly, Mike, Hector Frost, Smith). Groups read along with the audio and mime their character's actions.

14 Do the children want the diamonds? Why does Frost think that they want them? Discuss your answers.

- Have students discuss the questions in groups then invite one person to come to the front and write their group's answer on the board. Discuss all the different ideas.

Write the following statement on the board, *Australia is a better place for Polly and Mike to live than Ice Island.* Divide students into groups and ask them to discuss the statement. Tell one group to agree with the statement, and the other group to disagree with the statement. They might like to write their answers/ideas in their notebooks. Ask both groups to write their reasons on the board.

Pop Quiz: Close books. Read out sentences from the story. Students have to say who said them, e.g., *There are some children in the forest*. (*Hector Frost*) *There aren't any roads to Bollington Hall.* (*Mike*)

Homework WB page 42

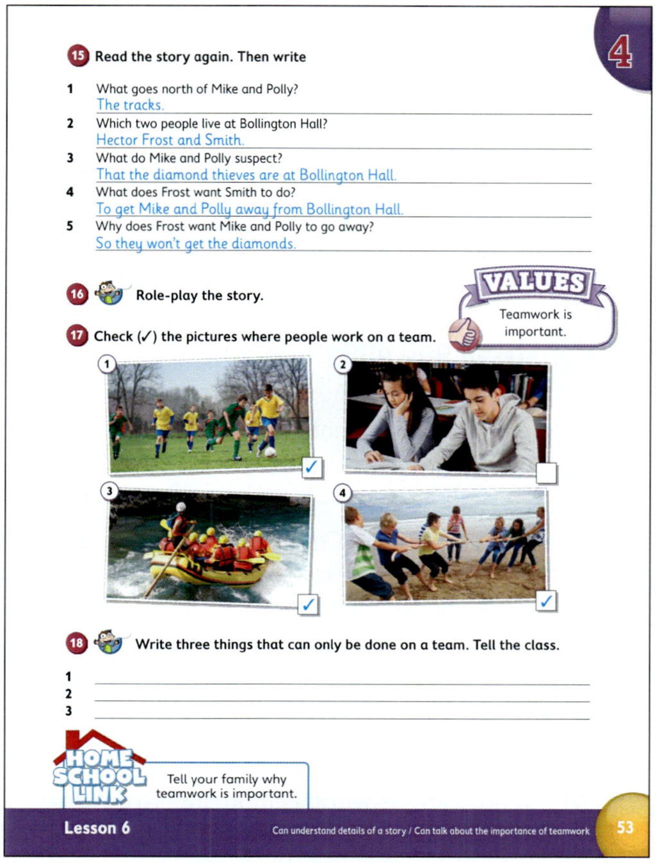

15 Read the story again. Then write

1 What goes north of Mike and Polly?
The tracks.

2 Which two people live at Bollington Hall?
Hector Frost and Smith.

3 What do Mike and Polly suspect?
That the diamond thieves are at Bollington Hall.

4 What does Frost want Smith to do?
To get Mike and Polly away from Bollington Hall.

5 Why does Frost want Mike and Polly to go away?
So they won't get the diamonds.

16 Role-play the story.

VALUES
Teamwork is important.

17 Check (✓) the pictures where people work on a team.

1 ✓ 2 ☐ 3 ✓ 4 ✓

18 Write three things that can only be done on a team. Tell the class.

1
2
3

HOME SCHOOL LINK
Tell your family why teamwork is important.

Lesson 6 Can understand details of a story / Can talk about the importance of teamwork 53

Lesson 6 SB Page 53 or Poptropica English World

Learning Objectives
Can understand details of a story
Can talk about the importance of teamwork

Value
Teamwork is important.

Warm-up

- Ask students to think about how Polly and Mike work together as a team. Ask, *Are they a good team?* (*Yes, they help each other.*) Give students a few minutes before asking them to think about Hector Frost and Smith. Ask, *Do they work as a team?* (*No, because Hector Frost just tells Smith what to do. No, because Hector Frost shouts at Smith.*)

Open books and ask students to look at the activities on the page. Ask, *What are we learning today?* Write the lesson objectives on the board: *We're reviewing the story, and we're learning about teamwork.*

15 Read the story again. Then write.

- Give students time to look at the story, and play the audio again.
- Allow time to do the activity.
- Check answers by having students switch books. Read the statements and elicit answers from the class.

16 Role-play the story.

- See the "How to use stories" section on page 23 for more ideas on how to build your students' confidence with role-plays.
- Divide students into groups of four. Give each group a set of cut-out Story Cards (see page 88), and have students place them in order.
- Play the audio again (track B:11). Put the class into groups to role-play the story.
- Give groups time to practice the role-play, then ask them to show the class.

You might like to give students feedback on their role-play.

17 Check (✓) the pictures where people work on a team.

- Read the value, *Teamwork is important.* Tell students about a team you are on. Ask, *Are you on a team? Do you think teamwork is important? Why?,* and elicit responses.
- Draw students' attention to the pictures in Activity 17. Check for comprehension by asking, *What are they doing?* Allow time to do the activity on the page. Check answers as a class.

18 Write three things that can only be done on a team. Tell the class.

- Pair students and allow time to work on the activity. Invite pairs of students to talk about their list to the class.
- Ask the class, *Do you think this class is a team?,* and elicit responses.

- **Home-School link:** Read the instruction with the class: *Tell your family why teamwork is important.* Ask students to do this at home.

Pop Quiz: Have a discussion about what types of teams there are (e.g., *a team of people at work, a team of people playing sport, a group of people putting on a play, a group of musicians playing together, a team building a bridge*). Brainstorm by having students call out examples of good teams (*doctors working together to save someone's life, a basketball team winning a game*). Make two lists together as a class: *What makes a team work well together.* and *What makes a team not work well together.*

Materials
Unit 4 cut-out Story Cards

Homework WB page 43

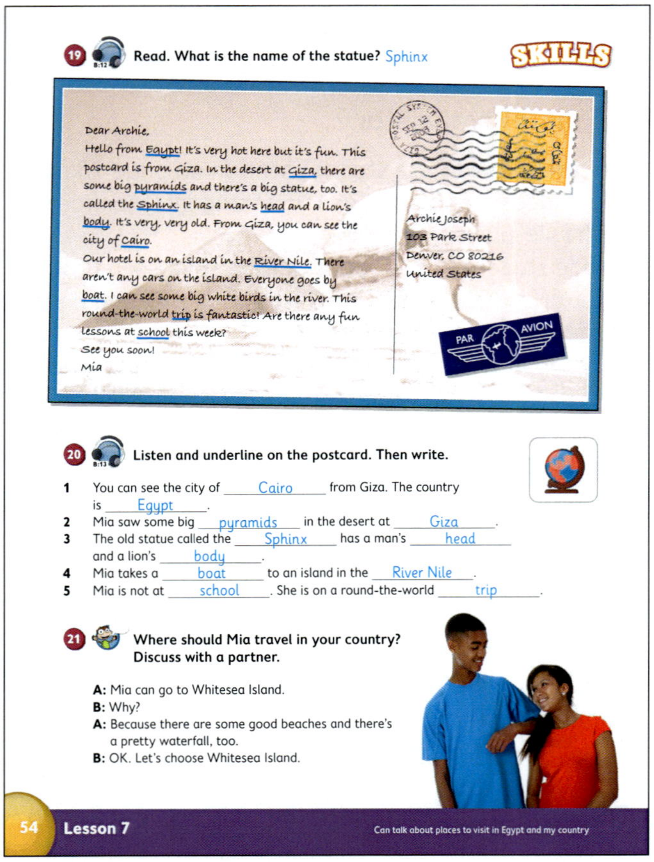

19 Read. What is the name of the statue? Sphinx

SKILLS

Dear Archie,
Hello from Egypt! It's very hot here but it's fun. This postcard is from Giza. In the desert at Giza, there are some big pyramids and there's a big statue, too. It's called the Sphinx. It has a man's head and a lion's body. It's very, very old. From Giza, you can see the city of Cairo.
Our hotel is on an island in the River Nile. There aren't any cars on the island. Everyone goes by boat. I can see some big white birds in the river. This round-the-world trip is fantastic! Are there any fun lessons at school this week?
See you soon!
Mia

Archie Joseph
103 Park Street
Denver, CO 80216
United States

20 Listen and underline on the postcard. Then write.

1 You can see the city of Cairo from Giza. The country is Egypt.
2 Mia saw some big pyramids in the desert at Giza.
3 The old statue called the Sphinx has a man's head and a lion's body.
4 Mia takes a boat to an island in the River Nile.
5 Mia is not at school. She is on a round-the-world trip.

21 Where should Mia travel in your country? Discuss with a partner.

A: Mia can go to Whitesea Island.
B: Why?
A: Because there are some good beaches and there's a pretty waterfall, too.
B: OK. Let's choose Whitesea Island.

54 Lesson 7 Can talk about places to visit in Egypt and my country

Lesson 7 SB page 54 or Poptropica English World

Learning Objective
Can talk about places to visit in Egypt and my country

Additional Language
Giza, Sphinx, Cairo, River Nile

Warm-up

- Divide the class into two. Talk about your country, giving information that students know. Students raise their hands to say *true* or *false* responses to your statement. A correct response gets a point.

Open books and ask students to look at the activities on the page. Ask, *What are we learning today?* Write the lesson objective on the board: *We're learning to talk about places to visit.*

19 Read. What is the name of the statue?

- Write _ *g* _ *p* _ on the board and invite a student to fill in the blanks. Ask another student to find the correct Picture Card from Picture Cards 55–68.
- Direct students' attention to the postcard and ask questions, *Where does this postcard come from? (Egypt) Who wrote this postcard? (Mia) Where does Archie live? (the United States).*
- Play the audio and have students listen and follow.
- Check students' understanding of the postcard by asking questions, *How's the weather in Egypt? (It's hot.) What did Mia see? (Cairo, River Nile, pyramids, big white birds, etc.)*

20 Listen and underline on the postcard. Then write.

- Play the audio. Give students time to read the postcard on their own and complete the activity.

1 Egypt is a country and Cairo is a city. You can see Cairo from another city called Giza.
2 There are some big pyramids and a big statue in the desert at Giza.
3 A famous statue in Egypt is called the Sphinx. It looks like a lion, but it has the head of a man.
4 Our hotel is in the Nile River on an island. On the island, there aren't any cars.
5 The trip around-the-world is fantastic! Are there any fun classes this week at school?

- Check answers as a class.

21 Where should Mia travel in your country? Discuss with a partner.

- Invite two confident students to read the exchange to the class. Say, *Now, let's talk about where Mia can travel in your country.* Pair students and give them time to do the activity. Invite pairs to share their ideas with the class.

Tell students you are Mia. Give students answers, and ask them to provide possible questions, e.g., you say, *No, there aren't.*, and students ask, *Are there any pyramids on the island?*

Pop Quiz: Have students read Mia's postcard again. Then have one student stand, choose a student, and ask him/her a question, e.g., *(Name), is there a river in Cairo? (Yes, there is. The River Nile is in Cairo.)* That student then chooses another student and asks a question, and so on.

- Direct students' attention to the globe card on page 54. Tell students to go online to the Poptropica English Island Adventure Game and find the item. Once students click on it, they are taken to a supplementary language task.

Materials
Picture Cards 55–68

Homework WB page 44

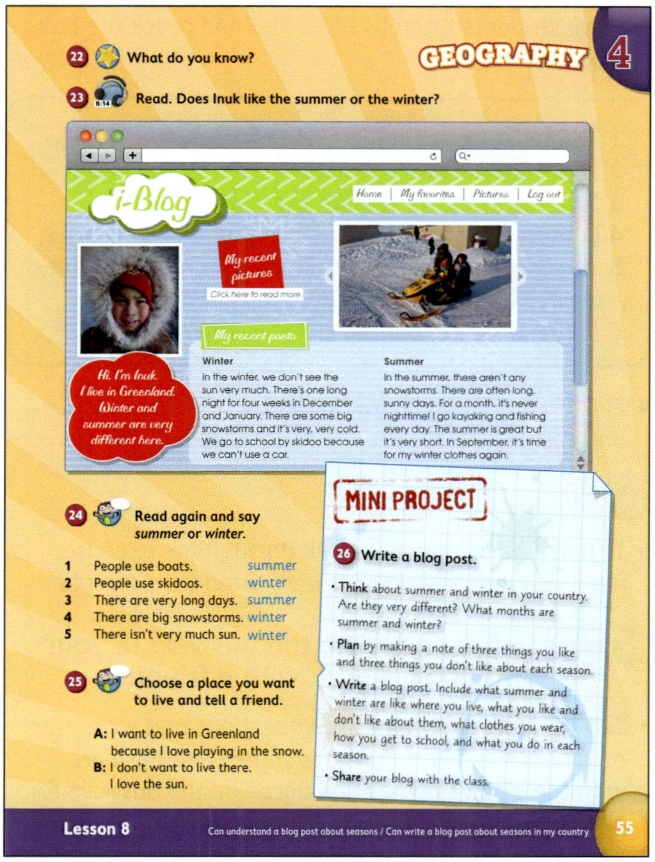
22 What do you know?

GEOGRAPHY 4

23 Read. Does Inuk like the summer or the winter?

i-Blog

Home | My favorites | Pictures | Log out

My recent pictures

Click here to read more

Hi. I'm Inuk. I live in Greenland. Winter and summer are very different here.

My recent posts

Winter

In the winter, we don't see the sun very much. There's one long night for four weeks in December and January. There are some big snowstorms and it's very, very cold. We go to school by skidoo because we can't use a car.

Summer

In the summer, there aren't any snowstorms. There are often long, sunny days. For a month, it's never nighttime! I go kayaking and fishing every day. The summer is great but it's very short. In September, it's time for my winter clothes again.

24 Read again and say *summer* or *winter*.

1 People use boats. summer
2 People use skidoos. winter
3 There are very long days. summer
4 There are big snowstorms. winter
5 There isn't very much sun. winter

25 Choose a place you want to live and tell a friend.

A: I want to live in Greenland because I love playing in the snow.
B: I don't want to live there. I love the sun.

MINI PROJECT

26 Write a blog post.

- **Think** about summer and winter in your country. Are they very different? What months are summer and winter?
- **Plan** by making a note of three things you like and three things you don't like about each season.
- **Write** a blog post. Include what summer and winter are like where you live, what you like and don't like about them, what clothes you wear, how you get to school, and what you do in each season.
- **Share** your blog with the class.

Lesson 8 Can understand a blog post about seasons / Can write a blog post about seasons in my country 55

Lesson 8 SB page 55 or Poptropica English World

Learning Objectives
Can understand a blog post about seasons
Can write a blog post about seasons in my country

Additional Language
Greenland, recent, snowstorms, nighttime, kayaking

Warm-up

- Point to a country on the world map, and explain what you know about it, using target language.
- Invite students to talk about countries they have learned about in this unit.

22 What do you know?

- Open books and ask students to look at the activities. Ask, *What are we learning today?* Write the lesson objective on the board: *We're learning to blog about seasons.*
- Refer to the learning adventure poster and say, *Great! You are moving along your learning adventure!*

23 B:14 Read. Does Inuk like the summer or the winter?

- Ask students if they know of any countries like Ice Island. Point to Greenland on the map and ask, *What do you know about Greenland?,* and elicit responses. Tell them, *Greenland is the world's largest island. There are 57,000 people living in Greenland. It is very cold. There are underground volcanoes in Greenland.*
- Tell students they are going to hear about a boy named Inuk. Draw attention to his picture. Play the audio and have students read along.

24 Read again and say *summer* or *winter.*

- Ask students to read the text one more time.
- Pair students and have them identify *summer* or *winter* for each.

25 Choose a place you want to live and tell a friend.

- Draw students' attention to the target language in this activity. Ask two confident students to model it. Give students time to do the activity.

26 Write a blog post.

- Ask students what steps they will take to make sure they include all the necessary information. Remind students of the steps to success: Think, Plan, Write and Share.
  Think Brainstorm ideas as a class if necessary.
  Plan Ask students to make notes on three things they like/dislike about each season.
  Write Give students time to write their blog. Remind them to check their work afterwards.
  Share Nominate students to read their blogs in class.

You may also wish to give students feedback on their projects.

Ask students, *What do you know about different weather and climates now?* Elicit responses. Ask students, *Where are you on your learning adventure?* Tell students, *Good job!* to reinforce the progress they are making.

Pop Quiz: Call out different scenarios, e.g., *I wear warm clothes. (winter) I go swimming. (summer).* Students respond with *summer* or *winter.*

Materials
Poster, map of the world

Homework WB page 45

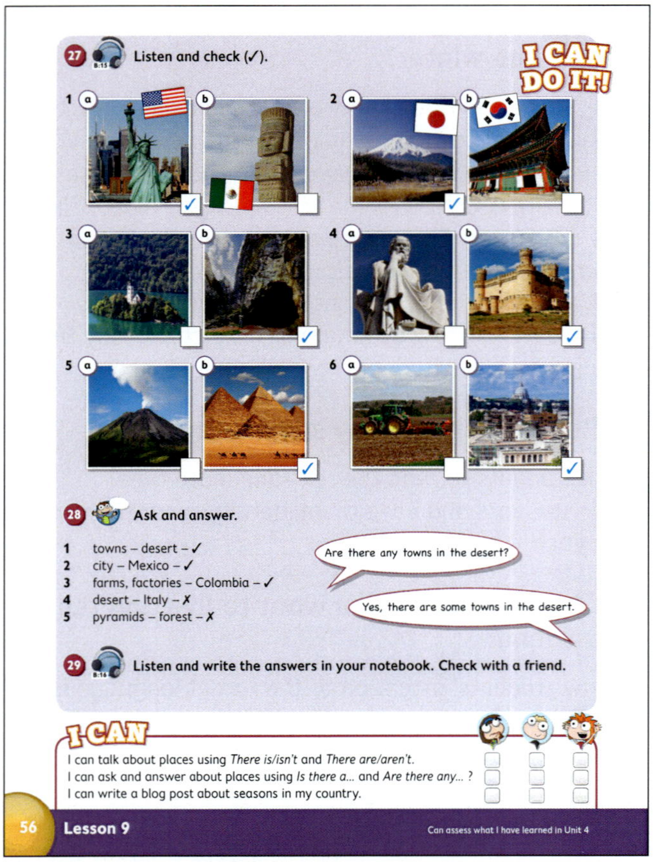

Lesson 9 SB page 56 or Poptropica English World

Learning Objective
Can assess what I have learned in Unit 4

Warm-up

- Give each student a card from Picture Cards 55–77 and tell them they have to find partners and make sentences about a place using the words on their cards.

Open books and ask students to look at the activities. Write the lesson objective on the board: *We're thinking about our learning adventure.*

- Ask students what they have been learning in the unit. Put their ideas on the board, e.g., *different countries.*
- For each idea, ask students to tell their partner where they think they are on their learning adventure. Reassure students who are less confident that they will have opportunities for more practice.

27 Listen and check (✓).

- Have students look at the pictures, and the flags. Invite students to talk about the pictures randomly, e.g., *Number 4a is a statue. It is a man.*
- Have students listen to the audio and check the box next to the item.

1 There's a statue in the United States.
2 There's a mountain in Japan.
3 Is there a cave in China? Yes, there is.
4 Is there a castle in Spain? Yes, there is.
5 Are there any volcanoes in the desert? No, there aren't. There are some pyramids in the desert.
6 Is there a desert in the city? No, there isn't.

- Play the audio again for students to check their answers.

28 Ask and answer.

- In pairs, have students work through the exercise, making questions, and answers using the prompts.

29 Listen and write the answers in your notebook. Check with a friend.

- Tell students to listen to the questions and write their own answers. Have students share their answers with the class. Do the class agree on the answers for questions 1–6?

1 Where do you live?
2 Are there any caves in your country?
3 Is there a desert in your country?
4 Are there any forests in your country?
5 What animals are there in your country?
6 Which countries do you want to visit? Why?

Ask students how they feel about their learning in this unit. Ask students to tell you what they found easy and what they found the most difficult to learn in the unit.

- Read the three *I can* statements with students and invite students to check the boxes according to how confident they feel about the language point.
- Ask students, *Where are you on your learning adventure?* Students indicate where they think they are on the learning adventure poster. Tell students, *Good job!* to reinforce the progress they are making.

Pop Quiz: In groups of four, students tell the others the answers to the following questions: *Which is your favorite activity in the unit? Why? Which activity don't you like? Why? What is your favorite new word? Which word is the most difficult for you?*

Materials
Poster, Picture Cards 55–77

Homework WB page 46

Lesson 10 SB page 57 or Poptropica English World

Learning Objective
Can use what I have learned in Unit 4

Warm-up

- Have a country and play spelling bee. Divide the class into two long lines. Show a card from Picture Cards 55–77 to the first person in each team. Give a point if the first person in a team spells it correctly. For the next picture, the first person from the second team gets to try first. Play until all students have had a turn.

Open books and ask students to look at the pictures. Ask, *What are we learning today?* Write the lesson objective on the board: *We're playing a game about places to review Unit 4 language.*

Write on the board, *Visiting different countries makes you a better person.* Divide the class into small groups, and ask them to discuss the statement, and take notes on why they agree or disagree with it. Ask the groups to present their reasons to the class. Write the reasons on the board. Take a class vote.

Ask students to work in pairs to make sentences/ questions with target language based on different people around the world. Tell students to choose three different countries and to write about what the people of that country look like, are good at and what their daily lives are like. Explain to students that they should use the words *often, usually,* and *sometimes*, not *always/ never*. Say, e.g., *Spain: People in Spain usually have brown eyes. They are often good at dancing.*

30 Look at the pictures and circle the words in the puzzle.

- Direct students' attention to the puzzle and ask questions about each picture.
- Allow students time to do the activity and find the hidden words.

31 Unscramble the words and find the secret message.

- Direct students' attention to the activity and allow them time to complete it.
- After a few minutes, invite students to work in pairs.
- Check answers as a class.
- To decode the secret message, ask students to write one of the code letters on the board, one at a time, starting from sentence *a* - number 6 (the 'o' in Mexico) so: 6 = o. Repeat for all thirteen numbers/letters. Then write 1 to 13 across the board, and invite students to decode the sentence together.

32 I want to know more!

- Ask students to choose anything they enjoyed from the unit and to go and find out more. You might like to set this activity as homework with a quick feedback session at the beginning of the next class.
- You can also suggest that students write one or two questions about what they want to know, then switch question(s) with a partner. Students then find answer(s) to their partner's question(s) as a homework activity, with feedback the next lesson.

Are you ready for Unit 5?

- Ask students if they are ready to move onto the next unit. Tell students that it is fine if they do not remember everything as they will continue to practice throughout the level.
- Encourage students to ask if they have any questions about what they learned in Unit 4.

You may wish to give Unit 4 Test (see page 194) at this time.

Materials
Picture Cards 55–77

Homework WB page 47

Unit 4 Story Cards

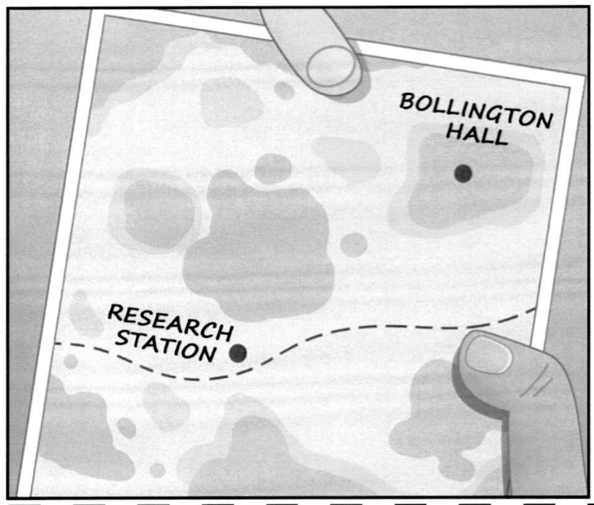

Review Units 3 and 4

SB pages 58–59 or Poptropica English World

Learning Objectives
Can talk about free-time activities and hobbies
Can talk about countries and places of interest

Warm-up

- Review activities and hobbies using Picture Cards 38–54. Give spelling practice by using the word-side of the cards. Hold a spelling bee.

Open books and ask students to look at the pages. Ask, *What are we learning today?* Write the lesson objective on the board: *We're reviewing language from Units 3 and 4.*

Direct students to pages 36–39 if they should like to refresh their memories on the vocabulary and grammar structures needed for Activities 1 and 2.

- Activities 3–5 are based on vocabulary and grammar structures from pages 48–51. To challenge students further, ask them to think of (or research) countries starting with each letter of the alphabet. If this is too challenging, ask them to think of (or research) countries starting with the letters A–K in English. (They only need to find new countries for D (Denmark/Djibouti), F (Finland/France), G (Greenland/Germany), H (Hungary/Hong Kong) – the others are taught on page 48).

1 Read. Then write.

- Read the words in the word box chorally, then give students time to read the speech bubbles.
- Ask students to say what they know about the people in these pictures. Let them turn back to earlier pages in the book, for reference.
- Allow students time to do the activity.
- Have students read the texts chorally, and check their own work.

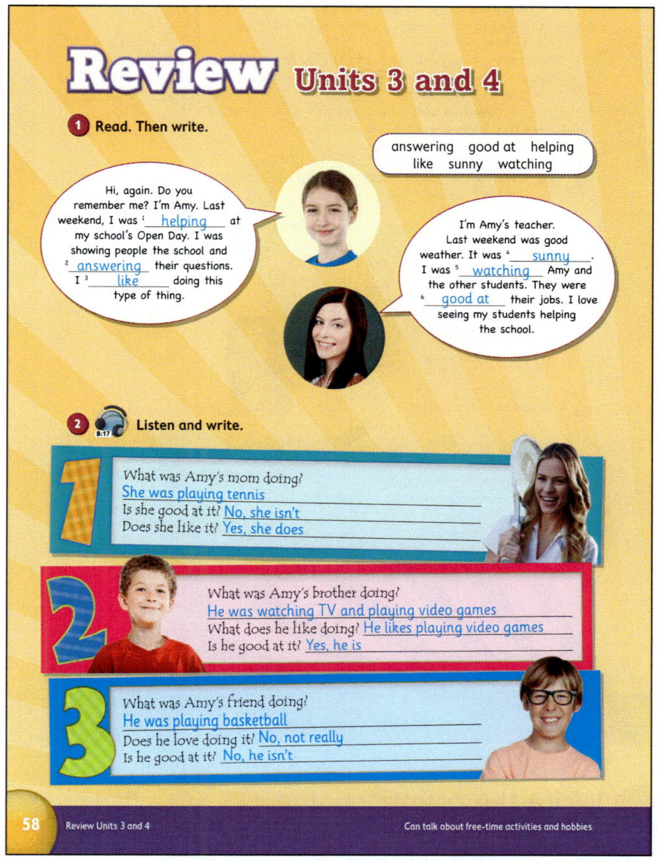
Review Units 3 and 4

1 Read. Then write.

answering good at helping like sunny watching

Hi, again. Do you remember me? I'm Amy. Last weekend, I was [1] helping at my school's Open Day. I was showing people the school and [2] answering their questions. I [3] like doing this type of thing.

I'm Amy's teacher. Last weekend was good weather. It was [4] sunny. I was [5] watching Amy and the other students. They were [6] good at their jobs. I love seeing my students helping the school.

2 Listen and write.

1 What was Amy's mom doing? She was playing tennis
Is she good at it? No, she isn't
Does she like it? Yes, she does

2 What was Amy's brother doing? He was watching TV and playing video games
What does he like doing? He likes playing video games
Is he good at it? Yes, he is

3 What was Amy's friend doing? He was playing basketball
Does he love doing it? No, not really
Is he good at it? No, he isn't

58 Review Units 3 and 4 Can talk about free-time activities and hobbies

2 Listen and write.

- Ask students to say what they know about the people in these pictures. Let them turn back to the Review for Units 1 and 2.
- Play the audio. Tell students to listen and follow.

> **1** Last weekend I was playing tennis. I usually play on Saturday. I'm not good at playing, but I like playing tennis. It's fun.
> **2** Last weekend I was watching TV, and playing video games with friends. I like video games because I'm good at playing.
> **3** Hi. I'm Fergus. Last weekend I was playing basketball at the school Open Day. I don't really like basketball because I am not good at it. I'm too short, but the teacher asked me to play.

- Play the audio again. You may wish to pause between each item to allow students time to complete the sentences.
- To check answers, have students switch their books with a partner, and elicit answers from the class.

Materials
Picture Cards 38–54, flag cards

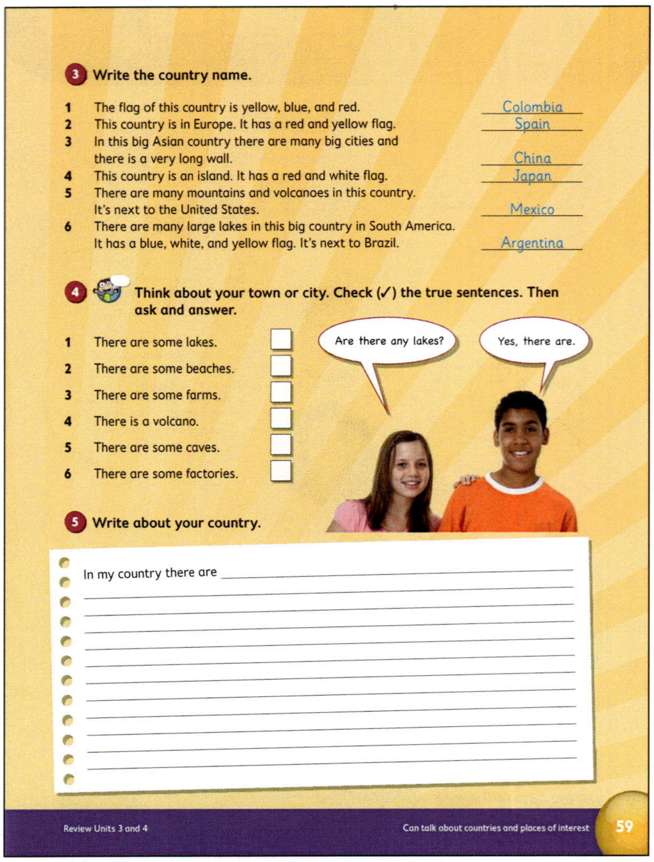

3 Write the country name.

1 The flag of this country is yellow, blue, and red. Colombia
2 This country is in Europe. It has a red and yellow flag. Spain
3 In this big Asian country there are many big cities and there is a very long wall. China
4 This country is an island. It has a red and white flag. Japan
5 There are many mountains and volcanoes in this country. It's next to the United States. Mexico
6 There are many large lakes in this big country in South America. It has a blue, white, and yellow flag. It's next to Brazil. Argentina

4 Think about your town or city. Check (✓) the true sentences. Then ask and answer.

1 There are some lakes.
2 There are some beaches.
3 There are some farms.
4 There is a volcano.
5 There are some caves.
6 There are some factories.

5 Write about your country.

In my country there are

Review Units 3 and 4 Can talk about countries and places of interest 59

3 Write the country name.

- Read the statements chorally. Place the cards with country names on them around the room for reference, if you wish. Also, at some point, remove the Picture Cards to make the activity more challenging.
- Allow students time to do the activity.
- Have students discuss their answers in pairs.
- Finally, check answers together as a class. Show the corresponding country flags.

4 Think about your town or city. Check (✓) the true sentences. Then ask and answer.

- Ask, *What are they saying?* Read the speech bubble exchange chorally.
- Read the six statements chorally. Allow students time to do the activity.
- Brainstorm questions that correspond to the six statements in Activity 4 and write them on the board. Read them chorally.
- Pair students and have them ask and answer questions about their home towns or cities.
- Invite students to talk about their towns or cities to the class, based on the boxes they have checked. Encourage students that are listening to ask questions. Encourage students presenting to say, *isn't/aren't* for the statements that they did not check.
- To check comprehension, after each student reports to class, ask some questions about what he/she said about their town or city. To make this more interesting, award points for correct answers.

5 Write about your country.

- Ask students to tell you one or two things about their country. Invite others to add information if they can.
- Give students time to complete the activity.
- Invite students to share their work with the class.

- Watch the video story *The Super Freeze machine* on Poptropica English World. Ask students what happened in the story. Watch again, stopping at key points, and ask them about the language, the images, or the story. Ask the students to role-play the story. Assign the roles of two of the characters to confident speakers and let other students play the other parts. Encourage them to say as much of the dialog as they can and prompt them where necessary.

Pop Quiz: Play a *Memory Game* on the board with flag cards and cards with the name of the country written on them. In random order, stick all the cards face down on the board in a grid. Divide the class into two teams. One by one, students from each team alternate turning over two cards, showing the class the cards they turn over. If they turn over a matching pair (flag and correct country name), their team gets to keep that card. If the cards don't match, they put them back in the same place. The aim is to remember where the cards are, so that you can try to turn over matching cards. The team with the most pairs wins.

You may wish to give Review Test 2 (see page 208) at this time.

5 Shopping

Unit Overview

Unit Objective

- I can talk about shopping and belongings

Language

Target Vocabulary	Clothing and accessories: jacket, swimsuit, watch, bracelet, wallet, handbag, umbrella, gloves, sunglasses, hoodie, belt Adjectives to describe clothing and accessories: cheap, expensive, tight, baggy, old-fashioned, modern
Target Structures	How much is this/that jacket? It's ninety dollars and fifty cents. How much are these/those sunglasses? They're thirty dollars. Whose watch is this? It's Maddy's/mine/yours/his/hers. Whose pens are these? They're Dan's/mine/yours/his/hers.
Features	**Cross-curricular:** Science: Properties of materials **Values:** Dress correctly for each occasion.

Skills

Reading	• Can understand a simple story • Can understand details of a story • Can understand a text about choosing shoes
Writing	• Can complete simple sentences about who things belong to • Can write about a pair of shoes I have designed • Can complete simple sentences about how much things cost *(Workbook)* • Can write simple sentences to describe clothes *(Workbook)* • Can write simple ads *(Workbook)*
Listening	• Can identify clothing and accessories • Can identify words that describe clothing and accessories • Can understand a simple story
Speaking	• Can ask and answer about how much things cost • Can ask and answer about who things belong to • Can discuss a story • Can talk about dressing correctly for different occasions • Can talk about different places to shop

Lesson 1 SB page 60 or Poptropica English World

Learning Objective
Can identify clothing and accessories

Target Language
jacket, swimsuit, watch, bracelet, wallet, handbag, umbrella, gloves, sunglasses

1 What do you know?

- Open books and ask students to look at the pictures. Ask, *What are we learning today?* Write the lesson objective on the board: *We're learning words for things we wear.*
- Close books. Ask students what English words they know for clothes, e.g., *T-shirt, dress.* Write on board.
- Refer to the learning adventure poster and say, *Great! You are already moving along your learning adventure!*

2 B:18 Listen and read. Does Emma buy the jacket?

- Ask students to look at the scenes in their books and listen as you play the audio. Play the audio again, pausing for students to repeat.
- Divide the class into three parts and assign the three roles. Have each group read their role.
- Ask comprehension questions, e.g., *What does Emma love? (a jacket) How much are the sunglasses? (fifteen dollars) Does Emma buy the jacket?*

3 B:19 Listen and say.

- Focus on the pictures. Play the audio and have students repeat.
- Put Picture Cards 78–86 on the board for students to refer to. Number them. Pair students and have them play a game. One student in each pair says a number. His/her partner has to say the item, and mimes the action of putting it on.

4 Look and say. Use words from Activity 3.

- Pair students and give them time to do the activity. Remind them to use the target language, *I like/don't like...* and *I love...* .

5 Shopping

1 What do you know?

2 B:18 Listen and read. Does Emma buy the jacket? no

3 B:19 Listen and say.

4 Look and say. Use words from Activity 3.

60 Lesson 1 Can identify clothing and accessories

Ask students, *How many clothes words do you know now?* Give students a minute to tell their partner the new words they know.

- Ask students to say where they are on their adventure now. Ask students which words they find easiest or most difficult to remember. Tell students, *Good job!* to reinforce the progress they are making.

Pop Quiz: Play *Clothes Closet*. Have students sit in a circle on chairs. Assign every fourth student the same clothing items. Stand in the middle and start talking. Explain to students that when they hear the clothing item, the ones who are assigned that item have to switch chairs. Also take a chair for yourself, leaving one student in the middle. That student does the same, although students can also talk about their "clothes closet", in which case all students move to a new chair.

Materials
Poster, Picture Cards 78–86

Homework WB page 48

LOOK!

How much is this/that jacket?	It's ninety dollars and fifty cents.
How much are these/those sunglasses?	They're thirty dollars.

5 Listen and write. Then ask and answer.

1 $15 2 $116 3 $29 4 $1000 5 $20 6 $360 7 $59.50 8 $30 9 $9.99

How much is that handbag?

It's fifty-nine dollars and fifty cents.

6 Look and imagine prices. Then role-play the conversation.

A: How much is that pen?
B: It's three dollars and fifty cents.
A: May I buy it, please?

1 pen 2 candy 3 guitar 4 drum set 5 computer 6 T-shirt 7 scarf 8 sandals

Lesson 2 Can ask and answer about how much things cost 61

Lesson 2 SB page 61 or Poptropica English World

Learning Objective
Can ask and answer about how much things cost

Warm-up

- Have a clothing and accessory spelling bee by dividing the class into two, showing students Picture Cards 78–86, and eliciting spellings. Correct spellings earn points for the teams.

Open books and ask students to look at the activities and the Look! box. Ask, *What are we learning today?* Write the lesson objective on the board: *We're learning to ask and answer questions about how much things cost.*

5 Listen and write. Then ask and answer.

- Draw students' attention to the Look! box and play the audio (track B:20). Students repeat chorally.
- Have students look at the pictures. Tell students they will listen to some statements and they need to write the price next to the pictures.

1 How much are those gloves? They're fifteen dollars.
2 How much are those sunglasses? They're one hundred and sixteen dollars.
3 How much is that swimsuit? It's twenty-nine dollars.
4 How much is that dress? It's one thousand dollars.
5 How much is that umbrella? It's twenty dollars.
6 How much is that jacket? It's three hundred and sixty dollars.
7 How much is that handbag? It's fifty-nine dollars and fifty cents.
8 How much is that wallet? It's thirty dollars.
9 How much is that watch? It's nine dollars and ninety-nine cents.

- Have students check answers in pairs. Point to item *7*, and ask, *How much is that handbag? (It's fifty-nine dollars and fifty cents.)* Then ask students to practice saying these statements in pairs.

6 Look and imagine prices. Then role-play the conversation.

- Draw students' attention to the items in Activity 6. Have the students repeat the words after you.
- Divide the class into pairs and give them time to do the activity, using the target language. Check answers as a class.
- To extend the lesson, pair students and pass each pair Activity Sheet 9 (see Poptropica English World). Ask them to cut out the items and the price tags. Students take turns putting prices to the items, and then model the target language from the lesson together.

Pop Quiz: Stick pictures of different clothing items and accessories from pages 60 and 61 on the board. Write prices next to each item. Get pairs of students to ask and answer how much two of the items cost in front of the class, e.g., *How much are those sunglasses? (They're fifty-one dollars.)* The student who answers can then change the price of the item.

- Direct students' attention to the skis card on page 61. Tell students to go online to the Poptropica English Island Adventure Game and find the item. Once students click on it, they are taken to a supplementary language task.

Materials
Picture Cards 78–86, Activity Sheet 9, scissors

Homework WB page 49

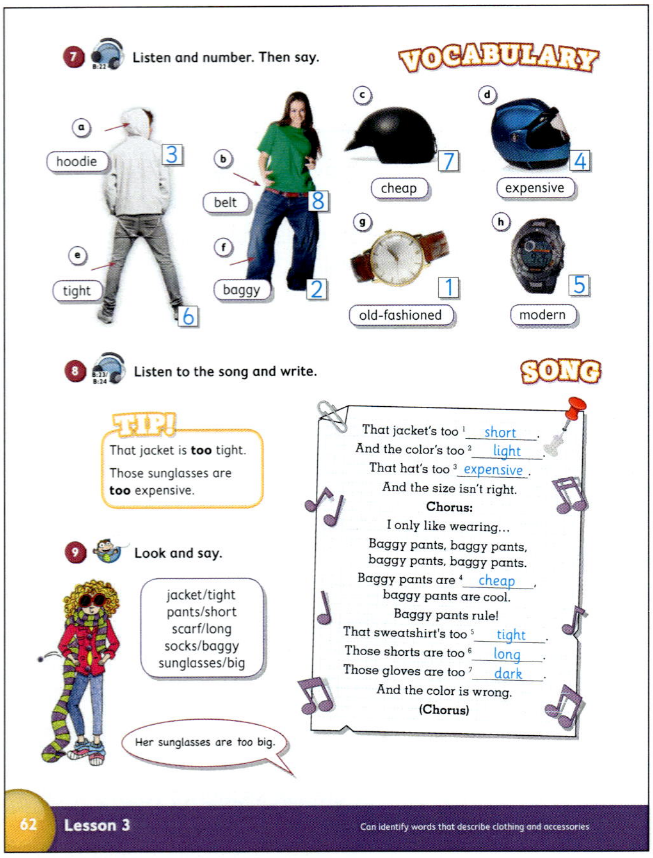

7 Listen and number. Then say. VOCABULARY

a hoodie 3; b belt 8; c cheap 7; d expensive 4; e tight 6; f baggy 2; g old-fashioned 1; h modern 5

8 Listen to the song and write. SONG

TIP!
That jacket is **too** tight.
Those sunglasses are **too** expensive.

That jacket's too [1] short.
And the color's too [2] light.
That hat's too [3] expensive.
And the size isn't right.
Chorus:
I only like wearing...
Baggy pants, baggy pants,
baggy pants, baggy pants.
Baggy pants are [4] cheap,
baggy pants are cool.
Baggy pants rule!
That sweatshirt's too [5] tight.
Those shorts are too [6] long.
Those gloves are too [7] dark.
And the color is wrong.
(Chorus)

9 Look and say.

jacket/tight
pants/short
scarf/long
socks/baggy
sunglasses/big

Her sunglasses are too big.

62 Lesson 3 Can identify words that describe clothing and accessories

Lesson 3 SB page 62 or Poptropica English World

Learning Objective
Can identify words that describe clothing and accessories

Target Language
hoodie, belt, cheap, expensive, tight, baggy, old-fashioned, modern
That jacket is too tight. Those sunglasses are too expensive.

Warm-up

- Review clothing items and prices. Divide the class into two lines. Model the activity by pointing to an item of clothing and saying, e.g., *My bracelet is thirty dollars. How much is that/your watch?* Students ask and answer down the line. Stress that they can invent any price they like. The first line to finish is the winner.

Open books and ask students to look at the pictures. Ask, *What are we learning today?* Write the lesson objective on the board: *We're learning words to describe clothes.*

- Close books. Ask students what English words describing clothes they know, e.g., *small, blue*. Write on board.
- Refer to the learning adventure poster and say, *Great! You are moving along your learning adventure!*

7 Listen and number. Then say.

B:22

- Introduce the new vocabulary with Picture Cards 87–94. Hold the Picture Cards up one by one, then turn them to the word-side and ask students to repeat the words after you. Then ask students to look at the pictures and read the words.
- Play the audio and ask students to number the pictures as they listen.

1 old-fashioned	**2** baggy	**3** hoodie	**4** expensive
5 modern	**6** tight	**7** cheap	**8** belt

- Play the audio again and have students repeat.

Tip!
Draw students' attention to the Tip! box. Explain the use of the word too + an adjective.

8 Listen to the song and write.

B:23
B:24

- Point to the boy in Activity 7 and say, *He likes wearing tight pants. What do you like wearing?* and elicit responses.
- Draw students' attention to Activity 8. Play the song audio and have students listen.
- Play the audio again and ask students to write the correct words. Have students check their answers with a partner.
- Play the karaoke version of the song and have students sing if they feel confident enough.

9 Look and say.

- Draw students' attention to the adjectives and clothing words.
- Model the language with a confident student. Pair students and have them make sentences about the girl's clothes. Invite students to say sentences to the class.

Ask students, *How many words for clothing do you know now?* Give students a minute to tell their partner the new words they know.

- Ask students to say where they are on their adventure now. Ask students which words they find easiest or most difficult to remember. Tell students, *Good job!* to reinforce the progress they are making.

Pop Quiz: Show students pictures of people wearing different clothing. Ensure that the pictures have examples of baggy, tight, old-fashioned, cheap, expensive and modern clothes, as well as examples with a belt and a hoodie. Ask students to describe the clothes in each picture, e.g., *That dress is old-fashioned. That hoodie is too tight.*

Materials
Poster, Picture Cards 87–94, clothing pictures (cut from magazines)

Homework WB page 50

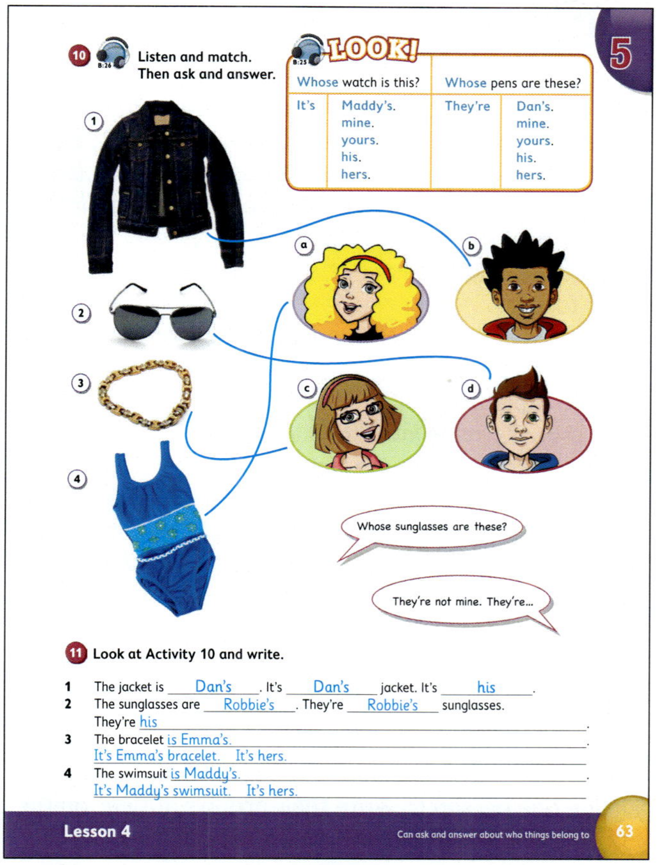

5

10 B:26 Listen and match. Then ask and answer.

B:25 LOOK!

Whose watch is this?		Whose pens are these?	
It's	Maddy's. mine. yours. his. hers.	They're	Dan's. mine. yours. his. hers.

11 Look at Activity 10 and write.

1 The jacket is Dan's. It's Dan's jacket. It's his.
2 The sunglasses are Robbie's. They're Robbie's sunglasses.
They're his.
3 The bracelet is Emma's.
It's Emma's bracelet. It's hers.
4 The swimsuit is Maddy's.
It's Maddy's swimsuit. It's hers.

Lesson 4 Can ask and answer about who things belong to 63

Lesson 4 SB page 63 or Poptropica English World

Learning Objective
Can ask and answer about who things belong to

Target Language
Maddy's, mine, yours, his, hers

Warm-up

- Review clothing items with a memory game. Have everyone stand up at the desks. Say, *Hoodie!* The first person in the first row says, *Hoodie! Sunglasses!* Repeat down the rows, adding a new word each time. If a person cannot remember, they have to sit down.

Open books and ask students to look at the activities and the Look! Box. Ask, *What are we learning today?* Write the lesson objective on the board: *We're learning to ask and answer about who things belong to.*

10 B:26 Listen and match. Then ask and answer.

- Draw students' attention to the Look! box and play the audio (track B:25). Students repeat chorally.
- Point to Picture 1 and ask, *What is it?* and elicit responses. Continue with other items.
- Have students listen to the audio and match the item to the people.

1
Robbie: Emma, whose jacket is this?
Emma: It's not mine and it's not Maddy's. It's too big for her. Maybe it's Dan's. Yes, it's his because his name is on the inside.
2
Emma: Robbie, whose sunglasses are these?
Robbie: They're mine.
Emma: Aren't they Dan's?
Robbie: They were his. But now they're mine, because they were too small for him.
3
Dan: Maddy, is this yours?
Maddy: No, I don't wear expensive bracelets like that.
Dan: Well, whose is it?
Maddy: It's Emma's. It was a birthday present from her mom and dad.
4
Woman: Robbie, whose swimsuit is this?
Robbie: Well, it's not mine. Ha-ha-ha! And it's not Dan's.
Woman: Emma, is this yours?
Emma: No, It's Maddy's. It's her new swimsuit. Last year's was too tight.

- Have students check answers with a partner.
- Play the audio again, and have students repeat.

11 Look at Activity 10 and write.

- Have students read the sentence beginnings and complete them.
- Check answers as a class. Invite confident students to offer answers for checking.
- To extend the lesson, pair students and give each pair Activity Sheets 9 and 10 (see Poptropica English World). They cut out the cards and combine them to make sentences about items of clothing they own, e.g., *My jacket and my watch are old-fashioned. And they're ugly.*

Pop Quiz: Tell students, *I would like to use some of your belongings for the Pop Quiz. Watch carefully who gives me each thing!* Gather a few items, e.g., pens, erasers, books, hoodies, that belong to different students, and place them in front of the class. Choose one item and say, e.g., *Whose pen is this?* Elicit an answer from the class. Students then take turns asking and answering about who the items belong to, e.g., *Whose eraser is this? (It's Sam's. It's his eraser.)*

Materials
Clothing items and accessories from class, Activity Sheets 9–10, scissors

Homework WB page 51

Lesson 5 SB page 64 or Poptropica English World

Learning Objectives
Can understand a simple story
Can discuss a story

Additional Language
Can you show us the way to the lake?

Functional Language
Sure! Get away from me!

Open books and ask students to look at the story. Ask, *What are we learning today?* Write the lesson objective on the board: *We're reading and discussing a story.*

Warm-up

- Ask students, *Why do you think people like going to lakes?* (e.g., *They're beautiful. They like water.*) Then ask, *What do people do at lakes in summer and in winter?* (e.g., *summer: swimming, fishing, kayaking; winter: ice-skating, fishing*).

12 B:27 Talk about the pictures. Then listen and read.

- Direct students' attention to the pictures and ask questions about the characters and the scenes, e.g., *Who can you see in Picture 3? (Mike, Polly, Gizmo, the explorers, Smith) What are they wearing? (warm clothes, boots, scarves, gloves...) Who is hiding? (Smith)*
- Play the audio and have students listen to the story and follow.
- Check students' understanding of the story by asking questions and pointing to the pictures. Ask, *What do the explorers want to buy? (clothes/a jacket) What can they see in the lake? (fish) Why is Smith hiding? (He doesn't want them to see him.)*
- Play the audio again. Divide students into five groups and assign each group a role (male explorer, female explorer, Polly's mom, Mike, Smith). Ask groups to read along with the audio and mime their character's actions.

13 Why does Smith push Polly into the water? Discuss your answers.

- Have students discuss the question in groups and then invite one person to write their group's answer on the board. Discuss all the different ideas.

Divide the class into small groups. Ask students in each group to take turns being Polly. The rest of the group asks him/her questions about the story, e.g., *Where did you meet the explorers? (in my mom's store) Where did they want to go? (the lake) Who pushed you in the lake? (Smith) How did you feel? (cold and scared)* This activity will give students practice at thinking of and phrasing interesting and relevant questions.

Pop Quiz: Say one word from the text (e.g., *fish*) and students put up their hands to say who said it, and to read the whole sentence aloud (*Male explorer: There are a lot of fish in this lake.*)

Homework WB page 52

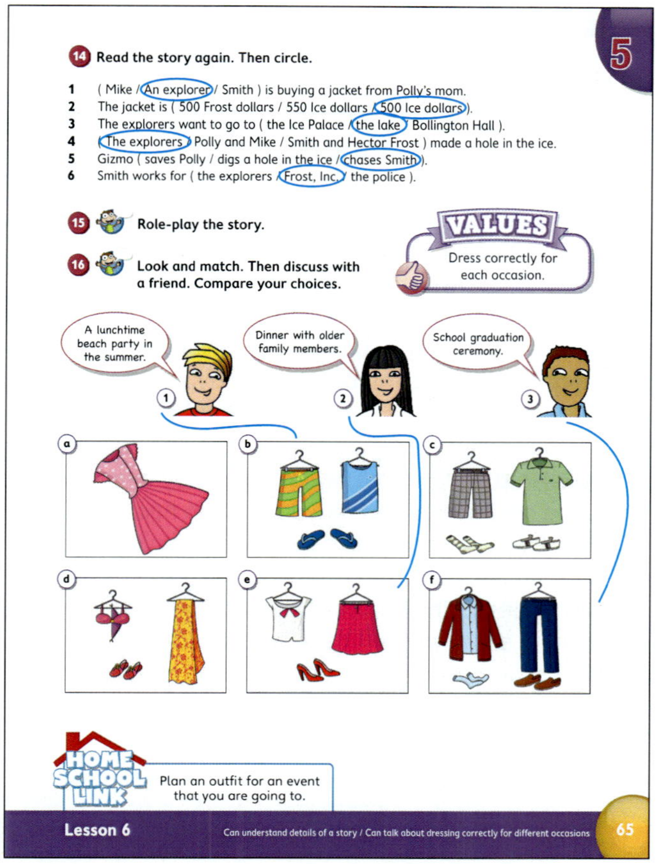
5

14 Read the story again. Then circle.

1 (Mike / An explorer / Smith) is buying a jacket from Polly's mom.
2 The jacket is (500 Frost dollars / 550 Ice dollars / 500 Ice dollars).
3 The explorers want to go to (the Ice Palace / the lake / Bollington Hall).
4 (The explorers / Polly and Mike / Smith and Hector Frost) made a hole in the ice.
5 Gizmo (saves Polly / digs a hole in the ice / chases Smith).
6 Smith works for (the explorers / Frost, Inc. / the police).

15 Role-play the story.

16 Look and match. Then discuss with a friend. Compare your choices.

VALUES
Dress correctly for each occasion.

HOME SCHOOL LINK Plan an outfit for an event that you are going to.

Lesson 6 Can understand details of a story / Can talk about dressing correctly for different occasions 65

Lesson 6 SB page 65 or Poptropica English World

Learning Objectives
Can understand details of a story
Can talk about dressing correctly for different occasions

Value
Dress correctly for each occasion.

Warm-up

- Draw a line down the middle of the board and write the headings: *inside / outside.* Invite student to list the kinds of clothes that one would wear in these places. Give students time to look at the list while you write them down, then erase the words. Divide the class into two and give each team a chance to name a clothing item under the heading of your choice. Keep score.

Open books and ask students to look at the activities. Ask, *What are we learning today?* Write the lesson objective on the board: *We're reviewing a story, and we're learning about dressing correctly for different occasions.*

14 Read the story again. Then circle.

- Give students time to look at the story and play the audio again.
- Allow students time to do the activity.
- Check answers by having students switch books with another student. Elicit answers from the class.

15 Role-play the story.

- See the "How to use stories" section on page 23 for more ideas on how to build your students' confidence with role-plays.
- Divide students into groups of five. Give each group a set of cut-out Story Cards (see page 102), and have students place them in order.
- Play the audio again (track B:27), and have students follow along. Put the class into groups to role-play the story.
- Give groups time to practice the role-play, then ask them to show the class.

You might like to give students feedback on their role-play.

16 Look and match. Then discuss with a friend. Compare your choices.

- Read the value, *Dress correctly for each occasion.* Brainstorm occasions with the class, e.g., *going to the cinema, going to watch a ballet at the theater, going to a public swimming pool, going to the library, visiting a church or temple*, and elicit good clothing items for each. Ask, *Why do you think dressing correctly is important?* and elicit responses.
- Draw students' attention to the pictures and speech bubbles in Activity 16. Allow students time to do the activity.

- **Home-School link:** Read the instruction with the class: *Plan an outfit for an event that you are going to.* Ask students to do this at home.

Pop Quiz: Ask students about their favorite recent purchase of clothing. Ask, *Why do you like it? Did you need it? Do the colors match your other clothes? Is it warm/cool? Is it good for the season? What occasions can you wear it to?*

Materials
Unit 5 cut-out Story Cards

Homework WB page 53

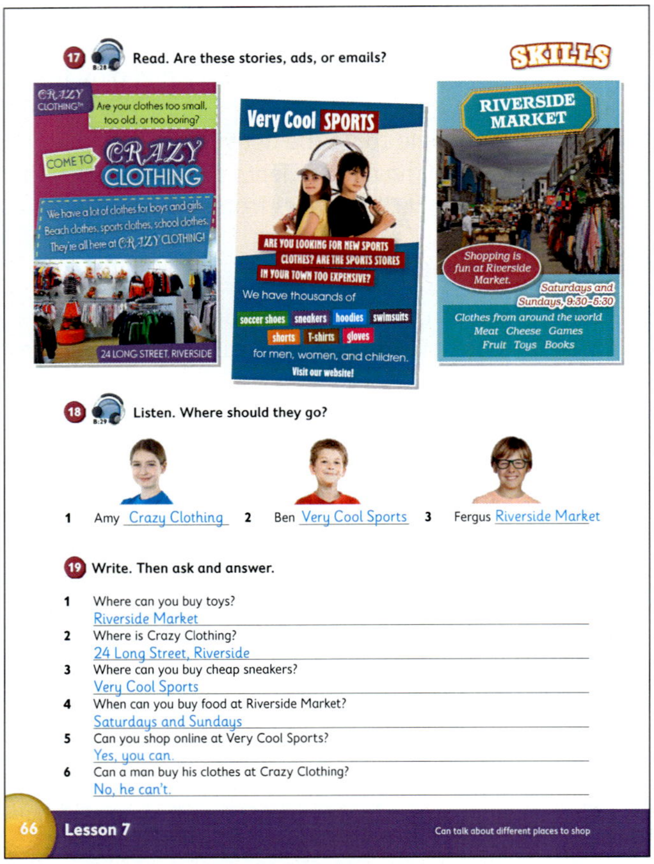
17 Read. Are these stories, ads, or emails?

SKILLS

CRAZY CLOTHING
Are your clothes too small, too old, or too boring?
COME TO CRAZY CLOTHING
We have a lot of clothes for boys and girls. Beach clothes, sports clothes, school clothes. They're all here at CRAZY CLOTHING!
24 LONG STREET, RIVERSIDE

Very Cool SPORTS
ARE YOU LOOKING FOR NEW SPORTS CLOTHES? ARE THE SPORTS STORES IN YOUR TOWN TOO EXPENSIVE?
We have thousands of
soccer shoes sneakers hoodies swimsuits shorts T-shirts gloves
for men, women, and children.
Visit our website!

RIVERSIDE MARKET
Shopping is fun at Riverside Market.
Saturdays and Sundays, 9:30–5:30
Clothes from around the world
Meat Cheese Games
Fruit Toys Books

18 Listen. Where should they go?

1 Amy Crazy Clothing 2 Ben Very Cool Sports 3 Fergus Riverside Market

19 Write. Then ask and answer.

1 Where can you buy toys?
Riverside Market
2 Where is Crazy Clothing?
24 Long Street, Riverside
3 Where can you buy cheap sneakers?
Very Cool Sports
4 When can you buy food at Riverside Market?
Saturdays and Sundays
5 Can you shop online at Very Cool Sports?
Yes, you can.
6 Can a man buy his clothes at Crazy Clothing?
No, he can't.

66 Lesson 7 Can talk about different places to shop

Lesson 7 SB page 66 or Poptropica English World

Learning Objective
Can talk about different places to shop

Additional Language
ads, emails, Crazy Clothing, thousands, Riverside Market

Open books and ask students to look at the activities. Ask, *What are we learning today?* Write the lesson objective on the board: *We're learning to talk about different places to shop.*

Warm-up

- Ask the class, *Who do you go shopping with? Do you look at information before you go?*, and elicit answers.

17 B:28 Read. Are these stories, ads or emails?

- Give students time to look at the three graphic items on the page, then ask them to close their books. Ask, *Are these stories, ads, or emails? (They are ads.)* Discuss what things are found in an ad.
- Play the audio and have students listen and follow.
- Play the audio again and have students read along.

18 B:29 Listen. Where should they go?

- Play the audio and have students listen.

1 I am going to a beach party on Saturday. But my swimsuit is too tight! I also need to buy a new belt. My jeans are always falling down. Oh, I must also buy a new school shirt. I got black paint all over my old shirt last week! Where should I go?

2 I can't wait for our snowboarding vacation! But before we go, it's my dad's birthday. I need to buy him a gift. He's very sporty, but he doesn't like buying expensive things. His old gloves have holes in them! Hmmm, where can I buy him some new gloves and maybe a warm hoodie?

3 My cousin is visiting us. She loves shopping! I don't, I like being outside. Or reading a book! But I guess I should take her shopping. Maybe there is somewhere that sells lots of different things. Somewhere I can eat and she can shop! Do you have any suggestions?

- Play the audio again and have students match the characters and the ads.
- Have students switch their books with a partner. Check answers by asking students who goes where.

19 Write. Then ask and answer.

- Tell students to read the questions, then write answers.
- Ask them to ask and answer the questions in pairs to check answers.

Write on the board, *Online shopping is better than going to the store.* Divide the class into two teams. Tell one team to brainstorm reasons why the statement is true. Tell the other team to brainstorm reasons why the statement is false. Give students enough time to put together their argument. Ask the teams to present their reasons to the class.

Pop Quiz: Divide the class into small groups. Say an item of clothing, e.g., *belt*. Each group have to write a statement using the word *belt*, e.g., *That belt is too long*. Groups read out their sentences, and every group with a unique sentence (not repeated by any other group) gets one point for that round. Then say another item of clothing for the second round, and so on.

Homework WB page 54

SCIENCE 5

20 What do you know?

21 Read. Then number.

Choose the right shoes!

We all love wearing our favorite sneakers. But for some activities, sneakers aren't a good idea. Find out how to choose the right shoes.

a 3 b 1 c 2

1 In good weather, sneakers are great for walking in a city. But on a rainy day, your feet get wet. Sneakers are too soft for walking in the mountains. They can be dangerous. Always wear stiff walking shoes or boots.

2 Dancers move and bend their feet a lot. The sneakers in this picture are good for dancers because the soles are soft in the middle. The soles of other sneakers are too stiff.

3 For rock climbing, you want to feel the rock with your feet. Sneakers are too big for this. Climbing shoes are small and tight.

What shoes do you wear for your favorite sport?

22 Read again and say *walking*, *rock climbing*, or *dancing*.

1 You can't wear shoes with hard soles.
2 Your feet bend a lot.
3 The right shoes are very tight.
4 Soft shoes can be dangerous.

23 Talk about the activities.

A: I don't like rock climbing because it's too dangerous.
B: Really? I love rock climbing!

MINI PROJECT

24 Design a pair of shoes.

- **Think** about the shoes you have. What are they for? What activities do you like? What shoes do you need to do it?
- **Plan** a perfect pair of shoes for an activity. Think about the soles, laces, weight, and what they are made of.
- **Write** about the shoes' features and why you chose them. Design and create a poster.
- **Share** your poster with the class.

Lesson 8 Can understand a text about choosing shoes / Can write about a pair of shoes I have designed 67

Lesson 8 SB page 67 or Poptropica English World

Learning Objectives
Can understand a text about choosing shoes
Can write about a pair of shoes I have designed

Additional Language
sneakers, dancers, soles, soft, stiff

Warm-up

- Invite students to describe their shoes.

20 What do you know?

- Open books and ask students to look at the activities. Ask, *What are we learning today?* Write the lesson objectives on the board: *We're learning to design, and write about, a pair of shoes.*
- Refer to the learning adventure poster and say, *Great! You are moving along your learning adventure!*

21 Read. Then number.

B:30

- Ask, *What can you see in Picture a? (A person is climbing.) What are the people doing in Pictures b and c? (They're walking/dancing.)*
- Play the audio and have students read along in their books, and then write numbers.

22 Read again and say *walking, rock climbing,* or *dancing.*

- Have students read the text aloud. Then read the four statements chorally.
- Pair students and have them complete the activity. Ask for volunteers to share their answers with the class.

Tell students you are talking about shoes and they need to work out the activity you are thinking of, e.g., say, *My shoes must be strong and have a small heel for going faster. (horseback-riding) I don't want my shoes to have slippery soles because I don't want to fall in the water! (sailing)* This will give students practice at thinking and forming questions.

23 Talk about the activities.

- Draw students' attention to the target language in this activity. Ask two confident students to model it.

24 Design a pair of shoes.

- Ask students what steps they will take to make sure they include all the necessary information. Remind students of the steps to success: Think, Plan, Write and Share.
  Think If students need some help, suggest activities.
  Plan Ask students to make some notes about features the shoes would need.
  Write Give students time to create their poster. Remind them to check their work afterwards.
  Share Nominate students to read their sentences in class.

You may also wish to give students feedback on their projects.

Ask students, *What do you know about types of shoes for different activities now?* Give students a minute to tell their partner the new ideas and words they can remember. Ask students, *Where are you on your learning adventure?* Tell students, *Good job!* to reinforce the progress they are making.

Pop Quiz: Pair students. One student mimes an activity.The other student guesses the activity (*dancing/rock climbing*, etc.). The student has to then talk about the kind of shoe needed for the activity.

Materials
Poster, sheet of paper for each students, colored pens or pencils

Homework WB page 55

25 Listen and check (✓).

B:31

I CAN DO IT!

1 a ✓ b

2 a b ✓

3 a b ✓

4 a $200 b $60 ✓

26 Listen and number the three things they buy.

B:32

a b c 3 d 1 e f 2

27 Look at Activity 26. Use the key to ask and answer.

Key:
1 = $95.50
2 = $62.30
3 = $22.99

28 Write. Then role-play with a partner to check your answers.

Maddy: 1 Whose pens are these? And 2 whose hoodie is 3 this ?
Robbie: They're not mine. Are 4 they Emma's?
Maddy: No, they're not 5 hers . Maybe they're Dan's? Hey, Dan. Are these 6 your pens? And 7 is this your 8 hoodie ?
Dan: Let's see... Oh, yes, the pens are 9 mine , thanks. But the hoodie 10 isn't mine.
Maddy: Well, 11 whose hoodie is it? It's 12 too big for a student.
Robbie: I don't know. Let's ask Mr. Smith. Maybe it's 13 his .

I CAN

I can ask and answer about how much things cost.
I can ask and answer about who things belong to.
I can write about a pair of shoes I have designed.

68 Lesson 9 Can assess what I have learned in Unit 5

Lesson 9 SB page 68 or Poptropica English World

Learning Objective
Can assess what I have learned in Unit 5

Warm-up

- Place Picture Cards 78–94 around the room. Invite students to take one, come to the front of the class, and talk about the items.

Open books and ask students to look at the activities. Write this lesson objective on the board: *We're thinking about our learning adventure.*

- Ask students what they have been learning in the unit. Put their ideas on the board, e.g., *different clothes/ accessories.*
- For each idea, ask students to tell their partner where they think they are on their learning adventure. Reassure students who are less confident that they will have opportunities for more practice.

25 Listen and check (✓).

B:31

- Have students listen to the audio and check the box next to the item that is being spoken about.

1 Some scarves are too long, and some are too short. But this purple and black one is great.
2 I like blue. It is a good color for me. The red jacket is too big.
3 This gold one is too big and old-fashioned – I don't like big bracelets. The silver one is smaller and modern. I think I should buy the silver bracelet.
4 I love this long dress, but look at the price! It's too expensive. It's $200. I should buy the cheaper skirt.

- Have students check answers in pairs.

26 Listen and number the three things they buy.

B:32

- Play the audio. Have students number the correct images.

1 Black shoes are good for school. I like the brown shoes but I need shoes for school. Can I buy the black pair, please? **2** I like this style of sunglasses but this green color is too... well um... the color is wrong. Can I buy the yellow sunglasses, please? **3** This red belt is cool but it is too short. The black belt is longer. It's not too short.

27 Look at Activity 26. Use the key to ask and answer.

- In pairs, have students ask and answer questions.

28 Write. Then role-play with a partner to check your answers.

- Have students complete the blanks in the sentences.
- Have students check their answers in pairs.

Ask students how they feel about their learning in this unit. Ask students to tell you what they found easy and what they found the most difficult to learn in the unit.

- Read the three *I can* statements with students and invite students to check the boxes according to how confident they feel about the language point.
- Ask students, *Where are you on your learning adventure?* Students indicate where they think they are on the learning adventure poster. Tell students, *Good job!* to reinforce the progress they are making.

Pop Quiz: In groups of four, students tell the others the answers to the following questions: *Which is your favorite activity in the unit? Why? Which activity don't you like? Why? What is your favorite new word? Which word is the most difficult for you?*

Materials
Poster, Picture Cards 78–94

Homework WB page 56

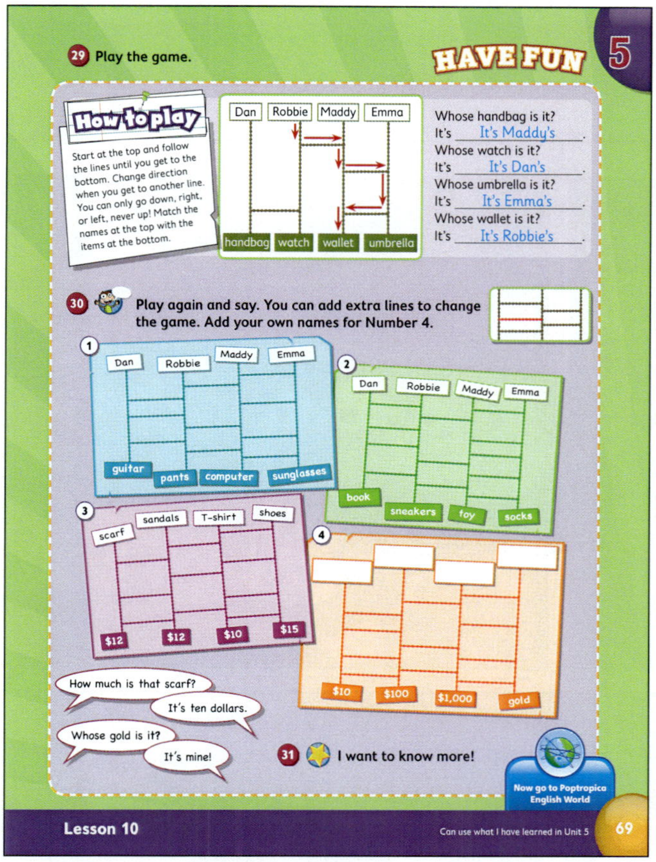

Lesson 10 SB page 69 or Poptropica English World

Learning Objective
Can use what I have learned in Unit 5

Warm-up

- Place Picture Cards 78–94 around the room. A student says, *I see something orange. I see something baggy.* Students try to guess and point at the picture. Repeat.

Open books and ask students to look at the pictures. Ask, *What are we learning today?* Write the lesson objective on the board: *We're doing a fun activity to review Unit 5 language.*

29 Play the game.

- Direct students' attention to the game-board and ask questions about the picture/activity. Ask, *What are the names? What accessories can you read in the game?*
- Give students time to do the activity and to match the names and accessories.
- Have students check answers in pairs.

30 Play again and say. You can add extra lines to change the game. Add your own names for Number 4.

- Direct students' attention to the activity and allow them time to complete it.
- After a few minutes, invite students to work in pairs. Say, *Teamwork makes it easier.*
- Draw students' attention to the exchange at the bottom of the page. Read chorally. Ask students to make sentences that go with the matching items in each game-board.

Write on the board, *You should only buy what you need.* Divide the class into small groups and ask them to discuss the statement and take notes on why they agree with it or disagree with it. Ask the groups to present their reasons to the class. Write the reasons on the board under *Agree* and *Disagree*. Take a class vote.

31 I want to know more!

- Ask students to choose anything they enjoyed from the unit and to go and find out more. You might like to set this activity as homework with a quick feedback session at the beginning of the next class.
- You can also suggest that students write one or two questions about what they want to know, then switch question(s) with a partner. Students then find the answer(s) to their partner's question(s) as a homework activity, with feedback the next lesson.

Are you ready for Unit 6?

- Ask students if they are ready to move onto the next unit. Tell students that it is fine if they do not remember everything as they will continue to practice throughout the level.
- Encourage students to ask if they have any questions about what they learned in Unit 5.

You may wish to give Unit 5 Test (see page 196) at this time.

Materials
Picture Cards 78–94

Homework WB page 57

Unit 5 Story Cards

Wider World 3

SB pages 70–71 or Poptropica English World

Learning Objectives
Can understand texts about shopping for food
Can talk about the different places to buy food

Additional Language
floating market, coconuts, dulce de leche, pastries, bakery

Wider World 3

Shopping for food

1 What do you know?

2 Listen and read. Then underline the foods.

1 Bao's blog

In Vietnam, we buy our food at the floating market. It opens at four o'clock in the morning. There are a lot of boats and you can climb from one boat to another to buy things. You can buy fish, rice, coconuts, bananas, ... and snakes, too! Some of the snakes can dance. I love watching them. Some people buy snakes for dinner but I don't eat snakes – they're too expensive.

Bao, 12, Vietnam

2 Silvia's blog

In Buenos Aires, Argentina, there are some amazing bakeries. You can buy a lot of different pastries there. There's a lot of *dulce de leche* or milk caramel in the pastries. I often go to a bakery after school with my friends. Pastries are my favorite food.

Silvia, 11, Argentina

70 Wider World 3 Can understand texts about shopping for food

Warm-up

- Ask any students if they have been to a different country. What food did they eat? Did they like it? Write any names of countries, and any new food items, on the board. Go over them together, correcting pronunciation if necessary. Invite students to come to the front and find countries on the world map.

1 What do you know?

- Open books and ask students to look at the pictures. Ask, *What are we learning today?* Write the lesson objective on the board: *We're learning about food shopping in different cultures.*
- Close books. Ask students what English words they know for places, e.g., *school, bank.*
- Refer to the learning adventure poster and say, *Great! You are moving along your learning adventure!*

2 Listen and read. Then underline the foods.

- Ask students to guess which countries the pictures are of. Tell them the names of the countries (*Vietnam*, *Argentina*, and *the United Kingdom*). Volunteers point to them on the world map. Invite students to say anything they know about these countries.
- Ask the class about the foods in each picture, e.g., *Picture 1. What foods can you see? Picture 2. What do they sell in this type of store? Picture 3. What do you think is growing in this garden?* Write students' ideas on the board. Pre-teach, *coconut, bakery, grow,* and *floating market,* by using the pictures.
- Play the audio and have students listen and follow.
- Give students time to read the blogs and underline the food items.
- Check answers as a class – have students brainstorm the food items and volunteers write them on the board. Students check their own work.

Write *fresh food / frozen food* on the board. Divide the class into small groups and ask them to argue which is right and which is wrong. Give them a few minutes, then ask groups that agree to join together. After a few more minutes, get the groups' arguments for which is right and which is wrong. Write their reasons on the board. Let students decide which group put forward the strongest argument. Remind students that there is no real correct answer.

3 Circle. Check with a friend.

- Read the sentences and the answer choices chorally.
- Tell students to underline the answers in the blogs, and not just pick an answer from memory. See if they can tell you why you have requested this. (If they pick from memory, they do not get more reading practice.)
- Allow students time to read the blogs silently to themselves.
- Remind students of the importance of context to work out the meaning of new words.

Materials
Poster, map of the world

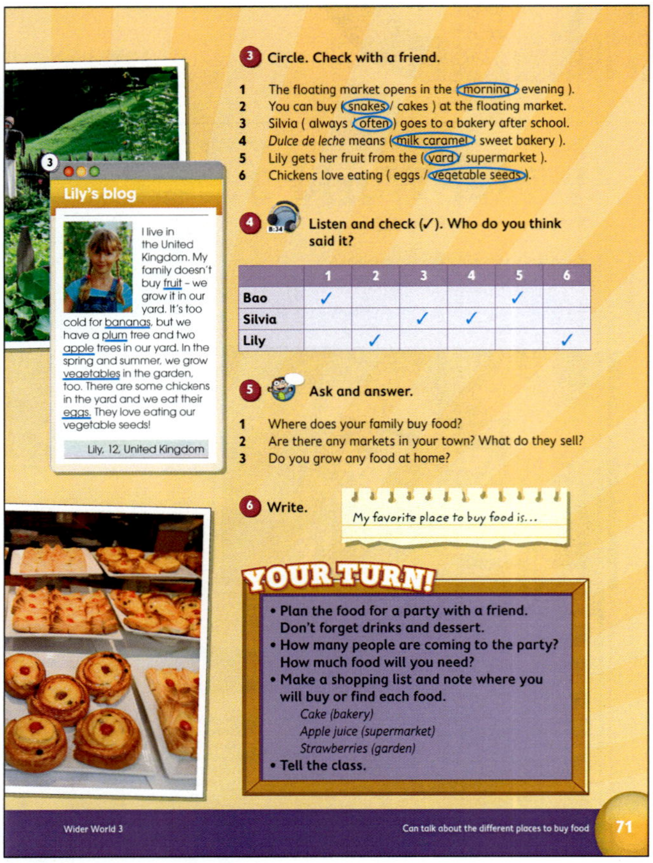
3 Lily's blog

I live in the United Kingdom. My family doesn't buy fruit – we grow it in our yard. It's too cold for bananas, but we have a plum tree and two apple trees in our yard. In the spring and summer, we grow vegetables in the garden, too. There are some chickens in the yard and we eat their eggs. They love eating our vegetable seeds!

Lily, 12, United Kingdom

3 Circle. Check with a friend.

1 The floating market opens in the (morning / evening).
2 You can buy (snakes / cakes) at the floating market.
3 Silvia (always / often) goes to a bakery after school.
4 *Dulce de leche* means (milk caramel / sweet bakery).
5 Lily gets her fruit from the (yard / supermarket).
6 Chickens love eating (eggs / vegetable seeds).

4 Listen and check (✓). Who do you think said it?

	1	2	3	4	5	6
Bao	✓				✓	
Silvia			✓	✓		
Lily		✓				✓

5 Ask and answer.

1 Where does your family buy food?
2 Are there any markets in your town? What do they sell?
3 Do you grow any food at home?

6 Write. My favorite place to buy food is ...

YOUR TURN!

- Plan the food for a party with a friend. Don't forget drinks and dessert.
- How many people are coming to the party? How much food will you need?
- Make a shopping list and note where you will buy or find each food.
  Cake (bakery)
  Apple juice (supermarket)
  Strawberries (garden)
- Tell the class.

Wider World 3 Can talk about the different places to buy food 71

4 Listen and check (✓). Who do you think said it?

- Tell students they are going to hear some sentences that aren't on the page, but are said by Bao, Silvia, or Lily.
- Ask students to listen carefully and then check who they think said it.
- Play the audio.

1 Most people wear hats because it gets hot on the water.
2 Our chickens' eggs taste so good for breakfast.
3 I am learning to bake my favorite food at home.
4 I want to open a bakery one day.
5 But it's not fun shopping when it rains. Everyone gets wet!
6 Tomatoes are really easy to grow in our garden.

- If necessary, play the audio again and have students check their answers in pairs.

5 Ask and answer.

- Ask volunteers to read the questions to the class. Different students answer.
- Encourage students to explain their answers, e.g., *My family buys food from the supermarket because it's big and there are a lot of things. It's cheap, too.*
- You may like to adapt question number three to make it appropriate for your country. If most of the students live in apartments, ask if their family has any place they can grow food, e.g., an allotment, or a family house in the country. Ask if they know anyone who has.

6 Write

- Have students write about where they like buying food, e.g., *My favorite place to buy food is the bakery because I love bread. I also love sweet pastries. Bakeries always smell really good!*
- Remind students to check their work when they are finished.

YOUR TURN! Pair students and ask pairs to think about what food they need for a party. Ask some prompt questions: *How many people are coming? How much food do you need? Where can you buy it?* Ask them to write a shopping list, noting where they will buy or find each item.

- Have students present their shopping list to the class. Remind pairs to think about one question to ask each group after their presentation.

Pop Quiz: Play a definitions team game – write a food on the board behind a student, and his/her team members need to say where you can buy/find it, and what it tastes like, in two sentences: *You can pick it from a tree in a garden. It tastes sweet. (apple)* The student at the front has five guesses to find the food word on the board.

6 Party time

Unit Overview

Unit Objective

- I can talk about events in the past

Language

Target Vocabulary	Irregular part tense verbs: make/made, have/had, come/came, give/gave, get/got, sing/sang, bring/brought, meet/met, eat/ate, see/saw Ordinal numbers: first, second, third, fourth, fifth, sixth, seventh, eighth, ninth, tenth, eleventh, twelfth, thirteenth, fourteenth, fifteenth, sixteenth, seventeenth, eighteenth, nineteenth, twentieth, thirtieth
Target Structures	I made a cake. / I didn't make a cake. Where did you go? I went to Ghana. When did you go to Ghana? I went on August 1st. What did you see? I saw giant butterflies. Who did you meet? I met relatives.
Features	**Cross-curricular:** History: The first Thanksgiving **Values:** Being a creative problem solver.

Skills

Reading	• Can understand a simple story • Can understand details of a story • Can understand a text about the first Thanksgiving
Writing	• Can complete simple sentences about the past using irregular verbs • Can write a mini-play • Can write simple sentences suggesting solutions to problems *(Workbook)* • Can write simple sentences about events in the past *(Workbook)*
Listening	• Can understand a simple story • Can understand a text about the first Thanksgiving
Speaking	• Can use irregular verbs to talk about the past • Can talk about what did and didn't happen in the past • Can use ordinal numbers as dates • Can ask and answer about past events • Can discuss a story • Can talk about being a creative problem solver • Can talk about a party in the past

Lesson 1 SB page 72 or Poptropica English World

Learning Objective
Can use irregular verbs to talk about the past

Target Language
make/made, have/had, come/came, give/gave, get/got, sing/sang, bring/brought, meet/met, eat/ate, see/saw

1 What do you know?

- Open books and ask students to look at the pictures. Ask, *What are we learning today?* Write the lesson objective on the board: *We're learning to use irregular verbs to talk about the past.*
- Close books. Ask students what English irregular past tense verbs they know, e.g., *have/had, eat/ate*. Write them all on board.
- Refer to the learning adventure poster and say, *Great! You are already moving along your learning adventure!*

2 Listen and read. Why is there a cake?

B:35

- Ask, *Who can you see in the pictures? (Maddy, her family, and Kipper) Where are they? (Students guess: at Maddy's house) Who do you think Maddy is speaking to in Picture 1? (Grandpa)*, etc.
- Ask students to look at the scenes in their books and listen as you play the audio.
- Have the class read the story chorally.
- Ask comprehension questions: *Why is there a cake? (It's Grandpa's birthday.) Did they eat cake? (No, they did not.) Why not?*

3 Listen and say.

B:36

- Focus students on the pictures. Play the audio and have students repeat.
- Put Picture Cards 95–104 on the board for students to refer to. Number them. Pair students and have them play a game. One student in each pair says a number. His/her partner has to say the verb in the past tense, and mime the action.

4 Read and say. Use words from Activity 3.

- Pair students and give them time to do the activity. Tell them to use the target language, and the irregular past tense verbs in Activity 3.

6 Party time

1 What do you know?

2 Listen and read. Why is there a cake?

3 Listen and say.

1 make/made 2 have/had 3 come/came 4 give/gave 5 get/got
6 sing/sang 7 bring/brought 8 meet/met 9 eat/ate 10 see/saw

4 Read and say. Use words from Activity 3.

Maddy Maddy's aunts Mom the family

The family gave Grandpa presents.

72 Lesson 1 Can use irregular verbs to talk about the past

Ask students, *How many irregular past tense verbs do you know now?* Give students a minute to tell their partner the new words they know.

- Ask students to say where they are on their adventure now. Ask students which words they find easiest or most difficult to remember. Tell students, *Good job!* to reinforce the progress they are making.

Pop Quiz: Make statements in the present tense and ask students to repeat them in the past tense, e.g., *I eat chocolate cake. (I ate chocolate cake.)* Then make statements in the past tense, and again ask students to repeat them, but in the present tense, e.g., *He got a present. (He gets a present.)*

Materials
Poster, Picture Cards 95–104

Homework WB page 58

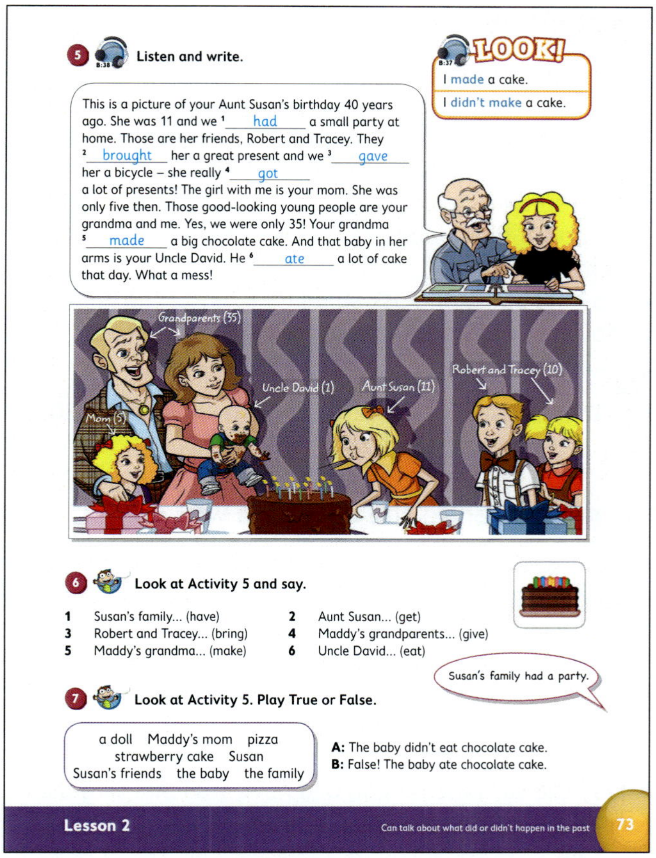

5 B:38 Listen and write.

This is a picture of your Aunt Susan's birthday 40 years ago. She was 11 and we [1] had a small party at home. Those are her friends, Robert and Tracey. They [2] brought her a great present and we [3] gave her a bicycle – she really [4] got a lot of presents! The girl with me is your mom. She was only five then. Those good-looking young people are your grandma and me. Yes, we were only 35! Your grandma [5] made a big chocolate cake. And that baby in her arms is your Uncle David. He [6] ate a lot of cake that day. What a mess!

LOOK! B:37
I made a cake.
I didn't make a cake.

6 Look at Activity 5 and say.

1 Susan's family... (have)
2 Aunt Susan... (get)
3 Robert and Tracey... (bring)
4 Maddy's grandparents... (give)
5 Maddy's grandma... (make)
6 Uncle David... (eat)

Susan's family had a party.

7 Look at Activity 5. Play True or False.

a doll Maddy's mom pizza
strawberry cake Susan
Susan's friends the baby the family

A: The baby didn't eat chocolate cake.
B: False! The baby ate chocolate cake.

Lesson 2 Can talk about what did or didn't happen in the past 73

Lesson 2 SB page 73 or Poptropica English World

Learning Objective
Can talk about what did or didn't happen in the past

Warm-up

- Have a short-snapper quiz by saying a verb (regular or irregular) and inviting students to shout out the correct past tense form. This can also be played as a team game by dividing the class into two, and saying a verb to two players (one from each team) at a time, and awarding points to the quickest correct response.

Open books and ask students to look at the activities and the Look! box. Ask, *What are we learning today?* Write the lesson objective on the board: *We're learning to talk about what did and didn't happen in the past.*

5 B:38 Listen and write.

- Draw students' attention to the Look! box and play the audio (track B:37). Students repeat chorally.
- Have students look at the picture of Grandpa and Maddy, and the picture of an old birthday party. Tell students they will listen to Grandpa. Play the audio and have students listen.
- Play the audio again, giving students time to write answers in the blanks.
- To check answers, students switch books, and elicit answers from the class.

6 Look at Activity 5 and say.

- Ask a confident student to model the target structure for number 1.
- Draw students' attention to the verbs in Activity 5. Have the students repeat the words after you.
- Divide the class into pairs and give them time to do the activity, using the target language.

7 Look at Activity 5. Play True or False.

- Ask two confident students to model the dialog.
- Draw students' attention to the words in the word box. Have students repeat the words after you. Divide the class into pairs, and give them time to do the activity, using the target language.
- To extend the lesson, hand out copies of Activity Sheet 11 (see Poptropica English World) and ask students to cut out the items. Then give each a sheet of paper and have them write down matching words, and cut them out as well. Students play *Concentration*, using picture/word card combinations, or word card only matches. When they get a match, they have to also model the target language.

Pop Quiz: Bring in an old picture of one of your early birthday parties. Ask students to ask you questions about who the people in the picture are, e.g., *Who is the man with the beard? (my dad).* Then ask students to make statements about the picture, e.g., *Mr./Ms. (Teacher's name) had a party in the park. He/She got a bike. His/Her mom made a cake.*

- Direct students' attention to the birthday cake card on page 73. Tell students to go online to the Poptropica English Island Adventure Game and find the item. Once students click on it, they are taken to a supplementary language task.

Materials
Activity Sheet 11, scissors, old picture of a birthday party

Homework WB page 59

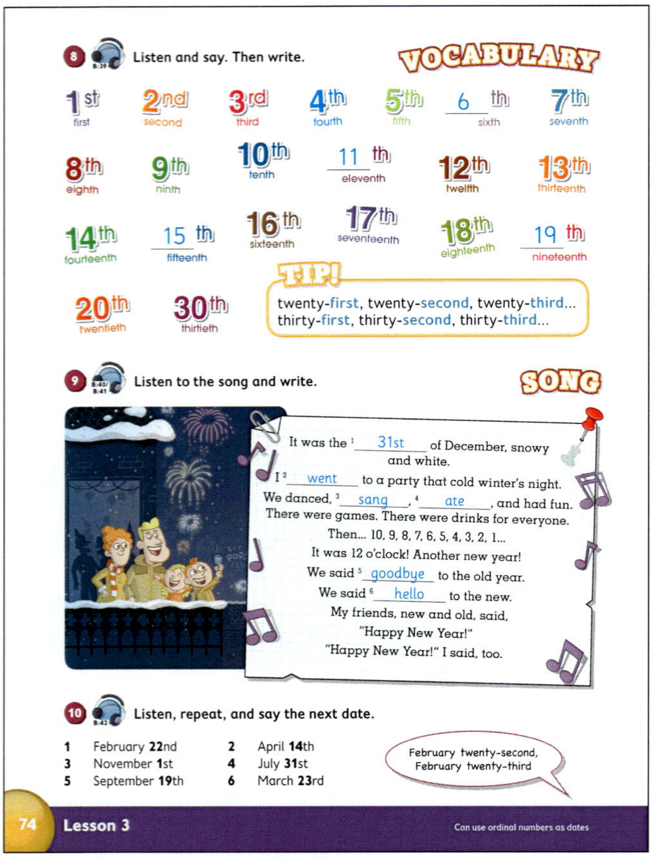

8 Listen and say. Then write. VOCABULARY

1st first, 2nd second, 3rd third, 4th fourth, 5th fifth, 6th sixth, 7th seventh, 8th eighth, 9th ninth, 10th tenth, 11th eleventh, 12th twelfth, 13th thirteenth, 14th fourteenth, 15th fifteenth, 16th sixteenth, 17th seventeenth, 18th eighteenth, 19th nineteenth, 20th twentieth, 30th thirtieth

TIP!
twenty-first, twenty-second, twenty-third…
thirty-first, thirty-second, thirty-third…

9 Listen to the song and write. SONG

It was the 1 31st of December, snowy and white.
I 2 went to a party that cold winter's night.
We danced, 3 sang, 4 ate, and had fun.
There were games. There were drinks for everyone.
Then… 10, 9, 8, 7, 6, 5, 4, 3, 2, 1…
It was 12 o'clock! Another new year!
We said 5 goodbye to the old year.
We said 6 hello to the new.
My friends, new and old, said,
"Happy New Year!"
"Happy New Year!" I said, too.

10 Listen, repeat, and say the next date.

1 February 22nd
2 April 14th
3 November 1st
4 July 31st
5 September 19th
6 March 23rd

February twenty-second, February twenty-third

74 Lesson 3 Can use ordinal numbers as dates

Lesson 3 SB page 74 or Poptropica English World

Learning Objective
Can use ordinal numbers as dates

Target Language
first, second, third, fourth, fifth, sixth, seventh, eighth, ninth, tenth, eleventh, twelfth, thirteenth, fourteenth, fifteenth, sixteenth, seventeenth, eighteenth, nineteenth, twentieth, thirtieth

Warm-up

- Divide the class into two teams and assign everyone a month randomly. When you say, *Go!*, students have to arrange themselves in order, those with the same month will stand together. The first team to arrange themselves in a proper order is the winner.

Open books and ask students to look at the pictures. Ask, *What are we learning today?* Write the lesson objective on the board: *We're learning ordinal numbers.*

- Refer to the learning adventure poster and say, *Great! You are moving along your learning adventure!*

8 Listen and say. Then write.

- Introduce ordinal numbers with Picture Cards 105–127. Hold them up one by one, then turn them to the word-side and ask students to repeat the words after you. Emphasize the use of *st, nd, rd* and *th* and have students practice the sounds. Then, ask students to look in their books, and look at the words and numbers.
- Play the audio and ask students to write the numbers.
- Play the audio again and have students repeat.

Tip!
Use the information in the Tip! box to explain how to form higher ordinal numbers.

9 Listen to the song and write.

- Point to the family in Activity 9 and ask, *What are they doing? What is in the sky? When is it?*, and elicit responses and guesses.
- Play the song audio and have students listen.
- Play the audio again and ask students to write the correct word in the spaces. Have students check their answers with partners.
- Play the karaoke version and have students sing the song if they feel confident enough.

10 Listen, repeat, and say the next date.

- Draw students' attention to the dates in this activity. Have students say the dates chorally.
- Play the audio, pausing to give students time to respond.

1 February twenty-second / What's the next date?
2 April fourteenth / What's the next date?
3 November first / What's the next date?
4 July thirty-first / What's the next date?
5 September nineteenth / What's the next date?
6 March twenty-third / What's the next date?

Ask students, *How many ordinal numbers do you know now?* Give students a minute to tell their partner the new verbs they know.

- Ask students to say where they are on their adventure now. Ask students which words they find easiest or most difficult to remember. Tell students, *Good job!* to reinforce the progress they are making.

Pop Quiz: Show students Picture Cards 105–127 and ask them to call out the words as a class. Then have students take turns to come to the front and write three ordinal numbers on the board in a row, as called out by another student, e.g., *first, eighteenth, twenty-second* (*1st, 18th, 22nd*).

Materials
Poster, Picture Cards 105–127

Homework WB page 60

6

11 B:44 Read. Then listen and write the dates.

LOOK! B:43

Where did you go?	I went to Ghana.
When did you go to Ghana?	I went on August 1st.
What did you see?	I saw giant butterflies.
Who did you meet?	I met my relatives.

This diary belongs to: Jenny Amoako

August

1st	I went to Ghana and met my relatives from Africa for the first time.
3rd	I went to Kakum National Park and saw beautiful giant butterflies.
5th	I went to a soccer game in Accra. Ghanaians love soccer! I danced and sang soccer songs with my new friends.
10th	I went to the north of Ghana. I saw the giant baobab trees and ate some baobab fruit, but I didn't like it!
22nd	I went to Lake Volta and sailed in a pirogue, a type of boat. It was cool!
28th	We had a party. My African friends gave me a lot of presents. "Come back soon!" they said. I cried at the airport.
30th	I came back home! I brought lots of presents for my mom, dad, and brother. It was a great experience!

12 Look at Activity 11. Ask and answer.

1 She... (meet) 2 She... (see)
3 She... (dance) 4 She... (sing)
5 She... (eat) 6 She... (have)
7 She... (come) 8 She... (bring)

When did she go to Ghana?

She went on August 1st.

Lesson 4 Can ask and answer about past events 75

Lesson 4 SB page 75 or Poptropica English World

Learning Objective
Can ask and answer about past events

Warm-up

- Ask students to write four sentences in the past tense about their last vacation. Choose a few confident students and ask the questions, *Where did you go?*, and *When did you go?*

Open books and ask students to look at the activities and the Look! box. Ask, *What are we learning today?* Write the lesson objective on the board: *We're learning to ask and answer about past events.*

11 B:44 Read. Then listen and write the dates.

- Have students listen to the Look! box audio (track B:43), then listen and repeat after you.
- Give students time to read the diary page. Then tell them they will hear a conversation, and have to write the dates next to the correct activity.
- Have students listen to the audio and fill in the blanks.

Woman:	When did you go to Ghana?
Girl:	Well, I went in August. I arrived on August first. It was very exciting. I met my relatives from Africa.
Woman:	Where did you go in Ghana?
Girl:	Well, on August third I went to Kakum National Park.
Woman:	What did you see there?
Girl:	I saw some amazing animals. The giant butterflies, for example. Very beautiful. Very, very big butterflies. Then on August fifth, we went to a soccer game in Accra. Ghanaians love soccer and they are very good at it. I danced and sang soccer songs with my new friends. Then on August tenth, I went to the north of Ghana to see the giant baobab trees, and ate some baobab fruit, but I didn't like it! On August twenty-second, I went to Lake Volta and sailed in a pirogue, a type of boat. It was cool!
Woman:	What did you do before you came home?
Girl:	On August twenty-eighth, we had a party. My African friends gave me a lot of presents. "Come back soon!" they said. I cried at the airport.
Woman:	When did you come back?
Girl:	I came back on August thirtieth. I brought lots of presents for my mom, dad, and brother. It was a great experience.

- Play the audio again, and have students say the answers at the appropriate time.

12 Look at Activity 11. Ask and answer.

- Give students time to do the activity. Invite students to share their answers with the class.

Pop Quiz: Ask students to imagine an exciting three-day vacation to a new country. Tell them to choose a month, dates (using ordinal numbers), a country and an activity per day. Pair students and ask them to talk about their vacations. If there is time, quiz the students about other people's vacation activities.

Lesson 5 SB page 76 or Poptropica English World

Learning Objectives
Can understand a simple story
Can discuss a story

Additional Language
tore, logo

Functional Language
What happened? Really! I see. Come on, let's go.

Warm-up

- Put the pictures of a polar bear, a wolf, and a fish on the board. Ask, *What is a fish good at? (It's good at swimming.)* Repeat for all pictures. To extend the activity, you can ask, *What animal is good at fishing? (polar bear).* Invite students to ask similar questions.

Open books and ask students to look at the story. Ask, *What are we learning today?* Write the lesson objective on the board: *We're reading and discussing a story.*

13 B:45 Talk about the pictures. Then listen and read.

- Direct students' attention to the pictures and ask questions about the characters and the scenes: *Who can you see in Picture 4?* (*Mike, Polly, Police Chief*) *What do you think they are saying?* (*That Smith pushed Polly into the lake. / That they think the thieves are at Bollington Hall.*)
- Play the audio and have students listen and follow.
- Check students' understanding of the story by asking questions and pointing to the pictures, *Did Smith really see a polar bear and a wolf?* (*No, he didn't.*) *Did Gizmo really tear Smith's pants?* (*Yes, he did.*) *What did the Police Chief tell them?* (*Hector Frost lives at Bollington Hall.*)
- Play the audio again. Divide students into five groups and assign each group a role (Hector Frost, Smith, Polly, Mike, Police Chief). Groups read along and mime their character's actions.

14 Does Smith tell Frost the truth about what happened? Why? Discuss your answers.

- Have students discuss the questions in groups, and then invite one person to write their group's answer on the board. Discuss all the different ideas. Encourage students to use the past simple with their answers.

Write the following statement on the board, *You should always tell the truth.* Divide students into groups and ask them to discuss the statement. Tell one group to agree with the statement, and the other group to disagree with the statement. They might like to write their answers/ideas in their notebooks. Ask both groups to write their reasons on the board, and extend the discussion.

Pop Quiz: Close books. Read out sentences from the story. Students have to say who said them, e.g., *And this is Hector Frost's logo. (Police Chief) I was fighting the wolf. (Smith)*

Materials
Pictures of a polar bear, a wolf and a fish (cut from magazines)

Homework WB page 62

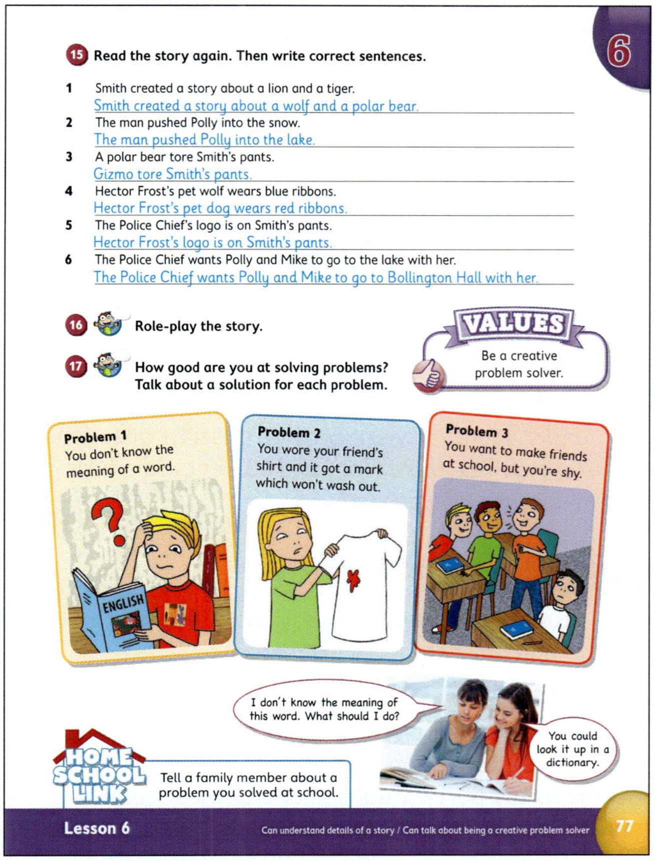
6

15 Read the story again. Then write correct sentences.

1 Smith created a story about a lion and a tiger.
Smith created a story about a wolf and a polar bear.
2 The man pushed Polly into the snow.
The man pushed Polly into the lake.
3 A polar bear tore Smith's pants.
Gizmo tore Smith's pants.
4 Hector Frost's pet wolf wears blue ribbons.
Hector Frost's pet dog wears red ribbons.
5 The Police Chief's logo is on Smith's pants.
Hector Frost's logo is on Smith's pants.
6 The Police Chief wants Polly and Mike to go to the lake with her.
The Police Chief wants Polly and Mike to go to Bollington Hall with her.

16 Role-play the story.

17 How good are you at solving problems? Talk about a solution for each problem.

VALUES
Be a creative problem solver.

HOME SCHOOL LINK
Tell a family member about a problem you solved at school.

Lesson 6 Can understand details of a story / Can talk about being a creative problem solver 77

Lesson 6 SB page 77 or Poptropica English World

Learning Objectives
Can understand details of a story
Can talk about being a creative problem solver

Value
Be a creative problem solver.

Warm-up

- Tell the class, *I have a problem. I forgot my lunch. What can I do?* Brainstorm with the class, by having students say a solution and you write it on the board. *(Ask a friend for some lunch. Buy something from the cafeteria. Go home and get it at lunchtime.)* Invite students to share how they solved recent problems, using past tense.

Open books and ask students to look at the activities. Ask, *What are we learning today?* Write the lesson objectives on the board: *We're reviewing a story, and we're learning about solving problems.*

15 Read the story again. Then write correct sentences.

- Give students time to look at the story and play the audio again.
- Give students time to do the activity.
- Have students check answers in pairs.

16 Role-play the story.

- See the "How to use stories" section on page 23 for more ideas on how to build your students' confidence with role-plays.
- Divide students into groups of five. Give each group a set of cut-out Story Cards (see page 116), and have students place them in order.
- Play the audio again (track B:45), and have students follow along. Put the class into groups to role-play the story.
- Give groups time to practice the role-play, then ask them to show the class.

You might like to give students feedback on their role-play.

17 How good are you at solving problems? Talk about a solution for each problem.

- Review the problems that were discussed in the warm-up activity. Draw students' attention to the Values box and read the value, *Be a creative problem solver.*
- Draw students' attention to the pictures and the problems in Activity 17. Pair students and give them time to do the activity.
- Invite pairs to stand and ask/answer the questions.

- **Home-School link:** Read the instruction with the class: *Tell a family member about a problem you solved at school.* Ask students to do this at home.

Pop Quiz: Prepare a few more problem scenarios before class, e.g., *You forgot to take your swimsuit to the beach. You forgot to take your glasses to the cinema. You left your school books at your friend's house after school. You dropped a glass which broke on the floor. You hear someone crying in the bathroom. You see someone bullying another child. You find some money that isn't yours.* Present the problems to the students and ask them how they would solve them.

Materials
Unit 6 cut-out Story Cards

Homework WB page 63

18 Read. Was yesterday fun for Harry?

SKILLS

Sally's Welcome Party

Who? Sally's friends, classmates, and teachers
Where? Hope School
When? Saturday, April 18th
What time? 6:30–9:00 p.m.

Harry's blog

Sunday, April 19th

Yesterday, we had a welcome party for Sally, a new student at school. Before the party, I went to my friend Mark's house for pizza. Then we went to school together in his dad's car. We saw all our friends there. Sally's parents were there, too. There was cool music but the room was too hot. We talked and played games. Then there was a dancing competition. A lot of the girls were good at dancing and Mark was good, too. He and Sally got a prize! We had a lot of fun!

19 Circle.

1 The party was at (school / Mark's house).
2 Harry met Mark (before / after) the party.
3 The party was on (Saturday / Sunday).
4 There was good (food / music) at the party but the room was too (hot / cold).
5 The children (talked / ate), played, and danced.
6 (Mark / Harry) and Sally got a prize.

20 Listen and write.

1 Who is talking? Sally
2 What did she eat before the party? A hot dog.
3 Was she good at her favorite game? No, she wasn't. She was laughing.
4 What did they do in the car on the way home? They sang.

21 Imagine you are Mark. Talk about the party.

Harry was at my house before the party.

78 Lesson 7 Can talk about a party in the past

Lesson 7 SB page 78 or Poptropica English World

Learning Objective
Can talk about a party in the past

Additional Language
welcome party, dancing competition

Warm-up

- Ask the class, *Do you like going to parties? What do we do at parties? Do you like listening to music? What types of music to do you like? Do you like dancing? What types of dancing do you like?*, and elicit answers.

Open books and ask students to look at the activities. Ask, *What are we learning today?* Write the lesson objective on the board: *We're learning to talk about a party in the past.*

18 Read. Was yesterday fun for Harry?

- Ask students what type of text they think it is *(a blog)*. Point out the date at the top.
- Give students time to read the text and answer the question. *(Yes, yesterday was fun for Harry.)*
- Play the audio and have students listen and follow.
- Play the audio again and have students repeat.
- Check students' understanding by inviting students to stand up and ask questions about the text to the student of their choice.

19 Circle.

- Give students time to complete the activity.
- Check answers as a class.
- Ask students to close their books. Invite confident students to ask and answer questions about the blog from memory. You can turn this into a team game if you like.

Sit in front of the class as Harry. Provide answers and students have to provide possible questions, e.g., you say, *Yes, there was.*, and students say, *Was there a dancing competition?*

20 Listen and write.

- Tell students to read the questions first. Play the audio and have students just listen.

Last night was my welcome party. Before the party I ate a hot dog with my parents. They also came to the party! I danced and got a prize! We played some games too. My favorite game was Musical Statues. You had to freeze like a statue when the music stopped. I wasn't good at Musical Statues because I was laughing so much. My new friend Meg got the prize for that game. She made it look easy! After the party, we sang in the car all the way home. I really like my new school!

- Ask students to be ready to write answers. Play the audio again.
- Have students switch their books with another student for marking. Ask them to read out their answers.

21 Imagine you are Mark. Talk about the party.

- Pair students and give them time to complete the activity.
- Have student check answers in new pairs.

Pop Quiz: Make statements as Harry, Sally or Mark. Students have to guess who you are, e.g., *I loved my party! (Sally) / Harry came to my house for pizza. (Mark) / Sally and Mark won prizes. (Harry)*. Have students take turns making statements.

Homework WB page 64

Lesson 8 SB page 79 or Poptropica English World

Learning Objectives
Can understand a text about the first Thanksgiving
Can write a mini-play

Additional Language
Thanksgiving, settlers, North America, Native Americans

Warm-up

- Talk about festivals that you know by showing some pictures of festivals (if possible ones students are unlikely to know), and having students guess the name of, and reason for, the festival.

22 What do you know?

- Open books and ask students to look at the activities. Ask, *What are we learning today?* Write the lesson objectives on the board: *We're learning about Thanksgiving, and we're learning to write a mini-play.*
- Close books. Ask students, *What do you know about Thanksgiving?*
- Refer to the learning adventure poster and say, *Great! You are moving along your learning adventure!*

23 B:48 Read. Then act out the mini-play in class.

- Play the audio and ask students to follow.
- Ask for volunteers to act in the mini-play.
- Ask the class to discuss and agree on how to set the stage, using classroom items and furniture as props.
- Have students act out the mini-play.
- Encourage students to give positive feedback.

Write on the board, *Why did the settlers arrive at the start of winter?* Ask students to discuss this question in small groups and present their ideas to the class. What do they feel is the most likely reason?

24 Circle T = True or F = False. Then correct the false sentences.

- Ask students to read the six statements chorally.
- Pair students and give them time to do the activity. Ask for volunteers to share the statements and the responses with the class.

25 Write a mini-play.

- Ask students what steps they will take to make sure they include all the necessary information. Remind students of the steps to success: Think, Plan, Write and Share.
  Think If they need some help, suggest activities.
  Plan Ask students to make some notes about their mini-play.
  Write Give students time to write their mini-play. Remind them to check their work afterwards.
  Share Have students perform their play.

You may also wish to give students feedback on their projects.

Ask students, *What do you know about Thanksgiving now?* Give students a minute to tell their partner the new ideas and words they can remember. Ask students, *Where are you on your learning adventure?* Tell students, *Good job!* to reinforce the progress they are making.

Pop Quiz: Ask pairs to briefly present their mini-play to the class, saying what celebration it's about, and what characters it involves.

Materials
Poster, pictures of festivals (cut from magazines)

Homework WB page 65

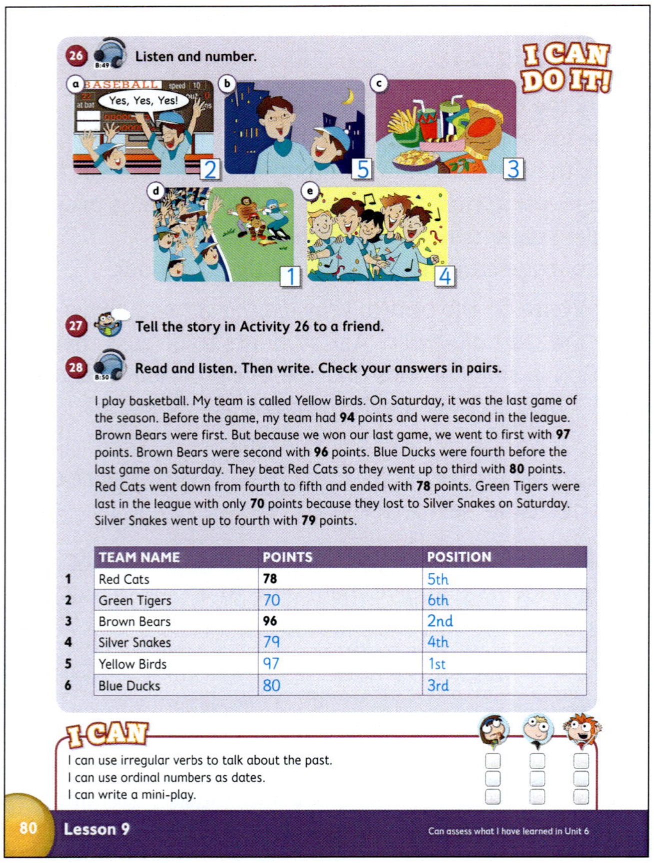

26 Listen and number.

a 2 b 5 c 3 d 1 e 4

27 Tell the story in Activity 26 to a friend.

28 Read and listen. Then write. Check your answers in pairs.

I play basketball. My team is called Yellow Birds. On Saturday, it was the last game of the season. Before the game, my team had **94** points and were second in the league. Brown Bears were first. But because we won our last game, we went to first with **97** points. Brown Bears were second with **96** points. Blue Ducks were fourth before the last game on Saturday. They beat Red Cats so they went up to third with **80** points. Red Cats went down from fourth to fifth and ended with **78** points. Green Tigers were last in the league with only **70** points because they lost to Silver Snakes on Saturday. Silver Snakes went up to fourth with **79** points.

	TEAM NAME	POINTS	POSITION
1	Red Cats	**78**	5th
2	Green Tigers	70	6th
3	Brown Bears	**96**	2nd
4	Silver Snakes	79	4th
5	Yellow Birds	97	1st
6	Blue Ducks	80	3rd

I CAN

I can use irregular verbs to talk about the past.
I can use ordinal numbers as dates.
I can write a mini-play.

80 Lesson 9 Can assess what I have learned in Unit 6

Lesson 9 SB page 80 or Poptropica English World

Learning Objective
Can assess what I have learned in Unit 6

Warm-up

- Place Picture Cards 95–127 around the room. Invite students to take one verb and one number, come to the front of the class, and say something in any way they like, e.g., *On August third, I got a lot of presents, it was my birthday.* Repeat until all students have a turn.

Open books and ask students to look at the activities. Write this lesson objective on the board: *We're thinking about our learning adventure.*

- Ask students what they have been learning in the unit. Put their ideas on the board, e.g., *ordinal numbers.*
- For each idea, ask students to tell their partner where they think they are on their learning adventure. Reassure students who are less confident that they will have opportunities for more practice.

26 Listen and number.

- Have students listen to the audio and write the correct number in the box next to the item that is being spoken about. Allow them time to complete the activity.

> **1** On Saturday, I went to watch the last game of the season for my favorite baseball team. There were lots of people there.
> **2** My team won! My dad said, "Yes, yes, yes!" We were very happy.
> **3** Our friends brought a lot of food and drinks.
> **4** We sang and danced.
> **5** We went home at ten o'clock. It was a great night.

- Have students switch their books with a partner. Play the audio again for students to check their answers.

27 Tell the story in Activity 26 to a friend.

- In pairs, have students tell the story to each other. Remind students to use the past tense verbs they have learned in the unit. Remind students of the verb list on Student Book pages 116–119 if they need to check any verbs in the past tense.

28 Read and listen. Then write. Check your answers in pairs.

- Play the audio and have students follow.
- Draw students' attention to the chart below the text. Give students time to fill in the blanks.
- To check answers, ask students to ask and answer questions about the information in the chart. Students can correct their own work.

Ask students how they feel about their learning in this unit. Ask students to tell you what they found easy and what they found the most difficult to learn in the unit.

- Read the three *I can* statements with students and invite students to check the boxes according to how confident they feel about the language point.
- Ask students, *Where are you on your learning adventure?* Students indicate where they think they are on the learning adventure poster. Tell students, *Good job!* to reinforce the progress they are making.

Pop Quiz: In groups of four, students tell the others the answers to the following questions: *Which is your favorite activity in the unit? Why? Which activity don't you like? Why? What is your favorite new word? Which word is the most difficult for you?*

Materials
Poster, Picture Cards 95–127

Homework WB page 66

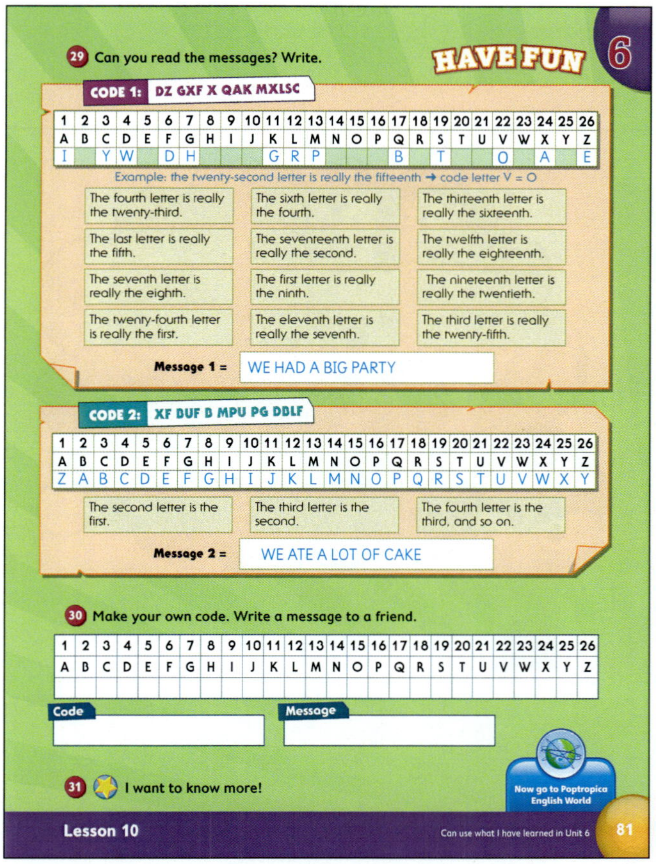

29 Can you read the messages? Write.

HAVE FUN 6

CODE 1: DZ GXF X QAK MXLSC

1	2	3	4	5	6	7	8	9	10	11	12	13	14	15	16	17	18	19	20	21	22	23	24	25	26
A	B	C	D	E	F	G	H	I	J	K	L	M	N	O	P	Q	R	S	T	U	V	W	X	Y	Z
I		Y	W		D	H				G	R	P				B		T			O		A		E

Example: the twenty-second letter is really the fifteenth → code letter V = O

The fourth letter is really the twenty-third.	The sixth letter is really the fourth.	The thirteenth letter is really the sixteenth.
The last letter is really the fifth.	The seventeenth letter is really the second.	The twelfth letter is really the eighteenth.
The seventh letter is really the eighth.	The first letter is really the ninth.	The nineteenth letter is really the twentieth.
The twenty-fourth letter is really the first.	The eleventh letter is really the seventh.	The third letter is really the twenty-fifth.

Message 1 = WE HAD A BIG PARTY

CODE 2: XF DUF D MPU PG DDLF

1	2	3	4	5	6	7	8	9	10	11	12	13	14	15	16	17	18	19	20	21	22	23	24	25	26
A	B	C	D	E	F	G	H	I	J	K	L	M	N	O	P	Q	R	S	T	U	V	W	X	Y	Z
Z	A	B	C	D	E	F	G	H	I	J	K	L	M	N	O	P	Q	R	S	T	U	V	W	X	Y

The second letter is the first.	The third letter is the second.	The fourth letter is the third, and so on.

Message 2 = WE ATE A LOT OF CAKE

30 Make your own code. Write a message to a friend.

1	2	3	4	5	6	7	8	9	10	11	12	13	14	15	16	17	18	19	20	21	22	23	24	25	26
A	B	C	D	E	F	G	H	I	J	K	L	M	N	O	P	Q	R	S	T	U	V	W	X	Y	Z

Code

Message

31 I want to know more!

Now go to Poptropica English World

Lesson 10 Can use what I have learned in Unit 6 81

Lesson 10 SB page 81 or Poptropica English World

Learning Objective
Can use what I have learned in Unit 6

Warm-up

- Review ordinal numbers with Picture Cards 105–127. Make sure the Cards are not in order, then show the number and have the students say the word.

Open books and ask students to look at the pictures. Ask, *What are we learning today?* Write the lesson objective on the board: *We're doing a puzzle to review Unit 6 language.*

Ask students to work in pairs to make sentences/questions with target language, based on different celebrations around the world. Tell students to choose three different celebrations, and to write about which countries celebrate them, when they occur (date/time of year), how people celebrate them, and the stories behind them, e.g., *Halloween is on October 31st in the U.S.A. Children wear scary clothes to look like ghosts or witches. They eat lots of candy and chocolate! Halloween was for scaring away bad spirits.* Give pairs a few minutes then ask them to share their sentences with the class.

29 Can you read the messages? Write.

- Direct students' attention to the puzzle. Give students time to do the activity and find the hidden message. To check students' work, pair students and have them go over their work, and agree on the message.
- Tell students to find a new partner. Direct students' attention to the second puzzle. Give students time to do the activity and find the hidden message. To check students' work, invite students to call out the message.

Write on the board, *Big parties with lots of people are better than small parties.* Divide the class into small groups, and ask them to discuss the statement and take notes on why they agree with it or disagree with it. Ask the groups to present their reasons to the class. Write the reasons on the board under *Agree* or *Disagree*. Take a class vote.

30 Make your own code. Write a message to a friend.

- Direct students' attention to the activity. Pair students and give them time to do the activity.

31 I want to know more!

- Ask students to choose anything they enjoyed from the unit and to go and find out more. You might like to set this activity as homework with a quick feedback session at the beginning of the next class.
- You can also suggest that students write one or two questions about what they want to know, then switch question(s) with a partner. Students then find answer(s) to their partner's question(s) as a homework activity, with feedback the next lesson.

Are you ready for Unit 7?

- Ask students if they are ready to move onto the next unit. Tell students that it is fine if they do not remember everything as they will continue to practice throughout the level.
- Encourage students to ask if they have any questions about what they learned in Unit 6.

You may wish to give Unit 6 Test (see page 198) at this time.

Materials
Picture Cards 105–127

Homework WB page 67

Unit 6 Story Cards

Review Units 5 and 6

SB pages 82–83 or Poptropica English World

Learning Objectives
Can talk about shopping and belongings
Can talk about events in the past

Warm-up

- Review clothing and accessories, using Picture Cards 78–94. If you want to practice spelling, use the word-side of the Cards. Hold a spelling bee if you have time.

Open books and ask students to look at the pages. Ask, *What are we learning today?* Write the lesson objective on the board: *We're reviewing language from Units 5 and 6.*

Direct students to pages 60–63 if they should like to refresh their memories on the vocabulary and grammar structures needed for Activities 1–3. To challenge students further, ask them to think of presents for each of the story characters (Mike, Polly, etc.) and to tell a partner how much the items cost.

- Activities 4–6 are based on vocabulary and grammar structures from pages 72–75. To challenge students further, ask them to make a birthday calendar for the class, writing everyone's birthdays on the board under the months of the year, then saying, *Amy's birthday is on March twenty-seventh.*, etc.

1 Choose a present. Write the letter. Then ask and answer.

- Have students read the speech bubbles chorally.
- Ask, *What's this? What are these?* for items **a** to **e**. Elicit responses.
- Allow students time to choose, and then write the letters in in the boxes.
- Check answers as a class. Encourage students to use complete sentences, e.g., *Number one. Let's choose sunglasses for Dan's grandparents.*

2 Order the sentences in the dialog. Then listen and check.

B:51

- Allow students time to read the questions and answers and then to number the boxes in order.
- Play the audio. Tell students to follow along, and check their answers. If your class needs support, ask them to repeat each sentence chorally, too.

Review Units 5 and 6

1 Choose a present. Write the letter. Then ask and answer.

Whose scarf is this? It's Uncle Andy's.

1 My grandparents often go to hot places. d
2 My baby cousin, Ollie, likes animals. b
3 Aunt Caroline loves baggy clothes. e
4 My parents like sports and they love swimming. c
5 Uncle Andy often goes to cold places. He likes skiing. a

a $___ b $___ c $___ d $___ e $___

2 Order the sentences in the dialog. Then listen and check.

a	**Salesperson:**	Yes, of course. Eighteen dollars and fifty cents, please.	4
b	**Salesperson:**	They're eighteen dollars and fifty cents.	2
c	**Dan:**	May I buy the pants, please?	3
d	**Dan:**	How much are those baggy pants?	1

3 Write prices for the items in Activity 1. Then role-play using the dialog in Activity 2.

82 Review Units 5 and 6 — Can talk about shopping and belongings

Dan: How much are those baggy pants?
Salesperson: They're eighteen dollars and fifty cents.
Dan: May I buy the pants, please?
Salesperson: Yes, of course. Eighteen dollars and fifty cents, please.

3 Write prices for the items in Activity 1. Then role-play using the dialog in Activity 2.

- Allow students time to write the prices in the blanks in Activity 1. To begin with, ask students for suggested prices.
- Pair students and have them complete the activity. Invite confident students to role-play for the class.

Materials
Picture Cards 78–94

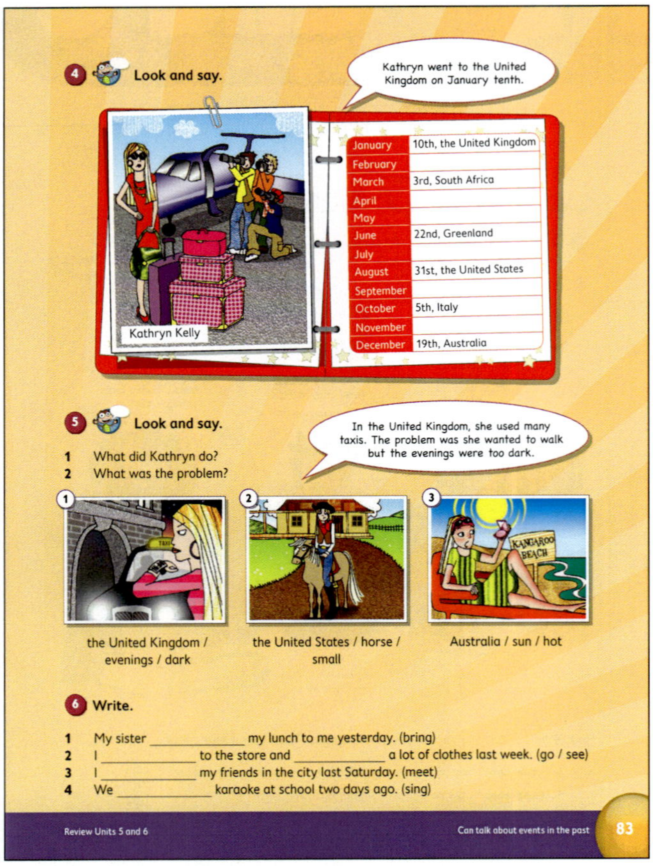
4 Look and say.

January	10th, the United Kingdom
February	
March	3rd, South Africa
April	
May	
June	22nd, Greenland
July	
August	31st, the United States
September	
October	5th, Italy
November	
December	19th, Australia

5 Look and say.

1 What did Kathryn do?
2 What was the problem?

1 the United Kingdom / evenings / dark
2 the United States / horse / small
3 Australia / sun / hot

6 Write.

1 My sister ____________ my lunch to me yesterday. (bring)
2 I ____________ to the store and ____________ a lot of clothes last week. (go / see)
3 I ____________ my friends in the city last Saturday. (meet)
4 We ____________ karaoke at school two days ago. (sing)

Review Units 5 and 6 Can talk about events in the past 83

4 Look and say.

- Ask individual students to describe the picture. This is a good opportunity to recycle language, e.g., ask, *What's Kathryn wearing? (She's wearing a red dress and red shoes.)*
- Ask a confident student to read the example speech bubble. Ask, *Is she in the United Kingdom now?*
- Put students in pairs and have them complete the activity.

5 Look and say.

- Ask about the pictures, e.g., *Picture 1. Is it light? (No, it isn't. It's dark.) What time is it? (It's four o'clock in the afternoon.)*
- Ask a volunteer to read out the example speech bubble.
- Allow students time to complete the activity.
- Invite volunteers to share their answers with the class.

6 Write.

- Allow students time to complete the activity.
- Invite volunteers to share their answers with the class, or have the class read the sentences chorally.
- To end the lesson, ask students what their favorite dates are and why.

- Watch the video story *Get the machine!* on Poptropica English World. Ask students what happened in the story. Watch again, stopping at key points, and ask them about the language, the images, or the story. Ask the students to role-play the story. Assign the roles of two of the characters to confident speakers and let other students play the other parts. Encourage them to say as much of the dialog as they can and prompt them where necessary.

Pop Quiz: Students imagine different countries or places they went to on a round-the-world tour. They write one sentence about each country, using *too* and an adjective, e.g., *I went to London. It was too big. I went to Africa. It was too hot.* They tell a friend or share their answers with the class.

You may wish to give Review Test 3 (see page 212) at this time.

7 School

Unit Overview

Unit Objective

- I can talk about school and school subjects

Language

Target Vocabulary	Adjectives: interesting, boring, exciting, scary, funny, difficult, easy, romantic, relaxing School subjects: computer science, math, geography, science, history, art, music, P.E.
Target Structures	Was it interesting? Yes, it was. / No, it wasn't. Was there an alien in it? Yes, there was. / No, there wasn't. Were there any exciting stories? Yes, there were. / No, there weren't. Did you have computer science on Tuesday? Yes, I did. / No, I didn't. Was P.E. relaxing? Yes, it was. / No, it wasn't. It was difficult.
Features	**Cross-curricular:** Social science: Life experiences **Values:** Learn about your older family members' youth.

Skills

Reading	• Can understand a simple story • Can understand details of a story
Writing	• Can complete simple sentences using adjectives to describe experiences in the past *(Workbook)* • Can write simple sentences describing activities or experiences *(Workbook)*
Listening	• Can identify school subjects • Can understand a simple story
Speaking	• Can use adjectives to describe experiences • Can ask and answer using *Was it…, Was there…,* and *Were there…?* • Can describe school subjects • Can ask and answer about a school schedule • Can discuss a story • Can talk about my older family members' youth • Can talk about school trips • Can talk about a star's childhood • Can talk about my grandparents' school life

Lesson 1 SB page 84 or Poptropica English World

Learning Objective
Can use adjectives to describe experiences

Target Language
interesting, boring, exciting, scary, funny, difficult, easy, romantic, relaxing

1 What do you know?

- Open books and ask students to look at the pictures. Ask, *What are we learning today?* Write the lesson objective on the board: *We're learning to use adjectives to talk about experiences.*
- Close books. Ask students what words they know in English for describing things (adjectives), e.g., *big/small, fat/thin.* Write them on the board.
- Refer to the learning adventure poster and say, *Great! You are already moving along your learning adventure!*

2 B:52 Listen and read. Why are Emma and Robbie scared?

- Ask, *What do you think Emma and Robbie are talking about? Who is on the bus with them? What does he have?*
- Ask students to look at the scenes in their books and listen as you play the audio. Ask, *Why are Emma and Robbie scared?*, and elicit answers.
- Have the class read the story chorally.
- Ask comprehension questions: *What happened at school today?* (*a story writing competition*) *Who was the winner?* (*Dan*) *What was his story about?* (*a green hand*)

3 B:53 Listen and say.

- Focus students on the pictures. Play the audio and have students repeat.
- Put Picture Cards 128–136 on the board for students to refer to. Number them. Pair students and have them play a game. One student in each pair says a number. His/her partner has to say the item, and mime the feelings/emotions related to the adjective.

4 Talk about these things. Use words from Activity 3.

- Read the words in the word box chorally. Then ask a confident student to read the example in the speech bubble.
- Pair students and give them time to do the activity. Tell them to use the target language, combining the phrases with the adjectives in Activity 3.

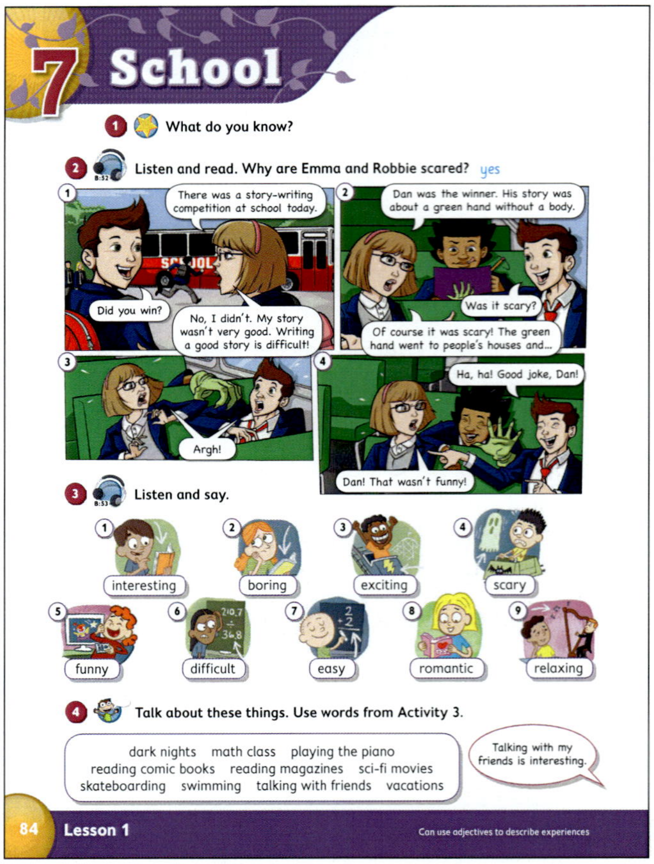

Ask students, *How many adjectives do you know now?* Give students a minute to tell their partner the new words they know.

- Ask students to say where they are on their adventure now. Ask students which words they find easiest or most difficult to remember. Tell students, *Good job!* to reinforce the progress they are making.

Pop Quiz: Write a word on the board and circle it. Then ask students to call out adjectives to describe it. Write each adjective around the circled word, e.g., *math (difficult/easy), Shrek (funny), Frozen (romantic/exciting/boring), sailing (exciting/difficult).*

Materials
Poster, Picture Cards 128–136

Homework WB page 68

LOOK!

Was it interesting?	Yes, it was. / No, it wasn't.
Was there an alien in it?	Yes, there was. / No, there wasn't.
Were there any exciting stories?	Yes, there were. / No, there weren't.

5 Listen and ✓ or ✗.

	1	2	3
exciting?	✓	✗	✓
scary?	✓	✗	✗
funny?	✗	✓	✗
children?	✓	✓	✗
an alien?	✗	✓	✗

6 Look at Activity 5. Ask and answer.

7 Look at Activity 5. Play the guessing game.

A: Was it exciting?
B: Yes, it was.
A: Were there any children in it?
B: Yes, there were.
A: It was *Island Adventure*!

Lesson 2 Can ask and answer using *Was it…*, *Was there…*, and *Were there…?* 85

Lesson 2 SB page 85 or Poptropica English World

Learning Objective
Can ask and answer using *Was it…*, *Was there…*, and *Were there…?*

Warm-up

- Write the adjectives on the board jumbled up. See who can unscramble them first. Then have an adjective spelling bee, using Picture Cards 128–136.

Open books and ask students to look at the activities and the Look! box. Ask, *What are we learning today?* Write the lesson objective on the board: *We're learning to use adjectives to ask and answer about the past.*

5 Listen and ✓ or ✗.

- Draw students' attention to the Look! box and play the audio (track B:54). Students repeat chorally.
- Play the audio and have students follow.

> 1 *Island Adventure* was exciting and sometimes scary, too. I don't think it was funny. There were some children in it, but there wasn't an alien.
> 2 *Mike Goes To Mars* wasn't exciting or scary, but it was funny. There were children in it, and there was an alien, too.
> 3 *Nile Princess* was exciting, but it wasn't scary or funny. There weren't any children in it, and there wasn't an alien.

- Play the audio again, giving students time to write answers in the blanks.
- To check answers, students switch books, and you elicit answers from the class.

6 Look at Activity 5. Ask and answer.

- Draw students' attention to the items in Activity 5. Put students into pairs and give them time to do the activity, using the target language.

7 Look at Activity 5. Play the guessing game.

- Pair students and allow them time to do the activity, using the target language.

Pop Quiz: Ask students to call out movies they have seen recently. Write the titles on the board. Try to pair students who have seen different movies. Have them ask and answer questions about the movies, e.g., *Was The Croods romantic? (Yes, it was.) Were there any animals in it? (Yes, there were. There were dinosaurs.)* Ask students to share their dialogs with the class.

- Direct students' attention to the backpack card on page 85. Tell students to go online to the Poptropica English Island Adventure Game and find the item. Once students click on it, they are taken to a supplementary language task.

Materials
Picture Cards 128–136

Homework WB page 69

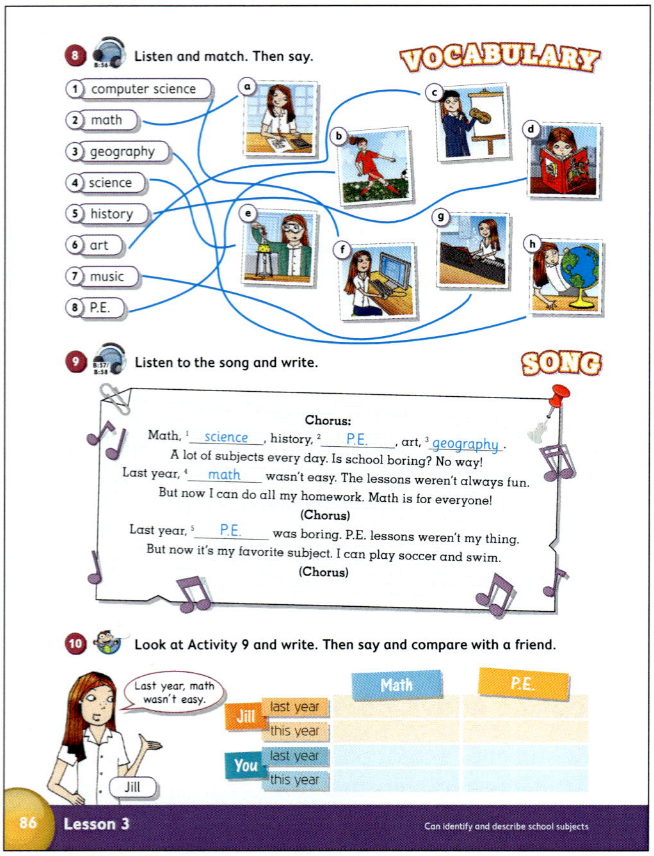
8 Listen and match. Then say.

VOCABULARY

1 computer science
2 math
3 geography
4 science
5 history
6 art
7 music
8 P.E.

9 Listen to the song and write.

SONG

Chorus:
Math, 1 science, history, 2 P.E., art, 3 geography.
A lot of subjects every day. Is school boring? No way!
Last year, 4 math wasn't easy. The lessons weren't always fun.
But now I can do all my homework. Math is for everyone!
(Chorus)
Last year, 5 P.E. was boring. P.E. lessons weren't my thing.
But now it's my favorite subject. I can play soccer and swim.
(Chorus)

10 Look at Activity 9 and write. Then say and compare with a friend.

Last year, math wasn't easy.

		Math	P.E.
Jill	last year		
	this year		
You	last year		
	this year		

Jill

86 Lesson 3 Can identify and describe school subjects

Lesson 3 SB page 86 or Poptropica English World

Learning Objective
Can identify and describe school subjects

Target Language
computer science, math, geography, science, history, art, music, P.E.

Warm-up

- Show students some school realia related to school subjects (e.g., compass, map, flute, paintbrush) and place them on the desk. Tell students these all represent school subjects, and ask them if they know the names for any of them.

Open books and ask students to look at the pictures. Ask, *What are we learning today?* Write the lesson objective on the board: *We're learning school subjects.*

- Close books. Ask students what English words they know for school subjects, e.g., *math*, *music*. Write on board.
- Refer to the learning adventure poster and say, *Great! You are moving along your learning adventure!*

8 Listen and match. Then say.

B:56

- Hold up Picture Cards 137–144 one by one, then turn them to the word-side and ask the students to repeat. Then ask students to look in their books and look at the words and pictures.
- Play the audio and ask students to match the words to the pictures.
- Play the audio again and have students repeat.

9 Listen to the song and write.

B:57 B:58

- Draw students' attention to Activity 9. Play the song audio and have students listen.
- Play the audio again and ask students to write the correct word in the spaces. Have students check their answers with partners.
- Play the karaoke version and have students sing the song if they feel confident enough.

10 Look at Activity 9 and write. Then say and compare with a friend.

- Draw students' attention to the chart. Have students say Jill's statement chorally.
- Allow time for students to complete the activity by writing *was (adjective) / wasn't (adjective)*.
- Pair students and have them practice asking and answering questions, and making statements, according to the information in the chart. Ask confident students to give statements to the class.

Ask students, *How many words for school subjects do you know now?* Give students a minute to tell their partner the new words they know.

- Ask students to say where they are on their adventure now. Ask students which words they find easiest or most difficult to remember. Tell students, *Good job!* to reinforce the progress they are making.

Pop Quiz: Play a guessing game with students. You think of a school subject and students need to ask you questions. You only answer, *yes* or *no*, therefore students have to think carefully about their questions.

Materials
Poster, Picture Cards 137–144, school realia

Homework WB page 70

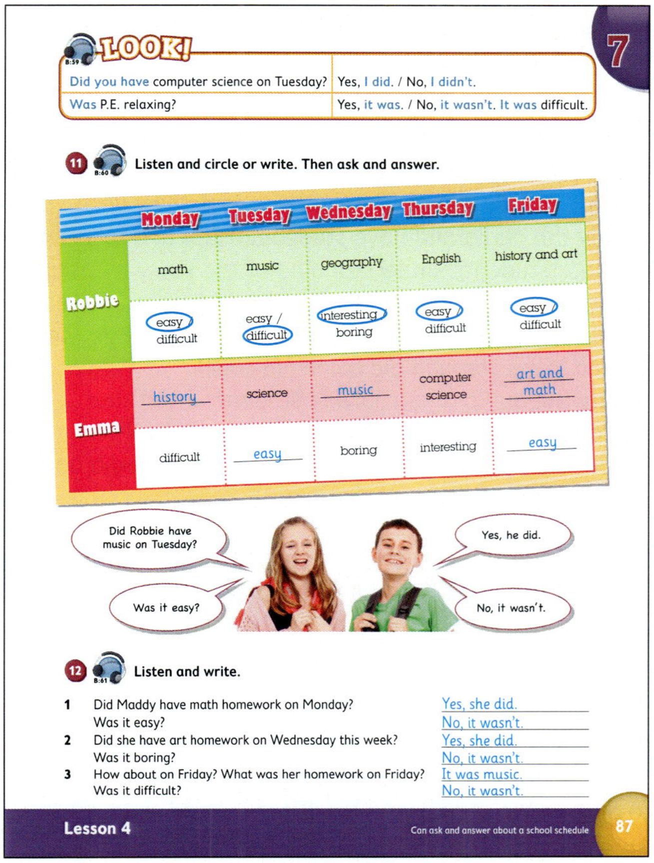

LOOK!

Did you have computer science on Tuesday?	Yes, I did. / No, I didn't.
Was P.E. relaxing?	Yes, it was. / No, it wasn't. It was difficult.

11 Listen and circle or write. Then ask and answer.

	Monday	Tuesday	Wednesday	Thursday	Friday
Robbie	math	music	geography	English	history and art
	easy / difficult	easy / difficult	interesting / boring	easy / difficult	easy / difficult
Emma	history	science	music	computer science	art and math
	difficult	easy	boring	interesting	easy

12 Listen and write.

1 Did Maddy have math homework on Monday? Yes, she did.
Was it easy? No, it wasn't.
2 Did she have art homework on Wednesday this week? Yes, she did.
Was it boring? No, it wasn't.
3 How about on Friday? What was her homework on Friday? It was music.
Was it difficult? No, it wasn't.

Lesson 4 Can ask and answer about a school schedule 87

Lesson 4 SB page 87 or Poptropica English World

Learning Objective
Can ask and answer about a school schedule

Warm-up

- Review school subjects using Picture Cards 137–144, and having the class guess as you show the picture. Then turn the cards to the word side, and repeat.

Open books and ask students to look at the activities and the Look! box. Ask, *What are we learning today?* Write the lesson objective on the board: *We're learning to talk about school schedules.*

11 B:60 Listen and circle or write. Then ask and answer.

- Have students listen to the Look! box audio (track B:59) and repeat chorally.
- Give students time to look at the two schedules, explaining that for Robbie's, the students listen and circle the correct adjective, and for Emma's they fill in the blanks. Play the audio.

Boy: On Monday, Robbie's homework was math, and on Tuesday it was music. Math was easy, but music was difficult.
On Wednesday, his homework was geography. Robbie likes geography, so the homework was interesting.
Thursday and Friday's homework was easy. His homework on Thursday was English, and on Friday it was history and art.
Girl: On Monday, Emma's homework was history. It was difficult for her.
On Tuesday, her science homework was easy, but music on Wednesday was boring. Emma likes computers, so her computer science homework on Thursday was interesting.
On Friday, her homework was art and math. Both of these were easy.

- Have students switch books for checking. Play the audio again, and have students say answers at the appropriate time.
- Pair students and have them ask and answer questions.

12 B:61 Listen and write.

- Draw students' attention to the activity. Play the audio.

1 On Monday, Maddy's homework was a lot. Her English homework was easy, but her math homework was very difficult.
2 Sometimes science is her homework on Wednesday, but this week she didn't have any. Her homework was drawing her friend's face for art. It was fun.
3 Friday was music homework. It wasn't difficult and it was interesting.

- Give students time to do the activity. Invite confident students to offer answers for checking.

Pop Quiz: Pair students and ask them to talk about their schedules. Invite pairs to come forward and talk about their partner's schedule to the class. Later, quiz the students about other people's schedules.

Materials
Picture Cards 137–144

Homework WB page 71

Lesson 5 SB page 88 or Poptropica English World

Learning Objectives
Can understand a simple story
Can discuss a story

Additional Language
tunnel

Functional Language
Cool! How strange! Great job, kids! Awesome! Quiet now.

Warm-up

- Write the following words on pieces of card then stick them on the board all in a row, *Police Chief, polar bear, skidoo, diamond necklace, red ribbon, lake, breakfast, ice cream, newspaper, explorers.* Ask students to order the words, to reflect the story so far. Have them do this in their notebooks. Then, work as a class and get students to come to the front one by one to move a word left or right, and explain why.

Open books and ask students to look at the story. Ask, *What are we learning today?* Write the lesson objective on the board: *We're reading and discussing a story.*

13 B:62 Talk about the pictures. Then listen and read.

- Direct students' attention to the pictures, and ask questions about the characters and the scenes: *Who can you see in Picture 2? (Mike, Polly, Police Chief, Gizmo) What is Polly doing? (She is picking something up.)*
- Play the audio and have students listen and follow.
- Check students' understanding of the story by asking questions and pointing to the pictures: *Who showed the children the tunnel? (the Police Chief) What do they need to get through the tunnel? (a code)*
- Play the audio again. Divide students into three groups and assign each group a role (Polly, Mike, Police Chief). Groups read along with the audio and mime their character's actions.

14 Who dropped the piece of paper Polly picked up? Discuss your answers.

- Have students discuss the question in groups and then invite one person to write their group's answer on the board. Discuss all the different ideas.

Write this question on the board, *Are codes important in the world today?* Give students time to discuss the question in small groups and then share their views with the class. Write their reasons on the board under two headings: *Yes, they are.* and *No, they aren't.*

Pop Quiz: Draw students' attention to the story. Ask them to describe what they see in each frame, using target adjectives, e.g., *In picture 1 there is a tunnel in the caves. It's exciting!*

Materials
Pieces of card

Homework WB page 72

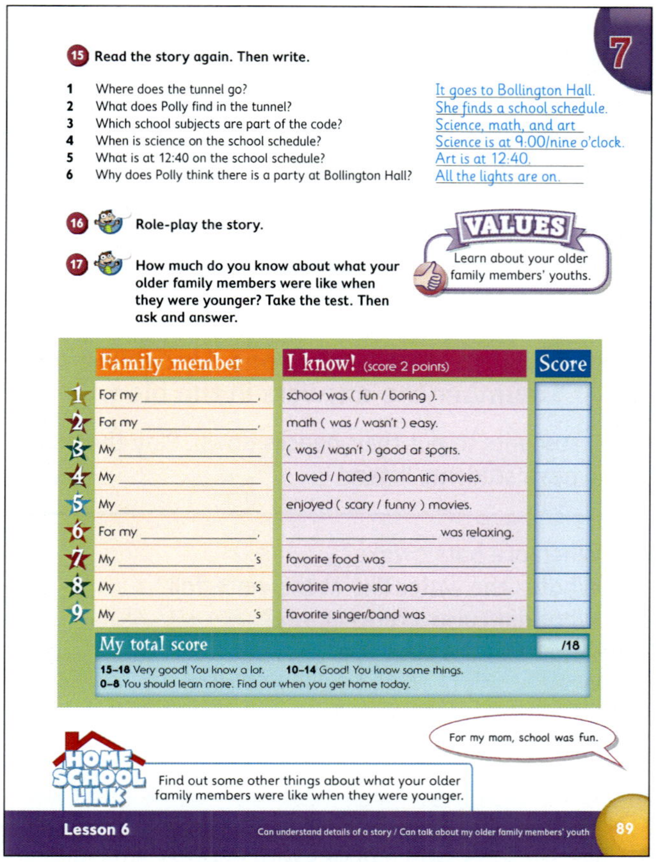

7

15 Read the story again. Then write.

1 Where does the tunnel go? It goes to Bollington Hall.
2 What does Polly find in the tunnel? She finds a school schedule.
3 Which school subjects are part of the code? Science, math, and art
4 When is science on the school schedule? Science is at 9:00/nine o'clock.
5 What is at 12:40 on the school schedule? Art is at 12:40.
6 Why does Polly think there is a party at Bollington Hall? All the lights are on.

16 Role-play the story.

17 How much do you know about what your older family members were like when they were younger? Take the test. Then ask and answer.

VALUES
Learn about your older family members' youths.

	Family member	I know! (score 2 points)	Score
1	For my ________,	school was (fun / boring).	
2	For my ________,	math (was / wasn't) easy.	
3	My ________	(was / wasn't) good at sports.	
4	My ________	(loved / hated) romantic movies.	
5	My ________	enjoyed (scary / funny) movies.	
6	For my ________,	________ was relaxing.	
7	My ________'s	favorite food was ________.	
8	My ________'s	favorite movie star was ________.	
9	My ________'s	favorite singer/band was ________.	
	My total score		/18

15–18 Very good! You know a lot. **10–14** Good! You know some things.
0–8 You should learn more. Find out when you get home today.

HOME SCHOOL LINK Find out some other things about what your older family members were like when they were younger.

For my mom, school was fun.

Lesson 6 Can understand details of a story / Can talk about my older family members' youth 89

Lesson 6 SB page 89 or Poptropica English World

Learning Objectives
Can understand details of a story
Can talk about my older family members' youth

Value
Learn about your older family members' youth.

Open books and ask students to look at the activities. Ask, *What are we learning today?* Write the lesson objectives on the board: *We're reviewing the story, and we're learning about older family members' youth.*

Warm-up

- Show pictures and tell the class about your grandmother or grandfather. Draw pictures on the board as you talk, to help comprehension. Invite students to talk about the youth of their family members, if they can.

15 Read the story again. Then write.

- Give students time to look at the story, and play the audio again.
- Give students time to do the activity.
- Check answers by having students pass their book to another student. Elicit answers from the class.

16 Role-play the story.

- See the "How to use stories" section on page 23 for more ideas on how to build your students' confidence with role-plays.
- Divide students into groups of three. Give each group a set of cut-out Story Cards (see page 130), and have students place them in order.
- Play the audio again (track B:62), and have students follow along. Put the class into groups to role-play the story.
- Give groups time to practice the role-play, then ask them to show the class.

You might like to give students feedback on their role-play.

17 How much do you know about what your older family members were like when they were younger? Take the test. Then ask and answer.

- Read the value, *Learn about your older family members' youth.*
- Draw students' attention to the test in Activity 17. Pair students and give them time to do the activity. Discuss in class.
- Check students' scores by saying the point range and having students raise their hands.
- Invite volunteers to stand and talk about family members.

- **Home-School link:** Read the instruction with the class: *Find out some other things about what your older family members were like when they were younger.* Ask students to do this at home.

Pop Quiz: Draw your family tree on the board, including your grandparents, your parents and their siblings, and your own siblings. Give each student a sheet of paper and ask them to draw their own family trees. Ask them to circle the person they interviewed for Activity 17. Have some students present their family tree to the class.

Materials
Unit 7 cut-out Story Cards, pictures of your grandmother/grandfather/older family members, sheet of paper for each student

Homework WB page 73

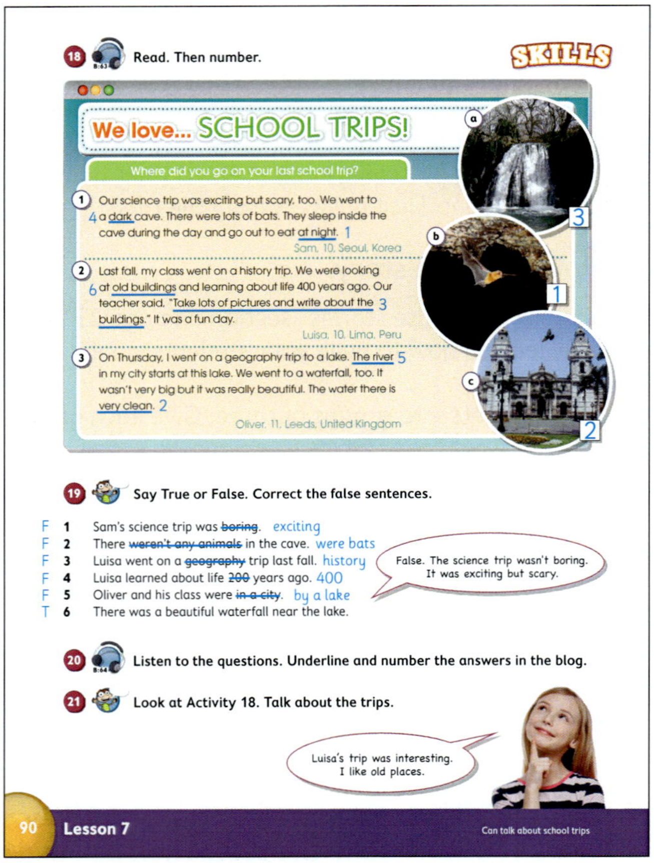
18 Read. Then number.

SKILLS

We love... SCHOOL TRIPS!

Where did you go on your last school trip?

1 Our science trip was exciting but scary, too. We went to 4 a dark cave. There were lots of bats. They sleep inside the cave during the day and go out to eat at night. 1

Sam, 10, Seoul, Korea

2 Last fall, my class went on a history trip. We were looking 6 at old buildings and learning about life 400 years ago. Our teacher said, "Take lots of pictures and write about the 3 buildings." It was a fun day.

Luisa, 10, Lima, Peru

3 On Thursday, I went on a geography trip to a lake. The river 5 in my city starts at this lake. We went to a waterfall, too. It wasn't very big but it was really beautiful. The water there is very clean. 2

Oliver, 11, Leeds, United Kingdom

a 3 b 1 c 2

19 Say True or False. Correct the false sentences.

F 1 Sam's science trip was ~~boring~~. exciting
F 2 There ~~weren't any animals~~ in the cave. were bats
F 3 Luisa went on a ~~geography~~ trip last fall. history
F 4 Luisa learned about life ~~200~~ years ago. 400
F 5 Oliver and his class were ~~in a city~~. by a lake
T 6 There was a beautiful waterfall near the lake.

False. The science trip wasn't boring. It was exciting but scary.

20 Listen to the questions. Underline and number the answers in the blog.

21 Look at Activity 18. Talk about the trips.

Luisa's trip was interesting. I like old places.

90 Lesson 7 Can talk about school trips

Lesson 7 SB page 90 or Poptropica English World

Learning Objective
Can talk about school trips

Additional Language
school trips, cave, bats, Seoul, Lima, Peru, waterfall, Leeds

Warm-up

- Ask the class, *Have you ever been on a school trip? Where did you go? Did you like it? Was it (exciting)?*, and elicit answers.

Open books and ask students to look at the activities. Ask, *What are we learning today?* Write the lesson objective on the board: *We're learning to find information from a website.*

18 Read. Then number.

B:63

- Ask, *What can you see in the pictures?* Review *bats, cave,* and *waterfall.*
- Give students time to read the text.
- Play the audio. Students listen and follow.
- Play the audio again and give students time to write the correct numbers in the boxes.

19 Say True or False. Correct the false sentences.

- Say the first statement then ask a student to model the text in the speech bubble.
- Pair students and allow them time to complete the activity.
- Ask students to close their books. Invite confident students to ask and answer questions from memory. You can turn this into a team game if you like.

20 Listen to the questions. Underline and number the answers in the blog.

B:64

- Tell students to put their pencils down. Play the audio and have students listen.

1 When are bats awake?
2 What is the water like at the waterfall?
3 What did Luisa's teacher say?
4 What was the cave like?
5 What starts at the lake Oliver visited?
6 What did Luisa look at?

- Play the audio again and have students complete the activity.
- Have students switch books with another student to check answers. Ask students to read out their answers.

Write the following pairs of words plus adjective on the board: *town/country (safe), old buildings/ new buildings (beautiful)*. Divide the class into four groups. Two groups argue that the first word in each pair is "right" (town/old buildings). The other two groups argue that the second word in each pair is "right" (country/new buildings).

- Give students some time to discuss their arguments, then have groups to present their arguments to the class. Remind them that there is no real correct answer.

21 Look at Activity 18. Talk about the trips.

- Have a confident student model the text in the speech bubble at the bottom of the page.
- Give students time to complete the activity. Invite students to talk in front of the whole class.

Pop Quiz: Prepare questions before class that Sam, Luisa and Oliver could ask on their school trips. Read out these questions to the class, and students have to guess who you are, e.g., *How old is that building? (Luisa) Is it cold in there? (Sam) What's that squeaking noise? (Sam) Can we drink this water? (Oliver).* Have students take turns asking questions.

Homework WB page 74

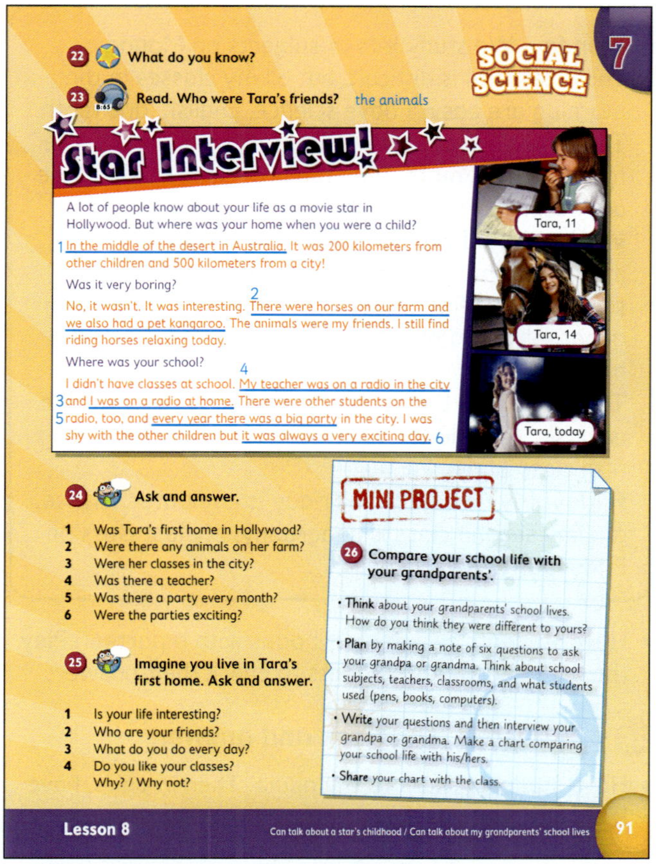
22 What do you know?

23 Read. Who were Tara's friends? the animals

SOCIAL SCIENCE 7

Star Interview!

A lot of people know about your life as a movie star in Hollywood. But where was your home when you were a child?

1 In the middle of the desert in Australia. It was 200 kilometers from other children and 500 kilometers from a city!

Was it very boring?

No, it wasn't. It was interesting. 2 There were horses on our farm and we also had a pet kangaroo. The animals were my friends. I still find riding horses relaxing today.

Where was your school?

I didn't have classes at school. 4 My teacher was on a radio in the city
3 and I was on a radio at home. There were other students on the
5 radio, too, and every year there was a big party in the city. I was shy with the other children but it was always a very exciting day. 6

Tara, 11

Tara, 14

Tara, today

24 Ask and answer.

1 Was Tara's first home in Hollywood?
2 Were there any animals on her farm?
3 Were her classes in the city?
4 Was there a teacher?
5 Was there a party every month?
6 Were the parties exciting?

25 Imagine you live in Tara's first home. Ask and answer.

1 Is your life interesting?
2 Who are your friends?
3 What do you do every day?
4 Do you like your classes? Why? / Why not?

MINI PROJECT

26 Compare your school life with your grandparents'.

- **Think** about your grandparents' school lives. How do you think they were different to yours?
- **Plan** by making a note of six questions to ask your grandpa or grandma. Think about school subjects, teachers, classrooms, and what students used (pens, books, computers).
- **Write** your questions and then interview your grandpa or grandma. Make a chart comparing your school life with his/hers.
- **Share** your chart with the class.

Lesson 8 Can talk about a star's childhood / Can talk about my grandparents' school lives 91

Lesson 8 SB page 91 or Poptropica English World

Learning Objectives
Can talk about a star's childhood
Can talk about my grandparents' school life

Additional Language
Hollywood, desert, kilometers, kangaroo, radio

Warm-up

- Ask a student to point at Australia on a map. Show students a map of Australia and invite students to find some desert areas. Then ask them to point at the United States, and ask them to find Hollywood. Ask, *What do people do in Hollywood? (make movies)*

22 What do you know?

- Open books and ask students to look at the activities. Ask, *What are we learning today?* Write the lesson objective on the board: *We're learning to compare different childhoods and school experiences.*
- Close books. Ask students, *Are all schools the same?* and elicit answers.
- Refer to the learning adventure poster and say, *Great! You are moving along your learning adventure!*

23 Read. Who were Tara's friends?

- Ask about the pictures, e.g., *How old was Tara in this picture? (She was eleven.)*
- Play the audio and have students read along.
- Play the audio again. Pause to check answers.

24 Ask and answer.

- Pair students and give them time to do the activity. Check answers as a class.

25 Imagine you live in Tara's first home. Ask and answer.

- Give students time to do the activity. Invite volunteers to give additional answers.

Write this statement on the board, *It is better to wear school uniforms at school.* Pair students and have them discuss and make notes of their arguments. Invite some pairs to share their views with the class.

26 Compare your school life with your grandparents'.

- Ask students what steps they will take to make sure they include all the necessary information. Remind students of the steps to success: Think, Plan, Write and Share.
  Think In pairs students think about questions to ask.
  Plan Give students time to make notes.
  Write Give students time to write their questions.
  Share Nominate students to share the information in class after they have conducted their interviews.

You may also wish to give students feedback on their projects.

Ask students, *What do you know about schools in the past now?* Give students a minute to tell their partner the new ideas and words they can remember. Ask students, *Where are you on your learning adventure?* Tell students, *Good job!* to reinforce the progress they are making!

Pop Quiz: Show the pictures of some of the following old-fashioned/obsolete/outdated/less common items before class: *a writing quill (feather) and ink, a typewriter, a gramophone, a horse and carriage, an old-fashioned telephone, an old-fashioned camera,* etc. Ask students what their modern equivalents are today.

Materials
Poster, map of the world, pictures of old-fashioned/obsolete/outdated/less common items (cut from magazines)

Homework WB page 75

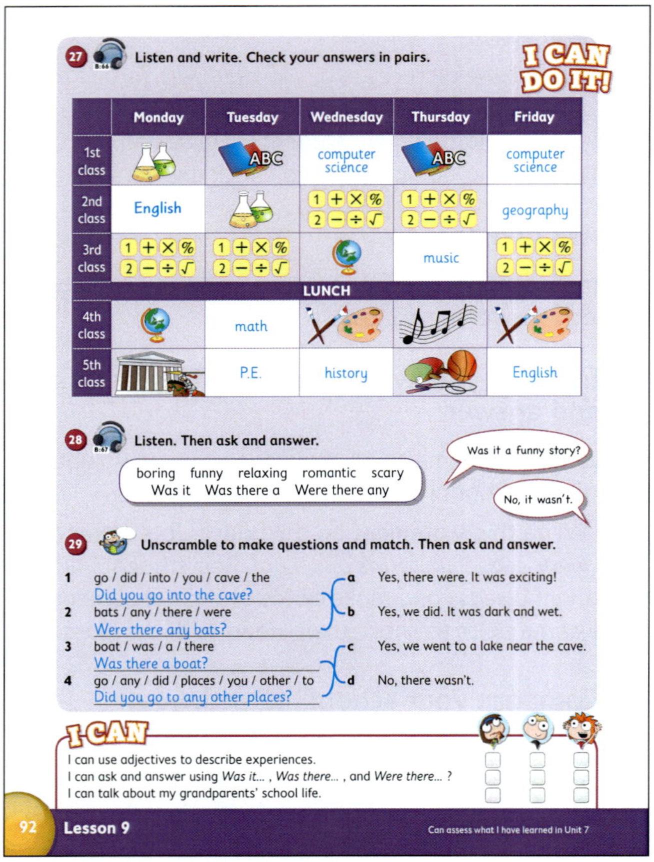
27 Listen and write. Check your answers in pairs. I CAN DO IT!

	Monday	Tuesday	Wednesday	Thursday	Friday
1st class			computer science		computer science
2nd class	English				geography
3rd class				music	
LUNCH					
4th class		math			
5th class		P.E.	history		English

28 Listen. Then ask and answer.

boring funny relaxing romantic scary
Was it Was there a Were there any

29 Unscramble to make questions and match. Then ask and answer.

1 go / did / into / you / cave / the
Did you go into the cave?
2 bats / any / there / were
Were there any bats?
3 boat / was / a / there
Was there a boat?
4 go / any / did / places / you / other / to
Did you go to any other places?

a Yes, there were. It was exciting!
b Yes, we did. It was dark and wet.
c Yes, we went to a lake near the cave.
d No, there wasn't.

I CAN
I can use adjectives to describe experiences.
I can ask and answer using *Was it...*, *Was there...*, and *Were there...* ?
I can talk about my grandparents' school life.

92 Lesson 9 Can assess what I have learned in Unit 7

Lesson 9 SB page 92 or Poptropica English World

Learning Objectives
Can assess what I have learned in Unit 7

Warm-up

- Place Picture Cards 128–144 around the room. Invite students to take one adjective and one school subject, and say a sentence using the words.

Open books and ask students to look at the activities. Write this lesson objective on the board: *We're thinking about our learning adventure.*

- Ask students what they have been learning in the unit. Put their ideas on the board, e.g. *different school subjects.*
- For each idea, ask students to tell their partner where they think they are on their learning adventure. Reassure students who are less confident that they will have opportunities for more practice.

27 Listen and write. Check your answers in pairs.

B:66

- Have students listen to the audio and write the correct school subject in the boxes.

Monday. We study lots of subjects on Monday. The afternoon is difficult, but all my classes in the morning are easy. I have science, English, and math.
Tuesday. Tuesday afternoon is difficult for me. The fourth class is math, then the fifth class is P.E. These are not my favorite subjects.
Wednesday. I like computers, so Wednesday morning is interesting because I have computer science in the first class. In the third class I have geography, and then the last class of the day is history.
Thursday. The third class on Thursday before lunch is music. After lunch, it's music, too. Then for the fifth class I have P.E.
Friday. My first class on Friday is computer science, and my second class is geography. My last class on Friday, after art, is English.

- Have students switch their books with a partner. Play the audio again for students to check their answers.

28 Listen. Then ask and answer.

B:67

- Have students listen to the audio. Then in pairs, have them ask and answer questions using the words.

go to page 132 for the script

29 Unscramble to make questions and match. Then ask and answer.

- Give students time to write questions using the words.
- Check answers as a class.

Ask students how they feel about their learning in this unit. Ask students to tell you what they found easy and what they found the most difficult to learn in the unit.

- Read the three *I can* statements with students and invite students to check the boxes according to how confident they feel about the language point.
- Ask students, *Where are you on your learning adventure?* Students indicate where they think they are on the learning adventure poster. Tell students, *Good job!* to reinforce the progress they are making.

Pop Quiz: In groups of four, students tell the others the answers to the following questions: *Which is your favorite activity in the unit? Why? Which activity don't you like? Why? What is your favorite new word? Which word is the most difficult for you?*

Materials
Poster, Picture Cards 128–144

Homework WB page 76

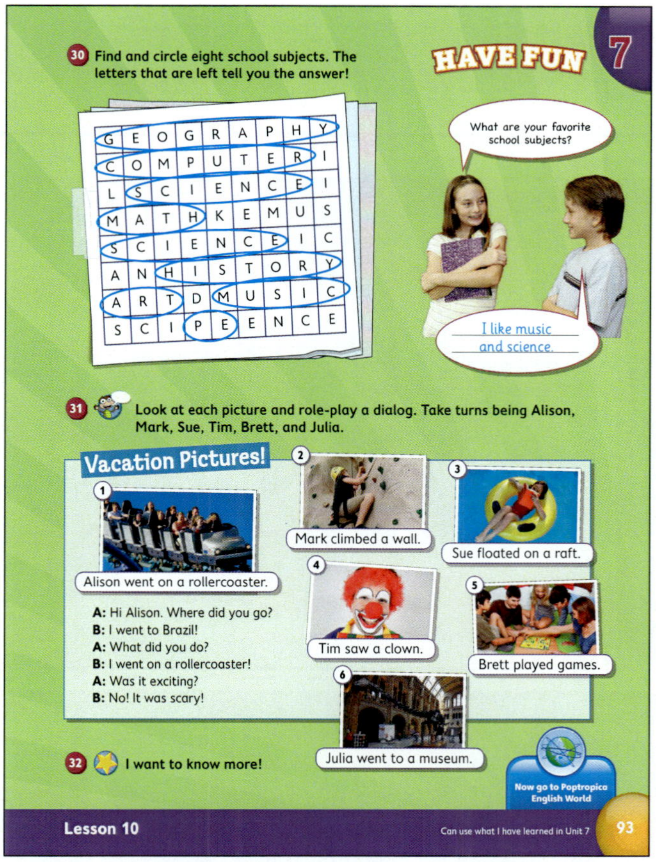

30 Find and circle eight school subjects. The letters that are left tell you the answer!

HAVE FUN 7

G	E	O	G	R	A	P	H	Y
C	O	M	P	U	T	E	R	I
L	S	C	I	E	N	C	E	I
M	A	T	H	K	E	M	U	S
S	C	I	E	N	C	E	I	C
A	N	H	I	S	T	O	R	Y
A	R	T	D	M	U	S	I	C
S	C	I	P	E	N	C	E	

What are your favorite school subjects?

I like music and science.

31 Look at each picture and role-play a dialog. Take turns being Alison, Mark, Sue, Tim, Brett, and Julia.

Vacation Pictures!

1 Alison went on a rollercoaster.

2 Mark climbed a wall.

3 Sue floated on a raft.

4 Tim saw a clown.

5 Brett played games.

6 Julia went to a museum.

A: Hi Alison. Where did you go?
B: I went to Brazil!
A: What did you do?
B: I went on a rollercoaster!
A: Was it exciting?
B: No! It was scary!

32 I want to know more!

Now go to Poptropica English World

Lesson 10 Can use what I have learned in Unit 7 93

Lesson 10 SB page 93 or Poptropica English World

Learning Objective
Can use what I have learned in Unit 7

Warm-up

- Review adjectives and school subjects with Picture Cards 128–144. Then have a spelling bee or a word scramble game.

Open books and ask students to look at the pictures. Ask, *What are we learning today?* Write the lesson objective on the board: *We're doing a fun activity to review Unit 7 language.*

30 Find and circle eight school subjects. The letters that are left tell you the answer!

- Direct students' attention to the word puzzle. Read the question chorally. Give students time to do the activity, and find the hidden answer to the question.
- To check students' work, pair students and have them go over their work and agree on the answer.

Write on the board, *Clowns are funny.* Divide the class into small groups, and ask them to discuss the statement and take notes on why they agree with it or disagree with it. Ask the groups to present their reasons to the class. Write the reasons on the board under *Agree* and *Disagree*. Take a class vote.

31 Look at each picture and role-play a dialog. Take turns being Alison, Mark, Sue, Tim, Brett, and Julia.

- Tell students they are going to create their own dialogs in pairs. Tell them to use adjectives from the unit. Have a confident student role-play the example with you.
- Ask a few pairs to role-play their dialogs in front of the class.
- To extend the lesson, divide the students into small groups and hand each group Activity Sheets 13 and 14 (see Poptropica English World), which they then cut into pieces. Ask them to turn all the slips with the word side down. They must turn over two slips and talk about schoolwork using the words, and the target language from this lesson.

32 I want to know more!

- Ask students to choose anything they enjoyed from the unit and to go and find out more. You might like to set this activity as homework with a quick feedback session at the beginning of the next class.
- You can also suggest that students write one or two questions about what they want to know, then switch question(s) with a partner. Students then find the answer(s) to their partner's question(s) as a homework activity, with feedback the next lesson.

Are you ready for Unit 8?

- Ask students if they are ready to move onto the next unit. Tell students that it is fine if they do not remember everything as they will continue to practice throughout the level.
- Encourage students to ask if they have any questions about what they learned in Unit 7.

You may wish to give Unit 7 Test (see page 200) at this time.

Materials
Picture Cards 128–144, Activity Sheets 13–14, scissors

Homework WB page 77

Unit 7 Story Cards

SB pages 94–95 or Poptropica English World

Learning Objectives
Can understand texts about unusual schools
Can talk about unusual schools and my ideal school

Additional Language
international, boarding school

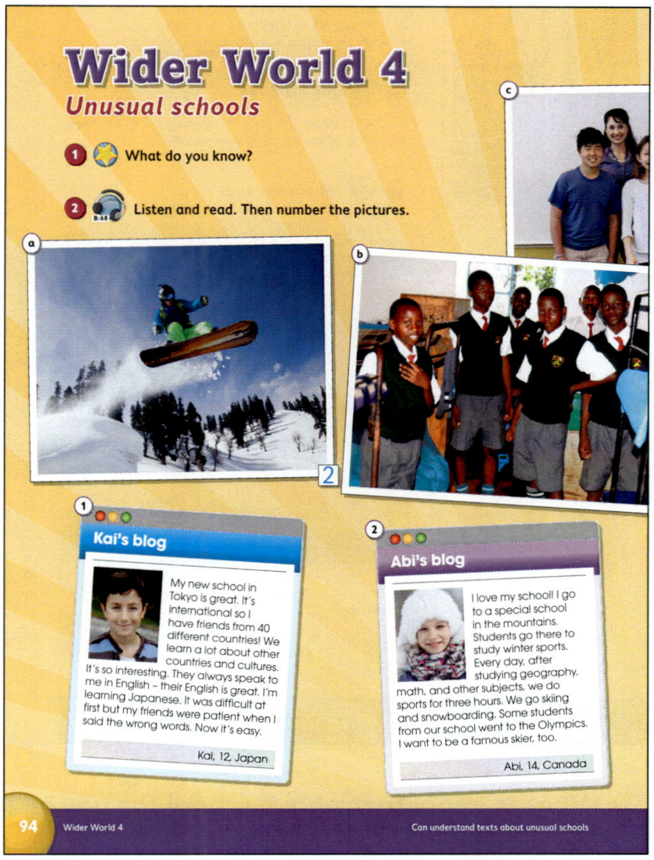
Wider World 4
Unusual schools

1 What do you know?

2 B:68 Listen and read. Then number the pictures.

a 2

b

c

1 **Kai's blog**

My new school in Tokyo is great. It's international so I have friends from 40 different countries! We learn a lot about other countries and cultures. It's so interesting. They always speak to me in English – their English is great. I'm learning Japanese. It was difficult at first but my friends were patient when I said the wrong words. Now it's easy.

Kai, 12, Japan

2 **Abi's blog**

I love my school! I go to a special school in the mountains. Students go there to study winter sports. Every day, after studying geography, math, and other subjects, we do sports for three hours. We go skiing and snowboarding. Some students from our school went to the Olympics. I want to be a famous skier, too.

Abi, 14, Canada

94 Wider World 4 Can understand texts about unusual schools

Warm-up

- Review school subjects by using Picture Cards 137–144. If you want to review spelling, use the word-side of the cards and have a spelling bee.

1 What do you know?

- Open books and ask students to look at the pictures. Ask, *What are we learning today?* Write the lesson objective on the board: *We're learning about schools in different cultures.*
- Close books. Ask students what English words they know about school, e.g., *classroom, teacher.*
- Refer to the learning adventure poster and say, *Great! You are moving along your learning adventure!*

2 B:68 Listen and read. Then number the pictures.

- Pre-teach *boarding/international school*. Say, *Children study and sleep at a boarding school. International schools are for children from different countries.*
- Pointing at the pictures, ask, *What country is he/are they in?* (Students guess.) Invite students to locate the countries (Japan, Canada, Kenya) on the world map.
- Ask the class about the pictures, e.g., *Picture a. What's the boy doing? (He's snowboarding.) What is there in the picture? (There's a mountain and there are some trees.)*
- Mime *skier* to pre-teach the word, and explain *Olympic Games*. Ask, *What can you see in Picture b? (six boys and a bedroom) Where are they? (At school. They're wearing school clothes.)*
- Play the audio. Students listen and follow. Then students match the pictures and write the correct number in the boxes.
- Play the audio again, pausing after each text to elicit and check answers.

3 Ask and answer.

- Give students time to read the blogs again on their own, and to underline relevant information.
- Pair students and allow them time to ask and answer the questions.
- Ask volunteers to point out Canada, Japan, and Kenya on the world map again.

Tell students you are going to give them an answer related to the blogs on the page, and they have to guess the question. For example, you say, *Canada*, and students guess the question, *Where does Abi live?*

4 Ask and answer.

- Read the questions chorally.
- Give pairs time to do the activity.
- Have volunteers share their answers to the class. Encourage them to explain, e.g. ask, *Why do you want to go to Abi's school?*

Materials
Picture Cards 137–144, map of the world

3 Ask and answer.

1 Who lives in a school? Matu
2 Who is learning Japanese? Kai
3 Who does sports for three hours a day? Abi
4 Who has friends from 40 countries? Kai

4 Ask and answer.

1 Which school in Activity 2 do you want to go to? Why?
2 What do you like about your school?

5 What is important about school for you? Tell a friend.

- good friends
- a swimming pool
- good teachers
- a lot of sports
- students from other countries

A swimming pool is important for me because I like swimming.

3 Matu's blog

I live in my school because it's a boarding school. My friends and I all live in rooms next to the school. I love living with my friends because I never get lonely and we have lots of fun together. The teachers are all very nice and patient. In the evening, there are a lot of activities. We can watch movies, play tennis, or go swimming but usually we have homework.

Matu, 12, Kenya

YOUR TURN!

- Think about your ideal school. How is it different from your school now?
- Make notes on your ideal school's subjects, sports, teachers, and number of students.
- What else is special about your ideal school? *There is a rock climbing wall. / We watch a movie once a week.*
- Tell the class.

5 Write.

At my ideal school...

Wider World 4 Can talk about unusual schools and my ideal school 95

5 What is important about school for you? Tell a friend.

- Ask a volunteer to read the example speech bubble.
- From the list, students decide what is and isn't important to them about school and why. Students discuss their ideas in pairs.
- Ask students to share their ideas with the class. Encourage other students to ask questions when someone is sharing their information.

YOUR TURN! Ask each student to think about his/her ideal school and how it is different to his/her school now. Ask students to make notes on their ideal school subjects, sports, teachers, number of students, etc. Tell students that their questions and answers will help them prepare Activity 6. Allow students time to think through their answers before they work with their partner. Have students present their ideas to the class.

- To give students a reason to listen, each student/pair will also think of one/two more questions to ask their partner.

6 Write

- Have students write about their ideal school using their ideas from the YOUR TURN! activity. Remind students to check their work when they've finished.

Pop Quiz: Tell the class that you are Kai, Abi or Matu. Read sentences from the blogs or make up likely statements, and have students guess who you are, e.g., *I live in my school because it's a boarding school. (Matu) We wear winter clothes all the time! (Abi)*

Unit 7, Lesson 9, Activity 28

This is the story I got a prize for in English today: It was June 2nd 1943. There was no moon in the night sky. The forest was dark and the family walking through the trees sometimes tripped and fell. There were no noises behind them, but they often looked back in fear. The girl helped her sick mother. Her father carried their suitcases. Suddenly they saw a light. It was a small house. "That's it!" whispered the mother. It was the house of her old school friend. The girl ran to the door and knocked softly. "Please, let us in!" she called. The door opened and a boy looked out. "We have come a long way," she told him. He knew it was dangerous, but he let them in. He showed them a secret room. "This is where you can hide," he said. The boy and his family hid the girl and her parents for two years until the soldiers left their country. The boy and girl fell in love and got married. They had four children and eight grandchildren. They told their brave story to each one, including me!

8 Entertainment

Unit Overview

Unit Objective

- I can talk about nationalities and entertainment

Language

Target Vocabulary	Nationalities: Chinese, Korean, Japanese, Australian, American, Mexican, Colombian, Brazilian, Argentinian, British, Spanish, Italian, Egyptian, Indian Occupations: cowboy, king, queen, scientist, spy, soldier, sailor, waiter, actor, musician
Target Structures	Is he/she from the United States? Yes, he/she is. / No, he/she isn't. Where's he/she from? He's/She's from Argentina. He's/She's Argentinian. Where are they from? They're from Australia. They're Australian. He's a cowboy. He likes playing the guitar. He's a cowboy who likes playing the guitar. It's an American movie. It's very famous. It's an American movie that's very famous.
Features	**Cross-curricular:** Technology: Video games **Values:** Be a good role model for others.

Skills

Reading	• Can understand a simple story • Can understand details of a story • Can understand short texts about TV shows
Writing	• Can complete simple sentences using *who* and *that* • Can write about a video game I like • Can complete simple sentences about where people are from *(Workbook)* • Can complete simple sentences about being a good role model *(Workbook)* • Can write simple sentences about my favorite entertainment *(Workbook)*
Listening	• Can identify occupations • Can understand a simple story • Can understand short texts about TV shows
Speaking	• Can talk about different nationalities • Can use *in, on* and *at* correctly • Can ask and answer about where someone is from • Can talk about people and things using *who* and *that* • Can discuss a story • Can talk about being a good role model • Can talk about video games

Lesson 1 SB page 96 or Poptropica English World

Learning Objective
Can talk about different nationalities

Target Language
Chinese, Korean, Japanese, Australian, American, Mexican, Colombian, Brazilian, Argentinian, British, Spanish, Italian, Egyptian, Indian

1 What do you know?

- Open books and ask students to look at the pictures. Ask, *What are we learning today?* Write the lesson objective on the board: *We're learning about different nationalities.*
- Close books. Ask students what English words they know for nationalities, e.g., *British, American*. Write on board.
- Refer to the learning adventure poster and say, *Great! You are already moving along your learning adventure!*

2 Listen and read. Is Carlos playing?

- Ask, *Where are Robbie and Dan? (They are at a soccer match.) Who are Robbie and Dan talking about?* (Students guess.)
- Ask students to look at the scenes in their books and listen as you play the audio.
- Have the class read the story chorally.
- Ask comprehension questions: *Who is Carlos? (a famous Spanish player) What teams was he on before? (American team/Italian team) Is Carlos playing now? (No, he isn't.) Why not? (He has a broken leg/foot.)*

3 Listen and say.

- Focus on the words. Play the audio and have students listen and repeat the nationalities.
- Put Picture Cards 145–158 on the board for students to refer to. Number them. Pair students and have them play a game. One student in each pair says a number. His/her partner has to say the item. If they know the name of a sports team from that country, they can say it.

4 Talk about famous people from different countries.

- Read the words in the speech bubbles chorally. Ask students, *Who is he?* and elicit answers. Pair students and give them time to do the activity.

8 Entertainment

1 What do you know?

2 Listen and read. Is Carlos playing?

3 Listen and say.

1	Chinese	2	Korean	3	Japanese	4	Australian
5	American	6	Mexican	7	Colombian	8	Brazilian
9	Argentinian	10	British	11	Spanish	12	Italian
13	Egyptian	14	Indian				

4 Talk about famous people from different countries.

96 Lesson 1 Can talk about different nationalities

Ask students, *How many nationalities do you know now?* Give students a minute to tell their partner the new words they know.

- Ask students to say where they are on their adventure now. Ask students which words they find easiest or most difficult to remember. Tell students, *Good job!* to reinforce the progress they are making.

Pop Quiz: Say a country name and have students put their hands up to say the nationality. You can turn this into a game with two teams. To make it more challenging, show flags of the countries without saying the name.

- Direct students' attention to the boots card on page 96. Tell students to go online to the Poptropica English Island Adventure Game and find the item. Once students click on it, they are taken to a supplementary language task.

Materials
Poster, Picture Cards 145–158

Homework WB page 78

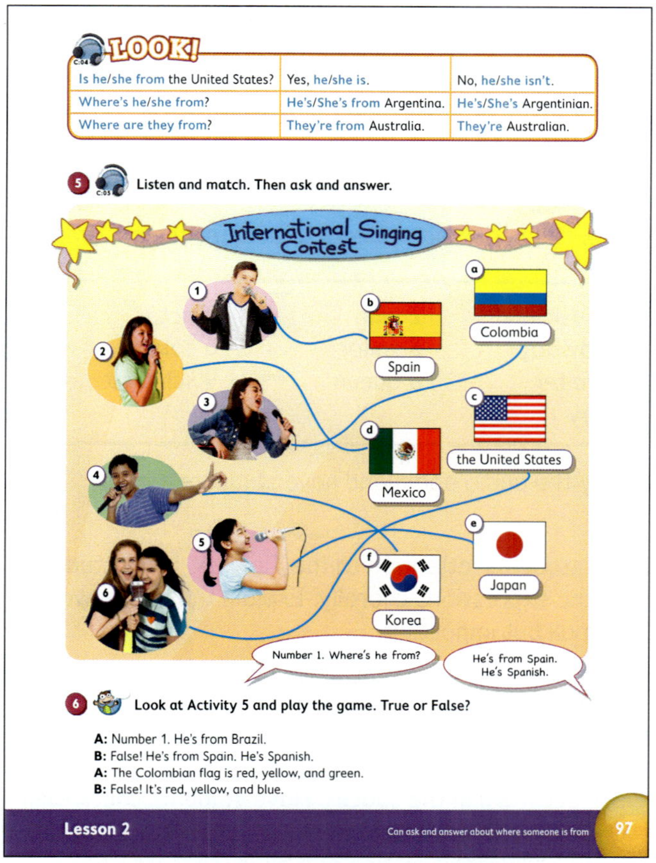

Lesson 2 SB page 97 or Poptropica English World

Learning Objective
Can ask and answer about where someone is from

Warm-up

- Write the nationalities on the board jumbled up. See who can unscramble them first. Then have a nationality spelling bee, using Picture Cards 145–158.

Open books and ask students to look at the activities and the Look! box. Ask, *What are we learning today?* Write the lesson objective on the board: *We're learning to ask and answer questions about where someone is from.*

5 Listen and match. Then ask and answer.

C:05

- Draw students' attention to the Look! box and play the audio (track C:04). Students repeat chorally.
- Give students time to look at the pictures. Read the title and the country names together. Invite student to talk about the students in the pictures.
- Play the audio and have students follow.

> **1** Where's he from? Is he American? / No, he isn't. He's from Spain.
> **2** Is she Mexican? / Yes, she is. She's from Mexico.
> **3** Is she Brazilian? / No, she isn't. She's Colombian.
> **4** Is he Korean? / Yes, he is. He's from Korea.
> **5** Is she from Japan? / Yes, she is. She's Japanese.
> **6** Where are they from? Are they from China? / No, they're from the United States. They're American.

- Play the audio, giving students time to match the student to their country flag.
- Invite two confident students to model the exchange in the speech bubbles. Pair students and have them ask and answer. Then ask students to ask and answer for the class to listen. Students check their own books.

6 Look at Activity 5 and play the game. True or False?

- Ask two confident students to model the dialog.
- Draw students' attention to the items in Activity 5. Divide class into pairs and give them time to do the activity, using the target language.

Pop Quiz: Place Picture Cards 145–158 around the room. Pair students and give each pair Activity Sheet 15 (see Poptropica English World) to cut out. Students take turns modeling the dialog in Activity 6, using all the pictures. Students look at the Picture Cards around the room for reference.

Materials
Picture Cards 145–158, Activity Sheet 15

Homework WB page 79

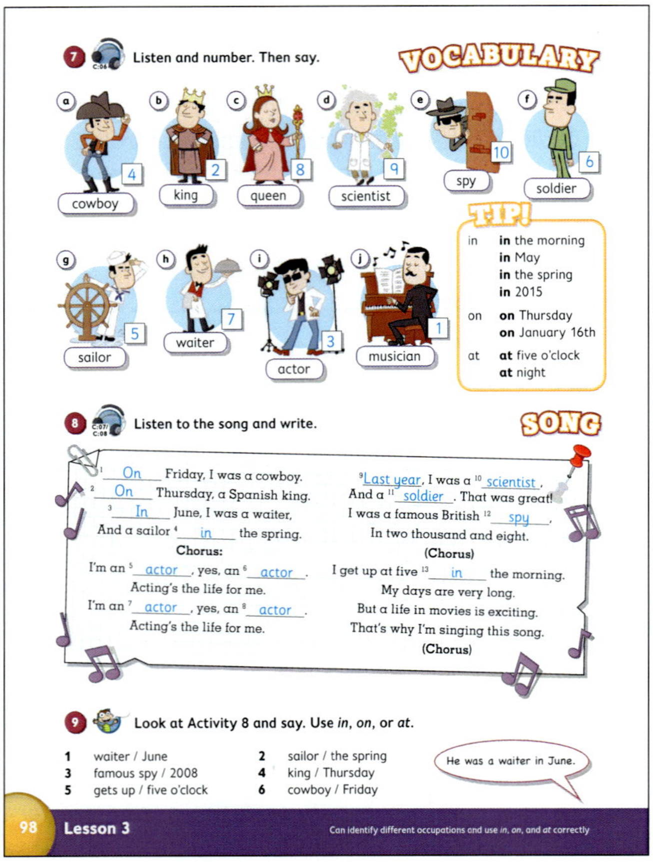

7 Listen and number. Then say. VOCABULARY

a cowboy 4 | b king 2 | c queen 8 | d scientist 9 | e spy 10 | f soldier 6

g sailor 5 | h waiter 7 | i actor 3 | j musician 1

TIP!
in — in the morning, in May, in the spring, in 2015
on — on Thursday, on January 16th
at — at five o'clock, at night

8 Listen to the song and write. SONG

[1] On Friday, I was a cowboy.
[2] On Thursday, a Spanish king.
[3] In June, I was a waiter,
And a sailor [4] in the spring.
Chorus:
I'm an [5] actor, yes, an [6] actor.
Acting's the life for me.
I'm an [7] actor, yes, an [8] actor.
Acting's the life for me.

[9] Last year, I was a [10] scientist.
And a [11] soldier. That was great!
I was a famous British [12] spy,
In two thousand and eight.
(Chorus)
I get up at five [13] in the morning.
My days are very long.
But a life in movies is exciting.
That's why I'm singing this song.
(Chorus)

9 Look at Activity 8 and say. Use *in*, *on*, or *at*.

1 waiter / June
2 sailor / the spring
3 famous spy / 2008
4 king / Thursday
5 gets up / five o'clock
6 cowboy / Friday

He was a waiter in June.

98 Lesson 3 Can identify different occupations and use *in*, *on*, and *at* correctly

Lesson 3 SB page 98 or Poptropica English World

Learning Objective
Can identify occupations and use *in*, *on*, and *at* correctly

Target Language
cowboy, king, queen, scientist, spy, soldier, sailor, waiter, actor, musician

Warm-up

- Show students the pictures of the King of Spain, Queen of England, James Bond (fictional British spy), Johnny Depp (American actor). Ask students, *Do you know him/her? Who is he/she? He/She is a (king/queen). Where is he/she from? He's/She's (British).*

Open books and ask students to look at the pictures. *Ask, What are we learning today?* Write the lesson objective on the board: *We're learning different occupations (jobs).*

- Close books. Ask students what English words they know for occupations, e.g., *teacher, doctor.* Write on board.
- Refer to the learning adventure poster and say, *Great! You are moving along your learning adventure!*

7 Listen and number. Then say.

C:06

- Introduce occupations with Picture Cards 159–168. Hold them up one by one, turn them to the word-side, and ask students to repeat the words after you. Then ask students to look in their books at the words and pictures.
- Play the audio for students to number the pictures.

1 musician	**2** king	**3** actor
4 cowboy	**5** sailor	**6** soldier
7 waiter	**8** queen	**9** scientist
10 spy		

- Play the audio again and have students repeat.

Tip!

Draw students' attention to the Tip! box. Have students read the expressions chorally. Explain that these words are small but important.

8 Listen to the song and write.

C:07 C:08

- Play the song audio and have students listen.
- Play the audio again and ask students to write the correct word in the spaces. Have students check their answers with partners.
- Play the karaoke version and have students sing the song if they feel confident enough.

9 Look at Activity 8 and say. Use *in, on,* or *at*.

- Draw students' attention to the speech bubble. Have students say the speech bubble text chorally.
- Give students time to complete the activity. Ask confident students to give statements to the class.
- To extend the lesson, put students in pairs and give each pair Activity Sheets 15 and 16 (see Poptropica English World), for them to cut into pieces. Students take turns handing their partner a card from each word group. The other student has to then talk about the person, using the target language, e.g. *This man is an actor. He's not famous. He's British.*

Ask students, *How many words for occupations do you know now?* Give students a minute to tell their partner the new words they know.

- Ask students to say where they are on their adventure now. Ask students which words they find easiest or most difficult to remember. Tell students, *Good job!* to reinforce the progress they are making.

Pop Quiz: Show students pictures of people from around the world doing different jobs. They can be any nationalities, but it's good to have a mix of Caucasian, Asian, Indian, and Latin American people. Ask students to create identities for each person. Say, e.g., *Where's he from and what does he do? (He's from Spain/Italy/Mexico. He's a cowboy.)*

Materials
Poster, Picture Cards 159–168, Activity Sheets 15–16, Internet pictures of the King of Spain, Queen of England, James Bond, Johnny Depp, pictures of people from around the world doing different jobs (cut from magazines)

Homework WB page 80

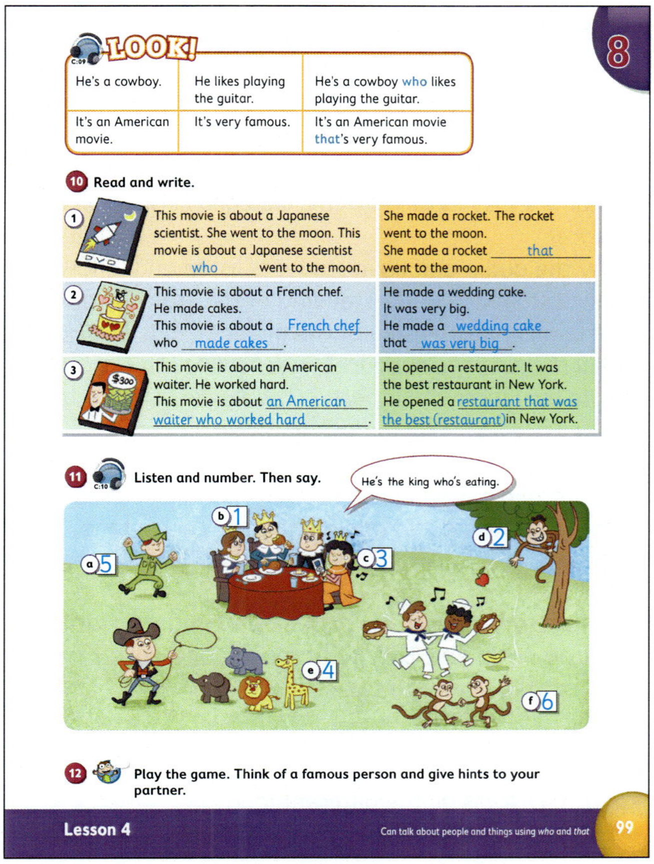
8

LOOK!

C:09

He's a cowboy.	He likes playing the guitar.	He's a cowboy who likes playing the guitar.
It's an American movie.	It's very famous.	It's an American movie that's very famous.

10 Read and write.

1	This movie is about a Japanese scientist. She went to the moon. This movie is about a Japanese scientist who went to the moon.	She made a rocket. The rocket went to the moon. She made a rocket that went to the moon.
2	This movie is about a French chef. He made cakes. This movie is about a French chef who made cakes.	He made a wedding cake. It was very big. He made a wedding cake that was very big.
3	This movie is about an American waiter. He worked hard. This movie is about an American waiter who worked hard.	He opened a restaurant. It was the best restaurant in New York. He opened a restaurant that was the best (restaurant) in New York.

11 C:10 Listen and number. Then say.

12 Play the game. Think of a famous person and give hints to your partner.

Lesson 4 Can talk about people and things using *who* and *that* 99

Lesson 4 SB page 99 or Poptropica English World

Learning Objective
Can talk about people and things using *who* and *that*

Warm-up

- Play a memory game by saying, e.g. *Channing Tatum is an American actor.* Have the first student repeat it and add a statement. Continue down the line. Those that forget a statement have to sit out.

Open books and ask students to look at the activities and the Look! box. Ask, *What are we learning today?* Write the lesson objective on the board: *We're learning to talk about people using* who *and* that.

10 Read and write.

- Draw students' attention to the Look! box and play the audio (track C:09). Students repeat chorally.
- Draw students' attention to the three pictures in Activity 10. Ask, *What is this? (It's a DVD/movie.)* Read the text in item 1 chorally. Emphasize the use of the words *who* and *that*.
- Allow students time to fill in the blanks in items 2 and 3.
- Have students switch books for checking. Invite some students to read the completed text, and have students say answers at the appropriate time.

11 C:10 Listen and number. Then say.

- Draw students' attention to the activity, and read the text in the speech bubble. Give them time to study the picture. Play the audio.

1 This is a man who is a king and who is eating chicken.
2 This is an animal that is throwing food at the sailors.
3 This is a woman who is a queen and who is listening to music.
4 This is an animal that has a long neck.
5 This is a man who is a soldier and who is dancing.
6 These are animals that are dancing.

- Give students time to do the activity. Invite confident students to offer the answers for checking.

12 Play the game. Think of a famous person and give hints to your partner.

- Give students time to do the activity. Invite confident students to come to the front to start off a quiz for the whole class.

Pop Quiz: Ask students to work in pairs and to each think of a movie. Each partner writes two sentences about the movie and its actors, one using *that* and one using *who*. Their partner tries to guess the movie, e.g. *This movie is about a boy who is small but smart. He has a pet dragon that he can ride.* (*How to train your dragon*). Suggest that they use the sentences in Activity 10 as a model. Have pairs read their sentences to the class.

Homework WB page 81

13 Talk about the pictures. Then listen and read. STORY

14 Hector and Smith don't run away when they first see the police officers. Why not? Discuss your answers.

100 Lesson 5 Can understand a simple story / Can discuss a story

Lesson 5 SB page 100 or Poptropica English World

Learning Objectives
Can understand a simple story
Can discuss a story

Additional Language
amusing, extraordinary

Functional Language
Quick! Catch them! You're welcome, any time!
Just call on the Ice Detectives!

Warm-up

- Review occupations with a spelling bee. Show a card from Picture Cards 159–168 and elicit the spelling of the word. Ask students to think of a statement using the word.

Open books and ask students to look at the story. Ask, *What are we learning today?* Write the lesson objective on the board: *We're reading and discussing a story.*

13 Talk about the pictures. Then listen and read.

- Direct students' attention to the pictures and ask questions about the characters and the scenes: *Who can you see in Picture 4? (Mike, Hector Frost, the Queen) What are they looking at? (the diamond necklace in the ice)*
- Play the audio and have students listen and follow.
- Check students' understanding of the story by asking questions and pointing at the pictures, e.g., *Did Hector steal the diamond necklace? (Yes, he did.) Did Hector invite the Queen to his party? (Yes, he did.) Did Hector invite Polly and Mike to the party? (No, he didn't.)*
- Play the audio again. Divide students into eight groups and assign each group a role. Groups read along with the audio and mime their character's actions.

14 Hector and Smith don't run away when they first see the police officers. Why not? Discuss your answers.

- Have students discuss the question in groups and then invite one person to write their group's answer on the board. Discuss all the different ideas.

Write the following question on the board, *Why did Hector Frost invite the Queen to his party at Bollington Hall?* Divide students into groups and give them time to discuss their answers and make notes. Ask the groups to present their ideas to the class.

Pop Quiz: Divide students into small groups, and tell them they are going to play *Parachute*. One student from each group comes to you and you quietly give them a word from the story, e.g. *astronaut*. These students go back to their groups and play the game.

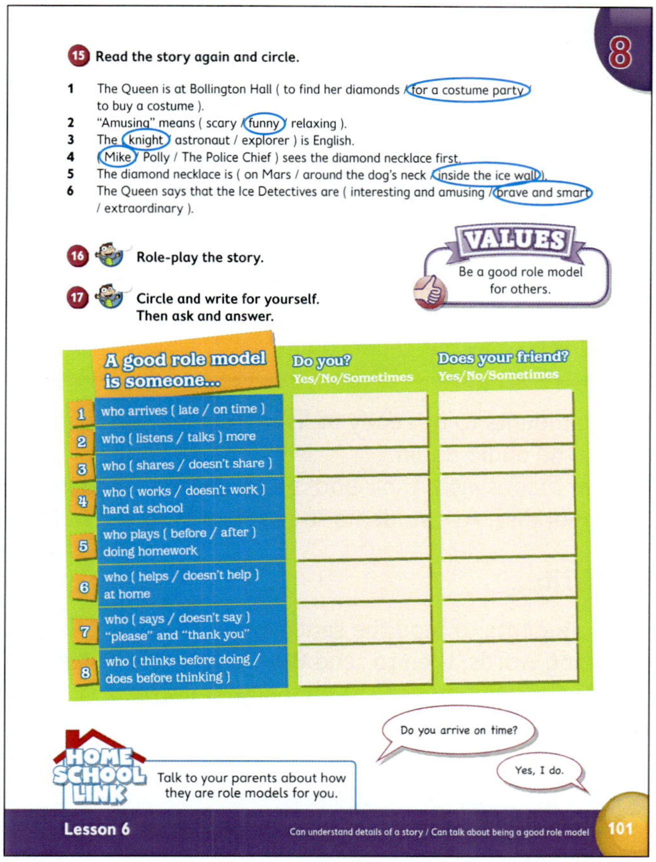
8

15 Read the story again and circle.

1 The Queen is at Bollington Hall (to find her diamonds / for a costume party / to buy a costume).
2 "Amusing" means (scary / funny / relaxing).
3 The (knight / astronaut / explorer) is English.
4 (Mike / Polly / The Police Chief) sees the diamond necklace first.
5 The diamond necklace is (on Mars / around the dog's neck / inside the ice wall).
6 The Queen says that the Ice Detectives are (interesting and amusing / brave and smart / extraordinary).

16 Role-play the story.

17 Circle and write for yourself. Then ask and answer.

VALUES
Be a good role model for others.

A good role model is someone...	Do you? Yes/No/Sometimes	Does your friend? Yes/No/Sometimes
1 who arrives (late / on time)		
2 who (listens / talks) more		
3 who (shares / doesn't share)		
4 who (works / doesn't work) hard at school		
5 who plays (before / after) doing homework		
6 who (helps / doesn't help) at home		
7 who (says / doesn't say) "please" and "thank you"		
8 who (thinks before doing / does before thinking)		

Talk to your parents about how they are role models for you.

Lesson 6 Can understand details of a story / Can talk about being a good role model 101

Lesson 6 SB page 101 or Poptropica English World

Learning Objectives
Can understand details of a story
Can talk about being a good role model

Value
Be a good role model for others.

Warm-up

- Show the occupations Picture Cards and ask, *What good things do they do?* and elicit answers. Invite students to suggest different occupations that involve doing good things for others, e.g. *nurse, doctor, police officer, teacher,* etc.

Open books and ask students to look at the activities. Ask, *What are we learning today?* Write the lesson objectives on the board: *We're reviewing the story, and we're learning about being a good role model for others.*

15 Read the story again and circle.

- Give students time to look at the story, and play the audio again.
- Give students time to do the activity.
- Check answers by having students pass their book to another student. Elicit answers from the class.

16 Role-play the story.

- See the "How to use stories" section on page 23 for more ideas on how to build your students' confidence with role-plays.
- Divide students into groups of eight. Give each group a set of cut-out Story Cards (see page 144), and have students place them in order.
- Play the audio again (track C:11), and have students follow along. Give groups time to practice the role-play, then ask them to show the class.

You might like to give students feedback on their role-play.

17 Circle and write for yourself. Then ask and answer.

- Read the value, *Be a good role model for others.*
- Draw students' attention to the text in Activity 17. Pair students and give them time to do the activity.

- **Home-School link:** Read the instruction with the class: *Talk to your parents about how they are role models for you.* Ask students to do this at home.

Pop Quiz: Ask students to name famous people who they think are good role models. Discuss as a class why they are good role models. Ask individual students to say who their famous role models are, and why.

Materials
Unit 8 cut-out Story Cards, Picture Cards 159–168

Homework WB page 83

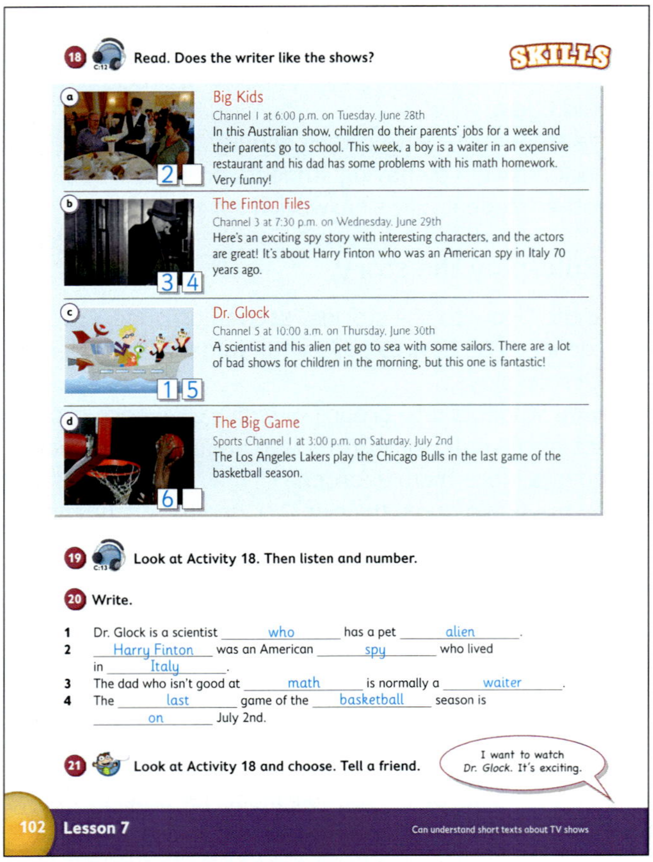

18 Read. Does the writer like the shows? SKILLS

a **Big Kids** 2
Channel 1 at 6:00 p.m. on Tuesday, June 28th
In this Australian show, children do their parents' jobs for a week and their parents go to school. This week, a boy is a waiter in an expensive restaurant and his dad has some problems with his math homework. Very funny!

b **The Finton Files** 3 4
Channel 3 at 7:30 p.m. on Wednesday, June 29th
Here's an exciting spy story with interesting characters, and the actors are great! It's about Harry Finton who was an American spy in Italy 70 years ago.

c **Dr. Glock** 1 5
Channel 5 at 10:00 a.m. on Thursday, June 30th
A scientist and his alien pet go to sea with some sailors. There are a lot of bad shows for children in the morning, but this one is fantastic!

d **The Big Game** 6
Sports Channel 1 at 3:00 p.m. on Saturday, July 2nd
The Los Angeles Lakers play the Chicago Bulls in the last game of the basketball season.

19 Look at Activity 18. Then listen and number.

20 Write.

1 Dr. Glock is a scientist __who__ has a pet __alien__.
2 __Harry Finton__ was an American __spy__ who lived in __Italy__.
3 The dad who isn't good at __math__ is normally a __waiter__.
4 The __last__ game of the __basketball__ season is __on__ July 2nd.

21 Look at Activity 18 and choose. Tell a friend.

I want to watch Dr. Glock. It's exciting.

102 Lesson 7 Can understand short texts about TV shows

Lesson 7 SB page 102 or Poptropica English World

Learning Objective
Can understand short texts about TV shows

Additional Language
channel, restaurant, characters, Los Angeles Lakers, Chicago Bulls, basketball season

Warm-up

- Show the class the TV schedule and elicit a response. Ask the class, *What TV programs do you like watching? Why?* and elicit answers.

Open books and ask students to look at the activities. Ask, *What are we learning today?* Write the lesson objective on the board: *We're learning to understand short texts from a TV schedule.*

18 Read. Does the writer like the shows?

- Ask, *What can you see in the pictures?*
- Give students time to read the text.
- Play the audio. Students listen and follow.
- Ask questions to check comprehension: *Who is the man by the telephone?* (*a spy*), etc. Ask, *Does the writer like the shows?*, and elicit responses.

19 Look at Activity 18. Then listen and number.

- Play the audio and have students just listen.

1 Which show is on Thursday?
2 Which show is funny?
3 Which show is at seven thirty?
4 Which show is about people a long time ago?
5 Which show is in the morning?
6 Which show has teams on it?

- Tell students to be ready to listen and number. Play the audio again.
- Have them switch their books with another student for marking. Ask students to read out their answers.

20 Write.

- Tell students to read the sentences with the missing words, then to read the TV schedule again, underlining or circling the important information.
- Have students write the missing words. Check answers as a class.

21 Look at Activity 18 and choose. Tell a friend

- Have a confident student model the text in the speech bubble at the bottom of the page.
- Give students time to complete the activity. Invite some students to come to the front to talk to the whole class.

Write this statement on the board, *Watching TV is bad for children.* Divide the class into small groups and ask them to agree or disagree with the statement, and to take note of their reasons. Elicit these reasons from the class and write them on the board in two columns: *Agree* and *Disagree*. Take a class vote to see what the majority view is.

Pop Quiz: Divide the class in half and start each team with five points. Invite a student to think of a TV show others may know of. Students ask, *Is it funny? Is it about soldiers? Is it at night?*, etc. The student says, *yes* or *no*. If a student thinks they know it, they may guess, but if they are wrong their team loses a point.

Materials
A TV schedule from a newspaper or the Internet

Homework WB page 84

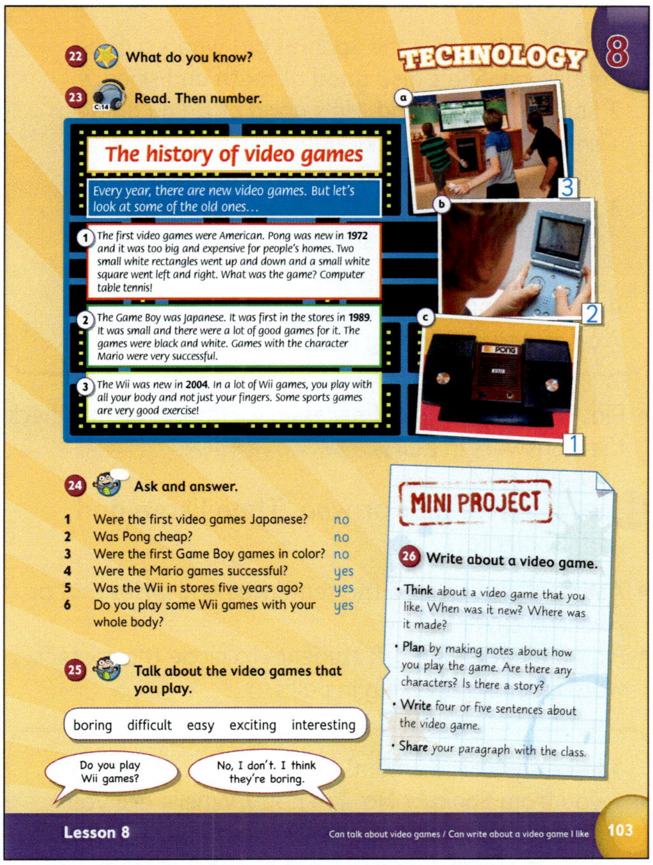

TECHNOLOGY 8

22 What do you know?

23 Read. Then number.

The history of video games

Every year, there are new video games. But let's look at some of the old ones…

1 The first video games were American. Pong was new in **1972** and it was too big and expensive for people's homes. Two small white rectangles went up and down and a small white square went left and right. What was the game? Computer table tennis!

2 The Game Boy was Japanese. It was first in the stores in **1989**. It was small and there were a lot of good games for it. The games were black and white. Games with the character Mario were very successful.

3 The Wii was new in **2004**. In a lot of Wii games, you play with all your body and not just your fingers. Some sports games are very good exercise!

a 3 b 2 c 1

24 Ask and answer.

1 Were the first video games Japanese? no
2 Was Pong cheap? no
3 Were the first Game Boy games in color? no
4 Were the Mario games successful? yes
5 Was the Wii in stores five years ago? yes
6 Do you play some Wii games with your whole body? yes

25 Talk about the video games that you play.

boring difficult easy exciting interesting

Do you play Wii games?

No, I don't. I think they're boring.

MINI PROJECT

26 Write about a video game.

- **Think** about a video game that you like. When was it new? Where was it made?
- **Plan** by making notes about how you play the game. Are there any characters? Is there a story?
- **Write** four or five sentences about the video game.
- **Share** your paragraph with the class.

Lesson 8 Can talk about video games / Can write about a video game I like 103

Lesson 8 SB page 103 or Poptropica English World

Learning Objectives
Can talk about video games
Can write about a video game I like

Additional Language
video games, Pong, Game Boy, Wii

Warm-up

- Invite students to talk about their favorite video game, saying what it is about and why they like it.

22 What do you know?

- Open books and ask students to look at the activities. Ask, *What are we learning today?* Write the lesson objective on the board: *We're learning to talk and write about video games we like.*
- Close books. Ask students, *What do you know about the first video games?* Write these on the board.
- Refer to the learning adventure poster and say, *Great! You are moving along your learning adventure!*

23 Read. Then number.

- Ask about the pictures, e.g., *Do you know this game? Do you like it?* Let students guess about picture *c*.
- Play the audio and have students read along.
- Play the audio again, giving students time to write the correct numbers in the boxes. Pause to check answers.

24 Ask and answer.

- Ask students to read the questions chorally.
- Pair students and give them time to do the activity. Check answers as a class.

25 Talk about the video games that you play.

- Draw students' attention to the target language. Pair students and have them do the activity.

26 Write about a video game.

- Ask students what steps they will take to make sure they include all the necessary information. Remind students of the steps to success: Think, Plan, Write and Share.
  Think Help students with ideas if necessary.
  Plan Ask students to make notes about the computer game. Allow students to do some research.
  Write Give students time to write their sentences. Remind them to check their work afterwards.
  Share Nominate students to share their work.

You may also wish to give students feedback on their projects.

Ask students, *What do you know about video games now?* Give students a minute to tell their partner the new ideas and words they can remember. Ask students, *Where are you on your learning adventure?* Tell students, *Good job!* to reinforce the progress they are making.

Write on the board, *What makes a good video game?* Ask students to discuss this question in small groups, thinking of all the different aspects of a video game, e.g., *How it looks, how easy it is to play, how competitive it is.* Ask students to present their ideas to the class.

Pop Quiz: Pass out a sheet of paper to each student, and tell them to design a computer game. They can write down the features in bullet point form. Give students time to do the activity, then invite some to present their ideas to the class.

Materials
Poster, sheet of paper for each student

Homework WB page 85

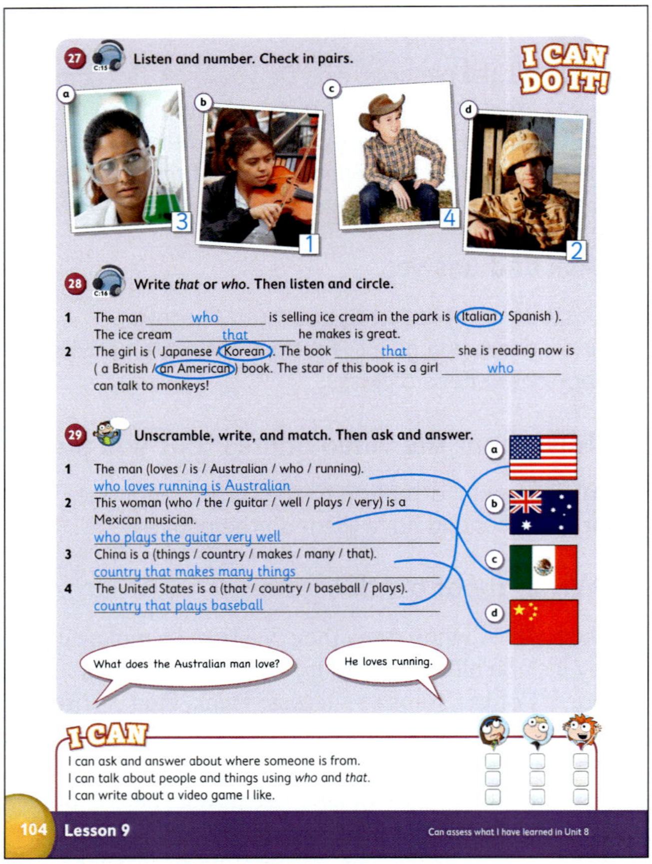

27 Listen and number. Check in pairs.

I CAN DO IT!

a 3 b 1 c 4 d 2

28 Write *that* or *who*. Then listen and circle.

1 The man ___who___ is selling ice cream in the park is (Italian / Spanish).
The ice cream ___that___ he makes is great.
2 The girl is (Japanese / Korean). The book ___that___ she is reading now is (a British / an American) book. The star of this book is a girl ___who___ can talk to monkeys!

29 Unscramble, write, and match. Then ask and answer.

1 The man (loves / is / Australian / who / running).
who loves running is Australian
2 This woman (who / the / guitar / well / plays / very) is a Mexican musician.
who plays the guitar very well
3 China is a (things / country / makes / many / that).
country that makes many things
4 The United States is a (that / country / baseball / plays).
country that plays baseball

What does the Australian man love?
He loves running.

I CAN

I can ask and answer about where someone is from.
I can talk about people and things using *who* and *that*.
I can write about a video game I like.

104 Lesson 9 Can assess what I have learned in Unit 8

Lesson 9 SB page 104 or Poptropica English World

Learning Objective
Can assess what I have learned in Unit 8

Warm-up

- Place Picture Cards 145–168 around the room. Invite students to take one nationality and one occupation, then say a sentence using both words.

Open books and ask students to look at the activities on the page. Write this lesson objective on the board: *We're thinking about our learning adventure.*

- Ask students what they have been learning in the unit. Put their ideas on the board, e.g. *different occupations.*
- For each idea, ask students to tell their partner where they think they are on their learning adventure. Reassure students who are less confident that they will have opportunities for more practice.

27 Listen and number. Check in pairs.

C:15

- Have students look at the pictures. Then ask students to listen to the audio and number the pictures.

1 That's Lily. She's the Spanish girl who's a good musician. She's also good at math and science.
2 Sam's from England. He's good at riding horses, snowboarding, and kicking. He's a soldier who likes playing soccer.
3 Alex is very musical. She plays the piano and the violin. But what she loves is science. She's a scientist who likes music!
4 This is Robin. He's an American boy who wears a hat and likes riding horses.

- Play the audio again if necessary. Have students check their answers in pairs.

28 Write *that* or *who*. Then listen and circle.

C:16

- Ask students to read the sentences and write *that* or *who* in the blanks.
- Play the audio and ask students to circle the correct words, before checking in pairs.

1 Here's your ice cream! / Thanks... Umm, are you from Spain? / No, I'm not. / Where are you from? / I'm from Italy.
2 Are you from Japan? / No, I'm not. I'm from Korea. / Oh, I see... What are you reading? / This book is about a girl who can talk to monkeys. It's an American book.

29 Unscramble, write, and match. Then ask and answer.

- Ask students to do the first part of the activity.
- Now ask students to match the sentences to the flags.
- In pairs, have students ask and answer.

Ask students how they feel about their learning in this unit. Ask students to tell you what they found easy and what they found the most difficult to learn in the unit.

- Read the three *I can* statements with students and invite students to check the boxes according to how confident they feel about the language point.
- Ask students, *Where are you on your learning adventure?* Students indicate where they think they are on the learning adventure poster. Tell students, *Good job!* to reinforce the progress they are making.

Pop Quiz: In groups of four, students tell the others the answers to the following questions: *Which is your favorite activity in the unit? Why? Which activity don't you like? Why? What is your favorite new word? Which word is the most difficult for you?*

Materials
Poster, Picture Cards 145–168

Homework WB page 86

30 Make a movie!

HAVE FUN 8

1 Your movie is... exciting funny interesting romantic scary

2 Choose and describe three characters for your movie.

actor cowboy king musician queen sailor scientist soldier spy waiter

1 Job: ______ Name: ______
2 Job: ______ Name: ______
3 Job: ______ Name: ______

Where are they from? 1 ______ 2 ______ 3 ______

What are they like? 1 ______ 2 ______ 3 ______

What do they look like? 1 ______ 2 ______ 3 ______

What are they good/bad at? 1 ______ 2 ______ 3 ______

3 What is your movie about? Tell the class.

31 I want to know more!

Now go to Poptropica English World

Lesson 10 Can use what I have learned in Unit 8 105

Lesson 10 SB page 105 or Poptropica English World

Learning Objective
Can use what I have learned in Unit 8

Warm-up

- Review nationalities and occupations with Picture Cards 145–168. Have students come to the front to choose a Card. They hold the Card up and other students say the word.

Open books and ask students look at the pictures. Ask, *What are we learning today?* Write the lesson objective on the board: *We're making a movie to review Unit 8 language.*

Pair students and ask each pair to choose a character from a movie, e.g. *Harry Potter*, *Hiccup*, *Shrek*, *Elsa*, etc. Pairs take turns sitting in front of the class and saying where their character comes from/lives, and what he/she looks like, without naming the movie or character. The pair then answers 10 questions from the class (e.g. *Is he/she a person or an animal?*), as they try to guess the character and movie.

Ask students to work in pairs to make sentences with target language based on different types of entertainment. Tell students to choose a different form of entertainment (not TV, reading, video games or movies), and to write about it – one student writes about liking this form of entertainment, and why. The other student writes about not liking this form of entertainment, and why. (Ideas could include listening to music, going to the theater to watch a play, watching ballet and other dancing, watching or playing sport, singing karaoke.) Give pairs a few minutes, and ask them to share their sentences with the class.

30 Make a movie!

- Ask students what they know about making a movie. Write suggestions on the board, e.g., *Find/write a story, find the right actors, build a set*, etc.
- Tell students to follow the steps 1–2 in making their own movie.
- Ask students to share their answers with the class. Have a class vote on the best movie idea.

31 I want to know more!

- Ask students to choose anything they enjoyed from the unit and to go and find out more. You might like to set this activity as homework with a quick feedback session at the beginning of the next class.
- You can also suggest that students write one or two questions about what they want to know, then switch question(s) with a partner. Students then find answer(s) to their partner's question(s) as a homework activity, with feedback the next lesson.

Ask students, *What do you think you have learned in Unit 8?* Give students a minute to tell their partner the new language they know. Ask students, *Where do you think you are on your learning journey?* Ask students if they are ready to move onto the next unit. Encourage students to ask any questions they might have before they move on. Tell students, *Good job!* to reinforce the progress they are making.

You may wish to give the Unit 8 Test (see page 202) at this time.

Materials
Picture Cards 145–168

Homework WB page 87

Unit 8 Story Cards

Review Units 7 and 8

SB pages 106–107 or Poptropica English World

Learning Objectives
Can talk about schools and school subjects
Can talk about nationalities and entertainment

Warm-up

- Show the class the pictures you brought to class. Ask students to name more famous people. Ask them to name some heroes and explain why they think they are heroic. Write them on the board, eliciting as many examples as you can. To extend the activity, ask the class to talk about the heroes they have named, giving as much detail as possible. Encourage students to ask questions.

Open books and ask students to look at the page. Ask, *What are we learning today?* Write the lesson objective on the board: *We're reviewing language from Units 7 and 8.*

Direct students to pages 84–87 if they should like to refresh their memories on the vocabulary and grammar structures needed for activities 1–3. To challenge students further, ask them to write a short school drama with a set character list written on the board, e.g., *musician, cowboy, actor, waiter.*

- Activities 4–6 are based on vocabulary and grammar structures from pages 96–99. To challenge students further, stick flag cards on the board on one side of a line, and a selection of pictures of people, animals, and occupations on the other side of the line. Ask students to take turns moving any picture to any flag, and sticking them together, while saying the nationality of the person/thing, e.g., *He's an Italian musician. They're Egyptian pyramids.*

1 Listen and match. Then ask and answer.

- Play the audio. Have students follow.

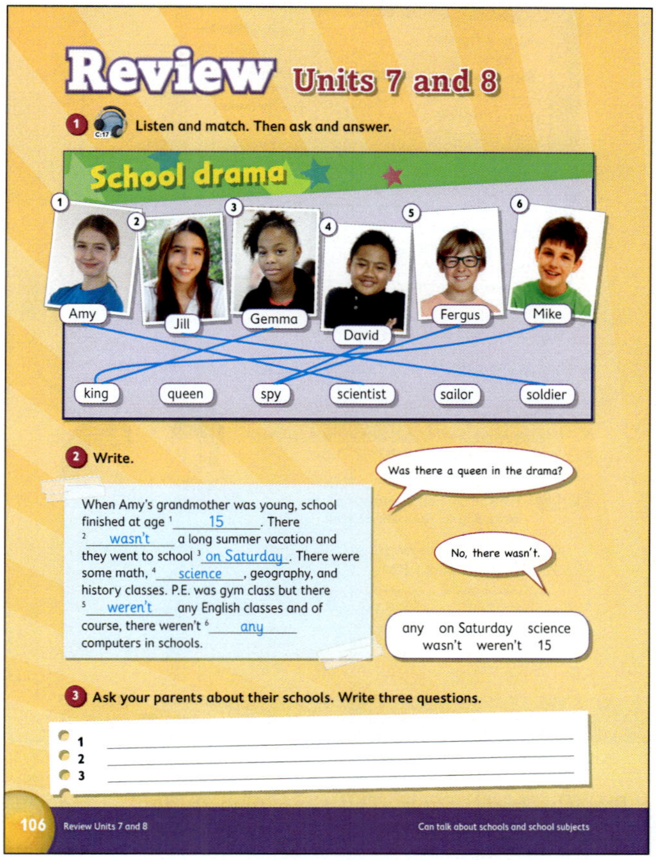
Review Units 7 and 8

1 Listen and match. Then ask and answer.

School drama

1 Amy 2 Jill 3 Gemma 4 David 5 Fergus 6 Mike

king queen spy scientist sailor soldier

2 Write.

Was there a queen in the drama?

No, there wasn't.

When Amy's grandmother was young, school finished at age 1 15. There 2 wasn't a long summer vacation and they went to school 3 on Saturday. There were some math, 4 science, geography, and history classes. P.E. was gym class but there 5 weren't any English classes and of course, there weren't 6 any computers in schools.

any on Saturday science wasn't weren't 15

3 Ask your parents about their schools. Write three questions.

1
2
3

106 Review Units 7 and 8 Can talk about schools and school subjects

Girl: Last week we made an exciting school drama in English class.
Woman: Sounds interesting, Amy. What was it about?
Girl: Well, there were two kings who both wanted to be the first king to fly to the moon.
Woman: Were you one of the kings?
Girl: No, Gemma and Mike were the kings. I was a scientist who was making a spaceship.
Woman: How about Fergus? Was he in the drama?
Girl: Yes, he was a spy who looked scary. There were two spies. David was the other spy. He didn't look scary.
Woman: Were there any other parts in the drama?
Girl: There was a soldier who guarded the spaceship. Jill was the soldier.

Materials
Picture Cards 128–168, pictures of people/heroes (cut from magazines)

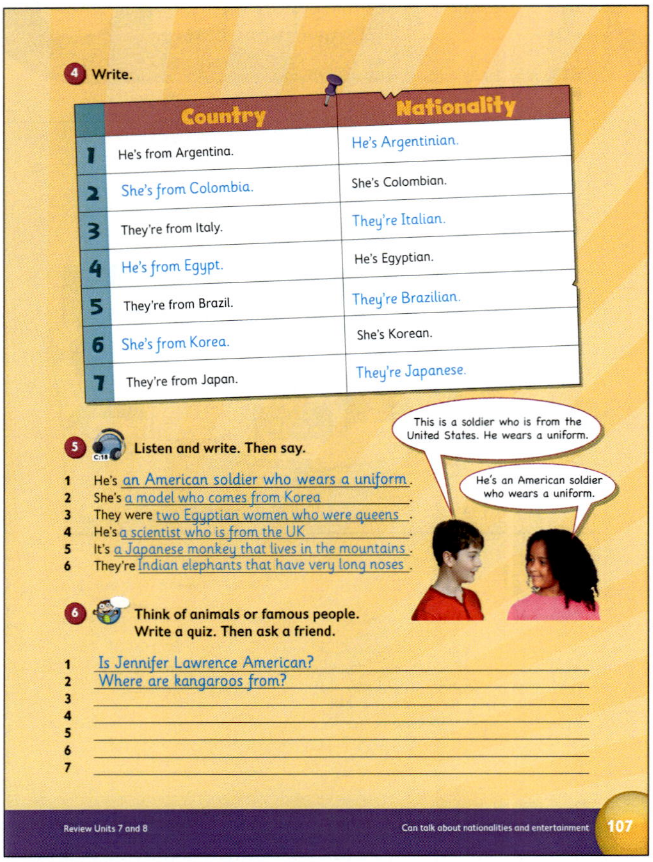

4 Write.

	Country	Nationality
1	He's from Argentina.	He's Argentinian.
2	She's from Colombia.	She's Colombian.
3	They're from Italy.	They're Italian.
4	He's from Egypt.	He's Egyptian.
5	They're from Brazil.	They're Brazilian.
6	She's from Korea.	She's Korean.
7	They're from Japan.	They're Japanese.

5 Listen and write. Then say.

1 He's an American soldier who wears a uniform.
2 She's a model who comes from Korea.
3 They were two Egyptian women who were queens.
4 He's a scientist who is from the UK.
5 It's a Japanese monkey that lives in the mountains.
6 They're Indian elephants that have very long noses.

6 Think of animals or famous people. Write a quiz. Then ask a friend.

1 Is Jennifer Lawrence American?
2 Where are kangaroos from?
3
4
5
6
7

Review Units 7 and 8 Can talk about nationalities and entertainment 107

- Play the audio again. This time, give students time to listen and match the student to the occupation by drawing a line. You may wish to pause the audio at times, to allow students enough time to complete their answers.
- Check answers by asking, e.g., *In the school drama, what role did Jill play? (She played the soldier.)* Students check their own work, or switch books with a partner.

2 Write.

- Allow students time to read the text and fill in the blanks.
- To check answers, have the class read the text chorally. Students check their own work.

3 Ask your parents about their schools. Write three questions.

- Pair students and give them time to discuss and write questions for their parents.
- Invite students to say a question, and write all the compiled questions on the board.
- Give students time to write down the additional questions in order to do the activity at home.

4 Write.

- Draw students' attention to the chart, and read the headings and the sentences chorally.
- Allow students time to do the activity.
- To check answers, have students switch their book with a partner. Elicit answers from the class.

5 Listen and write. Then say.

C:18

- Ask a volunteer to read out the example speech bubbles.
- Read the sentence beginnings chorally. Then play the audio, and tell students to listen only.

1 This is a soldier who is from the United States. He wears a uniform.
2 This woman is a model and she comes from Korea.
3 These are two women who were from Egypt. They were queens.
4 This is a man who is a scientist, and is from the UK.
5 This is a monkey that lives in the mountains of Japan.
6 These are elephants that live in India. Their noses are very long!

- Then play the audio again, pausing to allow students time to complete the answers.
- Invite volunteers to share their answers with the class, or say answers chorally. Students correct their own work.

6 Think of animals or famous people. Write a quiz. Then ask a friend.

- Give students time to write quiz questions.
- Pair students and give them time to ask and answer questions in pairs.
- To end the lesson, ask students what their favorite animal is. Have them say why.

- Watch the video story *He's escaping!* on Poptropica English World. Ask students what happened in the story. Watch again, stopping at key points, and ask them about the language, the images, or the story. Ask the students to role-play the story. Assign the roles of two of the characters to confident speakers and let other students play the other parts. Encourage them to say as much of the dialog as they can and prompt them where necessary.

Pop Quiz: Place Picture Cards 128–168 around the room and have students look at them. Tell them to close their eyes, and remove one of the Picture Cards. Whoever guesses first which card is missing, and can say a correct, complete sentence using that word, gets a point.

You may wish to give Review Test 4 (see page 216) at this time.

Goodbye

Unit Overview

Unit Objective

- I can review what I have learned

Skills

Speaking	• Can ask and answer about the story • Can use what I have learned
Writing	• Can write about the story • Can use what I have learned • Can complete simple sentences about characters in the story *(Workbook)* • Can complete simple sentences about my daily routine and favorite place *(Workbook)* • Can write simple sentences about my favorite person *(Workbook)*

Lesson 1 SB page 108 or Poptropica English World

Learning Objective
Can ask and answer about the story

Additional Language
jail

Warm-up

- Ask students to say things that happened in the story. Allow them to look back through the book to read their favorite sentences. Write these on the board. Have a vote to find out which sentence was the most popular with the class.

Open books and ask students to look at the pictures. Ask, *What are we learning today?* Write the lesson objective on the board: *We're reviewing the Ice Island story.*

1 Listen and number.

C:19

- Ask the class questions about each picture in turn. Students answer or guess, e.g., *What are they eating? (ice cream) Where are they? (in jail)*
- Play the audio and have students listen and look at the pictures.

1 She caught the thieves and she has a new pet.
2 They don't have the diamonds and they aren't at Bollington Hall. They are in jail.
3 They know Polly and Mike. They don't have any fish.
4 This boy has a dog and he loves eating strawberry ice cream.
5 She is also eating ice cream. Her mom is there, too.
6 He helped the Ice Detectives. He is a smart animal. He loves eating ice cream with his friends!
7 She is happy. She is wearing her diamond necklace.

- Give students time to do the activity. They have to listen and write the correct numbers in the boxes.
- Play the audio again, pausing for students to check their answers.

2 Ask and answer.

- Read the questions chorally.
- Pair students and give them time to do the activity.
- Invite students to come to the front and tell the class what their partner's thoughts are about the activities in Level 5.

Goodbye

1 Listen and number.

a 2 b 7 c 5 d 6 e 4 f 1 g 3

2 Ask and answer.

1 What was your favorite scene in the story? Why?
2 Who was your favorite character in the story? Why?
3 What was your favorite song in this book? Can you sing it?
4 Which *"Have Fun"* page was the best in this book?

108 Lesson 1 Can ask and answer about the story

- Find out what the class's favorite song is and sing it together.
- Find out what the class's favorite "HAVE FUN" page is, and do it again if possible.
- If there's time, ask students what part of the story was the most exciting part. Divide students into groups and have them role-play their favorite scene. Vote for the best role-play, and the best actress/actor.

Point to the lesson objective on the board. Ask students, *How did the story end?* Give students a minute to tell their partner. Ask students to point to where they think they are on the learning adventure poster. Ask students, *What was difficult? What do you want extra help with?* and help with pronunciation/extra practice.

Pop Quiz: Close books. Say the name of each character and ask students to say what happened to that character in the story, e.g., *Polly* (*She woke up at 2:00 a.m. on Thursday. She followed the skidoo. She ate ice cream. Smith pushed her in the lake.* etc.)

Homework WB page 88

3 Look and write. What unit are these pictures from?

1 Unit 2
2 Unit 8
3 Unit 5
4 Unit 7
5 Unit 4

4 Write. Who said it?

1 "Ah, those beautiful diamonds!" Hector Frost
2 "Eat your breakfast, guys." Polly's mom
3 "This is a job for the Ice Detectives." Polly
4 "The bear almost ate me." Smith
5 "A dog costume – how interesting!" The Queen of Ice Island

5 Write the answers.

1 What's the name of the big house in the story? Bollington Hall
2 What's the name of the bald thief? Smith
3 What's the name of the thief who loves diamonds? Hector Frost
4 What falls off a dog many times in the story? Red ribbons
5 Who wants to go to the lake? The explorers
6 Can Mike play soccer? Yes, he can.
7 What is Gizmo like? He's smart/brave.
8 Is Smith good at working out? Yes, he is.
9 What does Polly hear at 2:00 a.m.? She hears the skidoo.
10 What is the code in the tunnel? A school schedule (science 9:00, math 10:30, art 12:40)

Lesson 2 Can write about the story 109

Lesson 2 SB page 109 or Poptropica English World

Learning Objective
Can write about the story

Warm-up

- Hand out the cut-out Story Cards randomly. Students have to describe what is on the card. Then others have to explain what is happening in the story or guess the unit.

Open books and ask students to look at the book. Ask, *What are we learning today?* Write the lesson objective on the board: *We're remembering and writing about what happened in the story.*

3 Look and write. What unit are these pictures from?

- Draw students' attention to the pictures. Invite confident students to describe what is happening.
- Give students time to do the activity.
- Have students check answers in pairs. Elicit answers from the class.
- Invite students to give more details about the parts of the story that relate to the pictures.

4 Write. Who said this?

- Have students read the quotes chorally.
- To check answers, have students discuss in pairs. Elicit answers from the class. Students then check their own work.

5 Write the answers.

- Have students read the questions chorally.
- Give students time to do the activity.
- To check answers, hold a classroom quiz. Divide the class into two teams. Elicit answers from individual students. For each answer, have students raise hands when they got it correct. The team with the most hands raised gets a point.

Pop Quiz: Divide the class into two teams. Ask each team to write 10 difficult quiz questions on the story for the other team, with answers provided. Have the quiz in class, with different students asking the questions. See which team answers the most questions correctly.

Materials
Cut-out Story Cards (all units)

Homework WB page 89

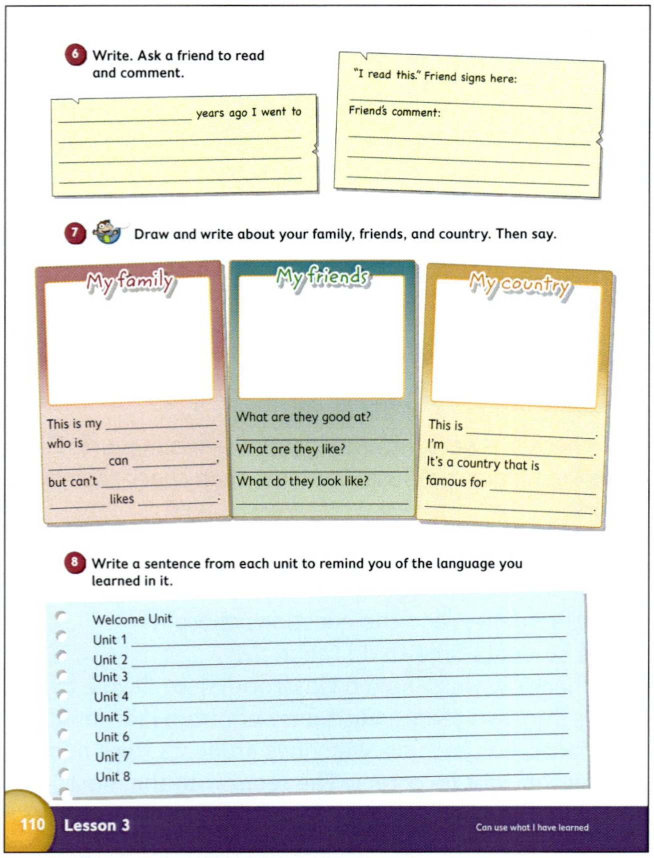

6 Write. Ask a friend to read and comment.

_____ years ago I went to

"I read this." Friend signs here:

Friend's comment:

7 Draw and write about your family, friends, and country. Then say.

My family

This is my _____
who is _____
_____ can _____.
but can't _____.
_____ likes _____.

My friends

What are they good at?
What are they like?
What do they look like?

My country

This is _____.
I'm _____.
It's a country that is famous for _____.

8 Write a sentence from each unit to remind you of the language you learned in it.

Welcome Unit
Unit 1
Unit 2
Unit 3
Unit 4
Unit 5
Unit 6
Unit 7
Unit 8

110 Lesson 3 Can use what I have learned

Lesson 3 SB page 110 or Poptropica English World

Learning Objective
Can use what I have learned

Warm-up

- Using Picture Cards 38–54, go over the activities and hobbies. Review spelling by using the word-side of the cards. Invite students to ask and answer question in small groups about what they are good / not good at. Have students report back to class about what other students are good or not good at.

Open books and ask students to look at the book. Ask, *What are we learning today?* Write the lesson objective on the board: *We're practicing what we learned in Level 5.*

6 Write. Ask a friend to read and comment.

- Allow students time to do the activity.
- Students switch books with a partner, who then reads the text, signs their name, and comments.
- Invite students to talk about their partner's comments. Discuss the comments that students have given their partners.

7 Draw and write about your family, friends, and country. Then say.

- Draw students attention to the three "introduction cards". Read the headings together, as well as the questions and sentence fragments. Give students time to do the activity.
- Invite students to come to the front and present to class. Keep notes for the Pop Quiz activity.

8 Write a sentence from each unit to remind you of the language you learned in it.

- Allow students time to do the activity.
- Invite students to present their sentences to class, and say why they are memorable. Have students vote for best presentation.

Pop Quiz: Based on your notes from Activity 7, ask questions of the class. To make the game more exciting, divide the class into two teams and play for points. (Those whose family, friends, or country are being referred to, cannot answer the question.)

Materials
Picture Cards 38–54

Homework WB page 90

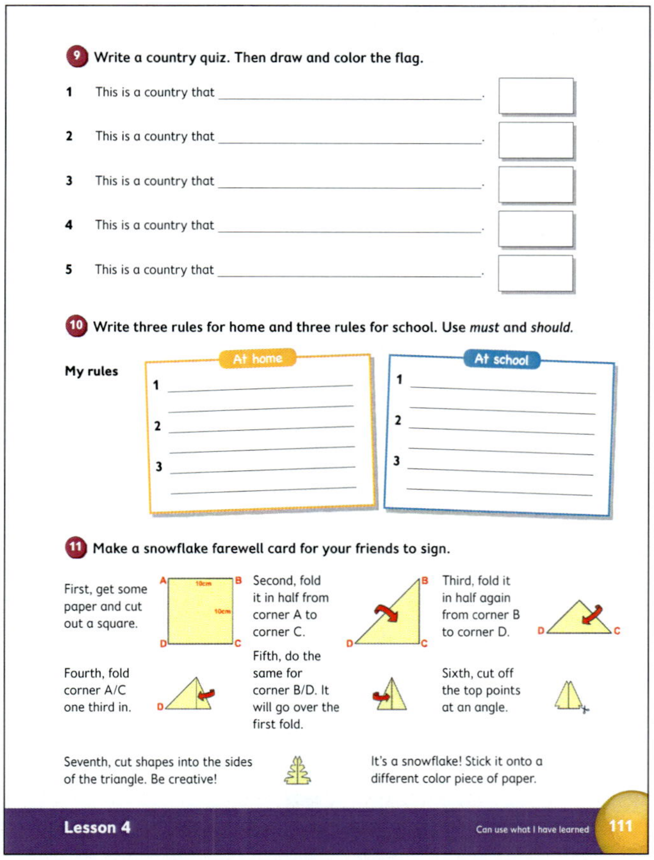

9 Write a country quiz. Then draw and color the flag.

1 This is a country that ________.
2 This is a country that ________.
3 This is a country that ________.
4 This is a country that ________.
5 This is a country that ________.

10 Write three rules for home and three rules for school. Use *must* and *should*.

My rules

At home
1 ________
2 ________
3 ________

At school
1 ________
2 ________
3 ________

11 Make a snowflake farewell card for your friends to sign.

First, get some paper and cut out a square.

Second, fold it in half from corner A to corner C.

Third, fold it in half again from corner B to corner D.

Fourth, fold corner A/C one third in.

Fifth, do the same for corner B/D. It will go over the first fold.

Sixth, cut off the top points at an angle.

Seventh, cut shapes into the sides of the triangle. Be creative!

It's a snowflake! Stick it onto a different color piece of paper.

Lesson 4 Can use what I have learned 111

Lesson 4 SB page 111 or Poptropica English World

Learning Objective
Can use what I have learned

Warm-up

- Using Picture Cards 23–37, review daily activities and adverbs of frequency. To check spelling, use the word-side of the card, then hold a spelling bee.

Open books and ask students to look at the book. Ask, *What are we learning today?* Write the lesson objective on the board: *We're practicing what we learned in Level 5.*

9 Write a country quiz. Then draw and color the flag.

- Allow students time to do the activity.
- Put students in groups of four to play the quiz game together.
- Hold a class quiz game for any of the countries not covered by the students. Ask students if they can draw any country flags of countries not yet discussed, and invite one or two to come to the front and draw on the board.

10 Write three rules for home and three rules for school. Use *must* and *should*.

- Draw students' attention to the rules cards. Give students time to do the activity.
- Put students into small groups to discuss. Invite some to present their ideas to class. Invite other students to ask questions. Vote on the best three rules for home/school, and write them on the board. Give students some time to remember them then erase the rules. At the end of class, test their memory.

11 Make a snowflake farewell card for your friends to sign.

- Prepare a snowflake card before class so that you can show students the finished product. Use white paper for the snowflake, and stick it on a different color card.
- Have students read the instructions chorally.
- Put students into small groups. It is best to do the activity together by giving the instructions, and working on another snowflake card yourself.
- When students have finished making the snowflake farewell card, have students mingle to ensure they get everyone's signature. Encourage students to write short notes as well, e.g., *Well done! / We finished Level 5! / Thanks for all your help!*
- Ask students if they have any questions about what they learned in Level 5.

Pop Quiz: Have students sit in a circle. Invite students to start off their favorite memory chants and sing their favorite songs. You can also ask students what their favorite games are, and play them.

Ask students if they can remember the things they learned in this level. Put their ideas on the board. Ask students to choose 2–3 ideas and write the words or sentences to show they understand the topic or language. Ask students to say where they are on their adventure and say, *Good job! Good luck with your new learning adventure!*

You may wish to give the End of Year Test (see page 220) at this time.

Materials
Picture Cards 23–37, white paper, glue, a prepared snowflake card (Activity 11)

Homework WB page 91

Activity Sheet 1

Activity Sheet 2

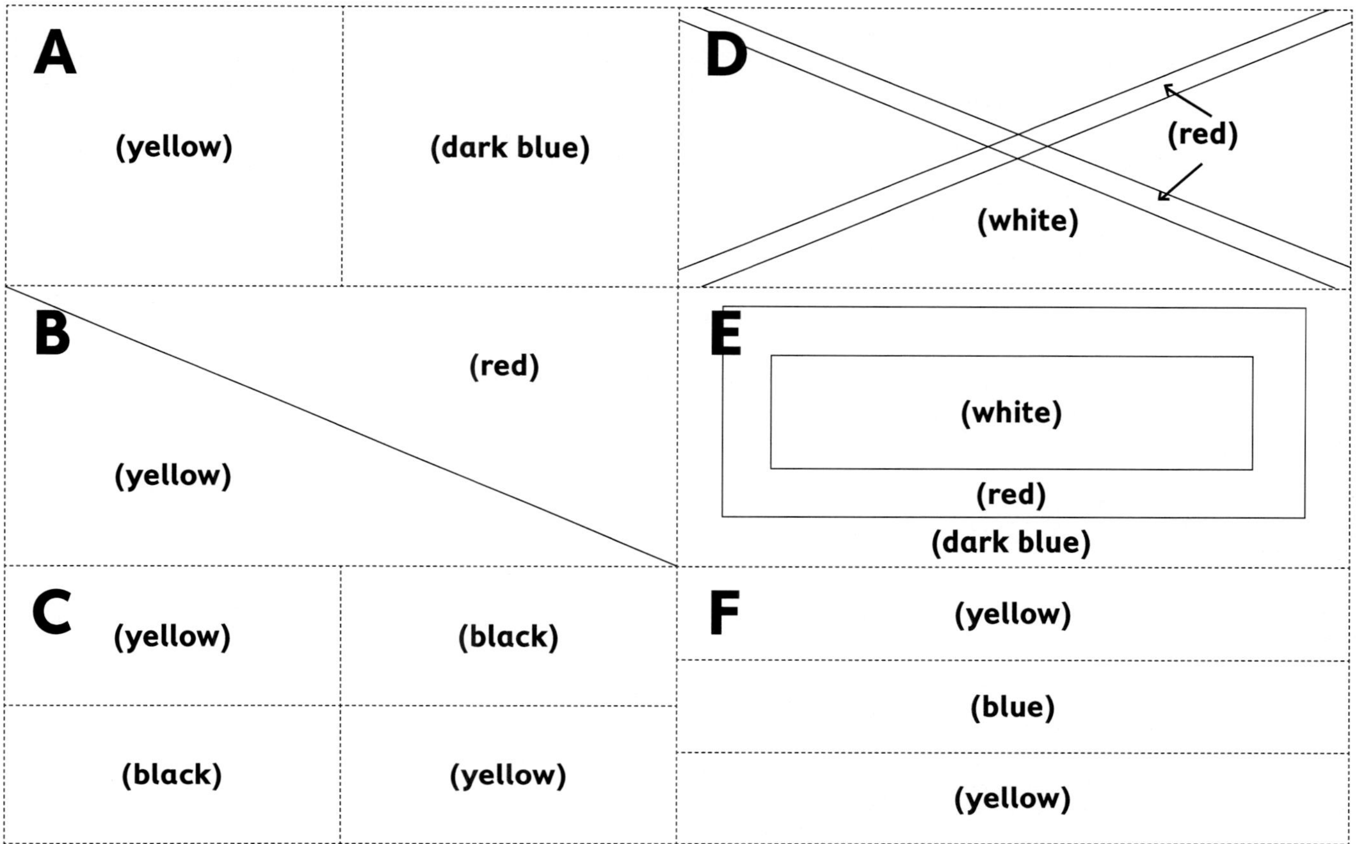

A I want to communicate with you.	**D** I need help.
B Man overboard.	**E** I need medical help.
C Stop your boat now!	**F** Stay clear! I am driving with difficulty.

Activity Sheet 3

every day

before school

after school

before bed

every morning

before a test

Activity Sheet 4

sometimes	never	usually	often	always
share music	small birthday gifts	birthday cards	show tickets	send text messages

Activity Sheet 5

Activity Sheet 6

Class Survey

What are we good at?
What do we like to do?

Name	Good at...	Not Good at...	Activities at "Dream Camp"

Workbook Script

Welcome

5 Listen and match. Then write.

1 Hi, I'm Mike. At nine o'clock, I'm studying. I get up early and study, so in the afternoon I can play soccer.
2 Hello. I'm Polly. At two o'clock, I'm swimming in the swimming pool. I'm not good at swimming, so I have swimming lessons.
3 I'm Smith. At ten o'clock, I'm working out. I like it. It makes me strong!

7 Listen and match.

1 She listened to some music on Monday morning.
2 He studied English on Thursday morning.
3 They played volleyball on Saturday afternoon.
4 She watched a soccer game on Wednesday evening.
5 They went to the park on Sunday afternoon.
6 He practiced the guitar on Tuesday evening.

11 Listen and match. Then write.

1 She danced at school on Monday morning.
2 He played baseball yesterday.
3 They cleaned the classroom two weeks ago.
4 She watched that movie two years ago.
5 They went to the library three days ago.

Unit 1, Friends

6 Listen and write.

So, Maddy, who is in your family? There's me, my mom and dad, and my grandpa... and Kipper the cat, of course. Dad is bald, and he has brown eyes. He's very tall. What about your mom? What does she look like? She has curly hair. And brown eyes? No, she doesn't have brown eyes. She has green eyes and glasses. And your grandpa? Grandpa has gray hair. He doesn't have glasses, but he has blue eyes and a mustache.

11 Listen and match. Then write.

1 Dan's a good hockey player. He practices every day. He likes talking to his friends.
2 Emma is very quiet in class. But she's always friendly to everyone.
3 Maddy doesn't always do her homework. And she usually gets up late! But she gets good grades.
4 Robbie helps his mom at home and his friends at school. He always works hard in his grandpa's yard.

20 Listen and match.

Hi, Grandma. Hi, Carlos. Are you having fun in the United States? Yes, I am! Seb's family is great. He has a sister, Megan. She's five and she's very funny. What does she look like? She's short – well, she's only five, so of course she's short... and she has curly, blond hair. She's very bossy, but she makes me laugh! And you're having a good time? Yes, it's fantastic! Seb's mom and dad are very creative. The food's nice. We do a lot of fun things. I'm very happy here! That's good, Carlos...

29 Listen and write.

My friend. What does she look like? My friend's name is Miki. She's tall and she has short, spiky hair. She has brown eyes and she wears glasses. She likes skirts and colorful T-shirts. What's she like? She's smart and sporty. She's a bit bossy, but it's OK. I like her because she's funny, talkative, and creative.

Unit 2, My life

2 Look and write. Then listen and check or cross for Dan.

I get up and brush my teeth in the morning. I make my bed every day. I wash my face before school. I'm on time for school every day. At school, classes are interesting. I take notes in class, and before a test I study a lot. I meet my friends after school, and then I do my homework before bed. I don't clean my room every day. I only clean it on Saturday.

4 What should they do before bed? Listen and match. Then write.

1 Robbie and Emma should say good night to their parents.
2 Emma should wash her hair.
3 Robbie should brush his teeth.
4 Dad should walk the dog.
5 Mom should clean the kitchen.

6 What must they do on Saturday? Listen and match. Then write.

1 Robbie and Emma must clean their rooms.
2 Mom and dad must take out the trash.
3 Maddy must practice the piano.
4 Dan must do his homework.

10 Listen and check. Then write.

I always brush my teeth before going to school and at night. Of course I do this every day. I should make my bed every day, but I only do it on Tuesday and Thursday. I do my homework after dinner on Monday, Wednesday, and Friday. My brother sets the table on Tuesday, but I set it on Monday, Wednesday, Thursday, and Friday. Sometimes I clean my room, but I never take out the trash – that is dad's job!

11 Listen and write.

I must get up at seven thirty. I must leave home at eight fifteen. I walk to school or sometimes run! I must be on time. School starts at eight forty-five, but I should be there at eight thirty. Today after school, I must buy a birthday present for my mom. It's her birthday tomorrow. At home, I always set the table. Today is Tuesday, so I must take out the trash before bed.

20 Read. Then listen and correct six differences. Then circle.

I get up at ten o'clock. I have chocolate and soda for breakfast. I never brush my teeth after breakfast. I often play computer games in the afternoon. After that, I watch a movie, eat dinner, and I go to bed at twelve o'clock.

24 Listen and write.

My evenings. In the evening I must do my homework. I always do my homework before dinner. After dinner I help my mom clean the table and wash the dishes. I often watch TV at seven thirty because my favorite show is on from seven thirty to eight. I sometimes email friends or play on my computer. I should go to bed at ten, but sometimes I'm late.

Unit 3, Free time

3 Look at Activity 2 and listen. Who is talking – Robbie or Dan?

I'm good at throwing and diving, but I'm not good at hitting.

16 Read. Then listen and correct six differences.

Dear Grandma, Action Camp is great! I'm here with Ellie because we both love sports. We go swimming every morning. I love swimming. I can swim fifteen meters underwater now. We have diving lessons, too. I'm not very good at diving because I feel scared, but Ellie can dive from the big diving board. She's fantastic! Ellie and I like jumping on the trampoline after lunch, and we love playing tennis together in the afternoon. Ellie is very good at running, and hitting the ball.
Mark

20 Listen to the music and check for yourself.

1 [dance music]
2 [reggae music]
3 [chart pop music]
4 [rap music]
5 [heavy metal music]
6 [opera music]
7 [indie rock music]
8 [classical music]

21 Listen again and choose your favorite. Then find that number and read about yourself.

[Repeat of the previous track]

23 Write. Then listen and circle T for True or F for False.

1 I love playing my guitar.
2 I win! I *can* play chess!
3 Oh, they aren't very good at singing.
4 Wow, do you like painting, Bill? I love it!

25 Listen and write.

My activities. I like playing tennis. I play tennis at a club. Yesterday, I was playing in the afternoon. We usually play games on Sunday, and we practice on Wednesday. I love swimming, too. I go swimming on Monday and Thursday. I love swimming in the ocean in the summer, too. At school, I'm good at sports and English. I'm not good at art, but the teacher helps me a lot.

Unit 4, Around the world

1 Listen and number.

1 the United Kingdom
2 Argentina
3 China
4 Mexico
5 Australia
6 the United States
7 Egypt
8 Spain
9 Italy
10 Brazil
11 India
12 Korea
13 Colombia
14 Japan

10 Read, guess, and write. Then listen and check your answers.

1 Are there any beaches in Australia? Yes, there are. In Australia, there are a lot of great beaches.
2 Is there a rain forest in Korea? Yes, there is.
3 Are there any volcanoes in Italy? Yes, there are.
4 Are there any volcanoes in Mexico? Yes, there are.
5 Is there a mountain taller than five thousand meters in Japan? No, there isn't.
6 Is there a river longer than the Amazon in China? No, there isn't.

13 Listen and circle the correct dog. Then write.

1 The dog is near the forest.
2 The dog is behind the skidoo.
3 The dog is between the forest and the skidoo.

17 Listen and circle.

Hi, Grandma. Hello, Mia. Where are you? I'm in Brazil. Are you in the rain forest? No, I'm not. I'm in a fantastic city – Rio de Janeiro. There are some nice places here. Are there any pyramids in Rio de Janeiro? No, there aren't. There are some beautiful beaches, though. There's a big statue, too – on a mountain next to the city. What's that music? It's the samba music of Brazil. I'm watching some people dancing. A lot of people here are very good at dancing!

20 Listen and write.

Come to Greenland! Ride on skidoos! Climb snowy mountains! See caves and waterfalls of ice! There aren't any big cities here, but there are some beautiful polar bears and reindeer in this cold place. Every day in Greenland is an adventure! Greenland – a world of ice!

24 Listen and write.

The river. There's a river near my house. I go there on my bike. There aren't any people near the river. There are a lot of trees and birds. The birds sing in the trees. There are fish in the river and sometimes they jump. There's a bridge over the river. Sometimes I sit under the bridge and read. I love the river.

Unit 5, Shopping

3 Listen. What does Maddy buy?

How much is that swimsuit, please? It's nineteen dollars and fifty cents. And how much are those sunglasses? They're fifteen dollars. May I buy the sunglasses, please? Yes, of course.

5 The prices in Activity 4 are wrong. Listen and circle the correct prices.

1 How much is that wallet? It's twenty-nine dollars.
2 How much is that bracelet? It's twelve dollars and fifty cents.
3 How much is that handbag? It's nineteen dollars.
4 How much is that jacket? It's two hundred and twelve dollars.
5 How much are those sneakers? They're forty-two dollars.
6 How much is that umbrella? It's twenty-five dollars and fifty cents.

14 Listen and write the prices. What does the Queen buy?

Hello. I like this hat. How much is it? It's nine dollars and ninety-nine cents. Oh... And the scarf? How much is that scarf? It's thirty dollars. It's very long. Yes, it is. Hmm. How much are those shoes? They're sixty-four dollars and ninety-nine cents. Sixty-four dollars and ninety-nine cents. That's more like it. What about these boots? How much are they? The boots are ninety-five dollars. They're new this week. Better and better! And the belt? How much is it? It's forty dollars. Ergh. OK. How much is that dress? That dress? It's nine hundred and ninety-nine dollars! I love it! May I buy it, please? Yes, of course!

18 Listen and check the ads the boys talk about.

Hey, Tom! There's an ad for a bike here. Great! My old bike is too small now. Can I see the ad? Here you are. Thanks. That bike is too big. I'm only a hundred and forty centimeters tall. What about that skateboard? You don't have a skateboard. The skateboard is thirty-eight dollars! It's too expensive. Hey, look! Those video games are cheap. Wow! Twenty games for seventeen dollars. I want to buy them. Good idea! Can I play the games with you?

19 Listen again and circle.

[Repeat of the previous track]

22 Listen and write.

1 What do you want to do, Jack? I want to go sailing. I have a warm jacket, my sunglasses, and sailing shoes.
2 What do you want to do, Pete? I want to go to dance class. I have dancing shoes, a T-shirt, and baggy pants.
3 What do you want to do, Sally? I want to go horseback riding. I have long boots, tight pants, and a hard hat.

25 Listen and write. Whose are these?

OK. These clothes were here in school last night. Whose are they? First is this dress. Whose is this? It's mine. Good. OK, here you go, Maddy. Next. Whose umbrella is this? That's mine. It's new. It was very expensive. OK. Be more careful, Dan. OK, next are these shoes – whose are they? Emma, are they yours? No, they aren't mine, but that hat is. They're my shoes. OK. Here you go, Robbie. Thank you. And here you go, Emma. Thank you.

26 **Listen and write.**

My clothes. My favorite T-shirt is white, with small letters on the back. It's really cool. My favorite shoes are my sneakers. They're red and black. I don't like my winter boots because they're old-fashioned, and my summer sandals are too small now. I like my school uniform. I really like the jacket. It's green and gold. They're my favorite colors.

Unit 6, Party time

3 **Listen and check the true sentences in Activity 2.**

Hello, Dan. How was your weekend? Hi, Mrs. Baker. It was great, thanks! Yesterday was my birthday. I'm twelve. Really? Happy Birthday! Did you get any nice presents? Yes, I got a new basketball, and Robbie gave me some cool sneakers. My birthday party was fun. All my friends were there, and of course they sang "Happy Birthday". What about your cousins, Saskia and Ollie? My cousins were in Hawaii with my aunt and uncle. But my grandparents were at the party. There were some games in the garden. But it was rainy yesterday! Yes. Later it was rainy, but we played a lot before the rain. After the games, we ate pizza and cake. Sounds great. Did your mom make the cake? No, Maddy made it. She gave it to me as a present. It was good.

7 **Listen and match.**

Hi, I'm Annabel. December was a really fun month – there were lots of parties! My cousin Taylor's birthday was on December second, and I went to her party. Then, on December eleventh, it was my mom's birthday. The dance show was on December thirteenth. That was a lot of fun! Then I went to my soccer club party on December seventeenth, and there was a party at school on December twentieth. And, of course, on December twenty-fifth it was Christmas Day, and there was a big meal with all my grandparents, uncles, aunts, and cousins.

10 **Listen and write the dates.**

Last year my family went on a long vacation. We went to China first. We arrived in Shanghai on July fifth. We went on a boat and saw a lot of tall buildings. On July ninth, we went to Beijing. We walked on the Great Wall of China. We walked for about an hour. The wall is very strong and very long. On July fourteenth, we went to Korea. We went to Seoul and met some new friends. We had a party and they gave us some presents! On July nineteenth, we said goodbye to our new friends in Seoul, and went to an island. We played on a beach – it was really fun! On July twenty-third, we were in Japan. We saw a temple and ate a lot of fish! On July twenty-fifth, we took a fast train to Mount Fuji and climbed to the top. It was very hot at the start but cool at the top. It was a really great vacation!

18 **Listen and number.**

Hi, Lucy. How was the party? It was fantastic. I met a lot of my friends from school. Oh, good. And was it very cold? No, it was sunny, but windy. Was the food nice? Yes, the food was great. We had fish and salad, then strawberries. Yum! Were there any games? Yes, we played soccer on the beach. That was fun, but I wasn't very good at kicking the ball. Was there dancing? No, but we sang after the meal. Some of the songs were very funny!

19 **Listen again and complete for Lucy.**

[Repeat of the previous track]

21 **Listen and check the things that were on the *Mayflower*.**

There was a doctor on the *Mayflower*. His name was Doctor Fuller. There were some chickens and pigs, but they were the only animals. There were some books, and there were some hats and clothes for the cold winters in America.

28 **Listen and write.**

A fun party. I went to a birthday party at my school. The school was fifty years old. Parents and grandparents came to the school party. There were drinks and food. We ate a lot. The teachers sang, and we played games outside. In the evening, we danced and talked with friends. The bakery in our town made a very big cake and gave it to the school. It was a fun party!

Unit 7, School

1 **Listen and write.**

The first class at school was easy. The second and third classes were difficult. There was an exciting game in the fourth class. Lunch was relaxing, but boring, too. The classes after lunch were interesting. In the last class, we read some poems. Some were funny, some were romantic, and some were scary.

2 **Listen and write for Maddy. Use words from Activity 1.**

1 Our school book last year was *Dinosaurs*. It was boring for me. But my friend liked it.
2 My mom has a book called *Summer Love*. I read it, too. It was a very romantic story.
3 Our school book in the summer was *Anna and the Aliens*. It was funny.
4 My first English book was the *First Book of Words*. It was easy.
5 Our teacher's favorite book last year was *Fun with Numbers*. It was difficult, but I like math.
6 Our school book in the spring was *The Adventures of 009*. It was exciting.

8 Write. Then listen and circle T for True or F for False.

Last week was a fantastic week! P.E. and geography are sometimes boring, but last week they weren't boring. Geography was interesting, but it wasn't easy. History and music were fun. Math was very interesting. Science and computer science were both very easy. There was an art class on Tuesday. I usually like art, but this week it was very boring.

10 Listen and circle. Then write.

On Monday, Dan's homework was computer science, and on Tuesday it was history. On Wednesday, his homework was science. Dan doesn't like science, but the homework was interesting. Thursday's art homework was easy, and on Friday Dan had music homework.

22 Listen and write.

And then we went to the United States, and I went to school there. Were you happy at your new school? No, I wasn't. It was very scary in a class with lots of other children. Were your teachers good? Yes, they were. But the math and English classes were too easy, and the history and geography classes were too difficult. What was your favorite subject? P.E. – I was on the basketball team. It was very exciting.

27 Listen and write.

My favorite subjects last year. My favorite subjects last year were English, P.E., and science. English was good because we read a lot of romantic poems. Science was difficult, but the teacher was very good. Her classes were interesting. She's my favorite teacher. P.E. was fun because I'm good at sports. Wednesday was my favorite day because we played sports all afternoon. P.E. was easy because there were no tests.

Unit 8, Entertainment

2 Listen and match.

Hey, Emma. Look at my magazine. Do you know these people? Nicole Kidman... hmm... Is Nicole Kidman a singer? No, she isn't. She's an Australian movie star. What about J.K. Rowling? Is she a movie star? No, she isn't. She's a writer – a British writer. What about Rafael Nadal? Is he Spanish? Yes, he is. He's a Spanish tennis player. And is Lionel Messi Spanish, too? No, he isn't. He's Argentinian. He's an Argentinian soccer player. And then there's Beyoncé. Yes. She's an American singer. I want to be a singer, too!

4 Listen and match.

1 Where's she from? She's from the United Kingdom.
2 Is he from Brazil? Yes, he is. He's Brazilian.
3 Is she from Egypt? No, she isn't. She's Italian.
4 Where's he from? He's from China.
5 Is she from Argentina? Yes, she is.
6 Is he from Egypt? Yes, he is. He's Egyptian.

8 Listen and number.

1 This is the girl who is walking her dog.
2 These are the girls who are playing badminton.
3 This is the boy who is catching a ball.
4 This is the boy who is throwing a ball.
5 This is the girl who is kicking the ball.
6 This is the boy who is running.
7 This is the girl who is wearing a big hat with her country's flag on it.
8 This is the Italian man who is selling ice cream.

17 Read. Then listen and number.

1 Well, we have an exciting game here today. The Spanish player, Miguel Leibar, is playing the Chinese player, Li Chan, and it's five games all. The two men are playing fantastic tennis. The game...
2 Last year, you were a king in your first movie. Now you're famous all around the world. How do you feel about that? Well, I don't think about it very often. I'm an actor, yes, but I'm a schoolboy, too. I do my homework, I play video games...
3 Where's the water? I'm thirsty! There isn't any clean water on the island. Oh, no! Here! Have some fruit. I got them two days ago.

25 Listen and write.

My favorite entertainment. My favorite kind of entertainment is watching TV. I love watching movies at home. I often watch one movie many times. I like watching movies that are in English. My favorite actor is Robert Pattinson, because he's handsome. I listen to music, too. I download music from the Internet. I love American music. I like playing many sports, and often play with my friends in the park.

Goodbye

5 Listen and write.

Captain Formosa went around the world in his submarine. He started from the United Kingdom on March first, and sailed to Spain. He got to Spain on March twenty-third. Next, on March thirtieth, he went to Italy, and then he had a long trip to the United States. He got to the United States on April twenty-ninth. He sailed down from the United States to Mexico on May sixth, and then down to Argentina on May twenty-seventh. To end his tour, he went to Asia, first to China, then Korea, then Japan. He visited China on June twenty-first, Korea on July second, and Japan on July eighth.

Workbook Answer Key

Welcome

page 4, Activity 1

1 Hector Frost **2** Smith **3** Polly **4** Mike
5 Gizmo **6** The Queen of Ice Island **7** Polly's mom

page 4, Activity 2

b 1 **c** 2 **d** 6 **e** 3 **f** 5 **g** 7

page 5, Activity 3

1 c **2** b

page 5, Activity 4

1 F **2** T **3** F **4** T **5** T **6** F

page 5, Activity 5

1 Mike, 9 o'clock, desk
2 Polly, 2 o'clock, swimming pool
3 Smith, 10 o'clock, training weights

1 He's studying. **2** She's swimming.
3 He's working out.

page 6, Activity 6

1 riding **2** are playing **3** He is climbing.
4 They are running. **5** They are singing.
6 They are drawing. **7** He is crying.
8 She is playing

page 6, Activity 7

1 c **2** e **3** b **4** f **5** a **6** d

page 6, Activity 8

1 listened **2** studied **3** played **4** watched
5 went **6** practiced

page 7, Activity 9

1 Monday **2** Sunday **3** Tuesday

page 7, Activity 11

1 on Monday morning **2** yesterday **3** two weeks ago **4** two years ago **5** three days ago

1 danced, on Monday morning **2** played baseball yesterday **3** cleaned the classroom two weeks ago **4** watched, movies two years ago **5** went to the library three days ago

Unit 1, Friends

page 8, Activity 1

1 light hair **2** bald **3** spiky hair **4** dark hair
5 cute **6** handsome **7** good-looking **8** beautiful

page 8, Activity 2

1 light **2** dark **3** spiky **4** handsome

page 9, Activity 4

1 What does she look like? **2** What do they look like?
3 What does he look like?

page 9, Activity 5

1 is ✓ **2** has **3** is ✓ **4** has **5** are **6** have ✓

page 9, Activity 6

Dad: brown, tall
Mom: curly, green, glasses
Grandpa: gray, blue, mustache

page 10, Activity 8

1 c **2** a **3** b **4** e **5** f **6** d

page 11, Activity 11

1 sporty, talkative **2** Emma like, friendly, talkative
3 What's Maddy like, smart, lazy
4 What's Robbie like, helpful, hard-working

page 11, Activity 12

1 because **2** and **3** and **4** because **5** but
6 but

page 12, Activity 14

1 Smith **2** Polly **3** Mike **4** Hector Frost

page 12, Activity 15

1 b **2** c

page 12, Activity 16

1 come on **2** beard **3** thieves **4** plan
5 strawberry **6** follow

page 13, Activity 18

a 1 **b** 4 **c** 2 **d** 1

page 14, Activity 20

1 funny, bossy **2** creative **3** nice **4** happy

page 15, Activity 24

1 picture **2** 1500 **3** thin **4** curly **5** short
6 mustache **7** young **8** 28

page 16, Activity 25

1 i **2** j **3** f **4** h **5** c **6** d **7** g **8** e
9 a **10** b

page 16, Activity 26

am/is/are: bald, beautiful, good-looking, tall
have/has: blue eyes, long hair, spiky hair, straight hair

page 16, Activity 27

1 does, She is **2** does, He is **3** do, They are
a 1 **b** 3 **c** 2

page 17, Activity 28

1 What is she like? She is tall and has spiky, black hair.
2 What are they like? They are beautiful and have long, straight hair.
3 What is your uncle like? He is short and bald.

page 17, Activity 29

1 name **2** tall **3** spiky **4** likes **5** smart
6 sporty **7** bossy **8** talkative **9** creative

Unit 2, My life

page 18, Activity 1

a 4 **b** 2 **c** 6 **d** 8 **e** 3 **f** 5 **g** 10 **h** 7
i 1 **j** 9

page 18, Activity 2

2 make my bed **3** on time **4** take notes **5** study
6 meet my friends **7** clean my room
1 ✓ **2** ✓ **3** ✓ **4** ✓ **5** ✓ **6** ✓ **7** ✗

page 19, Activity 4

1 c **2** e **3** a **4** b **5** d
1 Robbie and Emma should say good night to their parents.
2 Emma should wash her hair.
3 Robbie should brush his teeth.
4 Dad should walk the dog.
5 Mom should clean the kitchen.

page 19, Activity 6

1 b **2** c **3** d **4** a

page 20, Activity 7

2 always **3** sometimes **4** often

page 20, Activity 9

2 This is the dog's **3** This is Sasha's
4 This is Matt's

page 21, Activity 10

brush my teeth: Monday, Tuesday, Wednesday, Thursday, and Friday
make my bed: Tuesday and Thursday
do my homework: Monday, Wednesday, and Friday
set the table: Monday, Wednesday, Thursday, and Friday
take out the trash: never
2 She sometimes makes her bed.
3 She often does her homework.
4 She usually sets the table.
5 She never takes out the trash.

page 21, Activity 11

1 must **2** seven thirty **3** must **4** eight fifteen
5 walk **6** must **7** time **8** eight forty-five
9 should **10** eight thirty **11** must buy **12** always
13 before

page 22, Activity 12

1 Smith **2** igloo **3** fire **4** sleep **5** shopping
6 newspaper

page 22, Activity 13

2 He cleans his room at one fifteen.
3 He watches TV at two o'clock.
4 He washes the dog at three thirty.
5 He eats dinner at seven forty-five.
6 He goes to bed at ten o'clock.

page 23, Activity 15

a 4 **b** 1 **c** 3 **d** 2
b She should give John a ticket for a show.
c She should send Fiona some flowers.
d She should send Tom a text message.

page 24, Activity 17

2 watches, should not watch **3** makes, should make **4** washes, should wash **5** does, must do **6** brushes, should brush

page 24, Activity 18

1 always **2** must get up **3** sometimes sings **4** His **5** usually get up **6** often eat **7** always eats **8** should

page 25, Activity 19

2 O **3** N **4** E **5** S BONES

page 25, Activity 20

~~eggs on toast~~ chocolate and soda, ~~always~~ never, ~~soccer~~ computer games, ~~take a shower~~ watch a movie, ~~nine~~ twelve

page 26, Activity 21

1 g **2** d **3** h **4** c **5** a **6** b **7** e **8** f **9** j **10** i

page 26, Activity 22

1 You must make your bed every day. d
2 They should brush their teeth after breakfast. b
3 We should help our parents clean the house. c
4 I must finish this homework before 10 p.m. a

page 26, Activity 23

1 3 **2** 4 **3** 1 **4** 2

page 27, Activity 24

1 must **2** always **3** dinner **4** help **5** wash **6** often **7** sometimes **8** should

Unit 3, Free time

page 28, Activity 1

1 e **2** a **3** c **4** b **5** d **6** h **7** f **8** i **9** g

page 28, Activity 2

2 hitting **3** good at diving
4 not good at playing video games
5 good at catching **6** good at telling jokes

page 28, Activity 3

Robbie

page 29, Activity 4

1 What **2** I'm **3** at **4** isn't **5** they **6** Are **7** good **8** am **9** I'm not

page 29, Activity 5

2 Are you good at climbing?
3 Are you good at fishing?
4 Are you good at diving?

page 30, Activity 7

2 running races **3** playing the drums **4** playing chess **5** playing video games **6** acting **7** singing in a choir ***hidden word:*** singing karaoke

page 30, Activity 8

1 He loves jumping on the trampoline.
2 She is good at playing chess.
3 They love drawing.
4 They don't like singing.
5 They are good at running races.
6 She doesn't like singing in a choir.

page 31, Activity 9

1 sleeping **2** were, swimming **3** was, was eating lunch **4** were, were reading **5** was, doing, 5:00, He was playing **6** was, doing, She was meeting friends.

page 31, Activity 10

1 was **2** Were, eating, were, weren't
3 Was, working, he wasn't
4 Were, watching, they were, they weren't
1 Yes, she was. **2** No, they weren't. **3** No, he wasn't. **4** Yes, they were.

page 32, Activity 11

1 F Polly wants to go towards the mountains.
2 F Polly's mom made them breakfast.
3 T
4 F Mike always plays soccer on Saturdays.
5 F They see tracks, the roof of Bollington Hall, and a red ribbon.

page 32, Activity 12

1 running races 2 Yes, he is. 3 jumping on the trampoline, No, he doesn't. 4 Are they good at playing chess?

page 33, Activity 14

2 She should join a drama club. 3 They should take art classes. 4 She should join a sports team.
5 He should start a band.

page 34, Activity 16

~~50~~ 15, ~~dance~~ diving, ~~breakfast~~ lunch, ~~soccer~~ tennis, ~~morning~~ afternoon

page 34, Activity 17

1 He loves swimming in the morning. 2 Yes, he can. 3 No, he isn't. 4 Yes, she is. 5 They like jumping on the trampoline after lunch. 6 Yes, they do.

page 34, Activity 18

singing, playing, hitting, running, diving, riding

page 35, Activity 19

1 My 2 playing 3 good at 4 play 5 writing
6 write

page 36, Activity 22

1 d 2 i 3 g 4 h 5 f 6 a 7 b 8 e
9 j 10 c

page 36, Activity 23

1 Sam loves playing my guitar. T
2 Anna can't play chess. F
3 The children are good at singing. F
4 Bill doesn't like painting. F

page 36, Activity 24

1 was, She was playing baseball.
2 were,t They were playing video games.

page 37, Activity 25

1 playing 2 was 3 practice 4 go 5 love
6 in 7 good 8 not 9 but

Unit 4, Around the world

page 38, Activity 1

a 8 b 1 c 2 d 9 e 6 f 10 g 4 h 7
i 14 j 5 k 12 l 13 m 11 n 3

page 38, Activity 2

1 India 2 Italy 3 Japan 5 the United Kingdom 6 China 7 Argentina 8 Australia
9 Mexico 10 Egypt 11 Spain 12 Korea
13 Brazil 14 Colombia

page 39, Activity 3

1 the tree 2 There are, under the 3 There's, the beach 4 There aren't any, beach 5 There aren't any

page 39, Activity 4

1 some 2 a 3 any 4 some 5 a

page 39, Activity 5

1 There aren't any hippos in China.
2 There's a rain forest in Australia.
3 There isn't a snowy mountain in Egypt.
4 There aren't any elephants in Mexico.
5 There are beautiful beaches in Spain.

page 40, Activity 7

pyramid, castle, volcano, city, statue, cave, town, farm, factory ***hidden word:*** Australia

page 40, Activity 8

1 town 2 volcanoes 3 city 4 statues
5 pyramids 6 caves 7 castle 8 factories
9 farm

page 41, Activity 9

1 Are there any, in
2 Is there a, in, Yes, there is.
3 Are there any, in, No, there aren't.
4 Are there any, in, Yes, there are.

page 41, Activity 10

2 Yes, there is. 3 Yes, there are. 4 Yes, there are.
5 No, there isn't. 6 No, there isn't.

page 42, Activity 12

1 Polly and Mike have a map.
2 There aren't any roads to Bollington Hall.
3 There are some tracks going towards Bollington Hall.
4 There are some ribbons on the dog.
5 Frost isn't happy to see the children in the forest.

page 42, Activity 13

1 near the forest (Gizmo)
2 The dog is behind the skidoo. (Gizmo)
3 The dog is between the forest and the skidoo. (Tayler)

page 43, Activity 15

Writing: Sandra, Diego
Art: Peter, George
Computers: Sofia, Maria
Talking: Jenny, John

page 44, Activity 17

1 Brazil **2** grandma **3** city **4** beaches **5** statue **6** dancing

page 44, Activity 18

1 Grandpa **2** rain forest **3** trees **4** animals **5** river **6** beautiful

page 45, Activity 20

1 Ride **2** mountains **3** caves **4** any **5** some **6** bears **7** day

page 46, Activity 22

1 j **2** d **3** c **4** a **5** h **6** f **7** i **8** b **9** g **10** e

page 46, Activity 23

1 Is there a desert in Asia? Yes, there is.
2 Is there a rain forest in Italy? No, there isn't.
3 Are there any statues in Brazil? Yes, there are.
4 Are there any volcanoes in Egypt? Yes, there are.

page 47, Activity 24

1 on **2** There **3** any **4** are **5** birds **6** sing **7** fish **8** sometimes **9** There's **10** under

Unit 5, Shopping

page 48, Activity 1

1 jacket **2** swimsuit **3** watch **4** bracelet **5** wallet **6** handbag **7** umbrella **8** gloves **9** belt **10** sunglasses **11** hoodie

page 48, Activity 2

1 is, swimsuit **2** are, sunglasses **3** is, wallet **4** are, gloves

page 48, Activity 3

sunglasses

page 49, Activity 4

1 thirty dollars **2** twenty-one dollars and fifty cents **3** ninety-nine dollars **4** one hundred and twelve dollars **5** four hundred and twenty dollars **6** fifty-five dollars and fifty cents

page 49, Activity 5

1 c **2** a **3** b **4** a **5** c **6** b

page 49, Activity 6

1 much **2** dollars **3** how **4** hundred **5** please **6** course

page 50, Activity 7

a 2 **b** 3 **c** 6 **d** 4 **e** 5 **f** 1

page 50, Activity 8

1 tight **2** toy is too expensive **3** sweater is too baggy **4** hats are too old-fashioned

page 51, Activity 10

1 d **2** c **3** a **4** e **5** b

page 51, Activity 11

2 These pants are too baggy.
3 This sweater is too tight.
4 These shorts are too long.

page 51, Activity 12

1 It's Sky's. **2** They're Lee's. his **3** Whose sweater is this? his **4** Whose shorts are these? They're his.

page 52, Activity 13

1 Polly's mom **2** A jacket **3** The explorers
4 Smith **5** Polly **6** No, he doesn't.

page 52, Activity 14

2 $30 **3** $64.99 **4** $95 **5** $40
6 $999

page 54, Activity 18

1, 2, 4

page 54, Activity 19

1 big **2** expensive **3** video games

page 55, Activity 21

1 shorts and a T-shirt **2** a jacket **3** sunglasses
4 a hat **5** a swimsuit

page 55, Activity 22

1 sailing **2** jacket **3** sunglasses
4 sailing shoes **5** dance **6** dancing **7** T-shirt
8 baggy **9** horseback **10** boots **11** tight
12 hat

page 56, Activity 23

1 c **2** g **3** e **4** b **5** f **6** a **7** d

page 56, Activity 24

a 3 **b** 8 **c** 7 **d** 4 **e** 5 **f** 2 **g** 1 **h** 6

page 56, Activity 25

1 Maddy's **2** Dan's **3** Robbie's **4** Emma's

page 57, Activity 26

1 T-shirt **2** back **3** sneakers **4** red **5** because
6 old-fashioned **7** sandals **8** too **9** school
10 colors

Unit 6, Party time

page 58, Activity 1

1 made **2** had **3** came **4** gave **5** saw
6 brought **7** met **8** ate **9** got **10** sang

page 58, Activity 2

1 was **2** got **3** gave **4** sang **5** went **6** were
7 ate **8** made

page 58, Activity 3

1, 3, 4, 6, 7

page 59, Activity 4

1 had **2** came **3** brought **4** gave **5** made

page 59, Activity 5

1 come **2** make **3** sing **4** have

page 59, Activity 6

1 Emma **2** Emma **3** Robbie **4** Robbie
5 Emma **6** Robbie

page 60, Activity 7

2 b **11** c **13** f **17** e **20** d **25** a

page 60, Activity 8

2 December 25th **3** December 11th
4 December 2nd **5** December 17th
6 December 13th

page 61, Activity 10

1 fifth **2** ninth **3** fourteenth **4** nineteenth
5 twenty-third **6** twenty-fifth

page 61, Activity 11

1 fifth, China, went, saw **2** ninth, walked
3 fourteenth, Korea, met, had **4** nineteenth, played
5 twenty-third, Japan, saw, ate **6** twenty-fifth, climbed

page 62, Activity 12

a 4 **b** 6 **c** 1 **d** 3 **e** 5 **f** 2

page 63, Activity 15

1 c **2** e **3** a **4** d **5** g **6** f **7** b

page 64, Activity 18

a 2 **b** 3 **c** 4 **d** 1

page 64, Activity 19

2 sunny **3** windy **4** fish **5** soccer **6** No, didn't.
7 Yes, did.

page 65, Activity 21

a doctor, chickens, pigs, books, hats, clothes

page 65, Activity 22

1 were **2** were **3** was **4** went **5** was **6** had
7 ate **8** said

page 66, Activity 24

1 fourth **2** seventh **3** twenty-fifth
4 twenty-fourth **5** eleventh **6** seventh **7** sixth
8 second

page 66, Activity 26

1 went **2** met **3** made **4** had **5** played
6 bring **7** ate **8** were **9** was

page 66, Activity 27

1 It was yesterday. **2** It was in the town park.

page 67, Activity 28

1 went **2** came **3** were **4** ate **5** sang
6 played **7** danced **8** made **9** gave **10** was

Unit 7, School

page 68, Activity 1

1 easy **2** difficult **3** exciting **4** relaxing
5 boring **6** interesting **7** funny **8** romantic
9 scary

page 68, Activity 2

1 boring **2** romantic **3** funny **4** easy
5 difficult **6** exciting

page 69, Activity 4

1 c **2** a **3** f **4** d **5** b **6** e

page 69, Activity 5

1 How old were you?
2 Was your teacher patient?
3 Were there any scary things?
4 Were you happy?

page 70, Activity 7

geography, music, science, math, art, history
hidden word: English

page 70, Activity 8

1 P.E. and geography were boring. F
2 Geography wasn't easy. T
3 History and music were fun. T
4 Math wasn't interesting. F
5 Science and computer science weren't difficult. T
6 Art was exciting. F

page 71, Activity 10

computer science, history, science, art, music
1 Yes, he did. **2** No, he didn't. **3** No. He didn't.
4 Yes, he did. **5** Yes, he did.

page 71, Activity 11

1 English, No, it wasn't. It was easy.
2 Yes, it was.
3 No, it wasn't. It was boring.
4 geography, art, No, it wasn't. It was interesting.
5 No, it wasn't. It was relaxing.

page 72, Activity 13

1 A police officer **2** tunnel **3** a school schedule
4 code **5** 12:40 **6** night

page 72, Activity 14

1 a **2** a

page 72, Activity 15

1 party **2** cave **3** great job **4** tunnel **5** phew

page 73, Activity 17

1 What was your favorite food?
2 What was your favorite color?
3 Who was your favorite singer?
4 Was math easy for you?
5 Who was your favorite movie star?
6 Did you play an instrument?
7 Did you like scary movies?
8 What was your favorite subject?
9 Was school fun for you?
10 Were you good at P.E.?

page 74, Activity 19

1 Thursday **2** statues **3** art **4** interesting
5 tired **6** buses

page 75, Activity 21

2 Were there any horses on your farm? Yes, there were.
3 Was there a radio in your house? Yes, there was.
4 Were there any teachers near your house? No, there weren't.

page 75, Activity 22

1 school **2** Were **3** wasn't **4** scary **5** math
6 easy **7** history **8** difficult **9** P.E. **10** exciting

page 76, Activity 24

1 d **2** g **3** f **4** e **5** b **6** a **7** c

page 76, Activity 25

1 wasn't **2** Was **3** was **4** weren't **5** Were
6 there **7** were

page 76, Activity 26

1 Were **2** were **3** were **4** Was **5** was
6 wasn't **7** were **8** was

page 77, Activity 27

1 science **2** English **3** romantic **4** difficult
5 was **6** interesting **7** P.E. **8** because
9 favorite **10** easy

Unit 8, Entertainment

page 78, Activity 1

2 Egyptian **3** Japanese **4** American
5 Argentinian **6** Italian **7** Colombian **8** Chinese
9 Indian **10** Spanish **11** Mexican **12** Brazilian
13 British **14** Australian

page 78, Activity 2

1 Nicole Kidman, Australia, movie star
2 J.K. Rowling, the United Kingdom, writer
3 Rafael Nadal, Spain, tennis player
4 Lionel Messi, Argentina, soccer player
5 Beyoncé, the United States, singer

page 79, Activity 4

1 f **2** c **3** a **4** b **5** d **6** e

page 79, Activity 5

1 the United Kingdom, British
2 Yes, he is, Brazil
3 No, she isn't, Italy, Italian
4 China, Chinese
5 Yes, she is, Argentinian
6 Egypt, Egyptian

page 80, Activity 6

1 spy **2** sailor **3** cowboy **4** scientist **5** waiter
6 king **7** queen **8** musician **9** soldier **10** actor

page 80, Activity 7

in: December, the afternoon, the winter
on: August 25th, Tuesday
at: night, seven o'clock, three-thirty

page 81, Activity 8

a 2 **b** 1 **c** 5 **d** 8 **e** 4 **f** 3 **g** 7 **h** 6

page 81, Activity 9

1 Chinese, who, that
2 Egyptian, who, that
3 Brazilian, who, that

page 82, Activity 10

1 c **2** d **3** e **4** b **5** f **6** a

page 82, Activity 11

1 English, England, are you from, I'm, Mars
2 Are you, Canada, from, Where, Are you, Italy

page 83, Activity 14

Gwyneth: a, u
Marcela: n, s, n
Rob: a, u, o
Harry: u, s, s

page 84, Activity 17

a 2 **b** 1 **c** 3

page 84, Activity 18

1 exciting **2** Chinese **3** king **4** famous
5 water **6** days

page 85, Activity 20

1 In **2** at **3** Last **4** ago **5** playing
6 player **7** in **8** on

page 85, Activity 21

2 ✗ **3** ✓ **4** ✗ **5** ✓
The horse's name was Friday.

page 86, Activity 22

1 d **2** h **3** a **4** b **5** c **6** f **7** g **8** e

page 86, Activity 23

1 No, the soldier is from India.
2 He's/She's from Brazil.
3 The scientist is from Korea.
4 No, the king is from Egypt.
5 Yes, they are.
6 He's/She's from Japan.

page 86, Activity 24

1 The Chinese restaurant that I went to was very good.
2 I met a Mexican actor who was good-looking.

page 87, Activity 25

1 watching **2** home **3** movie **4** that **5** actor
6 listen **7** music **8** American **9** sports
10 friends

Goodbye

page 88, Activity 1

1 Polly and Mike
2 in jail
3 ice cream
4 the Police Chief
5 She has a picture of them.
6 They read about / saw it in the newspaper.

page 88, Activity 2

a 1 the Queen's **2** on TV
b 3 Hector Frost **4** Mike and Polly
c 5 Mike and Polly **6** Smith
d 7 Smith's **8** the training camp

page 89, Activity 3

1 Yes, there were some explorers on Ice Island.
2 Yes, there was a research station on Ice Island.
3 No, there weren't any pyramids on Ice Island.
4 No, there wasn't a volcano on Ice Island.

page 89, Activity 4

1 smart but lazy **2** doing her homework
3 kicking balls **4** playing video games **5** straight
6 jacket **7** one hundred and twenty-four dollars
8 reading a book **9** catching birds **10** brown
11 green **12** soccer **13** Carlos **14** Spanish

page 90, Activity 5

1 the United Kingdom **2** March 23rd **3** Italy
4 the United States **5** May 6th **6** May 27th
7 China **8** July 2nd **9** Japan

Assessment

Two types of assessment

1 Assessment *for* learning
2 Assessment *of* learning

There are many activities and techniques throughout the *Poptropica English* Teacher's Edition which will help you assess where your students are in their learning.

There is a wide range of tests to be used after each unit, to review multiple units, and at the end of the level. However, any test can be used either as an **assessment *for* learning** or **assessment *of* learning**. Using tests as an **assessment *of* learning** usually takes place after the learning, and this provides information about what the student is achieving by giving a grade. You can also use tests as an **assessment *for* learning**, providing specific feedback on students' strengths and weaknesses as part of the continuing learning process. It is a combination of both types of assessment which can provide powerful tools for helping students on their learning adventure.

Placement Tests

There are two *Poptropica English* Placement Tests. These will help you grade students and place them into the appropriate level of *Poptropica English*.

Placement Test A can be found in Teacher's Editions 1–3. It covers the language from Levels 1–3.

Placement Test B can be found in Teacher's Editions 4–6. It covers the language from Levels 4–6. Both Placement Tests are available on **Poptropica English World**.

Choosing the appropriate test

When choosing a test, try to find out if the student has studied English before, and to what level. Use this information to decide whether the student would fit better into a lower-level class or upper-level class. Give Placement Test A to students better suited to a lower-level class, and Placement Test B to students better suited to an upper-level class. If in doubt, have the student start with Placement Test A, and if necessary continue the assessment with Placement Test B.

Procedure

- Make a copy of the test pages, and complete the student's name and the date at the top of the page.
- Begin with the speaking part. Prepare the relevant Picture Cards.
- Give the rest of the Placement Test to the student. Play the audio for the student to complete the listening part.
- Allow student 20 minutes to complete the test.
- Check the answers against the Answer Key.

Placement Test A
10 points or below: Place in a Level 1 class.
11–40 points: Place in a Level 2 class.
41–80 points: Place in a Level 3 class.
81 points or above: Give Placement Test B.

Placement Test B
10 points or below: Give Placement Test A.
11–40 points: Place in a Level 4 class.
41–80 points: Place in a Level 5 class.
81 points or above: Assign to a Level 6 class.

Unit Tests

There are eight Unit Tests in each level of *Poptropica English*. These test the learning objectives from each unit. Have students take the Unit Test after studying each of the eight core units.

Review Tests

There are four Review Tests in each level of *Poptropica English*, covering Units 1–2, 3–4, 5–6, and 7–8. These can be given after completion of every two units in the Student Book.

End of Level Test

Each level of *Poptropica English* contains an End of Level Test, covering Units 1–8. This should be used in combination with ongoing assessment in class.

Exam preparation

For students taking the Cambridge Young Learner Exams, there are some exam-style activities in the Review Tests.

Procedure

- Copy the test for students, and have them write their name.
- Play the audio, and have students complete the listening activities. Then set students a time limit within which to complete the remainder of the test.
- Check the answers against the Answer Key on pages 179–182. Write the total score in the space provided.
- When handing tests back to students, go through the answers and explain any errors.

Tests Script

Placement Test B

B C:21 **Listen and draw a line from the name to the correct picture.**

1 Can you see that girl? Which girl? That one. That's Kim. Kim likes skateboarding.
2 Can you see her sister, Jenny? Which one is Jenny? She's skipping. Oh, yes, I can see her.
3 There's a boy cooking. Yes, I can see him. What's his name? That's Dan. Dan likes cooking.
4 There's Sam. Does Sam like walking the dog? Yes, he does.
5 And that's Bill. Bill likes skiing. Oh, yes, I can see him.

C C:22 **Listen and write.**

Hi. I'm Janet. I'm ten. I have short brown hair and green eyes. I love tennis. I am very sporty. What's your name?
I'm Pete. I'm ten. I have short dark hair and brown eyes. I am friendly and helpful. And this is Frank.
Yes, that's me! I'm Frank. I'm eleven. I have spiky brown hair and blue eyes. I love school, and I am hard-working. And, who are you?
Me... well, I'm Sophie. I'm eleven and, as you can see, I have long brown hair and blue eyes. I don't like sports. I am a little lazy. And this is my good friend, Emma.
Hi everyone. I'm Emma. I'm ten. I have short dark hair and brown eyes. I love drawing and painting. I am very creative.

D C:23 **Listen and write.**

This is Carl. He's my best friend. He's really helpful, but very lazy! He never makes his bed in the morning. And he lives right next to school, but always arrives late! He doesn't leave home until 9 o'clock! In class, he sometimes makes notes, but not always. Then he asks me for my notes! After school, we often meet up with our other friends. We talk or kick a ball around for ten minutes before our parents pick us up. I go home with Carl, and we do our homework together. We usually do our homework in the living room. Then Carl's mom takes me home.

E C:24 **Listen and check the box.**

1 I didn't know you could play percussion, Anna. I started playing the drums when I was four! My dad's a professional musician, and he wanted me to learn to play an instrument before I could write! Wow! Let's hear you play. OK. It gets very loud...
2 So what are you good at Harry? Me? Nothing in particular. I like playing video games, but I'm not that good. I play chess for the school. I like chess. We have a big competition coming up soon. Our school is one of the best in the country at playing chess! I think you are pretty good at chess, then.
3 Yesterday, I had a practice chess match at school, but I had to go shopping. Yes. I had to go shopping, too. It's summer vacation soon, and my parents wanted me to buy some new clothes. My parents did the same. They said they needed some new shorts and summer sandals.
4 So where are you going on vacation? Mom and dad decided they wanted to go somewhere warm. So we're going to the south of Spain. Where are you going? We're going to Spain, too. Somewhere near Malaga, I think.
5 I'll look out for you. I think we're going to Malaga, too! My dad wants to go walking in the mountains, and also to see some caves near there. We have to go, too. I like walking in the mountains, but I don't like going inside caves. I think they're dark and scary! I know the caves you mean. We're going there, too. Maybe we'll see you there!
6 Well I'm happy we're going somewhere warm this year. Last year my parents wanted to go to India but that was too expensive. So... we went to England! Can you imagine! It rained every day! We went to England, too. We stayed on a farm in the south west. It was very relaxing. But it rained every day as well! So, this year, it has to be warmer!

F C: 25 **Listen. Then choose the correct answer.**

1 How do you get to the movie theater, please? You go straight, then turn left after the bank, down Maple Street. The movie theater is at the end of Maple Street. Thank you!
2 Should we get something to eat after the movie, Rose? Yes, please, Dad! Do you want to get pizza or a burger and fries? Can we get noodles, Dad? I love them! Yes, of course.
3 Here you are, Mr. Smith. This is the name of the medicine I want you to take. Thank you, doctor. Can I get it at the supermarket? No, you have to go to the pharmacy. There's a pharmacy next to the hospital.
4 I'm sorry I'm late for class, Miss Trent. I missed my bus. What happened? Did you wake up late? No, Miss. My bus arrived, but then I dropped my bag, and everything went on the ground. I picked everything up, but the bus didn't wait for me.
5 Where do you live, Oliver? Do you know where the bookstore is? Yes, on Westport Drive? That's right. Well, go to the end of Westport Drive and turn left, and you'll see an Italian restaurant. Our house is on the opposite side of the road.
6 Hi, Tom. You don't look happy. What's the matter? Was the math test difficult? No, it was fine. How was

soccer practice? OK, but they didn't choose me for the school soccer team. I really wanted to be on the team this year. Oh, maybe next year. How about your favorite paella for dinner?

G C:26 **Read then listen. Correct ten differences.**

Hi, Jenny. It's Ben here. I am on an amazing trip. I am in Mexico. I am visiting some interesting places, and doing some exciting activities. Yesterday, I was diving in the ocean. It was blue, blue, blue! I saw a lot of fish. They were all different colors, shapes, and sizes. Yesterday evening, I went to a concert. The band was amazing! They were playing the drums and dancing. The dancing was so fast. It was so exciting. We were all dancing at the end! Today, I am visiting some pyramids. They are in the rain forest. Then, I am climbing a volcano. I'm not good at climbing but I am good at taking pictures! In the evening, we are swimming in the ocean.

Unit Tests

Unit 1

1 C:27 **Read. Then listen and circle.**

1 I'm Thomas. I'm nine. I have short, brown, spiky hair. I have a lot of friends, and I like talking. I'm very talkative. I'm not shy at all. I don't like homework, but I like doing different sports. I play soccer and basketball, and I go swimming every day. And I'm very creative. I love drawing and painting.

2 Hi. I'm Georgia. I'm ten. I'm tall, and I have long brown hair. It's straight and always tidy. I'm very hard-working and quite smart. I love homework and I love learning about everything. I'm talkative with my friends. There's always a lot to talk about. I'm not very sporty. I like reading and I like walking my dog.

2 C:28 **Listen. Then circle.**

1 Well... my uncle is very sporty. He isn't lazy. He's always doing things. He is shy and doesn't talk very much. But he's friendly and helpful with everyone.

2 So... my sister... well she's lazy. I have to do everything for her! She's always talking to her friends! Talk, talk, talk! She's talkative and very friendly.

3 Well... my cousin... he's very lazy. He never does anything. He's always reading, or listening to music, or watching TV! He's very smart but he never helps me with my homework! He is friendly and I like him a lot because he's talkative like me! He's my favorite cousin.

4 OK... so my aunt... she's great. She's very friendly and talkative. She's quite hard-working and helps my mom and dad in the yard. And she's very sporty. She loves playing tennis and soccer! She plays every day!

Unit 2

1 C:29 **Listen. Then match.**

1 We're doing a project at school on our lives. It's great. We give our friends different problems and they give us advice. Sometimes they give us orders! But that's OK. It's fun. My first problem is from Helen. What's your problem, Helen? My bedroom is always messy. I clean it every Saturday, but on Sunday it's messy again. What should I do? First, you should clean a little every day. Second, you should take out the trash from your room every day. Do you have a trash can in your bedroom? No, I don't. You don't have a trash can?! You must get a trash can! That's the first thing you must do. OK. Thanks.

2 Hi. I'm Bob. I'm going to talk to Victor and give him some advice. Hi, Victor. What's the problem? Hi, Bob. I have a big problem. I can't sleep and I'm very tired and can't study. I listen to quiet music and I go to bed early, but I can't remember anything! It's a big, big problem. Ah, yes. That is a big problem, Victor. What do you eat? I usually eat a lot of French fries and pizza and bread and jelly. Aha! You should eat more healthy food. You should eat some fruit and vegetables every day. If you eat healthy food, you will feel better and sleep better. But... I really don't like vegetables. First, eat more fruit. Then, choose one vegetable each day and have pizza and fries one day a week; don't eat it every day. You will feel much better. OK. Thanks.

2 C:30 **Listen. Then match.**

1 I always make my bed in the morning before I go to school.

2 I never make my bed, but I always clean my room.

3 I sometimes wash my face before going to bed, but I always wash my face in the morning.

4 I usually do my homework before I watch TV, and I always practice my guitar before I do my homework.

5 I take the dog for a walk with my mom every afternoon after school, but I never do the dishes!

6 I help my dad wash the car on the weekend, and I help my mom take out the trash on Tuesday.

Unit 3

1 C: 35 **Listen. Then circle.**

1 So... what are you good at Bobby? Well... I'm good at kicking a soccer ball and throwing balls. I'm good at sports. I'm not good at telling jokes or reading long books.

2 And, what about you, Sandy? What are you good at? I'm good at reading. I'm good at reading poetry and stories. I'm quite good at writing stories for little kids. I'm good at drawing and painting. I'm not good at sports. I can't kick a soccer ball or play volleyball. I'm not good at throwing or catching.

3 What about you, Charlie? What are you good at? Ummm. I'm not good at talking! I'm quite shy. I'm good at reading and playing the guitar and the piano. I'm good at working on my computer, and I'm quite good at playing tennis and soccer. I'm not good at telling jokes or singing, and I'm not good at acting!
4 And, Olivia. What are you good at? I'm good at playing the drums and singing karaoke. I love singing karaoke. I'm pretty good at drawing and I'm good at reading. I'm not good at in-line skating or running races. And I'm not good at playing volleyball or playing soccer.

2 C:36 **Listen. Then check.**

Hello, Betty! What were you doing yesterday? Yesterday, I was in-line skating in the park. I'm very good at in-line skating, but I can't go every day because I have a lot of homework to do.
Hello, Jed! What were you doing yesterday? Yesterday, I was drawing a picture in the art room. There's a drawing competition at school and I want to win!
Hello, Val! What were you doing yesterday? I was singing karaoke at my birthday party yesterday afternoon. I can't sing, but that wasn't a problem. I was happy and had a lot of fun.
Hello, Todd! Were you at a party yesterday? Yes, I was! I was at Val's party. I was playing the drums. I'm good at music and always play the drums at my friends' parties.

Unit 4

1 C:37 **Listen. Then circle.**

1 Mexico is in Central America. There are beaches and mountains. In Mexico, there are some volcanoes.
2 There are lots of pyramids in Egypt, but there aren't any pyramids in Spain.
3 Australia is an enormous country. There are mountains, rain forests, and deserts.
4 There are lots of forests in Canada, but there aren't any pyramids.
5 Ireland is a very green country. There are lots of lakes and forests in Ireland.
6 There are lots of forests in the United Kingdom, too. There are some very old forests in the United Kingdom.

2 C:38 **Listen. Then circle T for True or F for False.**

1 Hi. I'm Eliza and I'm from Brazil. In my country there is a long river called the Amazon. There is a very big forest called the Amazon rain forest. A lot of Brazil is rain forest. In this part of Brazil, it rains a lot. It usually rains every day in the rainy season.
2 Hi. I'm Dan. I'm from China. In China, there are some very high mountains. One side of Mount Everest, the highest mountain in the world, is in China. There are many rivers in China; some of the rivers are very long, like the Yangtze, and the Yellow Rivers.
3 Hi. I'm Monika. I'm from Poland. Poland is in Europe. There are seven countries next to Poland! There are beaches and mountains, and there are a lot of lakes. There aren't any deserts in Poland... or pyramids! But there are a lot of forests. And there are some bears in the forests!
4 Hi. I'm Sam. I'm from Greece. In Greece, there are some high mountains. I go skiing in the mountains in winter. There are a lot of forests and lakes, and we have a lot of islands. There aren't any deserts, and there aren't any pyramids, but there are some very old buildings.

Unit 5

1 C:42 **Listen. Then match.**

1 How much is that red jacket? It's sixty dollars. Oh. That's too expensive.
2 How much are these black wallets? They are usually twenty dollars but today they are only ten dollars. Oh. That's cheap. Are they leather? Yes, they are.
3 How much are those sunglasses? These ones? No, those ones. The black and yellow ones. Ah. Those are the most expensive sunglasses in the store. They're fifty dollars. Oh, dear. They're much too expensive.
4 Hi. How much is that umbrella? The black and white spotted umbrella at the back of the shelf. The spotted one... mmm... the normal price is thirty dollars but I think the umbrella is half-price so that's fifteen dollars. Fifteen dollars? That's OK. OK. Let me check.

2 C:43 **Listen. Then circle.**

1 Whose umbrella is this? It's green and brown, with white stripes. Is it mine? Does it have a name on it? Yes. What's your name? Michael. That's the name. Here you are.
2 Whose watch is this? It's a beautiful old-fashioned watch. Is it a brown, leather watch? Yes, it is. It's mine. Oh, thank you.
3 Whose are these baggy shirts? They're blue, purple, green, and yellow. I think they're Dan's. Yes. He has different colored shirts. Are you sure they're his? Do they have a small white pocket? No, they don't. Oh. Then they aren't his. Sorry.
4 Whose tight jeans are these? They look like Mary's. She was wearing tight jeans yesterday. Oh, yes. She was. They are hers. They have a leather pocket on them. Look. Yes. And there's her name. They are hers.

Unit 6

1 C:44 **Listen. Then write.**

Our town is five hundred years old. Yesterday we had a party for everyone in the town. There weren't any presents, but there were a lot of balloons. We put decorations on our houses, and the street looked amazing. There was a big barbecue, and a lot of food. There was too much food! There were hundreds of sandwiches, sausages, and potatoes, and salads to start with. Then there were big cakes, and small cakes, and cookies, and jello, and ice cream after. Everyone had to help. My family made two hundred cards. We gave one to every person who came to the party. My friends' family brought the music. They had music for the children and music for the adults. My friend's dad could play the guitar. He played at the end of the party, and we sang a lot of songs. It was great.

2 C:45 **Listen. Then match.**

Hi, Stef. Where did you go on vacation last year? Hi, Rob. I went to Greece with my family. When did you go? We went at the end of June – the twenty-eighth, I think. It was the beginning of the school vacation. It was hot and sunny every day. What did you do? It was too hot to do very much. Most days we sat by the pool or went to the beach. I don't like very hot weather, but my mom loves the sun. We saw some interesting historic places. They were amazing. We went to Athens one day. Athens is the capital of Greece. It's very noisy, and was very, very hot! We got some presents, and went to a museum, and then went back to the hotel. What did you see? Well... we saw people dressed in white costumes. They were guards. They were standing outside the important buildings. We saw lots of stone statues. I saw a lot of colorful fish in the ocean one day. I was swimming and hundreds of little blue and pink fish swam under me. It was a bit scary but they were beautiful. So... who did you meet? Did you meet any interesting people? Um. I can't remember. Everything was very interesting – the people, the food, the places... We met one of my school friends in Athens when we were shopping! Her family was on vacation in Greece, too. They were staying on one of the Greek islands. Where are you going next year? Somewhere cold! Hah! You should go to the UK then! That's quite cold in the summer. Do you like rain?

Unit 7

1 C:49 **Listen. Then write.**

1 When I was nine, I went to school in Argentina. My class had twenty-six children in it. My class teacher was Mr. Brown. He was a bit scary. He talked very loudly but he was kind and funny. My favorite subject was history. Mr. Brown taught history class in the park. We also had classes in museums and historic buildings. We did short plays about some of the buildings. We did short plays about some of the history topics. Our parents came to watch us. But... science class was difficult. I didn't like the teacher. It wasn't Mr. Brown. The teacher was very intelligent, but his class was boring. We listened to him talk and talk, and we made notes in our books! I like science now. In my new school, we do a lot of experiments and that's fun. But I liked that school. It was exciting going to school in a different country, and everyone was so interesting.

2 C:50 **Listen. Then write.**

1 Did you have geography on Wednesday? No, we didn't. We had geography on Friday afternoon.
2 Did you have science every day? No, we didn't. We had science on Tuesday morning and Thursday afternoon.
3 Did you have drama every week? Yes, we did. Every Wednesday afternoon.
4 Did you have sports in the morning or the afternoon? We had P.E. on Tuesday afternoon.
5 Did you have computer studies? Yes. We had computer studies on Monday, Wednesday, and Friday mornings.
6 And, did you have music lessons? Yes. We had class music lessons every Monday afternoon, and we had guitar lessons on Thursday morning. They were great!

Unit 8

1 C:51 **Listen. Then complete.**

1 This is my friend Carlos. He's from Mexico City. He's Mexican. He's going to school in England this year. Who is your friend? This is Abel. He's from Cairo. He's Egyptian. He's in England for two months. He's here for the summer vacation.
2 Hi. I'm Sue. I'm from Beijing. I'm Chinese. Where are you from? Hi, Sue. I'm Ruth. I'm from Tokyo. I'm Japanese.
3 Hi. This is my cousin Mariella. She's from Florence. She's Italian. Hi, Mariella. I'm Pablo. I'm from Buenos Aires. I'm Argentinian.
4 I'm Anna. I come from Delhi. I'm Indian. I'm Ryan. I come from Belfast. I'm British.

2 C:52 **Listen and number. Then find and match.**

1 He or she is someone who works in a band.
2 He or she is someone who works with horses on a farm.
3 He or she is someone who works on a ship.
4 He or she is someone who works in the theater, in movies, or in TV shows.
5 He or she is someone who works in a restaurant.
6 He or she is someone who does experiments.

Review Tests

Review Test 1

1 C:31 **Listen. Then write.**

1 Hi. I'm Janet. I'm ten. I have short, brown hair and green eyes. I love tennis. I am very sporty. What's your name?

2 I'm Pete. I'm ten. I have short, dark hair and brown eyes. I am friendly and helpful. And this is Frank.
3 Yes, that's me! I'm Frank. I'm eleven. I have spiky, brown hair and blue eyes. I love school and I'm hard-working. And, who are you?
4 Me... well, I'm Sophie. I'm eleven and, as you can see, I have long, brown hair and blue eyes. I don't like sports. I am a little lazy. And this is my good friend, Emma.
5 Hi, everyone. I'm Emma. I'm ten. I have short, dark hair and brown eyes. I love drawing and painting. I am very creative.

2 C: 32 Listen and check.

1 Hi. I'm Tom. I like school and I work hard. I usually study before a test.
2 My dad sometimes helps me with my homework when it's difficult.
3 My mom is great. She always makes my bed in the morning. I never do!
4 My brother, Mark, has a lot of friends. He usually meets them after school.
5 My sister never meets her friends. She loves reading. She is always reading something!

3 C: 33 Listen. Then write *usually, often, always, sometimes,* or *never* next to the pictures in Activity 2.

[Repeat of previous track]

4 C: 34 Listen. Then write.

This is Carl. He's my best friend. He's really helpful but very lazy! He never makes his bed in the morning. And he lives right next to school, but always arrives late! He doesn't leave home until 9 o'clock! In class he sometimes takes notes but not always. Then he asks me for my notes! After school we often meet up with our other friends. We chat or kick a soccer ball around for ten minutes before our parents pick us up. I go home with Carl and we do our homework together. We usually do our homework in the living room. Then, Carl's mom takes me home.

Review Test 2

1 C: 39 Read and listen. Correct ten differences.

Hi Jenny. It's Ben here. I'm on an amazing trip. I'm in Mexico. I am visiting some interesting places and doing some exciting activities. Yesterday, I was diving in the ocean. It was so blue! I saw a lot of fish. They were all different colors, shapes, and sizes. Yesterday evening, I went to a concert. The band was amazing! They were playing the drums and dancing. The dancing was so fast. It was so exciting. We were all dancing at the end! Today, I am visiting some pyramids. They are in the rain forest. Then, I am climbing a volcano. I'm not good at climbing, but I am good at taking pictures! In the evening, we are swimming in the ocean.

2 C: 40 Listen and circle.

I'm Jo, and I want to tell you about my vacation. I'm in Italy. It's really beautiful here! I'm visiting my Italian grandparents. I love them! They live in a small house on a farm. I am visiting a lot of places. There are some castles near their house. They are very old. There is also a big cave near their house. Today we are visiting the cave, and having a picnic.

3 C: 41 Listen and circle.

1 Hi, Anna. What are you doing? Hi, Harry. I'm practicing for a concert. What concert? The Young Percussionist Competition. I didn't know you could play percussion. I started playing the drums when I was four. My dad's a professional musician and wanted me to learn to play an instrument before I could write! Wow! Let's hear you play. OK. It gets very loud...
2 So what are you good at Harry? Me? Nothing in particular. I like playing video games but I'm not that good. I play chess for the school. I like chess. We have a big competition coming up soon. It sounds like you are pretty good at chess then. The school is one of the best in the country at playing chess, and you are playing for them!
3 So where are you going on vacation? Somewhere nice and warm? We were going to go to Argentina, but that's in the southern hemisphere so it will be winter in our summer. Mom and dad decided they wanted to go somewhere warm. So we're going to Spain. Where are you going? We're going to Spain, too. Somewhere near Malaga, I think.
4 I'll look out for you. I think we're going to Malaga as well! My dad wants to go walking in the mountains and also to see some caves near there. We have to go, too. I like walking in the mountains but I don't like going inside caves. They're dark and scary! I know the caves you mean. We're going there, too. Maybe we'll see you there!

Review Test 3

1 C: 46 Listen and circle.

1 The watch is $7.50.
2 The jacket is $30.
3 The bracelet is $62.20.
4 The sunglasses are $231.
5 The hoodie is $50.50.

2 Listen. Then write.

Look, Ben. An invitation. Who is it from? It's from Jamie. It's an invitation from Jamie. What is the invitation for? Umm. Let me read it! It's a party. It's Jamie's birthday. When is it? March 12th. That's next Saturday. Next Saturday! That's my friend's birthday, too. Where is the party? The invitation says: "South Beach." It must be a beach party! Yes! I love beach parties! Can you go swimming? Well... the invitation says "bring your swimsuit," so I guess we can go swimming! That's so cool! Oh, look. There's a number. That's their cell number. You have to tell them you are going. What's the number? It's 9-5-8-6-0-1-2-8-9-6. That's really strange. That's my friend's number. Jamie has a sister. Her name's Sandra. That's my friend's name. Look. There's another invitation in the envelope. It's to you. Wow! So we can both go to the beach party!

3 Listen and write the letters.

Hi, Matt. Hi, Jo. What are you taking on vacation? Not much. My new jacket and hoodie. Is that the blue jacket? Yes, that's the one. Are you taking sunglasses? No, I'm taking my old baggy jeans and belt. Oh, yes. They are really too big for you! Yes, but your jeans are really too tight! No, they're not! They're perfect! Are you taking your watch? No, I'm taking my bracelet. What about you? Yes, I'm taking my watch. Are you taking a swimsuit? Of course! I love swimming. My swimsuit is first on my list!

Review Test 4

1 Listen and circle.

Hi, Sarah. How was your day? Hi, Mike. It was good, thanks. I had a really interesting history class. How was your day? Not bad, thanks. We are reading a new story in English. It's a bit scary, but I think it will be good. I don't think stories are scary... but math... now that is scary! But you are so good at math! I'm good at geography but not math. What are you good at? Nothing, really. You must like doing something! Well... I like art, and I can draw... a little.

2 Listen. Then write.

I saw a really funny movie last night. What was it about? It was a romantic movie about some cowboys in Argentina. What happened? Well... there were some bad guys that wanted to steal the cowboys' cattle. I guess they rode horses? The cowboys did, yes, but the bad guys didn't. Can you imagine trying to steal cows on foot! So I guess that's why it was funny? Exactly! And the cowboys were Argentinian and speaking in Spanish. I didn't understand a word! Were there words in English underneath? Yes, there were. I think it was funny because it was difficult to read and watch the movie at the same time!

3 Listen. Then write.

Hi there. I'm Anna and I'm Colombian. Hi there. I'm Kim and I'm Korean. I have math class next. I like math. It's really easy. What do you like, Kim? I don't like math. That's for sure. I think it's very difficult. I like music. At school, I like playing the drums. I'm in the school band. What do you want to do when you leave school? Interesting question. I don't know. Maybe a soldier. What about you? I don't really know, either. At the moment I would like to be a scientist. I love doing experiments in science class. What do you do on vacation? Mmm. I love reading, so I spend a lot of time reading. I like funny stories the best. What about you? I write songs when I have time. I'm learning to play the guitar. It's difficult, but I really like learning new songs. Wow! I love listening to songs but I can't sing! I love watching movies but I can't act!

End of Level Test

1 Listen and circle.

Yesterday I watched my brother play basketball. It was very exciting. The game was very difficult. He practiced for weeks. I went with my mom and dad. It finished at a quarter after eleven. We got home at noon. My brother was very tired. He didn't do his homework! He watched TV. I talked to my friends. I was telling them funny jokes!

2 Listen. Then write.

1 Hi, Sue. Tell me about you. Where are you from? What do you like doing? Well... I'm from Australia. I'm Australian. I live in a beautiful house next to the beach. I go surfing. I go surfing every day after school.
2 And, Tony... what about you? Where are you from? What do you like doing? I'm from Argentina. I'm Argentinian. I live in the capital city. I like diving. I go diving with my parents. We usually go in the spring and the summer. There are some beautiful lakes in Argentina. I go diving with my dad, and my mom and brother climb the volcanoes!

3 Listen. Then match.

1 Look at these presents from my aunt. She was an international journalist. She was always visiting different countries and brought presents back for me. What do you have? This is Argentinian. It's a wallet. It was very cheap.
2 And, what are those? They're gloves. They're from Italy. They're Italian. They were expensive. She was in Italy last year.
3 And the watch? Where's that from? The watch is from Brazil. It's my favorite watch. It's very old-fashioned!
4 And the swimsuit? That looks a little tight! Ha! It is! But that's OK. My little sister can have it.
5 What's that? Those are pajamas. They are very baggy.

Tests Answer Key

Placement Test B

B

Kim-skateboarding, Jenny-skipping, Dan-cooking, Sam-walking the dog, Bill-skiing

C

1 Janet: 10; short brown; green; very sporty/loves tennis **2** Pete: 10; short dark; brown; friendly/helpful **3** Frank: 11; spiky brown; blue; hard-working/loves school **4** Sophie: 11; long brown; blue; doesn't like sports/is lazy **5** Emma: 10; short dark; brown; drawing and painting/creative

D

1 never **2** always **3** sometimes **4** often **5** usually

E

1 B **2** C **3** A **4** A **5** B **6** A

F

1 b **2** a **3** b **4** c **5** c **6** a

G

2 trip **3** Mexico **4** diving **5** playing the drums **6** dancing **7** pyramids **8** rain forest **9** volcano **10** swimming **11** in the ocean

H

1 yes **2** no **3** yes **4** no **5** no **6** yes **7** yes

I

1 No, it wasn't. **2** Yes, it was. **3** No, it wasn't, it was boring. **4** Yes, it was. **5** Yes, it was.

J

1 do **2** went **3** been **4** rode **5** Did **6** wasn't **7** lost **8** drove

Unit Tests

Unit 1

Reading and writing

1 1 Thursday **2** Tuesday **3** Monday
2 2 On Tuesday, Tom watched a DVD.
3 On Wednesday, Tom played tennis.
4 On Thursday, Tom practiced the piano.
5 On Friday, Tom went to the movies.
6 On Saturday, Tom danced at the party.
7 On Sunday, Tom cleaned his room.
3 1 intelligent **2** dark **3** face **4** today **5** played **6** listened **7** helpful **8** studied **9** ago **10** problems **11** patient
4 Student's own answers

Listening and speaking

1 Thomas: 1 nine **2** like **3** don't like **4** like **5** every day **6** creative
Georgia: 7 ten **8** long **9** tidy **10** talkative **11** I'm not
2 1 friendly **2** talkative **3** talkative **4** sporty
3 Student's own answers

Unit 2

Reading and writing

1 1 e **2** c **3** f **4** d **5** b **6** a
2 1 I always clean my bedroom on the weekend.
2 I always listen to my parents.
3 I sometimes eat unhealthy food.
4 I never go to bed after ten o'clock.
3 1 You should/have to study.
2 You should eat a sandwich.
3 You should go running.
4 You should/have to clean it.
5 You should/have to go to bed early.
6 You should buy her a present.
4 Student's own answers

Listening and speaking

1 Helen: a d e
Victor: b c f g h i
2 1 e **2** f **3** d **4** c **5** a **6** b
3 Student's own answers

Unit 3

Reading and writing

1 **2** not good at catching
3 not good at diving
4 good at telling jokes
5 good at playing video games
6 not good at throwing
2 **1** playing c **2** running b **3** singing e **4** going d
5 reading a
3 **1** play **2** playing **3** taking **4** afternoon
5 practice **6** at **7** Last **8** was
4 Student's own answers

Listening and speaking

1 **1** b **2** b **3** a **4** a
2 **Betty:** in-line skating
Jed: drawing
Val: singing karaoke
Todd: playing the drums
3 Student's own answers

Unit 4

Reading and writing

1 **1** Korea **2** Egypt **3** Spain **4** Australia
5 Mexico **6** the United Kingdom **7** India
8 Japan **9** Italy **10** Colombia
2 **1** some **2** a **3** any **4** a **5** an
3 **1** Are there any lakes in Egypt? No, there aren't.
2 Is there a rain forest in Brazil? Yes, there is.
3 Is there a desert in Italy? No, there isn't.
4 Are there any cities in China? Yes, there are.
4 Student's own answers

Listening and speaking

1 **1** a **2** b **3** b **4** a **5** b **6** b
2 **1** T, T, F **2** T, F, F **3** T, F, T **4** T, F, F
3 Student's own answers

Unit 5

Reading and writing

1 **1** 60 **2** 1,000 **3** 350 **4** sixteen
5 five hundred **6** one hundred and five
2 **2** pants Those are my tight pants.
3 bracelet That is my expensive bracewlet.
4 jeans Those are my short jeans.
5 gloves Those are my old-fashioned gloves.
3 **1** Harry's **2** hers **3** Ben's, his **4** your, yours
4 Student's own answers

Listening and speaking

1 **1** \$60 **2** \$10 **3** \$50 **4** \$15
2 **1** green, brown, and white, stripes
2 beautiful, old-fashioned
3 baggy, different colored
4 tight, leather pocket
3 Student's own answers

Unit 6

Reading and writing

1 **1** third **2** fifteenth **3** eleventh **4** eighth
5 fifth **6** sixteenth **7** first **8** thirteenth
2 **1** b **2** d **3** e **4** a **5** c
3 **2** went **3** didn't have **4** came
5 played **6** played
4 Student's own answers

Listening and speaking

1 **Decorations:** **1** balloons
Food: **2** sandwiches **3** sausages **4** cakes
5 jello **6** ice cream
Instrument: **7** guitar
2 **1** d **2** i **3** g **4** j **5** c
3 Student's own answers

Unit 7

Reading and writing

1 **1** b **2** a **3** d **4** c
2 **1** were, I was four years old.
2 Were, Yes, I was very excited.
3 was, It was very hot and sunny.
4 Was, It was a very interesting vacation.
5 did, I swam in the pool every morning. / Every morning, I swam in the pool.
3 **1** Did **2** Was **3** was **4** Were
5 Did **6** was
Student's own answers
4 Student's own answers

Listening and speaking

1 **2** scary **3** kind **4** history
5 museums **6** plays **7** difficult **8** intelligent
9 boring **10** science **11** exciting
2 **Monday:** M computer studies A music
Tuesday: A P.E.
Wednesday: M computer studies A drama
Thursday: M guitar lessons A science
Friday: M computer studies
3 Student's own answers

Unit 8

Reading and writing

1 **1** c **2** d **3** a **4** f **5** e **6** b
2 **2** f waiter **3** a scientist **4** d sailor **5** c spy
6 b musician
3 **1** who **2** that **3** that
4 Student's own answers

Listening and speaking

1 **1** Mexican **2** Egyptian **3** Chinese **4** Japanese
5 Italian **6** Argentinian **7** Indian **8** British
2 **1** d musician **2** b cowboy **3** e sailor
4 c actor **5** a waiter **6** f scientist
3 Student's own answers

Review Tests

Review Test 1

Reading and writing

1 **1** c **2** e **3** a **4** b **5** d
2 Student's own answers
3 **1** because **2** and **3** but **4** because **5** but
6 and **7** But **8** and **9** and **10** and
4 **2** brush my teeth **3** be on time
4 meet my friends **5** take notes in class
6 do my homework

Listening and speaking

1 **Janet:** short brown, green, loves tennis / sporty
Pete: 10, short dark, friendly and helpful
Frank: 11, blue, loves school / hard-working
Sophie: 11, long, brown, doesn't like sports / a little lazy
Emma: 10, short dark, brown, creative
2 **1** b **2** c **3** b **4** a **5** b
3 **1** usually **2** sometimes **3** always, never
4 usually **5** never, always
4 **1** never **2** always **3** sometimes **4** often
5 usually
5 Student's own answers
6 Student's own answers
7 Student's own answers

Review Test 2

Reading and writing

1 **1** yes **2** no **3** yes **4** no **5** no **6** yes
7 yes **8** yes
2 **1** good at... **2** good at...
3 are good at... **4** aren't good at...
Student's own answers
3 **2** pyramids **3** caves **4** town
5 castle **6** statues **7** lake **8** farm **9** factory
4 **1** was he doing/playing, chess
2 were they doing, were
3 she in-l ne skating, she
4 Were they (open answer), were running races
5 Student's own answers

Listening and speaking

1 **2** trip **3** Mexico **4** diving
5 playing the drums **6** dancing **7** pyramids
8 rain forest **9** volcano **10** swimming
11 in the ocean
2 **1** Italy **2** Italian **3** on a farm **4** castles
5 cave **6** cave
3 **1** b **2** c **3** a **4** b
4 Student's own answers
5 Student's own answers
6 Student's own answers

Review Test 3

Reading and writing

1 **1** c **2** c **3** f **4** e **5** b **6** d
2 **a** 3 **b** 8 **c** 7 **d** 4 **e** 5 **f** 2 **g** 9 **i** 6
3 **1** went **2** expensive **3** saw **4** first
5 swimsuit **6** cold **7** were **8** family's
4 **1** Whose belt is this? b **2** How much is that umbrella? a **3** What did you see? c
5 **2** (all) his good **3** near, town **4** eat and drink
5 (a game of) beach volleyball **6** After the game
7 parents **8** sang songs
6 Student's own answers

Listening and speaking

1 **1** c **2** c **3** b **4** b **5** c
2 **1** a birthday party **2** Saturday March 12th
3 South Beach **4** swimsuit **5** 9586012896
3 **Jo:** a b e f g
Matt: c d h
4 Student's own answers
5 Student's own answers
6 Student's own answers

Review Test 4

Reading and writing

1 **1** b **2** c **3** a **4** f **5** e **6** d
2 **1** Yes, but it was scary. **2** They were both Egyptian. **3** Yes, there were a lot. **4** No, but there were three sailors. **5** Yes, we did some exciting tests with water. **6** Yes, there were a lot of difficult questions.
3 **1** No, it wasn't. It was science.
2 Yes, it was.
3 No, it wasn't. It was boring.
4 Yes, it was.
5 No, it wasn't. It was easy.
4 **2** American **3** words **4** video **5** boring **6** changes **7** spy **8** difficult **9** exciting **10** funny **11** scientist
5 Student's own answers

Listening and speaking

1 **1** b **2** c **3** a **4** a **5** b
2 **1** No **2** Yes **3** No **4** Yes **5** No
3 **Anna:** Colombia, math, scientist, writing songs, act
Kim: Korea, music, soldier, reading, sing
4 Student's own answers
5 Student's own answers
6 Student's own answers

End of Level Test

Reading

1 **1** c **2** b **3** a **4** c **5** a

Writing

1 **1** went **2** love **3** are **4** am **5** In **6** played
2 **1** first **2** twenty-second **3** sixteenth **4** twenty-third **5** fiftieth
3 Suggested questions:
1 Is he from Egypt? / Is he Egyptian?
2 Where did you go last summer?
3 What are they good at?
4 Was the book/movie/class interesting?
5 Did you enjoy the book/movie/class?
4 **1** Why are you excited? **b** Because it's my birthday tomorrow.
2 Do you often clean your room? **c** I clean it every Saturday.
3 Where did you go last summer? **a** I went to Ibiza.

Listening

1 **1** watched **2** basketball **3** was **4** difficult **5** practiced **6** went **7** a quarter after eleven **8** at **9** tired **10** watched **11** talked to **12** telling
2 **Sue:** Australia, surfing, every day after school, beach next to her house
Tony: Argentina, diving, spring and summer, lakes
3 **1** cheap c **2** expensive a **3** old-fashioned e **4** tight d **5** baggy b

Speaking

1 Suggested answers:
1 In picture 1, there are some balloons. In picture 2, there aren't any balloons.
2 In picture 1, there are two presents. In picture 2, there is just one present.
3 In picture 1, there are five bottles on the table. In picture 2, there are four bottles.
4 In picture 1, there are two cups on the table. In picture 2, there aren't any cups.
5 In picture 1, there is one candle on the birthday cake. In picture 2, there aren't any candles on the cake.
2 Student's own answers

Placement Test B

Name: ______________________

Score: ___ / 120

A Ask students. (50 points)

Questions	Marks	Material
1 Do you...? What time do you...?	5 questions – score out of 5	Picture Cards of activities from Level 4, or draw on the board
Vocabulary: *have music/dance lessons, do karate/gymnastics, practice the piano/violin, learn to draw/cook, study English, study math; 2:15, quarter after 2, 2:30, two-thirty, 2:45, quarter to 3*		
2 What is it? Where is...?	5 questions – score out of 5	Picture Cards of natural features from Level 4, or draw on the board
Vocabulary: *valley, bridge, river, path, cave, waterfall, mountain, vines, lake, sea, coast, hills, around, through, toward, past*		
3 What time do you...? How often do you...?	5 questions – score out of 5	Picture Cards of natural features from Level 4, or draw on the board
Vocabulary: *brush my teeth, make my bed, wash my face, clean my room, do my homework, meet my friends, study before a test*		
4 What does he/she look like? What is he/she like?	5 questions – score out of 5	Picture Cards for adjectives from Level 5, or draw on the board
Vocabulary: *dark/light hair, light hair, handsome, beautiful, good-looking, bossy, kind, sporty, lazy, smart, shy, talkative, helpful, friendly, hard-working, creative, patient*		
5 Is there...? Are there...?	5 questions – score out of 5	Picture Cards of countries/places from Level 5, or use a map
Vocabulary *China, Korea, Japan, Australia, the United States, Mexico, Colombia, Brazil, Argentina, Spain, Italy, Egypt, India; statue, cave, volcano, city, town, farm, factory, castle*		
6 What's he/she wearing? How much...? It's/They're...dollars/euros.	5 questions – score out of 5	Picture Cards of clothes from Level 5, or draw on the board
Vocabulary: *jacket, swimsuit, watch, bracelet, wallet, handbag, umbrella, gloves, sunglasses, belt, hoodie; tight, baggy, cheap, expensive, old-fashioned, modern*		
7 When do you have...? Do you like...?	5 questions – score out of 5	Picture Cards of adjectives / school subjects from Level 5, or draw on the board
Vocabulary: *interesting, boring, exciting, scary, funny, difficult, easy, romantic, relaxing; computer science, math, geography, science, history, art, music, P.E.*		
8 Which animal is...?	5 questions – score out of 5	Picture Cards of animals from Level 6, or draw on the board
Vocabulary: *rhino, cheetah, panther, lemur, koala, whale, otter, sea turtle, tiger, meerkat, emu, scorpion; tallest, longest, shortest, biggest, smallest, heaviest, lightest, fastest, slowest*		
9 Where's the...? Is there a...?	5 questions – score out of 5	Picture Cards of places in town from Level 6, or draw on the board
Vocabulary: *library, park, movie theater, shopping mall, museum, bank, pharmacy, castle/tower, hospital, airport, bookstore, station, arcade, video store; turn left at the supermarket, then go straight*		
10 Are you going to...? What are you going to...?	5 questions – score out of 5	Picture Cards of activities from Level 6, or draw on the board
Vocabulary: *recycle paper, recycle bottles, pick up trash, reuse plastic bags, turn off the lights, use public transportation; save trees, save resources, keep the planet clean, reduce waste, conserve energy, reduce pollution*		

Placement Test B

B Listen and draw a line from the name to the correct picture. (5 marks)

Kim

Jenny

Dan

Sam

Bill

C Listen and write. (10 marks)

	Janet	Pete	Frank	Sophie	Emma
Age	10				
Hair			spiky brown		
Eyes		brown			
Other information					love drawing and painting

D Listen and write. (5 marks)

1 Carl ____________________ makes his bed in the morning.

2 He ____________________ gets to school late.

3 He ____________________ takes notes during class.

4 We ____________________ meet our friends after school.

5 We ____________________ do our homework in the living room.

Placement Test B

E C:24 **Listen and check (✓) the box. (6 marks)**

1 What is Anna good at?

A singing ☐ B playing the drums ☐ C acting ☐

2 What is Harry good at?

A playing video games ☐ B telling jokes ☐ C playing chess ☐

3 What were Anna and Harry doing yesterday?

A shopping ☐ B doing their homework ☐ C watching a movie ☐

4 Where are Anna and Harry going on vacation?

A Spain ☐ B Argentina ☐ C Italy ☐

5 What are they going to do on vacation?

A visit a volcano ☐ B visit some caves ☐ C visit a castle ☐

6 Where did they go on vacation last year?

A England ☐ B India ☐ C China ☐

F C:25 **Listen. Then choose the correct answer. (6 marks)**

1 The movie theater is

a at the corner of Maple Street.

b at the end of Maple Street.

c next to the bank.

2 Rose wants to eat

a some noodles.

b pizza.

c a burger and fries.

3 Mr. Smith has to go to

a the hospital.

b the pharmacy.

c the supermarket.

4 Kate missed her bus because

a she fell over.

b she was late.

c she dropped her bag.

5 Oliver lives

a next to the bookstore.

b at the end of Westport Drive.

c opposite a restaurant.

6 Tom was unhappy because

a he wanted to be on the soccer team.

b he failed his math test.

c he had paella for dinner.

G C:26 **Read then listen. Correct ten differences. (10 marks)**

Hi Jenny. It's [1] ~~Tom~~ *Ben* here. I am on an amazing [2] **boat**. I am in [3] **Colombia**. I am visiting some interesting places, and doing some exciting activities. Yesterday, I was [4] **fishing** in the sea. It was so blue! I saw a lot of fish. They were all different colors, shapes, and sizes. Yesterday evening, I went to a concert. The band was amazing! They were [5] **singing** and dancing. The dancing was so fast. It was so exciting. We were all [6] **singing** at the end! Today, I am visiting some [7] **statues**. They are in the [8] **town**. Then, I am climbing a [9] **castle**. I'm not good at climbing but I am good at taking pictures! In the evening, we are [10] **fishing** [11] **on the beach**.

H **Look and read. Write *yes* or *no*. (7 marks)**

1 There are two pyramids. ________

2 There are two volcanoes. ________

3 There is a statue in front of the pyramid. ________

4 There are some factories. ________

5 There are two girls running races. ________

6 Three children are kicking a soccer ball. ________

7 A child is jumping on the trampoline. ________

Placement Test B

I **Read the timetable and complete the questions and answers. (5 marks)**

Gemma's homework schedule				
Monday	**Tuesday**	**Wednesday**	**Thursday**	**Friday**
history	science	geography	English	music
boring	exciting	difficult	easy	interesting

1 Was Gemma's homework on Tuesday history? ____________________

2 Was Gemma's homework on Wednesday difficult? ____________________

3 Was Gemma's homework on Monday exciting? ____________________

4 Was Gemma's homework on Friday music? ____________________

5 Was Gemma's homework on Thursday easy? ____________________

J **Complete the conversation with the correct form of the verbs in the box. (16 marks)**

be drive do ride be lose go do

Hannah: Hi Rachel. What did you [1]____________________ on the weekend?

Rachel: I [2]____________________ to Greenfield Amusement Park with my family – it was great! Have you ever [3]____________________ there?

Hannah: Yes, I love it! Did you ride the rollercoaster?

Rachel: No, I was too scared! I [4]____________________ the Ferris wheel, and I went on the bumper cars.

Hannah: [5]____________________ you go on the water slide?

Rachel: Yes, I went on the water slide with my dad. He [6]____________________ very happy because he [7]____________________ his keys!

Hannah: Oh, no! What happened?

Rachel: My mom came in her car and [8]____________________ us home!

1 Friends

Reading and writing

1 Read. Then write. (3 marks)

Today is Wednesday.

1 Tomorrow is ____________________.

2 Yesterday was ____________________.

3 Two days ago was ____________________.

2 Look. Then write. There is one example. (6 marks)

1 On Monday, Tom studied English.

2 ____________________

3 ____________________

4 ____________________

5 ____________________

6 ____________________

7 ____________________

Tom's diary	
Monday	study English
Tuesday	watch a DVD
Wednesday	play tennis
Thursday	practice the piano
Friday	go to the movies
Saturday	dance at the party
Sunday	clean my room

3 Read. Then write. (11 marks)

ago dark face helpful intelligent listened patient played problems studied today

I have a friend called Bob. He's hardworking and [1] ____________. He always has good grades. He has [2] ____________ brown hair and a nice [3] ____________. It's Saturday [4] ____________ and we [5] ____________ soccer this morning and then [6] ____________ to some music. Bob is very [7] ____________. Sometimes he helps me with my homework. I [8] ____________ for a math test two days [9] ____________. I couldn't do one of the [10] ____________ so Bob helped me. He was very [11] ____________ because I took a long time to understand!

4 Think of a friend. Then write about him/her. (6 marks)

What does he/she look like? What is he/she like?

____

____

____

____

____

Score: ___ / 26

1 Friends

Listening and speaking

1 C:27 **Read. Then listen and circle. (11 marks)**

1 Thomas

I'm [1](eight / nine). I have short, brown, spiky hair. I have a lot of friends and I [2](don't like / like) talking. I'm very talkative. I'm not shy at all. I [3](like / don't like) homework, but I [4](like / don't like) doing different sports. I play soccer and basketball, and I go swimming [5](on the weekend / every day). And I'm very [6](creative / patient). I love drawing and painting.

2 Georgia

I'm [7](ten / eleven). I'm tall and I have [8](short / long), brown hair. It's straight and always [9](messy / tidy). I'm very hard-working and quite smart. I love homework and I love learning about everything. I'm [10](shy / talkative) with my friends. There's always a lot to talk about. [11](I'm / I'm not) very sporty. I like reading, and I like walking my dog.

2 C:28 **Listen. Then circle. (4 marks)**

1 Her uncle is (lazy / bossy / friendly).

2 Her sister is (talkative / shy / bossy).

3 Her cousin is (sporty / talkative / hard-working).

4 Her aunt is (lazy / shy / sporty).

3 **Think of the youngest person in your family. Then talk. (10 marks)**

What does he/she look like?

Is he/she...?

Is he/she taller/shorter...than...?

What is he/she like?

What does he/she like doing?

Score: ___ / 25

Whole test score: ___ / 51

1 Read. Then match. (6 marks)

1 make	a before a test	d my homework	4 do
2 wash	b my bedroom	e my bed	5 clean
3 meet	c my hands	f my friends	6 study

2 Order to make sentences. (4 marks)

1 always / my / weekend / I / the / bedroom / clean / on

____

2 parents / listen / my / always / to / I

____

3 eat / unhealthy / sometimes / food / I

____

4 o'clock / bed / never / ten / I / go / after / to

____

3 Read. Then give some advice. Use *have to* or *should*. (6 marks)

eat a sandwich go running go to bed early study buy her a present clean it

1 I have a test on Friday. _______________
2 I'm hungry. _______________
3 It's sunny today! _______________
4 My room is messy. _______________
5 I'm tired. _______________
6 It's my mom's birthday. _______________

4 You have a test tomorrow. What should you do? Write at least THREE things. Use *should* and *shouldn't*. (6 marks)

____

____

____

____

Score: ___ / 22

1 C:29 **Listen. Then match. (9 marks)**

a messy bedroom
b can't study
c can't sleep
d doesn't have a trash can
e cleans on Saturday

Helen

Victor

f listens to quiet music
g eat more healthy food
h eat one vegetable a day
i have pizza one day a week

2 C:30 **Listen. Then match. (6 marks)**

1 I always make my bed in the morning
2 I never make my bed,
3 I sometimes wash my face before going to bed,
4 I usually do my homework before I watch TV,
5 I take the dog for a walk with my mom every afternoon after school,
6 I help my dad wash the car on the weekend,

a but I never do the dishes!
b and I help my mom take out the trash on Tuesday.
c and I always practice my guitar before I do my homework.
d but I always wash my face in the morning.
e before I go to school.
f but I always clean my room.

3 **Look at the picture and think about healthy food. Then talk. (8 marks)**

What food is there?

Where is it?

You should/have to always/never...

I eat/need (to)...

Score: ___ / 23

Whole test score: ___ / 45

3 Free time

Reading and writing

1 **Look at the pictures. Then write. Use *good at* or *not good at*. There is one example. (5 marks)**

catching diving ~~kicking~~ playing video games telling jokes throwing

✓  **1** I'm good at kicking.

✗  **2** I'm ______________.

✗  **3** I'm ______________.

✓  **4** I'm ______________.

✓  **5** I'm ______________.

✗ 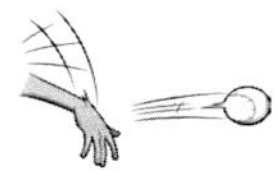 **6** I'm ______________.

2 **Unscramble and write verbs. Then match. (10 marks)**

1 glypani ______________ **a** poetry

2 gurninn ______________ **b** races

3 gnignsi ______________ **c** the drums

4 oigng ______________ **d** shopping

5 iderng a ______________ **e** karaoke

3 **Read. Then write. (8 marks)**

afternoon at last play playing practice taking was

Hi. I'm Jake. I [1] ______________ the drums. I like [2] ______________ the drums, but right now, I'm not very good. I'm [3] ______________ lessons. I have a lesson this [4] ______________. I [5] ______________ every day. My mom and dad aren't good [6] ______________ listening! [7] ______________ Saturday, I [8] ______________ playing the drums with my friends. We have a group. Paul plays the guitar and Rob sings. It's really fun!

4 **What are/aren't you good at? Think of at least THREE things. Write. (6 marks)**

____

____

____

____

Score: ___ / 29

1 C:35 **Listen. Then circle. (8 marks)**

1 Bobby's good at
  a telling jokes.
  b sports.
  c reading books.

2 Sandy's good at
  a playing soccer.
  b reading poetry.
  c catching a ball.

3 Charlie isn't good at
  a talking.
  b playing the guitar.
  c playing tennis.

4 Olivia isn't good at
  a in-line skating.
  b reading.
  c singing karaoke.

2 C:36 **Listen. Then check (✓). (8 marks)**

	Betty	Jed	Val	Todd
singing karaoke				
in-line skating				
playing the drums				
drawing				

3 **What were you doing yesterday? Think of at least FOUR things. Make some notes. Then talk. (8 marks)**

Yesterday morning: ______________________

Yesterday afternoon: ______________________

Yesterday evening: ______________________

Last night: ______________________

Score: ___ / 24

Whole test score: ___ / 53

4 Around the world

1 Unscramble and write. (10 marks)

1 aroke ________ 2 pytge ________

3 napis ________ 4 lautrasia ________

5 coxemi ________ 6 eth nutide gonkimd ________

7 danii ________ 8 panja ________

9 litya ________ 10 mobilaco ________

2 Read. Then write. (5 marks)

an a a some any

1 There are ________ waterfalls in Brazil.

2 There isn't ________ rain forest in the United States.

3 There aren't ________ elephants in Colombia.

4 There is ________ shark in the ocean. I can see it!

5 There isn't ________ island in Egypt.

3 Write the questions. Then answer. (4 marks)

1 Are there any ________? (lakes / Egypt)

No, ________. (✗)

2 Is ________? (rain forest / Brazil)

Yes, ________. (✓)

3 ________? (desert / Italy)

No, ________. (✗)

4 ________? (cities / China)

Yes, ________. (✓)

4 Write about your country. Use the prompts. (6 marks)

It is ________. *(location)*

There is ________. *(interesting place)*

There isn't ________.

There are ________.

Score: ___ / 25

1 Listen. Then circle. (6 marks)

1 In Mexico, there
- a are some volcanoes.
- b aren't any beaches.

2 In Egypt, there
- a aren't any pyramids.
- b are some pyramids.

3 In Australia, there
- a isn't a rain forest.
- b are some deserts.

4 In Canada, there
- a are some forests.
- b isn't a rain forest.

5 In Ireland, there
- a aren't any lakes.
- b are some forests.

6 In the UK, there
- a aren't any old forests.
- b are some old forests.

2 Listen. Then circle T = True or F = False. (12 marks)

1	Eliza is from Brazil.	T / F
	There are many rain forests in Brazil.	T / F
	It never rains in Brazil.	T / F
2	Some of Mount Everest is in China.	T / F
	There aren't many rivers in China.	T / F
	The Yangtze is the name of a mountain.	T / F
3	Monika is from Europe.	T / F
	There aren't any lakes in Poland.	T / F
	There are some bears in the forests.	T / F
4	There are some high mountains in Greece.	T / F
	There aren't any islands.	T / F
	There aren't any old buildings.	T / F

3 Make some notes about your country. Then talk. (8 marks)

My country is...

There are a lot of...

I like it/don't like it because...

There aren't any...

There is/isn't a...

Score: ___ / 26

Whole test score: ___ / 51

5 Shopping

Reading and writing

1 Read. Then write the numbers. (6 marks)

1 sixty ______
2 a thousand ______
3 three hundred and fifty ______
4 16 ______
5 500 ______
6 105 ______

2 Circle. Then write. Use *that* or *those*. There is one example. (8 marks)

1 baggy (sneakers / (pants)) Those are my baggy pants.
2 tight (pants / umbrella) ______
3 expensive (bracelet / pocket) ______
4 short (watch / jeans) ______
5 old-fashioned (teeth / gloves) ______

3 Read. Then answer. (6 marks)

1 Whose leather gloves are these?
They're (Harry) ______ gloves. They're his.
2 Whose black umbrella is this?
It's Sandra's umbrella. It's ______.
3 Whose silver bracelet is this?
It's (Ben) ______ silver bracelet. It's ______.
4 Whose old-fashioned swimsuit is this?
It's (you) ______ swimsuit. It's ______.

4 What do you usually wear? Write. Use some of the words in the box. (6 marks)

baggy tight expensive short long black white

At school, I ______ and ______.
At home on the weekend, I ______ and ______.

Score: ___ / 26

1 C:42 **Listen. Then match. (8 marks)**

1 jacket
2 leather wallets
3 sunglasses
4 spotted umbrella

$60 $50
$10 $15

2 C:43 **Listen. Then circle. (8 marks)**

1 **umbrella:**	green, brown, and white	beautiful	stripes
2 **watch:**	modern	beautiful	old-fashioned
3 **shirts:**	baggy	different colored	spotted
4 **jeans:**	black	tight	leather pocket

3 **Let's go shopping! Think about the questions and write your ideas. Then take turns to be the customer and the sales person. (6 marks)**

Sales person: What do you want to buy? What color? tight/baggy/expensive/cheap? How much money do you have?

Customer: What color? How much?

Customer:
Sales person:
Customer:
Sales person:
Customer:
Sales person:
Customer:
Sales person:

Score: ___ / 22

Whole test score: ___ / 48

6 Party time

1 Write the numbers. (8 marks)

1 3rd ______________________ 2 15th ______________________

3 11th ______________________ 4 8th ______________________

5 5th ______________________ 6 16th ______________________

7 1st ______________________ 8 13th ______________________

2 Read. Then match. (5 marks)

1 When did you go on vacation last year?
2 Where did you go on vacation last year?
3 How did you go there?
4 Who did you go with?
5 What did you do?

a I went with my parents and my sister.
b We went in August.
c We saw a lot of pyramids.
d We went to Mexico.
e We took a plane, and then went by bus.

3 Read. Then write. Use the past tense of the verbs. There is one example. (5 marks)

Yesterday we [1] ___had___ (have) a big soccer game at my club. I [2] ______________ (go) to the club right after school to get ready for the game. I [3] ______________ (not have) my soccer shorts and shirt. Mom washed them yesterday and I forgot to put them in my school bag this morning. My teacher [4] ______________ (come) to watch the game so we [5] ______________ (play) well. She loves soccer and comes to all our games. In the last game we won and our teacher said we [6] ______________ (play) really well. It was a great day!

4 What did you do on the weekend? Write. Use some of the words in the box. (6 marks)

bring	come	give	go	have	make	see

Last weekend, on Friday evening/Saturday/Sunday I ______________________________

____.

Then, on ______________________ I ______________________________

____.

I also ____

____.

Score: ___ / 24

1 Listen. Then write. (7 marks)

C:44

Decorations for the party	Food	Instrument
a lot of [1] ____________	hundreds of [2] ____________, [3] ____________ and potatoes and salads big and small [4] ____________ cookies and [5] ____________ and [6] ____________	My friend's dad played the [7] ____________

2 Listen. Then match. (5 marks)

C:45

1 Where did Stef go on vacation?

2 When did he go?

3 What did he do?

4 What did he see?

5 Who did he meet?

a On June 20th.

b He saw Greek islands.

c He met a school friend.

d He went to Greece.

e He went swimming every day

f The UK.

g He went to the beach and he went to Athens.

h He met one of his teachers.

i On June 28th.

j He saw buildings, guards, statues, and fish.

3 Think of something special you did last year. Make some notes. Then talk. (8 marks)

Who did you meet?

When did you go?

Where did you go?

What did you see?

What did you do?

Score: ___ / 20

Whole test score: ___ / 44

7 School

1 Read. Then match. (4 marks)

1 Did you play tennis yesterday?
2 Was Polly in the gym yesterday morning?
3 Were Janet and Flora shopping this morning?
4 Was Pete excited before his vacation?

a No, she wasn't.
b Yes, I did.
c Yes, he was.
d No, they weren't.

2 Write. Then reorder and write the answers. (10 marks)

1 How old ____________ you last year? was / old / I / years / nine

____

2 ____________ you excited? I / , / excited / was / Yes / very

____

3 What ____________ the weather like? was / sunny / It / and / hot / very

____

4 ____________ it interesting? It / interesting / vacation / a / very / was

____

5 What ____________ you do in the morning? swam / pool / I / the / morning / in / every

____

3 Write *was, were,* or *did*. Then answer. (12 marks)

1 ____________ you read a book last week? ______________________
2 ____________ your book interesting? ______________________
3 Who ____________ your English teacher last year? ______________________
4 ____________ you in the school play last year? ______________________
5 ____________ you enter a story competition last year? ______________________
6 What ____________ your favorite subject last year? ______________________

4 Think of a book or movie. Then write about it. (8 marks)

What was it called? ______________________
What was it about? ______________________
Did you like/finish it? ______________________
Was it scary/funny/boring/etc.? ______________________

boring exciting romantic scary funny interesting

Score: ___ / 34

1 Listen. Then write. (10 marks) C:49

boring exciting history difficult intelligent kind plays scary ~~school~~ science museums

When I was nine, I went to [1] ___school___ in Argentina. My class had twenty-six children in it. My class teacher was Mr. Brown. He was a bit [2] ________. He talked very loudly, but he was [3] ________ and funny. My favorite subject was [4] ________. Mr. Brown taught history class in the park. We also had classes in [5] ________ and historic buildings. We did short [6] ________ about some of the history topics. Our parents came to watch us. But science class was [7] ________. I didn't like the teacher. It wasn't Mr. Brown. The teacher was very [8] ________, but his class was [9] ________. We listened to him talk and talk, and we made notes in our books! I like [10] ________ now. In my new school, we do a lot of experiments, and that's fun. But I liked that school. It was [11] ________ going to school in a different country, and everyone was so interesting.

2 Listen. Then write. (8 marks) C:50

	Monday	Tuesday	Wednesday	Thursday	Friday
Morning		science			
Afternoon					geography

3 Think about a day at school last week. What did you do? Make some notes. Then talk. (6 marks)

In the morning/ afternoon, I...

I went to...

I didn't/wasn't...

I had my favorite/least favorite lessons...

It was/They were... With my friends, I...

Score: ___ / 24

Whole test score: ___ / 58

1 Read. Then match. (6 marks)

1 Where are Tom and Sue from?
2 Are Jan and Tina Australian?
3 Where are you from?
4 Is she Korean?
5 Is he from Mexico?
6 Are you Argentinian?

a I'm from Mexico.
b No, I'm Italian.
c They're from Egypt.
d Yes, they are.
e No, he isn't. He's from Colombia.
f No, she's not. She's Chinese.

2 Unscramble and write jobs. Then match. (10 marks)

a (cinstiset) ______ b (ucsiianm) ______ c (ysp) ______
d (osilra) ______ e (ratco) actor f (rwtaie) ______

[e] 1 I studied drama. I work in a theater.
[ ] 2 I work in a restaurant. I take the food to people.
[ ] 3 I studied science. I do experiments and make new discoveries.
[ ] 4 I love the ocean. I work on a ship and travel all over the world.
[ ] 5 I secretly find out information about other countries.
[ ] 6 I play in a band. I play the guitar.

3 Read. Then circle. (3 marks)

1 He's a waiter (who / that) comes from Brazil.
2 Australia is a big country (who / that) has rain forests.
3 It was a watch (who / that) he found in the theater.

4 Write the dates. Use *in, at,* or *on.* (6 marks)

1 After summer vacation, school starts again... ______
2 The festival of Halloween is... ______
3 My birthday is... ______
4 I get up because I have to go to school... ______
5 I usually make my bed... ______
6 I usually go to bed early but last night I went... ______

Score: ___ / 25

1 Listen. Then complete. (8 marks)

Name	Comes from...	Nationality
1 Carlos	Mexico City	
2 Abel	Cairo	
3 Sue	Beijing	
4 Ruth	Tokyo	
5 Mariella	Florence	
6 Pablo	Buenos Aires	
7 Anna	Delhi	
8 Ryan	Belfast	

2 Listen and number. Then find and match. (12 marks)

☐ sailor

☐ waiter

☐ musician

☐ scientist

☐ cowboy

☐ actor

a  ☐

b  ☐

c  ☐

d  ☐

e  ☐

f  ☐

3 Imagine you are a musician or scientist. Make notes. Then talk. (8 marks)

I'm a...

I work in a/an...

At work, I wear...

I start/finish work at...

In the morning/afternoon/evening, I...

I like/don't like...

Score: ___ / 28

Whole test score: ___ / 53

Review Test 1

(Units 1 and 2) Reading and writing

1 Read. Then match. (5 marks)

1 What does he look like?
2 What's she like?
3 Where does Jo do her homework?
4 What does Tom do each day?
5 What do your friends look like?

a She does her homework in the kitchen.
b He brushes his teeth.
c He's tall and thin, and he has short, brown hair.
d They are tall and beautiful, and have dark hair.
e She's very talkative and a bit bossy.

2 Read. Then draw and color. (8 marks)

1 This is my friend. He's tall and thin. He has light hair. It's short and spiky.

2 This is my cousin. She's beautiful. She has long, dark hair and brown eyes. She's tall and very thin.

3 My mom has short, light hair and blue eyes. She is short and thin.

4 My dad is very tall and thin. He has big, brown eyes and is bald. He is good-looking.

Review Test 1

(Units 1 and 2)
Reading and writing

3 Read. Then circle. (10 marks)

We have a new English teacher. I like her a lot [1] (but / because) she is always doing new things with the class. She is very strict [2] (and / because) creative. Yesterday, in class, she showed us how to make a helicopter out of paper. I listened very carefully to the instructions [3] (because / but) when I tried to make it, it didn't work! I asked my friend to help me [4] (but / because) she is really good at making things; [5] (but / because) I still didn't understand. Anyway, in the end, I asked my teacher to help. She came over to my desk [6] (but / and) looked at my helicopter. She asked me if I had all the things I needed. I said I did. [7] (But / Because), when I looked again, I saw that I needed a paper clip. I put the clip on the bottom of the helicopter [8] (but / and) threw it up in the air. To my surprise, it flew! Then it turned around [9] (and / but) around all the way down to the ground. It landed in the middle of the classroom! What a great lesson! Science [10] (because / and) English in the same lesson! My new teacher is great!

4 Read. Then choose and write. There is one example. (5 marks)

My name's Bill. Every week day I get up at seven o'clock. I go to the bathroom and [1] wash my face and [2] ____________. Then I go downstairs to the kitchen and have breakfast. I like to [3] ____________ for school because if we're late, we're sent to the school principal! I [4] ____________ in the playground and we plan what we are going to do after school. We always have a lot to learn so I [5] ____________ to help me remember! After school, I go home and [6] ____________. Then I watch TV or practice the guitar.

Score: ___ / 28

Review Test 1

(Units 1 and 2) Listening and speaking

1 C:31 Listen. Then write. (10 marks)

	Janet	Pete	Frank	Sophie	Emma
Age	10				
Hair			spiky brown		
Eyes		brown		blue	
Other information					loves drawing and painting

2 C:32 Listen and check (✓). (5 marks)

1 a  ☐ b  ☐ c 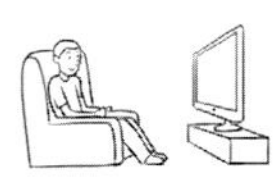 ☐ ____________________

2 a  ☐ b  ☐ c  ☐ ____________________

3 a  ☐ b  ☐ c  ☐ ____________________

4 a  ☐ b  ☐ c  ☐ ____________________

5 a  ☐ b  ☐ c  ☐ ____________________

3 C:33 Listen. Then write *usually, often, always, sometimes,* or *never* next to the pictures in Activity 2. (5 marks)

Review Test 1

(Units 1 and 2) Listening and speaking

4 C:34 **Listen. Then write. (5 marks)**

1 Carl ________________ makes his bed in the morning.
2 He ________________ gets to school late.
3 He ________________ takes notes during class.
4 We ________________ meet our friends after school.
5 We ________________ do our homework in the living room.

5 **Work with a friend. Look at the pictures. Ask and answer. (10 marks)**

1 Which things do you sometimes do?
2 When do you do them?
3 Which do you never do?
4 What should you do every day?
5 What should you do sometimes?

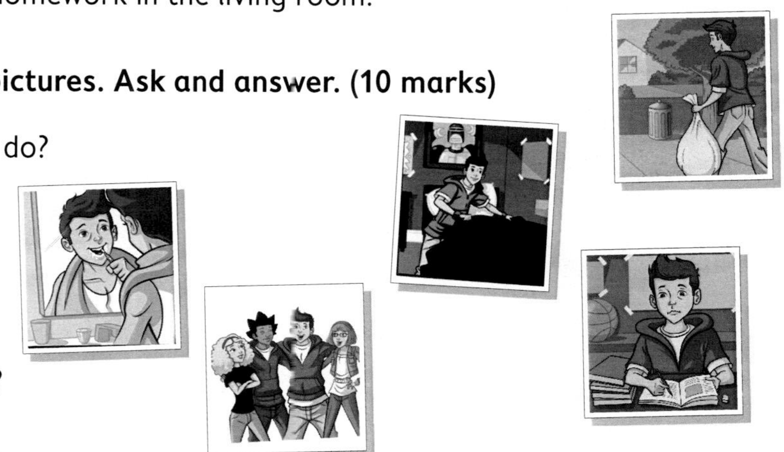

6 **Read and look. Then talk. (8 marks)**

1 What does she look like?

2 What is she doing?

3 What is he like?

4 How often should you brush your teeth?

7 **Look. Then describe the family. Use the prompts. (10 marks)**

Who is he/she?
What does he/she look like?
What is he/she like?
What is your family like?
What do your parents look like?

Score: ___ / 53

Whole test score: ___ / 81

Review Test 2

(Units 3 and 4)
Reading and writing

1 **Look and read. Write *yes* or *no*. (8 marks)**

1 There are two pyramids. ______
2 There are two volcanoes. ______
3 There is a statue in front of the pyramid. ______
4 There are some factories. ______
5 There are two girls running races. ______
6 Three children are kicking a soccer ball. ______
7 A child is jumping on the trampoline. ______
8 A boy and girl are throwing and catching a ball. ______

2 **What are/aren't you good at? What are/aren't your friends good at? (8 marks)**

1 (✓) I'm ______.
2 (✗) I'm not ______.
3 (✓) My friends ______.
4 (✗) My friends ______.

Review Test 2

(Units 3 and 4) Reading and writing

3 Look and read. Then match. There is one example. (8 marks)

castle caves factory farm lake pyramids ~~rain forest~~ statues town

1 This place has a lot of trees, and it rains a lot. rain forest
2 You can see these places in Egypt. ________
3 These go inside mountains and can be tunnels. ________
4 This place is bigger than a village but smaller than a city. ________
5 This place was built to protect people. ________
6 These are made out of stone. They are art. ________
7 You can go fishing and sailing here but it is not the ocean. ________
8 This is a place where you can find cows and sheep. ________
9 This is a place where different things are made. ________

4 Complete the questions and answers. (8 marks)

1 What ________, yesterday?
He was playing ________.

2 What ________, yesterday?
They ________ acting.

3 Was ________, yesterday?
Yes, ________ was.

4 ________, yesterday?
No, they weren't. They ________.

1 
2 
3 
4 

5 Write about a country you know. Use *there is/are* and *some/any*. (5 marks)

Name of country: ________

1 ________
2 ________
3 ________
4 ________
5 ________

Score: ___ / 37

Review Test 2

(Units 3 and 4)
Listening and speaking

1 C:39 **Read and listen. Correct ten differences. (10 marks)**

Hi Jenny. It's [1] ~~Tom~~ Ben here. I'm on an amazing [2] **boat**. I'm in [3] **Colombia**. I am visiting some interesting places and doing some exciting activities. Yesterday, I was [4] **fishing** in the ocean. It was so blue! I saw a lot of fish. They were all different colors, shapes, and sizes. Yesterday evening, I went to a concert. The band was amazing! They were [5] **singing** and dancing. The dancing was so fast. It was so exciting. We were all [6] **singing** at the end! Today, I am visiting some [7] **statues**. They are in the [8] **town**. Then, I am climbing a [9] **castle**. I'm not good at climbing, but I am good at taking pictures! In the evening, we are [10] **fishing** [11] **on the beach**.

2 C:40 **Listen and circle. (6 marks)**

1 Jo is in (Italy / Spain).
2 She is visiting her (Italian / Spanish) grandparents.
3 They live in a small house (in a town / on a farm).
4 There are some (statues / castles) near their house.
5 There is also a big (cave / volcano) near their house.
6 Today we are visiting a (cave / castle) and having a picnic.

3 C:41 **Listen and circle. (4 marks)**

1 What is Anna good at?
  a singing
  b playing the drums
  c acting

2 What is Harry good at?
  a playing video games
  b telling jokes
  c playing chess

3 Where are Anna and Harry going on vacation?
  a Spain
  b Argentina
  c Italy

4 What are they going to do on vacation?
  a visit a volcano
  b visit some caves
  c visit a castle

Review Test 2

(Units 3 and 4)
Listening and speaking

4 **Look at the pictures and read. Continue the story. Use the words/phrases in the box. (10 marks)**

Are/Is there...?	Let's visit...	I'm good at...
stay/farm house	visit castle	climb volcano

Gemma's family are planning to go to Mexico. Gemma is very excited. She wants to know a lot about Mexico, and asks her parents a lot of questions about places to visit and things to do.

aeroplane

farm

pyramids

castle

statues

volcanoes

5 **What were you doing yesterday? Write, using *in the morning/afternoon*, *at*, and *before*. Then talk. (8 marks)**

Yesterday: before school: played soccer

____

____

____

6 **Look. Then describe. (10 marks)**

Score: ___ / 48

Whole test score: ___ / 85

Review Test 3

(Units 5 and 6)
Reading and writing

1 Look and read. Then match. (6 marks)

a 

b 

c 

1 Women wear these on their arms.

2 You wear this to go swimming.

3 Women use these to keep things in.

4 You wear this with your pants.

5 You wear this on your wrist. It tells the time.

6 You put you money in this.

d 

e 

f 

2 Read. Then order. There is one example. (8 marks)

☐ a Oh! That's too expensive. I only have fifteen dollars. How much are those gloves?
☐ b Yes, of course. Ten dollars, please.
☐ c Great. May I buy it, please?
☐ d They're twelve dollars and fifty cents.
☐ e Well, they're cheap but they're too tight. How much is that scarf?
☐ f The jacket is thirty dollars.
☐ g Here you are. Ten dollars.
1 h Excuse me. How much is that jacket?
☐ i It's ten dollars.

3 Read. Then write. (8 marks)

cold expensive family's first saw swimsuit went were

Last year my parents and I 1 ________________ to Italy on vacation. Our hotel was quite 2 ________________ (120 euros) because it was next to a lake. Behind the lake, there was a very high mountain. We 3 ________________ some snow on the top of the mountain.

On the 4 ________________ day of our holiday, we had a walk by the lake. I didn't swim in the lake. I didn't have my 5 ________________ with me and the water was too 6 ________________. On the other side of the lake, there was a family – mom, dad, and two children. The children 7 ________________ throwing a ball. Next to mom and dad there was a basket of food. The 8 ________________ dog was eating a sandwich. It was funny!

4 **Reorder and write. Then match. (6 marks)**

1 belt / this / Whose / is

_______________________________?

2 is / much / How / that / umbrella

_______________________________?

3 you / did / see / What

_______________________________?

a It's twelve dollars.

b It's Sandra's.

c I saw the Great Wall.

5 **Read. Then complete the sentences. You can use 1, 2, 3, or 4 words. (7 marks)**

On the weekend, Jamie went to a beach party. He met all his good friends. The party was on the beach near his town. They had a lot to eat and drink. His friends didn't bring any food, but they ate it! Then they played a game of beach volleyball. They were very tired after the game. At the end of the party, Jamie's parents made a campfire on the beach. They all sang songs. It was a fantastic day!

1 Jamie went to a party. It was on the beach.

2 Jamie met ________________ friends there.

3 The beach was ________________ Jamie's ________________.

4 Everyone had a lot to ________________.

5 After eating, they played ________________.

6 ________________, they were very tired.

7 Jamie's ________________ made a campfire.

8 Then they all ________________.

6 **Write about a birthday party you went to. Use the prompts. (5 marks)**

I went to a birthday party (last weekend/last month/in the summer, etc.)

It was (exciting/boring, etc.)

I gave my friend a... We played/went/sang...

1 ____

2 ____

3 ____

4 ____

5 ____

Score: ___ / 40

Review Test 3

1 C:46 **Listen and circle. (5 marks)**

1 The watch is
- a $12.
- b $12.50.
- c $7.50.

2 The jacket is
- a $30.
- b $13.
- c $15.

3 The bracelet is
- a $52.20.
- b $62.20.
- c $62.30.

4 The sunglasses are
- a $200.
- b $231.
- c $213.

5 The hoodie is
- a $15.50.
- b $50.15.
- c $50.50.

2 C:47 **Listen. Then write. (5 marks)**

Invitation

Name	Jamie
1 What	______________
2 When	______________
3 Where	______________
4 What to bring	______________
5 Reply to	______________

3 C:48 **Listen and write the letters. (8 marks)**

a

b

c

h
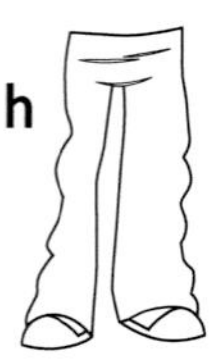

Jo	Matt

d

g

f

e

Review Test 3

(Units 5 and 6) Listening and speaking

4 Choose three things to buy. Ask and answer. Use the prompts. (6 marks)

$50

$12.50

$10

$17

$22

$15

How much is the belt?

It's ten dollars.

That's cheap. Can I buy it, please?

Here you are.

5a What did Jan do on vacation last year? Look at the diagram. Then talk. (5 marks)

Last vacation

- swim in ocean
- see penguins visit volcano
- buy sunglasses
- go to Argentina

Last year, Jan went to Argentina. When she was there, she...

5b Think about your last vacation. Then talk. (5 marks)

6 Describe the party. Make notes and then talk. (10 marks)

play see have bring eat drink sing come meet go

songs salad orange juice beach soccer picnic swimsuit

Yesterday, I...

Score: ___ / 44

Whole test score: ___ / 84

Review Test 4

(Units 7 and 8)
Reading and writing

1 **Read. Then match. (6 marks)**

1 Where was the winner from?	**a** Yes, there were.
2 Was it difficult?	**b** She was from Greece.
3 Were there any cowboys in the movie?	**c** No, it wasn't. It was easy.
4 Is she the girl who's in the play?	**d** No, it wasn't. It was very interesting!
5 Are they American?	**e** No, they aren't. They're Australian.
6 Was it boring?	**f** Yes, she is.

2 **Read. Then reorder and write the answers. (6 marks)**

1 Was the movie interesting? — scary / Yes / but / was / it / ,

____

2 Where were they from? — They / Egyptian / were / both

____

3 Were there any aliens in the movie? — a lot / there / Yes / were / ,

____

4 Were there any firefighters in the movie? — there / No / three / , / but / were / sailors

____

5 Was your science class interesting? — tests / with / Yes / did / some / , / exciting water / we

____

6 Were there any difficult questions in the test? — were / Yes / a lot / there / , / of / questions / difficult

____

Review Test 4

3 Read Gemma's homework diary. Then complete. (5 marks)

Monday	Tuesday	Wednesday	Thursday	Friday
history	science	geography	English	music
boring	exciting	difficult	easy	interesting

1 Was Gemma's homework on Tuesday history? ____________

2 Was Gemma's homework on Wednesday difficult? ____________

3 Was Gemma's homework on Monday easy? ____________

4 Was Gemma's homework on Friday music? ____________

5 Was Gemma's homework on Thursday funny? ____________

4 Read. Then circle. There is one example. (10 marks)

I love watching movies. My favorite movies are westerns about [1] cowboys. They are usually filmed in places like Mexico but the movies are [2] ____________! At school, we are making our own movie. We write our own script and then learn our [3] ____________, and act it out. Then our teacher makes a [4] ____________ of it. Some movies are really funny. Some are [5] ____________! But, if it isn't very good, we can edit it and make [6] ____________. My group's movie was about a [7] ____________ from space. It was easy to write the script. But it was a lot more [8] ____________ to find the clothes to wear. In the end, we had to make alien-like hats, and made a white coat out of paper! I think the best thing about making the movie was acting out the story. It was really [9] ____________. Some of my friends were really [10] ____________ and the teacher had to keep stopping the video and starting again! Next year, I want to make a movie about a [11] ____________ because I love science and I love doing experiments!

1 (cowboys) musicians teachers

2 Mexican American China

3 songs numbers words

4 video cartoon song

5 bored boring bore

6 good other changes

7 spy spies spi

8 different difficult easier

9 boring well exciting

10 funny fun famous

11 soldier musician scientist

5 Write about a famous person that you like. (10 marks)

What is his/her name? Where is he/she from? What is he/she like? What does he/she look like?

____

____

____

Score: ___ / 35

1 C:53 **Listen and circle. (5 marks)**

1 Sarah had a really __________ history class.

a boring

b interesting

c easy

2 Mike is reading a __________ story in English.

a romantic

b boring

c scary

3 Sarah thinks that __________ is a scary subject.

a math

b music

c P.E.

4 Sarah is good at

a geography.

b history.

c computer science.

5 Mike likes

a science.

b art.

c English.

2 C:54 **Listen. Then write Yes or No. (5 marks)**

1 Was the movie scary? ______________

2 Were there any cowboys in the movie? ______________

3 Did the bad guys ride horses? ______________

4 Were the cowboys Argentinian? ______________

5 Was the movie in English? ______________

3 C:55 **Listen. Then write. (10 marks)**

	Anna	**Kim**
From		
Likes		
Wants to be		
Free time activities		
Can't		

4 Describe the people in the pictures. (8 marks)

A soldier is a person who...

5a What movies does William like? Look at the diagram. Then talk. (5 marks)

Interesting movies

- Journey to Beyond (exciting)
- Aliens on the Move (scary)
- The Boy from Space (boring)
- Lost on Happy Island (exciting and funny)

William likes different movies. He likes Journey to Beyond because it is exciting. He...

5b On a sheet of paper, draw a diagram about movies you like. Then talk. (5 marks)

6 Look. Who's at the party? Make notes and then talk. (10 marks)

king queen sailor soldier cowboy monkey dancing singing in front of behind next to on the left/right

Score: ___ / 48

Whole test score: ___ / 83

1 **Read. Then circle. (5 marks)**

MY SCHOOL NEWS

VOL. 1, NO. 2 BARCELONA, SPAIN TODAY'S DATE

END OF TERM PARTY!

This year at school we had an end of term party. We hadn't had a party before. Every class had a job to do. My class had to bring the food and drinks. I made a fruit cake and a carrot cake. They were very tasty. My best friend, Sarah, made a mushroom and spinach pizza and some egg sandwiches. I took some salt and pepper and some sugar.

On the day, we were very excited. We listened to CDs and we had some competitions. I came second in the karaoke competition! Julia, who is in the class above mine, came first.

After singing we had some food. We ate and ate. There was a lot of food. There wasn't much fruit! The food was really unhealthy... but it was nice.

Then we danced. It was an excellent day. Everyone was so helpful and everyone really had a lot of fun. But the next day... oh, what a mess!

1 The school had an end of term party

a every year.

b sometimes.

c this year.

2 Every class

a made a cake.

b helped.

c sang.

3 Sarah

a didn't make a cake.

b brought some salt and pepper.

c won a competition.

4 The food

a was very healthy.

b was very good for us.

c tasted good.

5 After the party

a we didn't clean up.

b we danced.

c we had a lot of fun.

Score: ___ / 5

End of Level Test

1 Read. Then complete. (6 marks)

am are in played went love

Last winter, I [1] ________ to the mountains with my family. We [2] ________ skiing. My mom and dad [3] ________ good at skiing. I [4] ________ not good at skiing but I am good at snowboarding. [5] ________ the evenings, my dad [6] ________ the guitar and we sang. We love ski vacations!

2 Write the numbers. (5 marks)

1 1st ________ **2** 22nd ________

3 16th ________ **4** 23rd ________

5 50th ________

3 Read. Then write questions. (5 marks)

1 Is he ________?

Yes, he is. He's Egyptian.

2 Where did you ________?

I went to Turkey.

3 What are they ________?

They are good at skiing.

4 Was ________?

Yes, it was very interesting.

5 Did you ________?

No, I didn't. It was boring.

4 Order to make sentences. Then match. (9 marks)

1 you / Why / excited / are

________?

2 often / your / Do / you / clean / room

________?

3 last / you / Where / did / summer / go

________?

a to / went / I / Ibiza

____

b tomorrow / my / is / birthday / Because

____

c it / clean / I / Saturday / every.

____

Score: ___ / 25

1 Listen and circle. (12 marks)

C:56

Yesterday I [1] (watched / went) my brother play [2] (soccer / basketball). It [3] (was / were) very exciting. The game was very [4] (difficult / different). He [5] (practiced / studied) for weeks. I [6] (went / go) with my mom and dad. It finished at [7] (a quarter after eleven / ten-thirty). We got home [8] (at / on) noon. My brother was very [9] (tired / thirsty). He didn't do his homework! He [10] (listened to / watched) TV. I [11] (played / talked to) my friends. I was [12] (telling / talking) them funny jokes.

2 Listen. Then write. (8 marks)

C:57

	Where from	Activity	When	Where
Sue				
Tony				

3 Listen. Then match. (5 marks)

C:58

baggy

expensive

old-fashioned

tight

cheap

a
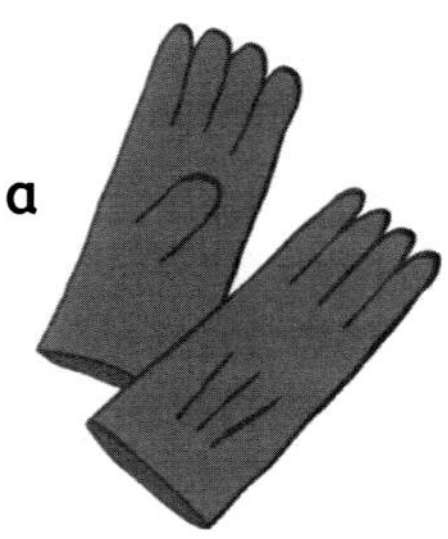

b

c
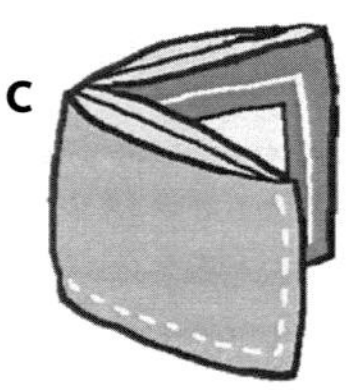

d

e

Score: ___ / 25

1 Look at the pictures. Find five differences. (10 marks)

1

2

2 Talk about the party in picture 1. (15 marks)

Score: ___ / 25

Whole test score: ___ / 80